Contributions to Political Science

More information about this series at http://www.springer.com/series/11829

Peter Drahn

Adoption of EU Business and Human Rights Policy

The Use of Discretion in the National Transposition of EU Directives

Springer

Peter Drahn
Jean Monnet Chair—Department of Political Science and European Affairs
University of Cologne
Cologne, Germany

ISSN 2198-7289 ISSN 2198-7297 (electronic)
Contributions to Political Science
ISBN 978-3-030-46934-4 ISBN 978-3-030-46935-1 (eBook)
https://doi.org/10.1007/978-3-030-46935-1

This Springer imprint is published by the registered company Springer Nature Switzerland AG
The registered company address is: Gewerbestrasse 11, 6330 Cham, Switzerland

For Dagmar Drahn

Acknowledgements

This Ph.D. project would not have been possible without the support of a number of people. First, I would like to thank my supervisors. Professor Wolfgang Wessels gave me the academic freedom to follow my interests, which led to my decision to explore a new policy area, EU Business and Human Rights policy. During our meetings, he encouraged me to develop and trust my own instincts, rather than trying to meet his expectations. I would also like to thank my co-supervisor Prof. Simon Bulmer for his helpful comments and valuable suggestions.

This study benefited considerably from the input of fellow academics at the Jean Monnet Chair of the University of Cologne. I thank my fellow Ph.D. colleagues Claudia Hefftler and Matthias Götz for our entertaining and scientifically instructive regular exchanges. I am also grateful to my Ph.D. colleague Deniz Ertin for his continuous support and for our enjoyable and insightful academic and political discussions. I also thank the participants of our 'Oberseminar' for critical questions and constructive suggestions.

During this Ph.D. project, I could always count on the support of my friends. I am especially grateful to Fabian, Tina, Christian, Eugen, Aron, Maren and Denis for their continuous encouragement, the occasional push, and the sometimes necessary distractions.

I could not have completed this Ph.D. project without the incredible support of my partner, Kristina Engels. She was there for me every step of the way, be it by providing a different academic perspective, by developing work plans together or by giving me the moral and practical support I needed. Thank you.

I am especially grateful for the continuous support of my family. My father Hans Joachim Drahn and my sister Claire Drahn always believed in me and were always there for me during difficult and stressful times.

Much of the strength and perseverance I needed to finish this project comes from my mother, Dagmar Drahn. This book is dedicated to her.

Contents

1 Introduction 1
1.1 Academic Relevance for Europeanization and Voluntarism in the EU 4
1.2 Political Relevance for Assessing EU Human Rights Commitments and Corporate Accountability 8
1.3 Theoretical Approach, Scope, and Structure of the Book 10
References 14

2 Business and Human Rights: A New and Contentious EU Policy Area 17
2.1 Legal and Living Constitution of Human Rights in the EU 19
2.1.1 The Development of a European Human Rights Regime 19
2.1.2 Assessing the European Human Rights Regime 22
2.2 The International Business and Human Rights Agenda 25
2.3 Forming EU Business and Human Rights Policy 28
2.3.1 The Development of EU BHR Policy 28
2.3.2 Discussion of EU BHR Policy 31
2.3.3 State of Play of EU BHR Policy 34
2.4 The Public Procurement Directives 36
2.5 The Non-financial Reporting Directive 41
2.6 Conclusion 44
References 45

3 Theoretical Explanations for the Domestic Impact of EU Law 49
3.1 New Institutionalist Theory 50
3.2 Europeanization and the Analysis of Directive Transpositions 56
3.2.1 The Emergence of Europeanization 56
3.2.2 Expounding the Concept 57
3.2.3 The Analysis of Directive Transpositions 61

3.2.4 The Concept of Misfit in Europeanization and Directive Transposition Research 63
3.2.5 The Roles of Facilitating Factors and Domestic Politics 66
3.2.6 The 'Worlds of Compliance' Typology 70
3.3 Policy Transfer 71
3.4 Voluntary Compliance with EU Rules 74
3.4.1 Conceptual Approaches to Explaining Voluntary Compliance with EU Rules 74
3.4.2 Observations from Studies on EU Directive Transposition 77
3.5 Constructing the Analytical Framework 78
3.5.1 Using 'Discretion' to Build the Dependent Variable 81
3.5.2 Determining Independent Variables and Formulating Hypotheses 81
3.5.3 Two Logics of Directive Transposition 88
References 91

4 Research Design 97
4.1 Methodological Approach 97
4.2 Selection of EU Directives 99
4.3 Selection of Cases 100
4.4 Dependent and Independent Variables 104
4.5 Operationalization of the Dependent Variable 105
4.6 Operationalization of the Independent Variables 109
4.6.1 Policy Misfit 109
4.6.2 Institutional Misfit 114
4.6.3 Government Composition 115
4.6.4 Political Salience Within the Policy Subsystem 116
4.6.5 International Policy Transfer 117
4.6.6 Administrative Effectiveness 118
4.7 Data Collection 118
References 119

5 Empirical Analysis I: Transposition of the Directives 121
5.1 Transposition of the Public Procurement Directives 121
5.1.1 Human Rights Provisions in the Public Procurement Directives 121
5.1.2 Comparative Transposition of the Three Public Procurement Directives 134
5.1.3 Overview of Transposition Results 146
5.2 Transposition of the Non-financial Reporting Directive 156

5.2.1 Human Rights Provisions in the Non-financial Reporting Directive . . . 156
5.2.2 Comparative Transposition of the Non-financial Reporting Directive . . . 160
5.2.3 Overview of Transposition Results . . . 168
5.3 Account of Transposition Variation . . . 172
References . . . 174

6 Empirical Analysis II: Explanation of Transposition Variation . . . 177
6.1 Country Transposition Background . . . 177
6.1.1 United Kingdom . . . 177
6.1.2 France . . . 180
6.1.3 Germany . . . 181
6.1.4 Denmark . . . 184
6.2 Testing Hypotheses for the Public Procurement Directives . . . 186
6.2.1 Policy Misfit . . . 186
6.2.2 Institutional Misfit . . . 189
6.2.3 Government Composition . . . 190
6.2.4 Political Salience Within the Policy Subsystem . . . 191
6.2.5 International Policy Transfer . . . 194
6.2.6 Administrative Effectiveness . . . 196
6.3 Testing Hypotheses for the Non-financial Reporting Directive . . . 197
6.3.1 Policy Misfit . . . 197
6.3.2 Institutional Misfit . . . 202
6.3.3 Government Composition . . . 203
6.3.4 Political Salience Within the Policy Subsystem . . . 204
6.3.5 International Policy Transfer . . . 206
6.3.6 Administrative Effectiveness . . . 208
6.4 Explaining Transposition Processes . . . 208
6.4.1 United Kingdom . . . 211
6.4.2 France . . . 213
6.4.3 Germany . . . 216
6.4.4 Denmark . . . 219
References . . . 223

7 Conclusion . . . 227
7.1 Discussion of Empirical Results . . . 229
7.1.1 Country-Specific Transposition Patterns . . . 229
7.1.2 Cross-Country Transposition Patterns . . . 237
7.2 Theoretical Conclusions . . . 242
7.3 Political Conclusions . . . 246
7.4 Outlook . . . 249
References . . . 250

Appendix A: List of Expert Interviews 253

Appendix B: Briefing note by the European Coalition for Corporate Justice (ECCJ) on the transposition of the NFR-Directive 255

Abbreviations

BHR	Business and Human Rights
CD	Concessions Directive
CDU	Christian Democratic Union (Germany)
CFSP	Common Foreign and Security Policy
CHES	Chapel Hill Expert Survey
CJEU	Court of Justice of the European Union
CME	Coordinated Market Economy
COREPER	Comité des représentants permanents (Committee of Permanent Representatives)
CSR	Corporate Social Responsibility
CSU	Christian Social Union (Germany)
DEFRA	Department for Environment Food and Rural Affairs
DG	Directorate-General
DGB	Deutscher Gewerkschaftsbund
DV	Dependent Variable
ECCJ	European Coalition for Corporate Justice
ECHR	European Convention on Human Rights
ECJ	European Court of Justice
ECtHR	European Court for Human Rights
EIDHR	European instrument for democracy and human rights
EP	European Parliament
ESG	Environmental, Social and Governance
EU	European Union
EURICO	EU-Richtlinien-Controlling
FDP	Free Democratic Party (Germany)
GPP	Green Public Procurement
GRI	Global Reporting Initiative
GSP+	Generalised Scheme of Preferences Plus
GWB	Gesetz gegen Wettbewerbsbeschränkungen
HGB	Handelsgesetzbuch

ICAR	International Corporate Accountability Roundtable
IFC	International Finance Corporation
ILO	International Labour Organization
IR	International Relations
ISO	International Organization for Standardization
IV	Independent Variable
KonzVgV	Konzessionsvergabeverordnung
KPI	Key Performance Indicator
LME	Liberal Market Economy
LREM	La République En Marche! (France)
MEAT	most economically advantageous tender
MEDEF	Mouvement des Entreprises de France
MEP	Member of the European Parliament
MNEs	Multinational Enterprises
NFR	Non-Financial Reporting
NGO	Non-Governmental Organization
NPE	Normative Power Europe
OECD	Organisation for Economic Co-operation and Development
OMC	Open Method of Coordination
PSD	Public Sector Directive
SektVO	Sektorenverordnung
SGAE	Secrétariat général des affaires européennes
SME	Small and medium-sized Enterprise
SPD	Social Democratic Party (Germany)
SRPP	Socially responsible public procurement
TEU	Treaty on European Union
TFEU	Treaty on the Functioning of the European Union
TNCs	Transnational Corporations
TTIP	Transatlantic Trade and Investment Partnership
UD	Utilities Directive
UK	United Kingdom
UN	United Nations
UNGPs	UN Guiding Principles on Business and Human Rights
USA	United States of America
VgV	Vergabeverordnung
VOB/A	Vergabe- und Vertragsordnung für Bauleistungen
VoC	Varieties of Capitalism

List of Figures

Fig. 2.1 Elements of EU BHR policy 18
Fig. 3.1 Classical design of top-down Europeanization research 59
Fig. 3.2 Magnitude and direction of national change in response to EU rules 60
Fig. 3.3 Directives in the EU multi-level process 62
Fig. 3.4 Independent variables and dependent variable 80
Fig. 4.1 Independent variables and dependent variable 105
Fig. 4.2 Categories for transposition analysis 107
Fig. 4.3 Thresholds for categorizing human rights scores for the public procurement directives 111
Fig. 4.4 Thresholds for categorizing human rights scores for the NFR-Directive 112
Fig. 4.5 Scale to measure the position of political parties on state intervention in the economy 116
Fig. 5.1 Stages of the EU public procurement process 125
Fig. 5.2 Transposition of public procurement directives by type 172
Fig. 5.3 Transposition of NFR-Directive by type 173

List of Tables

Table 2.1 Overview of EU measures in the EU BHR policy area 37
Table 3.1 Display of IVs with the assumed theoretical effects and associated transposition logics 90
Table 4.1 Spectrum of governmental approaches to BHR 103
Table 4.2 Possible transposition outcomes to measure commitment to human rights 108
Table 4.3 Calculation of yardsticks for the public procurement directives 110
Table 4.4 Calculation of yardsticks for the NFR-directive 112
Table 4.5 Siaroff's corporatism scores in 24 countries 115
Table 5.1 Provisions with human rights relevance in the three EU public procurement directives 128
Table 5.2 Transposition outcomes for the public procurement directives 147
Table 5.3 Transposition outcomes and human rights scores for the public procurement directives. 151
Table 5.4 Human rights score and transpositions by type for the public procurement directives 155
Table 5.5 Overview of human rights-related provisions in the NFR-Directive 161
Table 5.6 Transposition outcomes for the NFR-Directive 170
Table 5.7 Human rights score and transpositions by type for the NFR-directive 172
Table 5.8 Overview of transposition results for all directives. 174
Table 6.1 Results for the government effectiveness indicator 197
Table 6.2 Overview of all hypothesis tests. 209

List of Boxes

Box 1.1	Research question	3
Box 3.1	Hypothesis 1	82
Box 3.2	Hypothesis 2	84
Box 3.3	Hypothesis 3	84
Box 3.4	Hypotheses 4.1 and 4.2	86
Box 3.5	Hypothesis 5	87
Box 3.6	Hypothesis 6	88
Box 4.1	Research question	97
Box 4.2	Operationalization of the policy misfit for the public procurement directives	113
Box 4.3	Operationalization of the policy misfit for the NFR-directive	114
Box 6.1	Test of hypothesis 1 for the public procurement directives	189
Box 6.2	Test of hypothesis 2 for the public procurement directives	190
Box 6.3	Test of hypothesis 3 for the public procurement directives	191
Box 6.4	Test of hypotheses 4.1 and 4.2 for the public procurement directives	194
Box 6.5	Test of hypothesis 5 for the public procurement directives	196
Box 6.6	Test of hypothesis 1 for the NFR-Directive	202
Box 6.7	Test of hypothesis 2 for the NFR-Directive	203
Box 6.8	Test of hypothesis 3 for the NFR-Directive	204
Box 6.9	Test of hypotheses 4.1 and 4.2 for the NFR-Directive	206
Box 6.10	Test of hypothesis 5 for the NFR-Directive	208

Chapter 1
Introduction

> What is puzzling about member states' policies is that they respond differently to identical European policy demands and similar external and internal conditions [...]. (Héritier & Knill, 2000, p. 1)

To harmonize rules among its member states is one of the central goals of European integration and requires the constant reconciliation between 'community and autonomy' (Scharpf, 1994). Perhaps more than any other instrument of European integration, EU (European Union) directives, which must be transposed as the result to be achieved, represent the balancing act between ensuring a uniform application of EU rules and respecting the cultural and institutional diversity between member states. Because they give national governments the discretion to integrate domestic preferences, EU directives are neither purely supranational nor completely national (Ciavarini Azzi, 2000). How much flexibility is provided and how member states utilize the room for manoeuvre depends very much on the policy area in which the directive is used. When it comes to the promotion of human rights around the world, one would expect a large degree of uniformity among national transpositions. After all, EU member states share the respect for human rights as a common value, which is laid down as a general principle of European law (TEU, Article 2 & Article 6). With the EU Charter of Fundamental Rights (EU Charter), member states have bound themselves to the arguably most comprehensive human rights framework in Europe.[1] This far-reaching commitment to human rights is also set to guide all international activity of the EU.[2] This book analyses how the transposition of EU directives, which aim at ensuring and promoting the protection of human rights by internationally operating companies, shows surprising degrees of variation between member states.[3] The goal of this study is to determine and explain this variation.

[1] Poland and the United Kingdom have chosen to opt out from the EU Charter.

[2] See Article 21 TEU.

[3] The term transposition refers to the adoption of a national law by the government of an EU member state, whereby the directive provisions are converted into national law (Falkner, Treib, Hartlapp, & Leiber, 2005, p. 6).

P. Drahn, *Adoption of EU Business and Human Rights Policy*,
Contributions to Political Science, https://doi.org/10.1007/978-3-030-46935-1_1

The EU external impact on human rights around the world reaches beyond its foreign, development, and trade policies, where 'human rights clauses' establish the EU's normative commitment. Being a 'regulatory state' (Majone, 1996), the EU provides for the regulatory framework of EU-based companies that operate globally. Due to the "widening gap between global markets and the capacity of societies to manage their consequences" (United Nations, 2006, p. 7), human rights violations are known to occur in global supply chains. According to a report on human rights risks and impacts of large companies, half of all companies listed on the largest German, French, and British stock exchanges were identified in allegations regarding adverse human rights risks between 2005 and 2013 (International Peace Information Service, 2014). EU regulation has the potential to mitigate such human rights risks.

EU activities to foster corporate responsibility for human rights are subsumed under the emerging EU policy area *Business and Human Rights* (BHR). Measures in this field are closely related, but not similar to, activities in the area of Corporate Social Responsibility (CSR).[4] The EU drafted its BHR policy as a response to the United Nations Guiding Principles on Business and Human Rights (UNGPs), adopted by the United Nations (UN) human rights council in 2011. The *Protect, Respect and Remedy framework*, the core of the UNGPs, has become the global standard for addressing human rights violations, most notably by stressing the collective responsibility of both states and businesses to prevent human rights violations in global supply chains. With the support of international civil society organizations, a broad coalition of reform-minded businesses, and many accompanying international standards, the UNGPs globally advocate a 'smart mix' of voluntary and binding measures that every country in the world should implement. In response, the EU stressed the importance of "integrating human rights aspects into all policy areas of the European Union" (Council of the European Union, 2009, p. 1) and recognized the UNGPs as the "authoritative policy framework" (European Commission, 2015). Through a variety of legislative and coordinative measures, the EU has worked towards the implementation of the UNGPs.

A problem that arises when studying the EU's activity in this field is that most of the commitments to strengthen corporate responsibility for human rights are only 'soft' commitments and largely of declaratory nature. This corresponds with findings in the human rights literature, which point to a discrepancy between the EU's public commitment to human rights, and the implementation of policies that ensure the protection of human rights (see e.g. Alston & Weiler, 1999; Gatto, 2011). Legal obligations that would put teeth into human rights regulations by making responsible businesses conduct mandatory for companies are largely dependent on the EU member states. This is due to the complex allocation of competences within the EU multi-level system, according to which regulatory activity in the area of economic regulation or market power, which is crucial for BHR policy, lies largely at the member state level (Eberlein & Grande, 2005, p. 104). Moreover, harmonization

[4]The concept of CSR was developed in the business community and was only gradually brought into the regulatory policy context. It usually follows a broader understanding of sustainability and includes also environmental measures.

through EU directives provides member states with a large amount of leeway about which provisions to transpose and how to transpose them into national law. This large degree of discretion puts member states in the central position of EU BHR regulation because they can choose if they want to rely on binding measures or on 'voluntary regulation'.[5] The problem that this study addresses is that the transposition of directives which include EU requirements in the area of BHR is far from uniform. For example, EU reporting requirements on human rights risks in Germany apply only to listed companies with more than 500 employees and exceptions are possible. In Denmark, the same requirements exist for all Danish companies without exceptions.[6]

How can the considerable variation of the degree to which member states are willing to adopt stricter human rights requirements be explained? The policy input from the EU level is similar for all member states, but the policy output in the form of the transposition laws varies significantly. Primary EU law and the EU Charter equally bind all EU member states, which have all signed the UNGPs as individual countries, but at the same time, seek to protect their industries from regulation that could hamper their competitiveness in the global economy. Given that all member states are confronted with the same set of rules, why are some member states willing to go further than others? In this book, I address this research puzzle by answering the following research question:

> How and why do EU member states differ regarding the degree to which they transpose non-binding provisions of Business and Human Rights regulation in EU directives?

Box 1.1 Research question

As we can see, the research question consists of two parts, one descriptive and one causal question. Hence, I approach this research question in two steps. First, I compare how the four member states considered in this study (UK, France, Germany, and Denmark) transposed four EU directives in the policy area of BHR. The directives analysed are the three directives of the so-called 'public procurement package',[7] which contain several provisions on social and human rights concerns, and the Non-Financial Reporting Directive (NFR-Directive).[8] The public procurement directives

[5]The definition of voluntary regulation this study draws on the understanding by Potoski and Prakash, who define voluntary regulation as "rule structures [...] that seek to persuade firms to incur nontrivial costs of producing positive externalities beyond what the law requires of them" (Potoski & Prakash, 2009, p. ix).

[6]More specifically, Danish reporting requirements apply to companies that fall into accounting class D and have less than 500 employees, and to companies that are subject to accounting class C (Danish Business Authority, 2015, p. 6). For a more detailed comparison, see Chap. 5.

[7]Directive on public procurement (2014/24/EU), Directive for entities operating in the utilities sector (2014/25/EU), Directive on the award of concession contracts (2014/23/EU).

[8]Directive 2014/95/EU of the European Parliament and of the Council of 22 October 2014 amending Directive 2013/34/EU as regards disclosure of non-financial and diversity information by certain large undertakings and groups.

contain several clauses that require member states to integrate human rights concerns in their national procurement policies.[9] The NFR-Directive, which has become a poster child for BHR regulation, requires large European companies to disclose information about their policies and impacts on human rights as well as other social and environmental matters. In a comprehensive analysis of the national transposition laws, I compare how national governments transposed the mandatory and the voluntary provisions of these directives. The focus is put on the member states' usage of the 'discretionary room' of the directives, which I use as a yardstick to measure their willingness to adopt stricter human rights regulations. The second part of this analysis examines the reasons behind the variation. Relying on policy analysis and expert interviews, I attempt to explain the national transposition processes by testing the validity of six explanatory factors. At the core, this study therefore seeks to understand why member states react differently to flexible EU rules in a new and contentious policy area.

1.1 Academic Relevance for Europeanization and Voluntarism in the EU

This study contributes to our understanding of the EU BHR policy and advances the assessment of its effectiveness. At the same time, it sheds another light on the complicated relationship between the EU and its member states. By inquiring into the relationship between member states and EU in the new and interdisciplinary field of BHR policy, it contributes to the continuously evolving Europeanization research agenda. Ever since the early Europeanization studies in the mid-1990s (see e.g. Bulmer & Burch, 1998; Ladrech, 1994; Wessels & Rometsch, 1996), scholars in this field have been interested in explaining how European integration impacted structures, procedures, and norms at home. It was recognized that Europeanization included continuous feedback loops, which act as a "two-way-street" (Bomberg & Peterson, 2000, p. 7) between the EU and its member states. Efforts to methodologically grasp the reciprocal and continuously ongoing "processes of construction, diffusion, and institutionalisation" (Radaelli, 2003, p. 30) between the EU level and the member state level have brought about the concept of "circular Europeanization" (Saurugger, 2014, p. 183). Within this broad field of research, the study at hand limits itself to the top-down approach of Europeanization. While in a comprehensive study national bottom-up impacts on the EU-level cannot be ignored completely, it predominately focuses on member states' responses to EU rules.

This book contributes to the academic literature in two main ways. First, it responds to the Europeanization literature by assessing the relationship between the EU and its member states in a new, cross-sectional policy area. It examines member

[9] Public procurement can be defined as "the process by which public authorities, such as government departments or local authorities, purchase works, goods or services from suppliers that they have selected for this purpose" (European PPP Expertise Center, 2016, p. 5).

states' use of the 'discretionary room' of directives, by taking domestic politics seriously, and by taking into account the influence of international policy commitments. Secondly, it contributes to the understanding of voluntary governance by linking the debate on voluntary BHR regulation and the debate on voluntarism in the EU.

Europeanization is a continuously evolving research area because the relationship between the European integration process and member states is in constant flux. Even though the hype around this field has dampened down after the height of the Europeanization research agenda at the end of the 1990s and the early 2000s, the question of how the EU and its member states affect each other remains as topical as ever. In view of the vast regulatory challenges the EU faces, the interest in policy-specific directive transposition studies has increased over the last years (Fischer, 2017; Kaeding, Schmälter, & Klika, 2017; Thomann, 2015; Zhelyazkova, 2013; Zhelyazkova, Kaya, & Schrama, 2016; Zhelyazkova & Torenvlied, 2011). This is not surprising, because the responses to EU directives allow researchers to investigate a policy problem through the national lens and the community lens at the same time (Ciavarini Azzi, 2000). In this respect, the book contributes to the Europeanization research area by being the first work to study directive transposition in the field of BHR policy.

Second, I build on recent literature contributions to advance our understanding of flexible responses to EU directives. For the most part, previous directive transposition research has only applied simple frameworks to measure directive transposition, which often captured the transposition outcomes in a binary way. Scholars investigated if transpositions were on time or not on time, or if they were 'successful' or unsuccessful (see e.g. Kaeding et al., 2017; Zhelyazkova & Torenvlied, 2011). Recently some researchers have embraced a more comprehensive understanding of transposition responses that can capture varying degrees of transposition outcomes that go beyond the required minimum. Most notably, Thomann (2015) has analysed the transposition results beyond the minimum in four member states, using the example of veterinary drug regulations. She found that member states 'customize' their transpositions to individually solve a common problem. She states: "We evidently need to move beyond compliance […] to gain a fuller understanding of these often neglected, more fine-grained patterns of Europeanization" (p. 1384). With this book, I respond to this demand by providing an analytical framework that captures in how far member states are willing to go beyond the required minimum in the transposition of directives in the field of BHR. By taking the discretionary room seriously and using it as a tool to measure how far member states are willing to follow EU rules, I propose a more elaborate measure to assess how much European legislation influences national policymaking.

Third, this study contributes to Europeanization literature by advocating to pay more attention to the domestic political forces of transposition. Many Europeanization studies still depict directive transposition as a technical process, in which a specific interplay of functional variables will lead to a particular outcome. These works have their roots in classical implementation theory, which understands directive transposition essentially as an apolitical process, the success of which only depends on the clarity and coherence of the directive and the speed and efficiency of the national administrations (see e.g. Schwarze, Becker, & Pollak, 1993). Especially large quantitative studies that analyse the 'mass production of law' (Berglund, Gange, & Van Waarden, 2006) neglect the importance of political factors in the transposition. Even though the role of political factors has been recognized before (see e.g. Falkner et al. 2005; Thomann, 2015; Treib, 2003), such studies are still underrepresented, especially in recent contributions to the Europeanization literature. This study advances the understanding of political factors, such as government preferences or political salience, by examining their relative importance in domestic policy processes. Moreover, the goal is to examine the interplay between domestic political forces and the 'misfit', one of the central theses in directive transposition research, and to draw conclusions about their effect on transposition processes.[10]

Finally, this study is the first to take into account the effect of international norms on the national transposition process. As already mentioned, the primary impetus for the EU to become active on the issue of BHR came from the UNGPs. Even though the EU has adopted strategies concerning CSR before, the UN was and continues to be a driver for both the European institutions and the EU member states. While it is evident that BHR policy was transferred from the UN to the EU, this study also investigates, if transfer processes also affected the national transposition processes in this policy area.

Another area to which this book makes an academic contribution is the issue of voluntarism in EU governance. To set mandatory minimum standards while at the same time including a large number of non-binding regulations has become a well-establish practice across many policy areas (Fairbrass, 2011; Falkner et al., 2005). In this book, I use discretion as a tool to measure member states' policy commitment. Thereby, I seek to contribute to the ongoing debate about the effectiveness and voluntary regulation in the EU. In this debate, it was argued that in social policies and other 'market-correcting' policies, the EU was heavily relying on voluntarism instead of binding rules (see e.g. Leiber & Schäfer, 2008).[11] The question of voluntarism has even been integrated into typologies of European integration. Knill and Lehmkuhl (1999) argue that there are three types of integration, each of which corresponds to specific policy areas. Building on the works of Fritz Scharpf (e.g. Scharpf, 2008) and others, they distinguish between positive integration, negative integration, and 'framing' integration.[12] In the area of positive integration, the EU policy 'positively' prescribes an institutional model that the member states have to adopt. This type of integration refers to market-correcting measures, such as the exercise of

[10]The misfit refers to the "incompatibility between European-level processes, policies and institutions [...] and domestic-level processes, policies and institutions" (Börzel & Risse 2000, p. 1). As will be explained in Chap. 3, the misfit thesis holds that a greater misfit, i.e. a large degree of incompatibility, makes the adaptation to EU rules more difficult.

[11]Two examples for the reliance on voluntary regulation are the Open Method of Coordination and the 'social dialogue', a consultative dialogue between employers and labour unions.

[12]Scharpf defines negative integration as the form of integration that creates the single market, i.e. through the removal of barriers to free trade, and other distortions of competition, while positive integration refers to the exercise of competencies in the areas of economic policy and regulation (Scharpf, 2008, p. 50f).

competencies in the areas of economic policy and regulation (ibid, p. 50f). Negative integration describes the removal of barriers to the single market and the reduction of distortions to economic competition, which is achieved by changing domestic opportunity structures.[13] In *framing integration*, arguably the weakest mechanism, European policy alters beliefs and expectations of domestic actors. Framing integration is related to the concept of 'Neo-Voluntarism', which was coined by Wolfgang Streeck in 1995 when he criticised the development of European social policy in the post-Maastricht EU. He analysed the state of European social policy at the time and argued, in brief, that contrary to some expectations, European integration had not led to a European 'superstate' that would absorb and eventually replace national welfare states. Instead, the EU had developed to be a *sui generis* polity that was limited to market-making forces, which would partly undermine national social policy regimes. Following his argument, national social policy regimes would not be replaced with market-correcting forces on the EU-level, but with soft incentives and voluntary forms of regulation (Streeck, 1995). Schäfer (2005) comes to a similar assessment of the spreading application of 'soft modes of economic coordination' in the EU. He argues that the increasing heterogeneity among EU member states reduces the probability of a comprehensive policy consensus in EU economic policy, which is why voluntarist procedures have prevailed (see also Leiber & Schäfer, 2008). He holds that the effectiveness of soft coordination is much more dependent on the willingness of national governments than is the case with the community method (Schäfer, 2005, p. 223). In Chap. 2 of this book, I argue that the EU's BHR policy can be classified as a case of positive, market correcting integration, which addresses market deficiencies not only within, but also outside the EU.[14]

However, in the case of the directives analysed in this study, observers agree that the degree to which the measures are 'market-correcting' depends on national transpositions (Institute for Human Rights and Business, 2015; Kinderman, 2015; Spießhofer, 2014). In answering the research question, this study examines the interplay between domestic and external factors and explains why member states chose to transpose voluntary measures. This examination also underscores the tension between measures of positive integration on the one hand, and the large flexibility for national transposition and implementation on the other hand. Hence, this study addresses the scepticism some scholars have raised about the dissemination of 'voluntary regulation', who argued that flexible approaches would undermine normative command and control regulation (e.g. Leiber & Schäfer, 2008; Schäfer, 2005; Streeck, 1995). For example, Gerda Falkner has asked: "[I]s a flexible governance style necessarily a good thing? Could it even be a dangerous development?" (Falkner et al., 2005, p.1). The conclusion of this book tackles these questions by drawing on

[13] Scharpf (2008) argues that the enforcement of supranational European law by the Court of Justice of the European Union, which is in his view more effective than intergovernmental political decision-making, has mainly promoted negative integration, leading to an asymmetry between state and market that favours the latter over the former (ibid).

[14] Instead of arguing that increasing regulation would contribute to positive integration, other authors stress that relying on regulation would lead to a transition from a 'positive' to the 'regulatory' state (e.g. Bulmer, Dolowitz, Humphreys, & Padgett, 2007, p. 2).

the empirical insights gathered. Thereby, this study establishes a link between the debate on flexible governance in the EU and the debate on voluntary approaches to human rights regulation.

1.2 Political Relevance for Assessing EU Human Rights Commitments and Corporate Accountability

An analysis of EU BHR policy contributes to the political debate about the credibility of EU human rights commitments. The EU unambiguously presents itself as a standard-bearer and protector of human rights around the world. The EU's constituting texts stipulate that "[t]he Union's action on the international scene shall be guided by the principles which have inspired its own creation [...]: democracy, the rule of law, the universality and indivisibility of human rights [...]" (TEU, Title V, Chapter 1, Article 21). One of the most popular tools to conceptualize the EU as a 'force for good' has been the concept of 'Normative Power Europe' (NPE), introduced by Manners (2002). Key EU representatives, including the former Commission president José Manuel Barroso, endorsed the NPE concept (see Carta, 2008). Academics have challenged this appraisal on many accounts (Damro, 2012; Parker & Rosamond, 2013). One argument brought forward by critics points to a gap between the publicly stated commitment to human rights and policy implementation of this commitment (Wood, 2009).[15]

Politically, the claim that the EU is a normative power in the world is closely related to the EU's legitimacy, which has been challenged by Eurosceptic parties from the political left and the political right. The refugee crisis, the austerity policy in the Eurozone that followed the sovereign debt crisis, and the EU's limited capacity to prevent conflicts and human suffering in its wider neighbourhood have damaged the EU's image as a value-based community. One reason for the widespread success of Eurosceptic parties was the promise to protect local communities from globalization's and European integration's negative externalities. EU BHR policy presents a possibility for EU policymakers to underscore the EU's normative commitment, and to tackle one of globalization's negative effects, human rights abuses in global supply chains. According to Jacoby and Meunier (2010), such policies would meet the demand of the EU population, because "[i]n the eyes of most European citizens, the EU owes its legitimacy partly to being able to protect them from the negative side-effects of globalization while shaping aggressively a globalization in Europe's image" (p. 367). If the EU and its member states are able to hold corporations to account by introducing globally applicable human rights regulation, it has the

[15] A prominent response to NPE was formulated by Damro (2012), who proposed the concept of Market Power Europe (MPE). It does not promote any normative claims about the EU but positions the common market at the core of its identity. Damro (2012) argues: "The single market provides the material existence of the EU as an MPE that externalizes its economic and social market-related policies and regulatory measures" (p. 683).

potential to restore political accountability and credibility. The European Commission regards itself as "leading by example in business and human rights" (European Commission, 2015).[16] However, the credibility of this goal also depends on how effectively the EU and its member states transpose and implement BHR policies. In that respect, this book contributes to the assessment of this policy.

Just like the EU, the member states have committed themselves to respecting and promoting human rights. However, the cases where EU member states demonstrate their commitment to human rights are rare. The wider public seldom discusses the transposition of EU directives. Like with most EU policies, member states can 'hide' behind policies that were decided in Brussels. However, especially with directives that offer a large degree of discretion, it is politically important to make transparent, how member states used the freedom they had with the transposition. Concerning the NFR-Directive and the three public procurement directives, this study contributes to this transparency.

Next to governmental accountability, this book also contributes to policy discussion about the accountability of large corporations in Europe. In 2014 the world's top 100 Transnational Corporations (TNCs) held assets of 13.8 trillion US dollars and employed 16.8 million people, 57% of which did not work in the home country of that company (UNCTAD, 2015). The debate on trade agreements such as the Transatlantic Trade and Investment Partnership (TTIP) has brought to light public controversies over the influence of large multinational corporations have vis-à-vis the EU and its member states. Similarly, public discussions about the evasion of taxes by large international companies have raised doubts about the EU's regulatory authority over TNCs. Kobrin (2007) stated that TNCs had become "actors with private political authority in the international system: they can set standards, supply public goods and participate in international negotiations" (p.3). The European CSR agenda, the previous attempt to increase corporate accountability in Europe, has yielded little success in this respect, which was, as has been noted partly due to CSR's inherent ambiguity (Kinderman, 2013). EU BHR policy, on the other hand, has the potential to foster corporate accountability beyond the EU, because it entails extraterritorial state obligations[17] and describes a diagonal concept since it formulates state obligations towards individuals in other countries (Weber, 2009). It draws its legal bases from several international human rights treaties.[18] Legal scholars are debating, if the legal obligation of states to protect human rights extends beyond the state's territory, for example when a company domiciled in an EU member state is involved in human rights violations outside the EU. De facto existing European regulation in the areas of business regulation, environmental protection, or anti-corruption already entail provisions with extraterritorial effect (Augenstein, 2010). An example of EU

[16]Throughout this book I will use the term 'Commission' when referring to the European Commission.

[17]Other terms used in the debate are 'external obligations', 'transborder obligations', 'universal obligations', and 'international human rights obligations'.

[18]For example, the such as the UN Charter, the Vienna Convention on the Law of Treaties, and the International Covenant on Civil and Political Rights.

BHR regulation with extraterritorial effect is the so-called Victims Directive,[19] which confers rights on individuals, who became victims of extraterritorial human rights violations and who will become involved in criminal proceedings that take place in an EU country (European Commission, 2015). The four EU directives that are analysed in this study also have the potential to set extraterritorial obligations for companies. The empirical results can therefore contribute to our understanding of the EU's ability to establish corporate accountability vis-à-vis large multinational corporations.

1.3 Theoretical Approach, Scope, and Structure of the Book

How member states react to the rules formulated in the EU is contingent on a range of factors. Depending on the individual case, long-established policy legacies can be just as decisive as the political preferences of a newly elected government. As Héritier and Knill observe, "the scope and direction of domestic regulatory changes [...] are dependent upon the distinctive constellation of regulatory, ideological and institutional factors at the national level" (Héritier & Knill, 2000, p. 27). To approach the analysis of directive transposition in the field of BHR regulation from a theoretical perspective, I adopt a pluri-theoretical approach.[20] From different conceptual explanations for divergence in directive transposition in the literature, a set of relevant independent variables are derived that will be tested for their explanatory power. For the most part, this study relies on the three classic variants of new institutionalist theory: rational choice institutionalism, sociological institutionalism, and historical institutionalism. For scholars of Europeanization, new institutionalist explanations have been the starting point in efforts to find the "missing link" (Goetz, 2000, p. 222) between the increased European output and domestic change. The literature has recognized that institutions are central agents in political systems that play a vital role in the implementation of European rules (see e.g. Börzel, 1999; Börzel & Risse, 2000; Héritier, 2001; Olsen, 2002; Radaelli, 2000, 2003). Rational choice institutionalism assumes that political players act rationally, but within the confines of institutions, and behave according to a *logic of expected consequences*. This school of thought expects them to act in a highly strategic manner, where calculations are made about how other actors will behave. Historical institutionalism has been the theoretical basis for the formulation of the misfit thesis, which assumes that long-established national rules are 'sticky' and difficult to change. Sociological institutionalism, on the other hand, stresses the role of norms in the transposition processes. According to this school of thought, socialization and collective learning processes would cause key actors to internalize norms, who would then act according to a *logic of appropriateness* (Börzel & Risse, 2000). A similar logic is used in this study to take into

[19] 2012/29/EU.

[20] I adopted the term 'pluri-theoretical approach' from Falkner et al. (2005).

account the influence of policy transfer on the national transpositions, i.e. the transfer of international norms from international organisations to national governments.

The new institutionalist approaches from the directive transposition literature are complemented with theoretical approaches that are employed by the literature on corporate responsibility. This literature has established a link between the institutional setup of the political economy and state behaviour in the field of BHR (see Kinderman, 2009, 2013). This study is not the first to make the connection between the institutional setup of the political economy and the outcomes of directive transpositions (see e.g. Thomson, 2010). To make initial assumptions about the relationship between the institutional arrangements of a political economy and government behaviour in the field of BHR, I rely on the Varieties of Capitalism (VoC) approach by Hall and Soskice (2001). VoC puts firms in the centre of the analysis that seek to rationally advance their interests by coordinating with a range of internal and external actors across several spheres.[21] In different countries, this process happens according to distinct modes of coordination, from which Hall and Soskice draw the distinction between two sorts of political economies: liberal market economies (LMEs), and coordinated market economies (CMEs) (Hall & Soskice, 2001, p. 8). This typology provides the basis for the operationalization of the 'institutional misfit', the effect of which on the transposition outcome is tested. Lastly, classical implementation theory will also be considered to complete the setup of possible explanatory factors.

Based on these theoretical considerations I formulate hypotheses which are tested in the empirical analysis of this study. I conduct a qualitative comparison of the transposition of four EU directives in the policy area of BHR regulation. The methods used are policy analysis and expert interviews. Following the method of structured and focused comparison, I contrast the transpositions of four member states. The dependent variable (DV) is the transposition of human rights clauses in the four directives. It is operationalized by analysing how each member state transposed the human rights-related provisions in the directives. To explain the DV, six independent variables (IVs) are taken into consideration. The first IV is the policy misfit between the EU directive and the national laws before the adoption of the directive. This is a classical factor in implementation studies which relies on the historical institutionalist assumption of 'sticky' institutions. The second factor also assumes path-dependent institutions but builds on the institutional setup of the political economy. With this variable, I test if key characteristics of the political economy can explain how member states transpose the EU directives. The third and fourth factors take into account the politics of transposition, as they consider the influence of the composition of the domestic government and the salience of the transposition within the policy subsystem. The fifth factor looks at the effect on international policy transfer on the transposition outcome. Finally, functional determinants are also considered, since classical implementation theory holds that administrative efficiency of national authorities is highly relevant, both for implementation and transposition outcomes.

---

[21] Industrial relations, vocational training and education, corporate governance, inter-firm relations, and employees.

The scope of this book is largely determined by the limitation to the transposition analysis of four EU directives in four EU member states. The immediate explanatory power of the empirical results is limited to the units of analysis. However, the countries and directives were chosen to allow for a significant degree of generalizability of the results. The member states that are considered are the UK, France, Germany, and Denmark. The selection of these four cases followed the logic of diverse cases, which aims at "the achievement of maximum variance along relevant dimensions" (Gerring, 2007, p. 97). The approach has the objective to achieve large representativeness of the sample by choosing countries that show diversity in the dimensions that are relevant for the policy area in which the comparative analysis is conducted. The dimensions that were considered to be relevant were the positioning of the governments in the area of BHR and the institutional setup of the political economy. While the transposition process is unique in each member state, the fact that other EU member states share similar characteristics with the four selected countries increases the chance that the results can be generalized beyond the scope of this study.[22]

The second decision limiting the scope of this book was the choice of the directives. The directives analysed are the three directives of the so-called 'public procurement package', which contain several provisions on social and human rights concerns, and the NFR-Directive. The public procurement directives contain several clauses that require member states to integrate human rights concerns in their national procurement policies. The NFR-Directive, which has become a poster child for BHR regulation, requires large European companies to disclose information about their policies and impacts on human rights and other social and environmental matters. These directives are central elements of the EU's efforts to implement the UNGPs, which is why it is possible to draw more general conclusions for the policy area as a whole. The choice of directives also determines the period of investigation, which is set between February 2014 and August 2017. All four directives considered in this analysis were adopted in 2014 and the last transposition legislation was passed by the French parliament in August 2017.

This book is structured in seven chapters. Chapter 2 provides a comprehensive account of the development and features of the EU BHR policy area. It establishes that this policy area rests on two pillars: the EU human rights regime and EU CSR policy, both of which contain inherent contradictions which in turn also affect EU BHR policy. The review of previous research in these fields highlights an 'implementation gap' between the EU's commitment to human rights and the practical implementation of EU human rights policy. Moreover, I characterize EU BHR policy as a regulative policy area that was transferred from the UN level to the EU level and identify policy-specific factors that are integrated in the analytical framework of this study. Finally, this chapter briefly sets out the current state of play of EU BHR policy and substantiates, why the public procurement directives and the NFR-Directive were chosen for the empirical analysis.

[22]It can be assumed that member states for which the results can have explanatory power are for example the Benelux-countries, Sweden, Finland, Ireland, and Austria.

Chapter 3 addresses theoretical explanations for the domestic impact of EU law. It starts with an elucidation of the three schools of new institutionalism that are employed in this analysis: rational choice institutionalism, historical institutionalism, and sociological institutionalism. It then goes on to provide a review of the literature on Europeanization and directive transposition and identifies several factors that are suited to account for the transposition variation investigated in this book. Furthermore, the chapter gives a brief account of the concept of policy transfer, which informs one of the IVs. Finally, drawing on the previously gathered theoretical insights, I postulate several hypotheses and present the analytical framework. Chapter 4 describes the research design for the empirical analysis. It features the methodological approach and reviews the selection of directives. Moreover, the chapter explains that the country selection follows the logic of diverse cases in order to achieve the maximum variance along the dimensions relevant for the policy area of BHR. After outlining the Y-centred research perspective, the last sections operationalize the dependent and independent variables and describe the means of data collection.

Chapter 5 represents the first part of the empirical analysis and tackles the descriptive part of the research question, namely how the transpositions of the four directives investigated differ between member states. The first two sections give detailed accounts of the transpositions of the public procurement directives and the NFR-Directive by the UK, France, Germany, and Denmark. For each directive, one section will first present all pertinent directive provisions and rank them according to their relevance for human rights. Then, I explain how the national transposition laws in the four member states have transposed these provisions. At the end of each section, the transposition scores are set side by side to highlight the different degrees to which the discretionary room was used. Finally, the last section of Chap. 5 combines the results for all directives and visualizes the transposition variation.

Chapter 6 represents the second part of the empirical analysis and answers the causal part of the research question, namely why transposition outcomes differ. The first section of this chapter describes the political and institutional background in which the national transpositions took place. Sections 6.2 and 6.3 test the hypotheses formulated in Chap. 3 for the public procurement directives and the NFR-Directive in each country. The last section of Chap. 6 places the insights gathered from the hypothesis testing back into the domestic policy context. By relying on national policy documents and information from expert interviews, this section explains the relationship and relative importance of each of the factors for the transposition outcome.

The concluding chapter discusses the results gathered in Chaps. 5 and 6 and answers the research question of this study. First, I discuss the empirical results both from a country-specific and from a factor-specific perspective. The following section presents the theoretical conclusions and explains, why a combination of historical institutionalism and rational choice institutionalism is best suited to account for the transposition variation. The insights gathered in this study are contrasted with findings from the literature on Europeanization and directive transposition. The second section of this chapter draws political conclusions for the practice of directive transposition, the BHR policy area, and the EU's human rights regime. I discuss the political relevance of the findings and formulate policy recommendations. The last section presents a political outlook and suggests avenues for further research.

References

Alston, P., & Weiler, J. H. H. (1999). An "ever closer union" in need of a human rights policy: the European Union and human rights. In *The EU and Human Rights* (pp. 3–69).

Augenstein, D. (2010). *Study of the legal framework on human rights and the environment applicable to European enterprises operating outside the European Union*. University of Edinburgh. Retrieved from http://www.euenterpriseslf.ed.ac.uk/project_documents.

Berglund, S., Gange, I., & Van Waarden, F. (2006). Mass production of law. Routinization in the transposition of European directives: A sociological- institutionalist account. *Journal of European Public Policy, 13*(5), 692–716.

Bomberg, E., & Peterson, J. (2000). *Policy Transfer and Europeanization: Passing the Heineken Test? Queens Papers on Europeanization*. Retrieved from http://citeseerx.ist.psu.edu/viewdoc/summary?doi=10.1.1.530.7978.

Börzel, T. (1999). Towards convergence in Europe? Institutional adaptation to Europeanization in Germany and Spain. *Journal of Common Market Studies, 37*(4), 573–596.

Börzel, T., & Risse, T. (2000). When Europe hits home: Europeanization and domestic change. *European Integration Online Papers, 4*(No. 15).

Bulmer, S., & Burch, M. (1998). Organizing for Europe: Whitehall, the British State and European Union. *Public Administration, 76*(4), 601–628.

Bulmer, S., Dolowitz, D., Humphreys, P., & Padgett, S. (2007). *Policy transfer in European Union Governance: Regulating the utilities*. New York: Routledge.

Carta, C. (2008). EU's International image as seen by the commission's diplomats. *European Foreign Affairs Review, 13*.

Ciavarini Azzi, G. (2000). The slow march of European legislation: the implementation of directives. In K. Neunreither & A. Wiener (Eds.), *European integration after Amsterdam: Institutional dynamics and prospects for democracy* (p. 384). Oxford: Oxford University Press.

Council of the European Union. Council conclusions on Human Rights and Democratisation in third countries 2985th FOREIGN AFFAIRS Council meeting Brussels, 8 December 2009 (2009). Brussels.

Damro, C. (2012). Market power Europe. *Journal of European Public Policy, 19*(5), 682–699.

Danish Business Authority. (2015). Implementation in Denmark of EU Directive 2014/95/EU on the disclosure of non-financial information. Retrieved October 5, 2016, from http://csrgov.dk/file/557863/implementation-of-eu-directive.pdf.

Directive 2014/23/EU of the European Parliament and of the Council of 26 February 2014 on the award of concession contracts. (2014). Official Journal of the European Union, L 94.

Directive 2014/24/EU of the European Parliament and of the Council of 26 February 2014 on public procurement and repealing Directive 2004/18/EC. (2014). Official Journal of the European Union, L 94.

Directive 2014/25/EU of the European Parliament and of the Council of 26 February 2014 on procurement by entities operating in the water, energy, transport and postal services sectors and repealing Directive 2004/17/EC. (2014). Official Journal of the European Union, L 94.

Directive 2014/95/EU of the European Parliament and of the Council of 22 October 2014 amending Directive 2013/34/EU as regards disclosure of non-financial and diversity information by certain large undertakings and groups. (2014). Official Journal of the European Union, L 330.

Eberlein, B., & Grande, E. (2005). Beyond delegation: Transnational regulatory regimes and the EU regulatory state. *Journal of European Public Policy, 12*(1), 89–112.

European Commission. (2015). commission staff working document on implementing the UN guiding principles on business and human rights—state of play. Brussels.

European PPP Expertise Center. (2016). *PPPs and procurement—impact of the new EU Directives*. Retrieved from http://www.eib.org/epec/resources/publications/epec_ppp_and_procurement_en.

Fairbrass, J. (2011). Exploring corporate social responsibility policy in the EU: A discursive institutionalist analysis. *Journal of Common Market Studies, 49*(5), 949–970.

Falkner, G., Treib, O., Hartlapp, M., & Leiber, S. (2005). *Complying with Europe. EU Harmonisation and soft law in the member states*. New York: Cambridge University Press.
Fischer, S. (2017). *Die Energiewende und Europa—Europäisierungsprozesse in der deutschen Energie- und Klimapolitik*. Wiesbaden: Springer VS.
Gatto, A. (2011). *Multinational enterprises and human rights: Obligations under EU law and international law*. Cheltenham: Edward Elgar.
Gerring, J. (2007). *Case study research : Principles and practices*. Cambridge University Press.
Goetz, K. H. (2000). European integration and national executives: A cause in search of an effect? *West European Politics, 23*(4), 211–231.
Hall, P. A., & Soskice, D. (2001). An introduction to varieties of capitalism. In P. A. Hall & D. Soskice (Eds.), *Varieties of capitalism: The institutional foundations of comparative advantage* (pp. 1–68). Oxford: Oxford University Press.
Héritier, A. (2001). Differential Europe. The European Union Impact on National Policymaking. In M. G. Cowles, J. A. Caporaso, & T. Risse (Eds.), *Transforming Europe. Europeanization and Domestic Change* (pp. 1–22). Lanham, Md.: Rowman & Littlefield Publishers.
Héritier, A., & Knill, C. (2000). Differential responses to european policies: A comparison. *Max-Planck Project Group Preprint, No. 2000/7*.
Institute for Human Rights and Business. (2015). protecting rights by purchasing right—the human rights provisions, opportunities and limitations under the 2014 EU Public Procurement Directive.
International Peace Information Service. (2014). *The adverse human rights risks and impacts of European companies: Getting a glimpse of the picture*. Antwerp.
Jacoby, W., & Meunier, S. (2010). Europe and globalization. In *Research Agendas in EU Studies* (pp. 354–374). Springer.
Kaeding, M., Schmälter, J., & Klika, C. (2017). *Pharmacovigilance in the European Union*. Wiesbaden: Springer.
Kinderman, D. (2009). Why do some Countries get CSR sooner, and in Greater Quantity, than Others? The Political Economy of Corporate Responsibility and the Rise of Market Liberalism across the OECD: 1977-2007. Wissenschaftszentrum Berlin Für Sozialforschung, (Discussion Paper SP III 2009-301).
Kinderman, D. (2013). Corporate social responsibility in the EU, 1993–2013: Institutional ambiguity, economic crises, business legitimacy and bureaucratic politics. *Journal of Common Market Studies, 51*(4), 701–720.
Kinderman, D. (2015). Corporate social responsibility—Der Kampf um die EU-Richtlinie. *WSI-Mitteilungen, 2015/8*.
Knill, C., & Lehmkuhl, D. (1999). How Europe matters. Different mechanisms of Europeanization. *European Integration Online Papers, 3*(7), 1–19.
Kobrin, S. J. (2007). Private political authority and public responsibility: Transnational Poltics, multinational firms and human rights. *International studies association annual meeting*. Chicago: International Studies Association.
Ladrech, R. (1994). Europeanization of domestic politics and institutions: The case of France. *Journal of Common Market Studies, 32*(1), 69–88.
Leiber, S., & Schäfer, A. (2008). Der Doppelte Voluntarismus in der EU-Sozial- und Beschäftigungspolitik. In I. Tömmel (Ed.), *Die Europäische Union: Governance und Policy-Making* (pp. 116–135). VS Verlag für Sozialwissenschaften.
Majone, G. (1996). Regulating Europe. London: Routledge.
Manners, I. (2002). Normative power Europe: a Contradiction in terms? *Journal of Common Market Studies, 40*(2), 235–258.
Olsen, J. P. (2002). The many faces of Europeanization. *Journal of Common Market Studies, 40*(5), 921–952.
Parker, O., & Rosamond, B. (2013). "Normative Power Europe" meets economic liberalism: Complicating cosmopolitanism inside/outside the EU. *Cooperation and Conflict, 48*(2), 229–246.
Potoski, M., & Prakash, A. (2009). Voluntary programs: A club theory perspective. MIT Press.

Radaelli, C. M. (2000). Whither Europeanization? Concept stretching and substantive change. *European Integration Online Papers, 4*(8).

Radaelli, C. M. (2003). The Europeanization of public policy. In K. Featherstone & C. M. Radaelli (Eds.), *The politics of Europeanization* (pp. 27–56). Oxford: Oxford University Press.

Saurugger, S. (2014). Europeanisation in times of crisis. *Political Studies Review, 12*(2), 181–192.

Schäfer, A. (2005). *Die Neue Unverbindlichkeit—Wirtschaftspolitische Koordinierung in Europa*. Frankfurt/New York: Campus.

Scharpf, F. (1994). Community and autonomy: Multi-level policy-making in the European union. *Journal of European Public Policy, 1*(2), 219–242.

Scharpf, F. (2008). Negative und positive Integration. In M. Höpner & A. Schäfer (Eds.), *Die Politische Ökonomie der europäischen Integration* (61st ed., pp. 49–87). Frankfurt: Campus.

Schwarze, J., Becker, U., & Pollak, C. (1993). *Die Implementation von Gemeinschaftsrecht: Untersuchungen zur Gesetzgebungs- und Verwaltungspolitik der Europäischen Gemeinschaft und ihrer Mitgliedstaaten*. Baden-Baden: Nomos.

Spießhofer, B. (2014). Die neue europäische Richtlinie über die Offenlegung nichtfinanzieller Informationen—Paradigmenwechsel oder Papiertiger? *Neue Zeitschrift Für Gesellschaftsrecht, 1281*(33), 1281–1320.

Streeck, W. (1995). Neo-voluntarism: A new European social policy regime? *European Law Journal, 1*(1), 31–59.

TEU [Lisbon]. Consolidated Version of the Treaty on European Union. Official Journal of the European Union, C 326.

TFEU [Lisbon]. Consolidated Version of the Treaty on the Functioning of the European Union. Official Journal of the European Union, C 326.

Thomann, E. (2015). Customizing Europe: transposition as bottom-up implementation. *Journal of European Public Policy, 22*(10), 1368–1387.

Thomson, R. (2010). Opposition through the back door in the transposition of EU directives. *European Union Politics, 11*(4), 577–596.

Treib, O. (2003). Die Umsetzung von EU-Richtlinien im Zeichen der Parteipolitik: Eine akteurszentrierte Antwort auf die Misfit-These. *Politische Vierteljahresschrift, 44*(4), 506–528.

UNCTAD. (2015). *World Investment Report 2015*. Geneva.

United Nations. (2006). *Promotion and Protection of Human Rights—Interim report of the Special Representative of the Secretary-General on the issue of human rights and transnational corporations and other business enterprises*. New York: Economic and Social Council.

Weber, A. (2009). *Die rechtliche und politische Dimension von extraterritorialen Staatenpflichten bei Menschenrechtsverstößen durch transnationale Konzerne—Ein Literaturbericht. INEF Forschungsreihe Menschenrechte, Unternehmensverantwortung und Nachhaltige Entwicklung* (Vol. 02/2009). Duisburg: Institut für Entwicklung und Frieden, Universität Duisburg Essen.

Wessels, W., & Rometsch, D. (1996). Conclusion: European Union and national institutions. In D. Rometsch & W. Wessels (Eds.), *The European Union and member states: Towards institutional fusion?*. Manchester and New York: Manchester University Press.

Wood, S. (2009). The European Union: A normative or normal power? *European Foreign Affairs Review, 14*(1), 113–128.

Zhelyazkova, A. (2013). Complying with EU directives' requirements: the link between EU decision-making and the correct transposition of EU provisions. *Journal of European Public Policy, 20*(5), 702–721.

Zhelyazkova, A., Kaya, C., & Schrama, R. (2016). Decoupling practical and legal compliance: Analysis of member states' implementation of EU policy. *European Journal of Political Research, 55*(4).

Zhelyazkova, A., & Torenvlied, R. (2011). The successful transposition of European provisions by member states: Application to the Framework Equality Directive. *Journal of European Public Policy, 18*(5), 690–708.

Chapter 2
Business and Human Rights: A New and Contentious EU Policy Area

In a 2015 staff working document on the implementation of the UNGPs, the Commission formulated the first coherent policy strategy in the EU policy area of Business and Human Rights (European Commission, 2015).This was the first attempt to consolidate existing and forthcoming measures that contribute to the political objective to implement the UNPGs. Neither corporate responsibility nor the promotion of human rights were new to EU policy-making before the adoption of the UNGPs. While the term Business and Human Rights, which was coined at the UN, provided the framework for this new EU policy area, most of the content of EU BHR policy built on EU measures that took place before the inception of the international BHR agenda. EU BHR policy is thus a complex blend of EU human rights policy, EU CSR policy and specific measures adopted for the implementation of the UNGPs. This chapter aims at shedding light on this new and contentious policy area, by considering and discussing the various influences and contradictions it entails. Thereby, it contributes to the hitherto small body of research on the EU BHR policy area (Álvarez Rubio & Yiannibas, 2017; Augenstein, 2010; Augenstein, Dawson, & Thielbbrger, 2018; Buhmann, 2011, 2018; Kinderman, 2013, 2015; Santoro, 2015).

For the empirical analysis and the overall argumentation of this book, this chapter is relevant in three respects. First, this study has the goal to contribute to the political understanding of BHR as an EU policy area. To be able to draw wider policy conclusions, it is crucial to delineate and discuss BHR as a policy area and explain connections to related areas. From the analysis of these fields, I discern the EU's BHR policy to be resting on two pillars: the EU's human rights regime and the EU CSR policy (Fig. 2.1).

The first pillar, the EU's human rights regime, gradually developed over time, at first only through judge-made law by the European Court of Justice (ECJ) and later through the adoption of the EU Charter and ensuing policies. The second pillar, EU CSR policy, has been developed by the Commission since the 1990s and was first formulated as a policy in a 2001 CSR Green Paper. The Commission mostly promoted CSR through codes of conduct, social reporting, labels, and socially responsible investment initiatives. This chapter sheds light on the developments of both pillars, as they provide the foundation for understanding this emerging policy area. On this

P. Drahn, *Adoption of EU Business and Human Rights Policy*,
Contributions to Political Science, https://doi.org/10.1007/978-3-030-46935-1_2

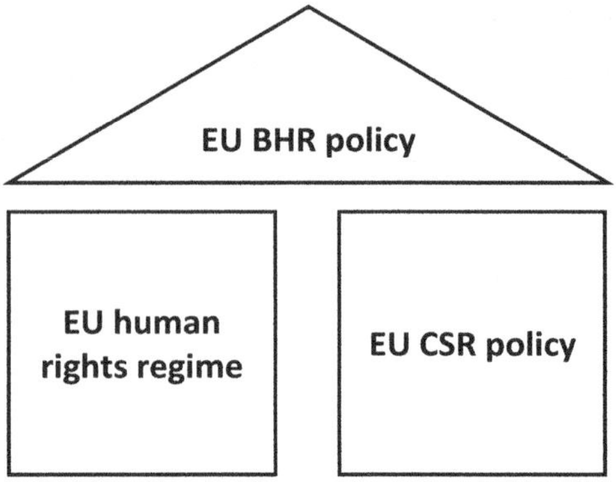

Fig. 2.1 Elements of EU BHR policy

basis, the conclusions from the empirical analysis of this book can be put in the broader context of the EU policy area of BHR. At the same time, this chapter also provides insights into the national policy subsystems, which are relevant for the transposition analysis. One of the six IVs of the empirical analysis investigates the impact of political salience within the policy subsystem.[1] This chapter provides the necessary background to understand such policy subsystems.

The second way in which this chapter is relevant for this study is to inform the selection of the policy-specific independent variables in the empirical analysis. While all explanatory factors are, to some degree, embedded in the policy background, the selection of two variables builds on the observations made in this chapter. The selection of the independent variable 'international policy transfer' is based on the description of the connections between the international BHR agenda and the policy formulation at the EU level. Moreover, the review of the literature on BHR provides the basis for the institutional misfit. This variable is one of the six factors investigated in this study, and it tests for the influence of the setup of the political economy. Lastly, this chapter is relevant for the empirical analysis because it explains the selection of the four EU directives that are analysed in the empirical analysis. Presenting the directives in relation to other measures shows the degree to which they hold explanatory power for the overall policy area.

This chapter is structured in four sections. The first section provides an account of the development of the EU's human rights regime and reviews the literature assessing it. The second section summarizes how the international BHR policy developed to become a globally accepted policy framework. The third section provides the synthesis of the previous two, as it explains how human rights and CSR policies fed into the development of the EU's BHR policy. It gives an account of the current state of play of BHR policy and describes the four EU directives that are analysed in the empirical analysis. The last section summarizes the findings of this chapter, which will contribute to the overall conclusion of this book.

---

[1] A policy subsystem "consists of actors from a variety of public and private organizations who are actively concerned with a policy problem or issue [...] and who regularly seek to influence public policy in that domain (Sabatier, 1998, p. 99). For a more detailed explanation of the use of the policy subsystem, see Chap. 3.

2.1 Legal and Living Constitution of Human Rights in the EU

2.1.1 The Development of a European Human Rights Regime

Human rights are one of the core values embedded in the EU treaties. The Treaty on European Union (TEU) mentions the term 'human rights' 16 times[2] and Articles 2 and 6 of the TEU define the respect for human rights as a common value of the EU and as a general principle of European law. Member states that seriously and persistently violate human rights can lose some of their rights and, in extreme cases, even lose voting rights in the Council under Article 7 TEU.[3] The EU Charter, which became legally binding with the adoption of the Treaty of Lisbon in 2009,[4] is the most comprehensive and far-reaching commitment to human rights the EU has made so far. Without any context, one could get the impression that European integration and the protection of fundamental rights have been intertwined from the beginning and that therefore European regulation in the area of BHR is a natural continuation of European integration. A closer look reveals a more complicated picture.

The first integration treaties forming the European Coal and Steel Community and the European Communities did not include any guarantees or even mentions of fundamental rights. With the drafting of the European Convention on Human Rights in 1950 and the adoption of the Universal Declaration of Human Rights by the UN General Assembly two years earlier, a foundation of fundamental principles had already been established, which allowed the European integration project to develop without a separate human rights foundation (Alston & Weiler, 1999). With the focus on creating a common market, the issue of human rights was initially ignored by European integration. The first institution to affirm that protecting fundamental rights was also a part of the Community's legal heritage was the ECJ[5] at the end of the 1960s (ibid). As the increasing transferral of competencies to the European level took place in incremental, often subtle steps, there was no occasion to formulate human rights on the European level (Schmidt, 2013). Instead, as the increasing community competence was not matched by any guarantees on a European level, the ECJ sought to ensure the protection of fundamental rights through *judge made law* (ibid). As Borowsky (2010, p. 148) points out, the ECJ sought to prevent national constitutional courts, especially the German *Bundesverfassungsgericht*, from providing this protection on the basis of national fundamental rights. This could have, as Douglas-Scott (2006, p. 633) notes, lead them to reject the supremacy of EC law.

---

[2]Seven of the mentions appear in the article provisions, nine in the protocols. The treaty on the functioning of the European Union (TFEU), being the more detailed and operational treaty, mentions the term 'human rights' eleven times.

[3]When I use the term 'Council', I refer to the Council of the European Union (also Council of Ministers).

[4]Poland and the United Kingdom have chosen to opt out from the EU Charter.

[5]The formal name of the highest court in the EU is Court of Justice of the European Union (CJEU). However, since the term ECJ is commonly used, it will also be used throughout this book.

The *Stauder*[6] case of 1969 was the first to formally recognize the basic rights of the person, while the *Internationale Handelsgesellschaft*[7] case of 1970 is widely regarded as the starting point in community jurisdiction in the area of human rights (Douglas-Scott, 2006; Schmidt, 2013). In their judgements, the ECJ was guided by the member states' constitutions and was later also influenced by the European Convention on Human Rights (ECHR), which all member states are party to. Through its rulings, the ECJ created a flexible system to protect fundamental rights, which included a wider variety of rights such as property rights, religious rights, and rights of the family (Borowsky, 2010; Schmidt, 2013). Alston and Weiler (1999, p. 10) argue that these initial moves of establishing fundamental rights in the community legal order through *judge made law* can be regarded as negative integration. By prohibiting the violation of a general principle of the Community (i.e. fundamental rights), the development of a community legal order of fundamental rights followed on a path similar to the establishment of the single market (ibid).

It was not until the Maastricht Treaty of 1993 that the (newly formed) EU could enshrine the protection of fundamental rights into primary Community law (Article F para 2 TEU [Maastricht]). Six years later the various claims for a codification of European fundamental rights, which date back to the 1970s, were met. At the Cologne European Council in June 1999, EU heads of state and government, following a German proposal, mandated the drafting of a catalogue of fundamental rights. The ensuing and hitherto novel convention, which was led by former German president Roman Herzog[8] and mainly composed of parliamentarians, government representatives and legal scholars,[9] developed the EU Charter in a remarkably short period. Borowsky (2010) identifies three reasons for this breakthrough. First, EU leaders wanted to overcome the credibility crisis that had led to the resignation of the Santer Commission by highlighting and re-assuring Europe's values and traditions. Second, they sought to signal to possible future members of the EU that they would join not merely an economic, but a value-based community. Third, as the integration process had changed its character, the EU Charter should serve as a normative foundation for the debate about the EU's *finalité* (Borowsky, 2010, p. 149). These arguments show that the inception of the EU Charter was not only the result of normative considerations but also driven by concrete political goals.

The content of the EU Charter is more than just a collection of previously existing rights. It touches on many issues that are relevant for modern societies such as data protection, biomedical guidelines, and discrimination based on genetic features and has therefore been described as the "most modern and arguably most comprehensive catalogue of fundamental rights" (Borowsky, 2010, p. 152). The EU Charter should

---

[6]Case 29/69, Stauder v. City of Ulm [1969] ECR 419.

[7]Case 11/70, Internationale Handelsgesellschaft, [1970] ECR 1125.

[8]Roman Herzog was only actively present at the beginning of the convention. In the later stages of the conference, when he was unable to attend for personal reasons, his formal leadership was still influential. Participants recount that they often asked themselves, 'what Herzog would advise for' (Borowsky, 2010, p. 150).

[9]Due to the high number of legal scholars present, the convention was also called a 'convention of professors' (Borowsky, 2010, p. 150).

have become legally binding with the treaty change following the Treaty of Nice. After the Constitutional Treaty had been rejected, the ensuing Treaty of Lisbon, adopted in 2009, did not make the EU Charter part of the treaties but granted it the same legal status. In addition to granting the EU Charter primary law status, the Lisbon Treaty also introduced human rights obligations concerning the EU's external action in the TEU and the Treaty on the Functioning of the European Union (TFEU). Thus the Treaty of Lisbon, which Bartels (2014) calls a "watershed for the human rights obligations of the EU and its Member States" (p. 15), provided a crucial legal basis for European regulation in the area of BHR.

With the EU Charter and the codification of human rights in the treaties, the European protection of fundamental rights through judge-made-law had been complemented by a second column, codified as EU primary law (Schmidt, 2013, p. 56). A third column of the system of fundamental rights could have been the EU's membership of the ECHR. But the accession of the EU to the ECHR, which had been debated for decades and even laid down in the Lisbon Treaty (see Article 6(2) TEU), was put to a halt by a ruling of the ECJ in 2014,[10] in which it argued that the accession agreement in question was not compatible with EU law.[11] This decision weighs heavily, because, as Augenstein (2010) stresses, under the ECHR "[s]tates are not merely permitted but required to protect human rights [...] in relation to extraterritorial activities of European corporations, and can be liable if they fail to do so" (p. 16). As the EU's path to ECHR membership is foreclosed for the foreseeable future, the EU will thus not be duty-bound by its provisions. This consequence highlights why some legal commentators have called the ECJ's rejection of ECHR membership a "clear and present danger to human rights protection" (Douglas-Scott, 2014, para. 18). However, since all EU member states are also members of the ECHR, the ECtHR's rulings are still of relevance for the EU's action in the area of BHR. Augenstein (2010) writes:

> [T]he procedural and substantive standards of protection developed in the jurisprudence of the ECtHR could serve as a basis for the European Union and its Member States to further clarify and develop normative standards on business and human rights. Such normative standards could feed into, for example, the new Commission's CSR policy and the EU Member State business and human rights strategies. (Augenstein, 2010, p. 31)

This comment shows that the ECHR is still of relevance for the EU, but the fact remains that the ECJ's rejection of the accession to the ECHR increases the reliance of the EU on its member states.

Under current EU human rights law, the EU "does not have an explicit general (internal or external) competence to legislate on human rights" (Augenstein, 2010, p. 17). Instead, the EU has endowed itself with European human rights law, which does not extend the EU's competence concerning human rights, but which the EU is bound to comply with when it legislates in other areas of the law (European Commission, 2015). It consists of the ECJ's judge-made law, the EU Charter, and the relevant provisions in EU primary law. Under EU primary law, i.e. the TEU and

---

[10]Opinion 2/13 of the Court of 18 December 2014.

[11]For a commentary on the ECJ's decision, see Douglas-Scott (2014).

TFEU, the EU has made further commitments to human rights. In addition to Article 2 TEU on the EU's core values, Article 3(5) TEU states that the EU shall promote human rights in relations with the wider world. Article 6(3) TEU defines general human rights as one of the principles of the Union's law. Article 21 TEU states that human rights shall guide the EU's international action, stipulating that

> "[t]he Union's action on the international scene shall be guided by the principles which have inspired its own creation [...]: democracy, the rule of law, the universality and indivisibility of human rights [...]" (TEU, Title V, Chapter 1, Article 21).

Article 10 TFEU states that in the implementation of its policies and activities, the EU shall aim to combat all forms[12] of discrimination. Furthermore, the TFEU provisions that outline the EU's external policies, namely trade policy (Article 207(1)), development policy (Article 208(1)), economic, financial, and technical cooperation (Article 212), and humanitarian aid (214), confirm that these policies shall be conducted in the context of the above principles.[13]

The above mentioned primary law provisions, as they are legally binding after the treaty of Lisbon, have substantially raised the EU's commitment as a global promoter of human rights. Articles 3(5) TEU and 21(3) TEU forbid any acts that affect the human right of individuals in third countries. Article 21(2) obliges the EU to "define and pursue common policies and actions" (TEU, Title V, Chapter 1, Article 21(2)) to promote human rights globally. As Bartels (2014) writes: "The significance of these obligations cannot be overstated. In most respects, they exceed anything on the international plane, [...] let alone in domestic constitutions" (p. 24).

As this section has shown, the EU has taken a long and complicated path until developing a human rights regime. While it has endowed itself with a comprehensive and modern constitution of human rights, the process was marked by complications and often followed political motives. The legal constitution of human rights in EU primary law has only been realized with the adoption of the Lisbon Treaty in 2009, whereas the membership of the ECHR has failed for now. As the next section will show, this basis has not been complemented with a comprehensive human rights policy which leads to contradictions for the living constitution of human rights in the EU.

2.1.2 Assessing the European Human Rights Regime

A conventional interpretation for the development of the EU human rights regime states that the more European integration progressed from a mere economic community to a political union with state-like functions, the more it needed a normative foundation that would justify such a union (De Schutter, 2005; Stobbe, 2011). The

[12]Discrimination based on sex, racial or ethnic origin, religion or belief, disability, age, or sexual orientation.

[13]In addition, the TFEU mentions human rights with regard to the modalities under which the EU should have acceded to the ECHR.

'No Demos Thesis', as Weiler (1995) described it, would argue that Europe cannot give itself a constitution, as the subject for such a constitution, a European *Staatsvolk* (constitutive people), is missing. In contrast to this, the European treaties are univocally based on shared ideals and values that have been formulated in the EU Charter. But to base European integration solely on universal human rights can lead to an impasse, because if human rights are truly universal, they cannot serve as a justification for a distinctly European integration project. Eurosceptics have thus accused the EU of only using human rights as a pretext for the political goal to advance European integration (Stobbe, 2011). Weiler (2004) tries to find a solution to this problem:

> [T]he specific definition of fundamental human rights often differs from polity to polity. Even in the relatively homogeneous cultural zone such as Western Europe, these differences might reflect fundamental societal choices and form an important part in the different identities of polities and societies. [...] Given that the rights are considered fundamental, so would be the differences among them. When the Court has to choose this or that variant of a right 'for Europe', it is making, implicitly, a choice about the cultural identity of Europe (p. 66f).

However, the critique of the EU's relation with human rights relies on other arguments as well. Already before the Lisbon treaty was adopted, some observers pointed to a disparity between the declaratory rhetoric of human rights and the implementation of human rights. Again, Weiler (2004) detects a "celebratory tone" (p. 59) in the European human rights discourse, stating that human rights had achieved an "iconographical position in European culture" (ibid). Others have merely noted the "rich, fertile, or perhaps even [...] excessive focus on human rights" (Douglas-Scott, 2006, p. 630). In 1999, Alston and Weiler noted a paradox in the EU's human rights policy. They argued that on the one hand, the EU was a "staunch defender of human rights in both its internal and external affairs" (Alston & Weiler, 1999, p. 3), while on the other hand, it lacked a comprehensive and coherent policy. Later, Weiler elaborates further on this, referring to the *Habeas Corpus syndrome,* stating that

> increasingly, the measurement of the efficacy of these documents, of their very reality as meaningful legal instruments, is in their invocability by individuals and their enforcement, at the instance of individuals, against public authority by courts. (Weiler, 2004, p. 60)

Therefore, he calls for a stronger European human rights policy, consisting of an EU human rights commissioner, a Directorate General, a budget, and a policy to enforce human rights more actively (ibid, p. 65). Another set of critique points to the divergence between the internal and external dimension of the EU's human rights policy: "[T]he internal and external dimensions of human rights policy can never be satisfactorily be kept in separate compartments. They are, in fact, two sides of the same coin" (Alston & Weiler, 1999, p. 8).

The codification of human rights as EU primary law through the Lisbon treaty in 2009 did not eliminate the criticism. More recent literature also notices a 'compliance gap', arguing that much of the EU's human rights regime is only declaratory and lacks a stringent policy that consists of clear procedures and implementation mechanisms (see Gatto, 2011). In 2011, before the EU's implementation of the UNGPs, Gatto (2011), detected a

> gap between the EU's commitment to the respect and the promotion of human rights, the potential to regulate to conduct of MNEs [Multinational Enterprises], and the EU's reluctance to impose human rights obligations on MNEs. (p. 275)

In the literature that responded to the claim that the EU was a 'normative power', a similar critique can be found. Responding to the claim that the EU understands itself as a 'different' kind of global actor that places normative considerations above others, Wood (2009) states:

> The EU's *mission civilisatrice* is susceptible to a relatively straightforward if unpleasant realpolitik that can expose **a rhetoric–behaviour gap**. [...] When faced with resistance to a (potentially) vigorous promotion of democracy and human rights, or when imperatives that compel it to modify or rescind such activity enter the equation, the EU appears a rather powerless normative power. (Wood, 2009, p. 128, emphasis added)

Moreover, De Búrca (2011) points to three essential shortcomings of the current European human rights system, stating that it lacks a serious human rights mechanism, it is insufficiently integrated into the international human rights system, and it contains a double standard as between internal and external human rights policies (De Búrca, 2011, p. 692 f).

Furthermore, she observes the political conflict between political actors about the way, in which these shortcomings should be addressed. In her view, the current European human rights regime is characterized by

> a dialectical tension manifest in the complex interaction between "mobilizing" actors seeking to strengthen the institutions for human rights protection—including civil society actors, transnational networks, and supranational actors like the European Commission and the Court of Justice—and "resistant" governmental actors seeking to curb and deter the same. (2011, p. 651)

This tension between mobilizing and curbing actors, the lack of a comprehensive, institutionally endowed human rights policy, and the double standard between the internal and the external human rights policy suggest the existence of a significant gap between the legal and the living constitution of human rights in the EU. The strong foundation of human rights in EU primary law and the abundance of declarations and public commitments to human rights stand in stark contrast to a lack of institutional instruments on the EU level that could help to promote human rights abroad. The EU has tried to alleviate this by adopting the EU Strategic Framework for Human Rights and Democracy. Such initiatives rely to a large extent on the member states, because, as the comment by De Búrca highlights, much of the implementation of human rights in the EU takes place at the national level. De Schutter (2005) notes that this form of "decentralized implementation of fundamental rights produces suboptimal consequences" (2005, p. 17). The EU's failed accession to the ECHR underlines how much the EU human rights regime depends on the implementation by member states, which is why the empirical part of this study looks at the transposition of directives in the field of BHR policy.

2.2 The International Business and Human Rights Agenda

When the Universal Declaration of Human Rights was adopted in 1948, the obligation to protect human rights was mainly attributed to states. However, in an increasingly integrated world economy, where business enterprises profit from open markets and global supply chains, businesses are increasingly being held accountable for human rights abuses as well. Capital mobility enables Transnational Corporations (TNCs) to relocate to the most efficient production sites, whereby they often operate outside the national regulation of their home states. Especially in areas of limited statehood, where institutions are underdeveloped, such diminution of regulatory authority is not equivalently replaced and has led to a "widening gap between global markets and the capacity of societies to manage their consequences" (United Nations, 2006, p. 7). Simply put, such governance gaps result from the fact that "[g]lobally operating firms are not regulated globally" (Ruggie, 2013, p. xvi).

In this situation, human rights abuses in global supply chains have become more frequent.[14] According to the ILO (2017), 40.3 Million people were victims of modern slavery in 2016. Of those, 24.9 million people are victims of forced labour, of which 16 million worked in the private economy (ibid). However, it is often difficult to directly link transnational corporations that have their headquarters in Europe to human rights abuses. With supply chains becoming ever more complex, many businesses are not directly involved but are indirectly connected to human rights violations through suppliers and sub-contractors. NGOs point to the abounding evidence of adverse consequences of corporate conduct, such as instances of dangerous working conditions, child labour, forced labour, land grabbing, displacement of indigenous populations, or other inhumane circumstances. Following what Spar (1998) called the *spotlight phenomenon*, NGOs and other advocacy organizations increasingly reported on such instances of human rights violations. Modern technology and the wide accessibility of cameras make it easier to globally publicize human rights abuses, which then stir up debates about the roles and responsibilities of business enterprises. One event that has received widespread international attention was the collapse of the Rana Plaza factory in Bangladesh in 2013. The tragedy, in which over 1,100 workers died and around 2,000 were injured, received considerable attention in the media and politics and intensified the debate about fair supply chains.

However, in the view of such events it should still be noted that in the debate about how businesses affect human rights, observers agree that the impact of TNCs on human rights is not necessarily negative (e.g. De Schutter, 2008; Kamminga, 1999). Investments of large corporations in developing markets often spur local growth and positively affect both economic and social rights. If economic growth translates into higher wages, citizens are empowered to assume their rights and invest in health, education, and a higher standard of living. While most scholars of BHR do not contest such effects, the emerging multi-disciplinary BHR field focusses on

---

[14]According to 2014 Human Rights Risk Atlas, published by the risks analytics firm Maplecroft, the human rights violations have increased between 2008 and 2014 by 70% (Verisk Maplecroft, 2014).

those instances, where business enterprises have yielded adverse effects. Scholars and practitioners from politics, law, and business management are looking for ways to prevent human rights abuses by third parties, such as TNCs and sector interests, through appropriate policies, regulation, and legal arbitration.

Moreover, BHR policy aims at changing corporate cultures and making businesses aware of their responsibility to protect and promote human rights. On the international stage, the most important milestone on the BHR agenda has been the adoption of the UN Guiding Principles on Business and Human Rights (UNGPs) by the UN Human Rights Council in June 2011. Developed by former Harvard professor and UN Special Representative for Business and Human Rights John Ruggie, the UNGPs, have become, though voluntary, the global standard for addressing adverse human rights impacts related to business activity. The adoption of the legally non-binding UN resolution and the following broad consensus among states and civil society were considered by many to be the watershed event for BHR. The core element of the principles, the *Protect, Respect and Remedy framework*, explicitly addresses the role of both states and businesses in ensuring the respect for human rights in the global economy. The framework rests on three pillars: The states' responsibility to respect, protect and fulfil human rights, businesses' role to comply with the laws and to respect human rights, and the availability for legal remedies after human rights abuses have occurred. In short, the framework stresses that "states must protect; companies must respect; and those who are harmed must have redress" (Ruggie, 2013, p. xxi).[15] The 31 principles make suggestions for each of the three pillars. With regard to states' duties, the principles demand that "home States take steps to prevent abuse abroad by business enterprises within their jurisdiction" (United Nations, 2011, p. 4). Thereby, the UNGPs argue that states should formulate the expectation that companies ensure respect for human rights throughout all business operations. Under current international law, states are not required to regulate businesses domiciled in their territory internationally. While there are cases of *extraterritorial legislation*, for example in the field of anti-corruption, the legal debate, if extraterritorial legislation should also be applicable for human rights protection, is still ongoing (see Methven O'Brian, 2016).[16]

The UNGPs do not unequivocally clarify, in how far the protection of human rights by businesses should be ensured through voluntary or compulsory measures. The UNGPs say that states should consider "a smart mix of measures—national and international, mandatory and voluntary" (United Nations, 2011, p. 5). However, as I argue in the operationalization of the variable 'international policy transfer', several phrases in the UNGPs suggest an inclination towards binding measures. The UNGPs also address the State-Business-Nexus and specifically mention public procurement. Principle 6 lays down that states should promote respect for human rights through procurement contracts. Human rights reporting receives even more attention in the

[15] I.e. victims must be granted greater access to effective judicial and non-judicial remedy.

[16] The term extraterritorial legislation refers to rules adopted in the national sphere that companies based in these states should abide by globally. Some countries, such as Germany, are opposed to the idea of extraterritorial obligations by states as a matter of principal (Bundestag, 2013).

UNGPs, which demand reporting elements that are similar to those in the EU NFR-Directive. The UNGPs underline that "[f]inancial reporting requirements should clarify that human rights impacts in some instances may be 'material' or 'significant' to the economic performance of the business enterprise" (United Nations, 2011, p. 6). Other demands of the UNGPs include specific indicators, reporting in sectors that have high human rights risks, and independent verification of the reports. A central element of the UNGPs was the call for the development of National Action Plans (NAPs), which are regarded as an essential tool to compare and explain national efforts.

After its adoption, the UNGPs were not only implemented by states and businesses; they also resonated with other international organizations. A central international BHR agreement is the *Tripartite declaration of principles concerning multinational enterprises and social policy* by the International Labour Organization (ILO). It provides detailed guidance for TNCs and is a widely embraced reference standard for governments, employers, and employees. The Organisation for Economic Co-operation and Development (OECD) included the UNGPs in their Guidelines for Multinational Enterprises[17] and continues to publish guidance reports for specific sectors and topics, the latest being a 2017 guidance for the garment and footwear sector.[18] The International Finance Corporation (IFC) of the World Bank has also adjusted its performance standards to the UNGPs.[19] The International Organization for Standardization (ISO) included elements of the UNGPs in the influential ISO 26,000 social responsibility standard. In 2016, the Council of Europe adopted non-binding recommendations on human rights and business, which encourages member states to review national legislation in order to implement the UNGPs.[20] In addition, civil society organisations and consultancies are using the UNGPs as a reference standard when they are collaborating with businesses, more recently also relying on the UNGP Reporting Framework that was launched in February 2015. These international agreements and frameworks constitute the corpus of international BHR obligations, which is also endorsed by the four EU member states that are investigated in this book. As I explain in Chap. 3, the hypothesis that tests the influence of international policy transfer on the transposition (H5), relies on these international agreements and frameworks.

The increasing private governance of BHR has raised questions about the role that governments still need to play in regulating global supply chains. Nowadays, few state or business representatives share the view of Milton Friedman, who famously

[17]The OECD Guidelines for Multinational Enterprises were first adopted in 1976 as part of the OECD Declaration and Decisions on International Investment and Multinational Enterprises. These guidelines were designed to ensure an open and transparent international investment climate and to encourage responsible business conduct, by promoting economic, environmental, and social progress.

[18]Other guidance reports were published for the minerals sectors, the extractive industry, the agricultural sector, institutional investors and for the issue of child labour.

[19]The IFC Performance Standards on Environmental and Social Sustainability came into effect in January 2012.

[20]Recommendation CM/Rec(2016)3 on human rights and business.

declared that the only social responsibility of businesses was to increase profits (Friedman, 1970). Today, the debate centres around the question if social standards should be voluntary or mandatory. Most NGOs dealing with BHR positioned themselves on the regulatory side of the debate. They welcomed the adoption of the UNGPs and are among the most tenacious proponents of their consistent implementation. Some NGOs also highlighted shortcomings, stating that the UNGPs should only be the first step on a path towards more comprehensive regulation.[21] Large globally operating organizations such as Transparency International, and Human Rights Watch, were soon joined by a vast number of new smaller national NGOs that specifically focussed on BHR policy. They are connected through umbrella organisations on the European or on the global level that coordinate lobbying efforts in the EU and in national capitals, and disseminate practical information and resources and diffuse ideas.[22] They create an 'epistemic community' (Haas, 1992), which consists of a group of "expert actors in policy-making who share norms, causal beliefs and political projects and who seek change in specific areas of policy" (Stone, 2000, p. 58). As the explanation of directive transposition processes in Chap. 6 shows, NGOs are central actors in national policy subsystems, where they advocated strongly for a far-reaching transposition of the EU directives.

2.3 Forming EU Business and Human Rights Policy

2.3.1 The Development of EU BHR Policy

EU BHR policy was instigated by the political decision to implement the UNGPs. While this decision entailed several new initiatives, in no small degree EU BHR policy formalized the status quo ante, as previously existing policies in the areas of human rights and EU policies in the area of CSR were integrated into a new policy framework. Before recounting the coming about of the EU BHR policy, it is crucial to delineate the terms BHR and CSR in the EU policy context. One significant difference is that the term CSR typically refers to a much broader understanding of sustainability. While the precise definitions changed over time and remain contested, CSR usually also includes environmental measures, while BHR is only concerned with human rights. Furthermore, the *protect, respect and remedy framework* structures and specifies BHR. CSR, on the other hand, lacks such concrete foundations and has therefore been called "contested and fuzzy" (Fairbrass, 2011, p. 952). Moreover, the concept was developed in the business community and was only gradually brought into the regulatory policy context. CSR served as a broader predecessor of BHR, which was from the beginning framed as a collective responsibility of both business and state actors.

---

[21] See for example Heydenreich et al. (2014).

[22] Examples for umbrella organisations are the European Coalition for Corporate Justice (ECCJ) and the International Corporate Accountability Roundtable (ICAR).

In Europe, the questions about the responsibility and accountability of businesses were debated long before the term CSR was coined. In the 1950s academics in Europe, inspired by debates in the US, started investigating the issue of corporate responsibility (Fairbrass, 2011). These debates took place only in the areas of management research and business ethics because state involvement was not considered at the time. The gradually increasing involvement of regulators led to discussions about if and how the state should structure activities of corporate responsibility. The evolution of an EU CSR policy, and later the development of a BHR policy, have been marked by the question, if measures of corporate responsibility should remain voluntary for businesses, or if binding regulatory rules should complement them. Kinderman (2013) traces the development of CSR in the EU and observes that the EU's positioning in this question has changed back and forth over the last 30 years. Under the presidency of Jacques Delors (1985–1995), the Commission understood CSR as a tool to regulate capitalism and to counter the liberal single market program. Delors organized business support for an agenda that aimed at alleviating social exclusion and poverty within the EU.[23] However, mainly due to employer resistance, the social-liberal understanding of CSR was abandoned, and a new market liberal interpretation of CSR was adopted. The first Barroso Commission replaced the officer previously in charge of CSR and the de facto leadership of CSR in the Commission was moved from DG Social Affairs to DG Enterprise (Kinderman, 2013, p. 709). During that time, the Commission built a coalition of actors that were opposed to regulation,[24] while side-lining pro-regulation actors (Fairbrass, 2011, p. 966f). This coalition prevailed and was, for the time being, able to establish a voluntary approach to CSR policy (ibid). The term CSR entered the EU-level discourse in 2001 when the Commission published the first CSR Green Paper. The Commission followed the voluntary approach and defined CSR as a "concept whereby companies integrate social and environmental concerns in their business operations and in their interaction with their stakeholders on a voluntary basis" (European Commission, 2001, p. 6).[25]

In the wake of the financial crisis, the question if CSR was "a means to regulate the economy, or a domain of voluntary activity" (Kinderman, 2013, p. 701) resurfaced again. Due to the political situation, the mood in all EU institutions changed towards a more regulatory interpretation of CSR (ibid). This development went hand in hand with the development of the international BHR agenda. When John Ruggie started his work on the UNGPs, the EU endorsed the process from the beginning. Under the Swedish presidency in 2009, the EU Foreign Affairs Council[26] endorsed the *Protect, Respect and Remedy framework* two years before the UN Human Rights Council

[23]In his article on the development of CSR in the EU, Kinderman (2013) analyses the influence of the two most important business lobby organisations.

[24]The Council, the Economic and Social Committee, the Committee of the Regions, some national governments, and business associations were part of this coalition.

[25]Green Paper: Promoting a European framework for Corporate Social Responsibility (COM (2001) 366 final).

[26]The Council conclusions on Human Rights and Democratisation in third countries, adopted by the 2985th Foreign Affairs Council meeting Brussels on 8 December 2009, referred to a CSR

adopted it. The development of the UNGPs, its support by the Swedish and Spanish presidencies, and general free-market fatigue caused by the financial crisis were central factors which changed the Commission's interpretation of CSR. In part, efforts to promote business responsibility in the EU were aimed at adding a social aspect to its free-market agenda (Kinderman, 2013). The realignment towards a more regulatory understanding resulted in a new definition of CSR. In the 2011 CSR strategy, the Commission interpreted CSR in more concrete terms as "the responsibility of enterprises for their impacts on society" (European Commission, 2011, p. 6). Moreover, CSR should now include 'complementary legislation'. The Commission justified the updated understanding by stating that "[c]ertain regulatory measures create an environment more conducive to enterprises voluntarily meeting their social responsibility" (European Commission, 2011, p. 3). It envisioned measures in the fields of global respect for human rights, social dialogue, and multi-stakeholder approaches.

The CSR strategy paper also stated that the EU would further promote the respect for human rights in the global economy by relying on "a mix of global advocacy and complementary legislation" (European Commission, 2011, p. 14). It announced the initiation of several legislative acts in this respect. In the EU Strategic Framework for Human Rights and Democracy of 2012, the Council stated that it would promote human rights in all external instruments, including CSR. In the 2015 Commission staff document mentioned in the beginning of this chapter, the Commission recognized the UNGPs as the "authoritative policy framework" (European Commission, 2015, p. 2), listed how existing EU regulation corresponds with the UNGPs, and announced further regulatory and non-regulatory initiatives, such as the NFR-Directive and the public procurement directives. For most member states, the transposition of these directives marked the first time they had to deal with BHR. Like CSR, which according to Kinderman (2013, p. 704) arrived at the European level earlier than in most EU member states, BHR policy was implemented in the EU mainly from the top down. Few member states, such as France and the UK, adopted measures in the field of BHR policy outside a European framework.[27] For the most part, however, legally binding corporate responsibility legislation on the national level was only adopted, if harmonization measures, such as EU directives, were taken on the European level (Interview 1).

The interplay between voluntary and mandatory approaches to CSR did not only take place on the community level. The Commission encouraged member states to develop guidance on best practices, benchmarking tools, and other instruments to acquaint national industries with the concept of corporate responsibility. In general, Western European member states adopted more legislation than their Eastern European neighbours (Wensen, Broer, Klein, & Knopf, 2011, p. 56). Albareda, Lozano, and Ysa (2007) developed a typology of four models of government action in the field of CSR that is used when explaining the case selection in Chap. 4 of this book. They hold that national CSR policies depend on political institutions and processes,

conference that was held in Stockholm on 10-11 November 2009 and that marks one of the first discussions on how BHR can be integrated in the EU legal framework.

[27]The UK adopted the modern slavery act in 2015 and France adopted the loi de vigilance in 2017.

social structure, historical traditions, and established views of the role of companies (ibid, p. 393).

In the EU, many of the requirements adopted early after the publication of the first CSR green paper in 2001 were loosened around 2005–2006 to avoid unnecessary burdens for businesses (Wensen et al., 2011). However, after the financial crisis, the trend began to change again towards more binding regulation (ibid). This included an increased combination of voluntary and mandatory rules. Often, voluntary standards operate as 'pre-law' because such non-binding guidelines are usually easier to adopt than binding legislation that has to be adopted in a complicated legislative process. At the same time, they prepare industries for binding legislation that might be adopted at a later stage. Rules in national legislations usually focus on some businesses that either exceed a specific size, are publicly listed or are active in a particularly risky industry.[28] National regulations differed concerning the degree of transparency that was required or the form of the disclosure. However, the overall interchange between the use of voluntary and mandatory rules in EU member states has followed a broadly similar pattern as the developments on the community level.

2.3.2 *Discussion of EU BHR Policy*

The brief overview of the development of BHR in the EU has displayed a complex policy area. In light of the recent nature and the diversity of the measures subsumed under it, one could even question, if BHR qualifies as a coherent policy area. When the Commission refers to BHR in the 2015 staff working document, the wording is not consistent. The Commission either speaks of the "EU's current regime relating to business and human rights" (European Commission, 2015, p. 3) or refers to "policy activities in the area of human rights" (p. 17). However, following the definition of a policy area as an organized set of rules that has the intention to make real-world changes (Lowi, 1972) then the Commission document allows us to answer this question affirmatively. The Commission formulates the intention to implement the UNGPs with a series of measures that are "structured around the three pillars of the UNGPs, taking into account internal and external dimensions of EU action" (p. 3), and stresses the importance of policy coherence. This shows that contents of the policy area's structure are provided for by an international source: the UNGPs. As the previous section has shown, the building of EU BHR policy is causally linked with the international BHR agenda. EU BHR policy, therefore, represents a case of vertical policy transfer from the UN level to the EU level.[29]

---

[28]For example, companies in the extractive industries or particularly energy-intensive companies.

[29]Policy transfer is defined as "a process in which knowledge about policies, administrative arrangements, institutions etc. in one time and/or place is used in the development of policies, administrative arrangements and institutions in another time and/or place" (Dolowitz & Marsh, 1996, p. 344). A more comprehensive discussion of policy transfer is provided in Chap. 3.

In order to classify BHR as a policy area, the classical policy taxonomy by Lowi (1972, p. 300) provides a suitable starting point. It distinguishes between four types of policy: distributive policy, constituent policy, regulative policy, and redistributive policy. BHR policy falls under the category of regulative policy, as it prescribes limits to the actions of private actors in the global economy, and it has immediate coercion effects. Thus, EU BHR policy can be understood as a regulative policy area that was transferred from the UN level to the EU level. This observation leads to the assumption that the international BHR agenda could also influence policy-making at the member state level. In the empirical analysis of this study, I test the impact of international policy transfer on the transposition of EU directives. In Chap. 3, I postulate the hypothesis (H5) that international BHR obligations cause member states to transpose more voluntary BHR directive provisions.

A central characteristic of EU BHR policy is the inherent ambiguity between voluntary incentives and mandatory regulation, which leads to diverging political understandings of EU BHR policy.[30] The voluntary understanding stresses soft-law and incentive mechanisms, while the regulative understanding underscores the importance of binding legal rules and regards BHR policy as a tool to regulate businesses.[31] Proponents of the soft-law approach, often stressed in liberal and conservative political parties, argue that outcomes desirable to society can be better achieved without binding rules. This view stresses the corrective role of market mechanisms, which are seen as more effective in achieving social and sustainable market conduct. It is acknowledged that in an interconnected global public, the reputational risk of tolerating abusive businesses practices has increased dramatically. Therefore, proponents of voluntary approaches stress that under the spotlights of media and international civil society, large corporations cannot afford to violate human rights in their business operations. The assumption is that well-informed responsible consumers, as well as shareholders concerned about the image and value of a company, will force business managers to adopt socially responsible business practices. Following the logic of this *spotlight phenomenon* (Spar, 1998), promoting human rights is in the commercial interest of businesses because it can increase company value. Under this view, the 'business case' of corporate responsibility builds on the observation that consumers and (potential) employees will value the image of a socially responsible company. Also, soft law rules are usually agreed in close cooperation with the industries that are affected, which results in less formalized rules than those of mandatory regulatory regimes. Such rules, it is argued, are easier to implement for businesses.

The opposing view to the soft-law approach, usually held by parties of the political left, advocates binding legislation on corporate responsibility. They are not opposed to the 'business case' but argue that legal requirements are necessary to establish the transparency necessary for reputational market mechanisms to work. The argument

[30] De Schutter (2008) also refers to a third interpretation, which would see businesses only responsible towards its shareholders, workers, customers, and its direct community.

[31] Majone (1996) defines regulation as "sustained and focused control exercised by a public agency, on the basis of a legislative mandate, over activities that are generally regarded as desirable to society" (p. 9).

is that only binding transparency requirements such as the binding elements of the NFR-Directive provide the media and civil society with the information that is needed to establish the reputational pressures that will lead to more responsible business behaviour. Proponents of this view stress that voluntary rules and company initiatives can quickly turn into mere marketing exercises, which focus on enhancing the public image of a company, rather than mitigating negative human rights impacts. Under this view, only compulsory rules can change business behaviour. The association of different political parties with the mandatory and the voluntary understanding of BHR regulation leads to the assumption that party politics is a relevant factor for the interpretation of BHR rules. For this reason, as I explain in more detail in Chap. 3, one of the factors in the analytical framework of this study tests the impact of the governing political parties on the transposition of BHR directives (Hypothesis H3).

Which of the two interpretations of BHR are preferred in a country is not only a party-political question. It also depends on long-established political institutions and traditions that are either conducive or unfavourable to mandatory business regulation. Comparative studies on capitalism have suggested that the degree of corporatism in a country is connected to the propensity to adopt binding business regulation (Streeck, 2010). According to Siaroff (1999), the main features of corporatism are

> within an advanced industrial society and democratic polity, the co-ordinated, co-operative, and systematic management of the national economy by the state, centralised unions, and employers (these latter two co-operating directly in industry), presumably to the relative benefit of all three actors". (p. 177)

Several authors have suggested that the degree of corporatism in a country is a relevant factor when trying to explain national differences in regulatory behaviour. In the EU context, studies have investigated how the level of corporatism affects a country's behaviour in social and employment regulation (Falkner, Treib, Hartlapp, & Leiber, 2005; Thomson, 2007, 2009). Zhelyazkova and Torenvlied (2011) use corporatism as a control variable to explain how member states transposed the Framework Equality Directive, which consists of business regulation in the field of non-discrimination.[32] These studies assume that corporatist and pluralist institutional configurations determine policy making and interest group participation in a country, which in turn affects the choice between voluntary and mandatory regulation.[33]

Among recent works on comparative capitalism, the VoC approach by Hall and Soskice (Hall & Soskice, 2001b) and their distinction between LMEs and CMEs has become a popular reference point in the literature. The authors make several statements regarding the links between institutional configurations in a political economy and a country's stance towards regulation. Regarding how states define their interests in international negotiations, they emphasize that

> [the varieties of capitalism approach] suggests that their stance toward new regulatory initiatives will be influenced by judgements about whether those initiatives are likely to sustain or undermine the comparative institutional advantages of their nation's economy. (Hall & Soskice, 2001a, p. 52)

[32]Council Directive 2000/78/EC.

[33]For the differentiation between corporatism and pluralism see Schmitter (1974).

Hall and Soskice hold that this approach can be applied to EU member states in many different situations of EU governance. For example, they state that Germany's favourable stance towards financial regulation in the 1990s or Britain's position on competition regulation can be explained with this logic. They make assumptions about LMEs' and CMEs' position towards regulation.

> In the face of more intense international competition, business interests in LMEs are likely to pressure governments for de-regulation, since firms that coordinate their endeavors primarily through the market can improve their competencies by sharpening its edges. The government is likely to be sympathetic because the comparative advantage of the economy as a whole rests on the effectiveness of market mechanisms. (ibid, p. 57)

For countries classified as CMEs, the authors expect the opposite positioning:

> In coordinated market economies, however, the political dynamic inspired by globalization should be quite different. Here, governments should be less sympathetic to deregulation because it threatens the nation's comparative institutional advantages. (ibid, p. 58)

Following these considerations, it is not surprising that scholars have used the VoC approach in analyses of countries' behaviour in the areas of BHR regulation as well (see Kinderman, 2008, 2015). Therefore, in the empirical analysis of this study, I will also take the institutional configurations within a political economy into account. In Chap. 3, I hypothesize that member states' institutional fit with the content of the EU directives can be explained by taking into account the institutional setup of the political economy (Hypothesis H2).

2.3.3 State of Play of EU BHR Policy

The previous sections have provided an account of the development of EU BHR policy and presented possible political and theoretical explanations for government behaviour in this policy area. Lastly, this sub-section provides a brief overview of the current state of play of this new policy area. Apart from the obligations under EU primary law and international law, the EU's BHR policy consists of legislative acts (secondary law) and several other policy measures. Within the EU's scope of action, which is determined according to the principle of conferral (Article 5 TFEU), the EU and its member states are obliged to comply with human rights standards whenever EU law is implemented. Therefore, potentially all policy areas that concern the impact of business conduct on human rights and in which the treaties have granted the EU competence could contain BHR legislation. In the 2015 staff working paper on the implementation of the UNGPs the Commission writes:

> "Business and human rights" is not a stand-alone issue, it touches upon a wide range of different legal and political areas, including but not limited to human rights law, labour law, environmental law, anti-discrimination law, international humanitarian law, investment and trade law, consumer protection law, civil law, and commercial law, corporate or penal law. (European Commission, 2015).

To bring issues from such diverse fields together, the Commission stresses explicitly the need for "[p]olicy coherence on business and human rights within the EU" (p. 16) and describes the institutional coordination to achieve that goal. 'Clusters' with the High Representative, with Commissioners and inter-service groups within the Commission are tasked to ensure policy coherence in BHR (ibid). Moreover, the policy goal to implement the UNGPs should be brought in line with the obligations under the EU Charter. Externally, coherence should be achieved with the activities in trade and investment, the generalised scheme of preferences, EU development policy, and with the human rights dialogues at the bilateral level and co-operation with regional organisations (ibid).

Up until now, the EU has adopted legislation and other measures of BHR policy in seven areas.[34] Accounting regulation has been identified by regulatory authorities around the world as a powerful tool to ensure the duty of care for human rights by companies, not least because the UNGPs specifically address it. Since businesses are accustomed to reporting on their financial situation, non-financial reporting requirements are considered a straightforward way to increase the transparency of businesses' human rights impacts. EU regulation in the field of labour rights addresses the problem of adverse human rights conditions of third-country nationals that reside in the EU. These measures constitute a particular case in EU BHR regulation because they address human rights violations inside the EU's territory, which is usually ensured by the national laws in the member states.

Nonetheless, due to the free movement of persons in the EU, several directives have addressed the protection of rights of third-country nationals. The prevention of human trafficking is another area that can be subsumed under EU BHR policy. EU Directive 2011/36/EU seeks to preclude human trafficking by requiring several measures, such as prevention policies, protection of victims and punishment of perpetrators. The area of civil justice is a vital aspect of the UNGPs, as it stresses the importance of legal remedy after human rights violations have occurred. Therefore, several EU regulations have been adopted, which make it easier for victims to sue companies before EU courts, even though the human rights violations took place outside the EU. Two measures that received attention in this respect are the Rome I regulation (EC 593/2008) and the Rome II regulation (EC 864/2007), which are relevant in cases when a court in an EU member state has to decide which law applies in a cross-border case. 'Rome II' has received more media attention, because, regarding tort, it states that in cases of human rights violations the applicable law is that of the state where the human rights violation occurs, while the application of the law can take place within the EU.[35]

In the field of criminal justice, the EU has adopted a number of measures that ensure the right to a fair trial, the right to interpretation and translation, and the right to information. Lastly, EU trade and investment agreements contain BHR measures.

---

[34]The information provided from this overview builds mostly on the Commission's 2015 staff working paper on the UNGPs (European Commission, 2015).

[35]On this basis, the German regional court (Landgericht) in Dortmund accepted a case against the clothing retailer KiK for injuries and deaths that were caused by a fire in a jeans factory in Karachi.

Since 1995 the EU has, as a rule, included so-called 'human rights clauses' in all trade and cooperation agreements.[36] Moreover, all trade agreements of the last years contain CSR provisions.

This short overview has displayed the various existing and new measures that contribute to the EU policy area of BHR. Table 2.1 provides an overview of all the measures and their intended purpose. Out of these measures, I have chosen to analyse the Non-Financial Reporting Directive and the three public procurement directives as subjects for this study, because they are central elements of the EU's BHR policy. The UNGPs specifically address the importance of both non-financial reporting and of public procurement (see United Nations, 2011 pp. 6, 8, 17, 24). Consequently, EU institutions committing to the implementation of the UNGPs put these two measures in the centre. In the 2016 conclusions on BHR, the Foreign Affairs Council underlined the importance of both areas. In the paragraph that stresses the relevance of business transparency for the respect of human rights, the Council "notes in this regard the contribution of the EU Directive on disclosure of non-financial and diversity information by certain large companies and groups" (Council of the European Union, 2016, p. 4). The Council emphasizes the relevance of public procurement similarly:

> The Council encourages EU Institutions and Member States to address their responsibilities as commercial actors (e.g. in public procurement) [...]. The Council calls on the Commission to consider what support can be provided to public authorities covered by the revised EU Procurement Directives, through tools and guidance for the implementation of the UN Guiding Principles, the OECD Guidelines and the ILO Tripartite Declaration. (Council of the European Union, 2016, p. 4)

The 2015 Commission staff working document also underscores both areas. The NFR-Directive is mentioned as the first measure in the field of accounting. The section on the 'state-business-nexus' mentions the three public procurement directives as a key tool to ensure the implementation of the UNGPs in this area (principles 4–6) (European Commission, 2015). Due to the high importance that EU institutions place on the NFR-Directive and on the public procurement directives, which is also reflected in the wide attention the directives received among lobby and civil society organizations, they have been singled out for the empirical analysis. The next two sections will present these directives in more detail.

2.4 The Public Procurement Directives

In the EU, public authorities spend about 1.9 trillion Euro every year on public procurement contracts (European Commission, 2016a). Within the member states, public procurement accounts for a considerable share of GDP. In the UK and Denmark,

---

[36]While the general EU investment agreements contain human rights clauses, sectoral agreements, for example in the steel or fisheries sector, do not contain such clauses, but can nonetheless have grave impacts on human rights (Bartels, 2014). This criticism was also expressed by the European Parliament in a 2006 resolution (OJ C 290E/107).

Table 2.1 Overview of EU measures in the EU BHR policy area

Year	Instrument	Function
Accounting regulation		
2014	Directive 2014/95/EU	The Non-Financial Reporting Directives introduces human rights-related reporting obligations for large companies
2017	Regulation (EU) 2017/821	EU importers of so-called 'conflict minerals' have to conduct human rights due diligence on suppliers
Public procurement		
2014	Directive 2014/24/EU	Includes a 'social clause' and other human rights-related provisions in EU procurement legislation
2014	Directive 2014/23/EU	Includes a 'social clause' and other human rights-related provisions on concession contracts
2014	Directive 2014/25/EU	Includes a 'social clause' and other human rights-related provisions on the procurement of utility contracts
Labour rights of third-country nationals		
2003	Council directive 2003/109/EC	Protection of third-country nationals who are long-term residents in the EU
2004	Council Directive 2004/114/EC	Protection of third-country nationals for the purposes of studies, pupil exchange, unremunerated training or voluntary service
2005	Council Directive 2005/71/EC	Protection of third-country nationals for the purposes of research
2009	Council Directive 2009/50/EC	'Blue Card Directive' ensures equal treatment to highly-qualified third-country nationals (working conditions, social security etc.)
2011	Directive 2011/98/EU	Framework directive on the protection of third-country nationals
2014	2014/36/EU	Protection of third-country nationals for the purpose of employment as seasonal workers
2014	2014/66/EU	Protection of third-country nationals in the framework of an intra-corporate transfer
Human trafficking		
2011	Directive 2011/36/EU	Prevention of human trafficking and protection of its victims

(continued)

Table 2.1 (continued)

Year	Instrument	Function
Civil justice		
2007	Regulation (EC) 864/2007	'Rome II regulation' specifies that with regard to non-contractual obligations, the applicable law is that of the state where the human rights violation occurs, while the application of the law can take place within the EU
2008	Regulation (EC) 593/2008	'Rome I regulation' allows victims of a human rights violations that have contractual relations with a European parent company or a third country subsidiary, to choose which law applies
2003	Directive 2003/8/EC	Facilitates access to justice in cross-border disputes by establishing minimum common rules relating to legal aid
2012	Regulation (EU) 1215/2012	'Brussels I regulation' sets out rules for the allocation of jurisdiction in cross-border disputes, including civil liability disputes concerning the violation of human rights
Criminal justice		
2009	Directive 2009/52/EC	Prohibits the employment of third-country nationals without a legal permit and foresees financial and criminal sanctions
2010	Directive 2010/64/EU	Ensures the right to interpretation and translation in criminal proceedings
2012	Directive 2012/13/EU	Ensures the right to information in criminal proceedings
2013	Directive 2013/48/EU	Ensures the right to access to a lawyer in criminal proceedings
Trade and investment agreements		
1995	Trade agreements	Trade/cooperation agreements shall contain human rights clauses
2010	Commission Communication on European investment policy (COM(2010)573)	Stresses that European investment policy should be guided by principles and objectives of EU external action, including human rights
2012	Regulation 1219/2012	If member states, authorised by the Commission, negotiate investment agreements, human rights clauses must be included
2012	Commission communication COM (2012) 22 final of 27.1.2012	Commission communication "Trade, Growth and Development—Tailoring trade and investment policy for those countries most in need" promotes responsible business conduct and CSR

public procurement accounts for 14% of GDP (European Commission, 2016b, e), while in Germany and France it accounts for 15% (European Commission, 2016d, c). Despite its economic importance, public procurement regulation has emerged much later than internal market rules regulating the private economy. In part, this stems from the fact that state-owned public enterprises have historically accomplished many of the functions that are now regulated by the public procurement directives. However, after the wave of privatization started in Europe during the 1980s, the regulatory mode changed from regulation through public ownership to statutory regulation (Majone, 1996).[37] Current procurement legislation has the aim to open the public procurement market and ensure the free movement of goods, services, and labour within the EU and thereby make public procurement more transparent and competitive.

In 1996, the Commission started preparations to streamline the existing EU legal framework, which resulted in the two public procurement directives, adopted in 2004.[38] The two pieces of legislation marked a general overhaul of EU procurement legislation and were intended to simplify and modernize procurement rules. Before the adoption of these two directives, complicated provisions and lengthy bureaucratic procedures made it difficult for companies in one member state to bid for a public tender in another (Hebly & Van Rooij, 2007). Apart from introducing electronic purchasing mechanisms and new procurement procedures, the new directives were also the first to mention social concerns in the procurement legislation. However, the few provisions alluding to the possibility of taking social concerns into account were only voluntary.[39]

In 2010, the Commission further advanced the issue of social considerations in procurement rules. The so-called ‘Monti Report’, which outlined a new strategy for the single market, proposed to use public procurement strategically in order to, inter alia, promote social objectives (see Monti, 2010). This represented a “significant shift” (Institute for Human Rights and Business, 2015, p. 14) for the EU procurement policy. Afterwards, the Commission published a guide on socially responsible public procurement (SRPP) for public authorities. In this guide defines SRPP as

> procurement operations that take into account one or more of the following social considerations: employment opportunities, decent work, compliance with social and labour rights, social inclusion (including persons with disabilities), equal opportunities, accessibility design for all, taking account of sustainability criteria, including ethical trade issues and wider voluntary compliance with corporate social responsibility (CSR), while observing the principles enshrined in the Treaty for the European Union (TFEU) and the Procurement Directives. (European Commission, 2010)

---

[37]Especially the regulation is the areas of utilities and concessions contracts lays down rules for industries that were formerly owned by the state.

[38]The two new directives were the ‘classical’ procurement directive (Directive 2004/18/EC of the European Parliament and of the Council of 31 March 2004 on the coordination of procedures for the award of public works contracts, public supply contracts and public service contracts) and the ‘Sector Directive’ (Directive 2004/17/EC of the European Parliament and of the Council of 31 March 2004 coordinating the procurement procedures of entities operating in the water, energy, transport and postal services sectors), which focused on utilities, transport and postal services.

[39]Recitals 1 and 46, as well as Article 26 mention social issues.

A reading of this guide shows that the Commission's approach to SRPP follows the structures and procedures of its Green Public Procurement (GPP) agenda. A similar observation has been made in an external report on the strategic use of public procurement, which states that "GPP is clearly the most dominant approach" (Kahlenborn, Moser, Frijdal, & Essig, 2011, p. 48) and that

> [p]olicy approaches integrating environmental objectives in public procurement generally date back longer, are far more elaborate, and are furnished with more supportive programs than those for socially responsible procurement or procurement promoting innovation. (ibid)

In 2011, the Commission published proposals to revise the two 2004 directives and proposed a new directive on the award of concession contracts. It aimed at simplifying procurement rules and modernizing some practices, for example, by gradually introducing new rules on e-procurement. The Commission also sought to integrate public procurement into the overall political goals of the Juncker Commission, among other things in order to create "a more innovative, green and socially-inclusive economy" (European Commission, 2016a, para. 1). The revised public procurement directives should induce public authorities to set positive examples and encourage businesses to respect social standards. In effect, the directives promote SRPP in three ways. First, by ensuring that the awarding of public contracts is no longer dependent on the lowest price alone. Instead, contracting authorities should award procurement contracts to the 'most economically advantageous tender' (MEAT). Second, by introducing a social clause, which stipulates that national or EU social and labour laws have to be respected. Third, by providing the possibility to reserve some public tenders for companies that promote the integration of people with disabilities (European Commission, 2016a).[40]

The negotiation of the directive texts took two years until adoption in February 2014. The results were three lengthy compromise texts.[41] The EP took an active part in shaping the directive. The responsible rapporteur tabled a total of 750 amendments to the Commission proposal of the public-sector directive, many of which addressed social issues. However, the Council was not opposed to ensuring that social concerns would play an important role in the common procurement rules (Semple, 2014). In comparison to the negotiation of the NFR-Directive (see below), the debates about the human rights provisions in the public procurement directives were much less contested among the co-legislators.[42] The EP proposed a stronger language of the social clause and placed it under the article dealing with procurement principles. As the Council did not object, this proposal was adopted. However, the essence of the human rights-related clauses and their degree of obligation as adopted in the final version of the directive was broadly similar to the language proposed by the Commission. Partly, the lack of controversy about the human rights clauses can be explained by the fact that unlike the NFR-Directive, the public procurement directives are not single-issue directives. Apart from the social criteria, co-legislators also

[40] A detailed breakdown of the human rights-related clauses is provided in Chap. 5.

[41] The PSD is 178 pages long, while the UD and CD have 132 pages and 64 pages respectively.

[42] One contested issue in the negotiations was the EP's proposal to introduce a 'European Procurement Passport', which was rejected by the Council.

had to negotiate about issues such as the access of SMEs to public procurement, electronic procurement rules, environmental criteria, and the detailed rules of procurement procedures. Still, given the significant advancement of SRPP in the EU brought about by the new procurement directives, more controversy could have been expected. After all, the new procurement directives addressed human rights concerns in all stages of the procurement process, while the 2004 directives only mentioned social issues concerning the contracting stage (Institute for Human Rights and Business, 2015). NGOs and civil society organizations have commended the 2014 public procurement directives as crucial milestones for the development of SRPP in the EU (CorA Netzwerk für Unternehmensverantwortung, 2014; Heydenreich, Paasch, & Kusch, 2014; Institute for Human Rights and Business, 2015).[43] However, most provisions that address human rights still have voluntary character, which is why the effectiveness of such rules depends on national transpositions.

2.5 The Non-financial Reporting Directive

Since its adoption in 2014, the NFR-Directive has become somewhat of a poster-child for European BHR regulation. It requires all European companies that have more than 500 employees "to disclose information on policies, risks and results as regards the respect for human rights, anti-corruption, bribery issues, environmental matters, social and employee-related aspects, as well as the diversity on boards of Directors" (European Commission, 2015). EU regulation of accounting practices dates back to 1978. As the latest in a series of accounting directives, the NFR-Directive has introduced the most extensive non-financial reporting requirements so far. Such requirements are often also called *sustainability reporting*, which refers to the "provision of environmental, social and governance (ESG) information within documents such as annual reports and sustainability reports" (Wensen et al., 2011, p. 14).[44]

The first input to make non-financial reporting obligatory came from an EP resolution, which was advanced by the British Member of the European Parliament (MEP) Richard Howitt and was adopted in 1999.[45] As a result of this resolution, the 2003 version of the accounting directive contained a provision whereby managers were encouraged, but not obligated to decide if they wanted to publish non-financial reports.[46] According to Kinderman (2015), the Commission was only willing to make such provisions mandatory after the experience of the financial crisis had resulted in

[43]One point of criticisms about the directives was the fact that all social criteria always have to be linked to the subject-matter of the public tender (see Semple, 2014).

[44]In this book I will use the terms sustainability reporting and non-financial reporting interchangeably.

[45]*Resolution on EU standards for European enterprises operating in developing countries: towards a European Code of Conduct* (A4-0508/98).

[46]The provision was Article 46 in Directive 2003/51/EC.

a more pro-regulatory stance. In 2011, after the mood about binding regulation had shifted, the CSR strategy formulated the ambition to introduce non-financial reporting obligations, which produced much activity among interest groups. Especially the German industry and employer representatives were reportedly adamant about preventing mandatory disclosure requirements (ibid). Negotiations among stakeholders became even more intense after the Commission published the directive proposal in 2013, which contained binding reporting requirements for companies with more than 500 employees.

The negotiations of the directive were reported to have been marked by the conflicts between member states and between interest groups. In the Council of ministers, the opposing positions of France and Germany dominated negotiations. While France was a strong supporter of the directive, advocating far-reaching reporting requirements, Germany rejected the proposal altogether (Kinderman, 2015, p. 5).[47] Even before the proposal was published, German ministries voiced their opposition to binding reporting requirements in front of the Commission (Heydenreich et al., 2014, p. 120). The UK positioned itself in between the two countries and played an essential role as a proposer of amendments (Kinderman, 2015, p. 5). Among interest groups, business associations were opposed to binding regulation, arguing that mandatory reporting requirements would dampen competitiveness.

On the other hand, a coalition of NGOs and other civil society organizations regarded mandatory regulation as the only effective instrument to prevent human rights abuses. The European Coalition for Corporate Justice (ECCJ) was the central coordinator for several national accountability associations and had, despite its small size, an impact on the negotiations, especially by influencing the report by the EP's committee on legal affairs (ibid, p. 8). Another force in favour of stricter reporting requirements were sustainable investors, who hold considerable economic resources and favour sustainability requirements because they would grow the market for sustainable investments.[48] A letter to Commissioner Tajani, which was co-signed by the Executive Director of the European Sustainable Investment Forum, stated that

> [t]he legislation shouldn't allow excessive discretion on companies' side to decide whether they should report on social, environmental and human rights aspects. The "comply or explain" approach, where companies can decide not to report on their non-financial risks and impacts by simply explaining why they don't, has proved insufficient to increase the quantity and quality of the non-financial reporting and it undermines the very rationale of the legislation. (Itschert, Passant, Chaplier, & Goyens, 2013, p. 3)

The EP's role was generally very supportive of the Commission proposal. As none of the major political groups was opposed to binding regulation, the EP acted as a strong supporter of reporting requirements in the legislative process (Kinderman, 2015; Spießhofer, 2014). The EP acted as the antagonist to the Council, which, despite

---

[47] The positions of France and Germany are explained in more detail in Sect. 5.1.

[48] According to Kinderman (2015, p. 7), the three large sustainable investors, the European Sustainable Investment Forum (Eurosif), Principles for Responsible Investment and Aviva Investors/ The Corporate Sustainability Reporting Initiative represent over 25 trillion Euro in assets.

the diverging positions between member states, introduced most of the amendments leading to greater discretion (ibid).

The final result of the NFR-Directive prescribes reporting obligations for companies, which are 'public-interest entities' and have more than 500 employees.[49] These companies have to publish an annual report, which contains information about, at least human rights, environmental and social matters. This information has to be provided in a way to make a businesses' development, performance, position, and its impact on society understandable. The requirement to report on a company's *impact* is an important innovation of this directive. Avoiding negative impacts on society goes further than to merely abide by the law. The aim is that companies acquire knowledge about their negative impact on society and seek to remove it by implementing due diligence procedures (Spießhofer, 2014). Moreover, companies should pre-emptively identify principal risks concerning human rights, environmental and social matters and specify how it manages such risks. Where relevant and proportionate, supply chains and business relationships also have to be taken into account in this respect. Due to these innovations, commentators were quick to point out the historical dimension of this "paradigm shift" (Spießhofer, 2014, p. 1281) in EU accounting regulation.

At the same time, many observers noted the differences between the Commission proposal and the final result of the directive. They argued that the directive had been "watered down substantially" (Kinderman, 2015, p. 2) during the legislative process. Most notably, the scope was reduced significantly. While the original Commission proposal sought to regulate all companies with more than 250 employees (about 18,000 companies), the directive as adopted applies only to those with more than 500 employees (about 6,000)—a reduction by two thirds. Moreover, many derogations were included. For example, a so-called *safe harbour clause* allows member states to exclude commercially sensitive information in exceptional cases. Critics state that the directive leaves too much room for implementation, which in the end would lead to a lack of consistency and comparability (e.g. Spießhofer, 2014, p. 1282). Other commentators argued that the directive would only focus on *ex-post* accountability, whereas it would have been more effective to also require organizational change within companies, which could proactively create awareness for potential human rights risks (Buhmann, 2018). However, most critics focus on the many derogations and a large amount of discretion that is provided in the directive (European Coalition for Corporate Justice, 2014; Heydenreich et al., 2014; Kusch, 2014). Kinderman (2015) stresses how the large degree of voluntarism underscores the importance of national transpositions:

> National parliaments and other stakeholders across the EU will determine whether this Directive will end as a paper tiger or whether it will make a lasting and meaningful contribution to corporate accountability across Europe and beyond. (p. 11)

Spießhofer (2014) states that in order to achieve the intended coordination of national regulations it would have been necessary to define clear benchmarks, the

[49] Public-interest-entities are large listed companies, credit institutions, insurance companies, and other companies which member states define as such.

standard of expected business conduct, clear goals, and methods of how to achieve them (p. 1285). She agrees that if member states make use of the numerous derogations, the directive would essentially become ineffectual. Such assessments underline the relevance of a comprehensive analysis of the national transpositions.

2.6 Conclusion

This chapter aimed to explain and discuss BHR as a policy area, to inform the selection of the policy-specific independent variables in the empirical analysis, and to explain the selection of the four EU directives that are investigated in the empirical analysis. In this chapter, I have shown that the development of an EU human rights regime was a complicated political process, which included elements of both negative and positive integration. While the EU human rights regime has a strong normative foundation, the emphasis on principles comes at the expense of a comprehensive implementation of a human rights policy. In this respect, scholars have noted a gap between the publicly stated commitment to human rights and the implementation of human rights policy. From a legal perspective, the EU member states are at the centre of a European human rights regime. As the ECJ has blocked the EU's accession to the ECHR, the member states are the only actors that can be held liable for extraterritorial activities of European corporations. This example shows that this book's goal to contribute to the understanding of member states' behaviour in BHR has implications beyond the transposition of EU directives. The review of the EU's BHR policy has shown that the EU is still in the process of building this policy area, by integrating previously existing measures from human rights policy and CSR policy, and new instruments into a novel policy framework. Since the UNGPs provide the source for this policy area, I argue that EU BHR policy can be understood as a regulative policy area that was transferred from the UN level to the EU level. Based on this observation, international policy transfer will also be used as a variable in the empirical analysis of this study.

The discussion of EU BHR policy has highlighted the inherent ambiguity between voluntary incentives and mandatory regulation, which informs diverging political understandings of EU BHR policy. This ambiguity also leads to different party-political and theoretical interpretations of BHR regulation. When trying to make assumptions about the regulatory behaviour of states, scholars have relied on categorizations of the political economy. Most notably, the VoC approach by Hall and Soskice (2001b) has been established as an instrument to predict state behaviour in the area of BHR. These considerations also inform the selection of the independent variables used in the empirical analysis.

The final sections of this chapter have given a detailed account of the EU's current BHR policy. This policy area combines measures from diverse fields such as accounting regulation, labour rights, and criminal justice. The three EU directives on public procurement and the NFR-Directive stand out from these measures, because they are recently adopted directives, which, on the one hand, entail considerable economic consequences for business enterprises, and which, on the other hand, are of high relevance for the protection of human rights in global supply chains. In addition, member states are given a significant degree of discretion when transposing these directives, which renders them suitable for the empirical analysis.

References

Albareda, L., Lozano, J. M., & Ysa, T. (2007). Public policies on corporate social responsibility: The role of governments in Europe. *Journal of Business Ethics, 74*(4), 391–407.

Alston, P., & Weiler, J. H. H. (1999). An "ever closer union" in need of a human rights policy: the European Union and human rights. In *The EU and Human Rights* (pp. 3–69).

Álvarez Rubio, J. J., & Yiannibas, K. (Eds.). (2017). *Human rights in business: Removal of barriers to access to Justice in the European Union*. New York: Routledge.

Augenstein, D. (2010). *Study of the legal framework on human rights and the environment applicable to European enterprises operating outside the European Union*. University of Edinburgh. Retrieved from http://www.euenterpriseslf.ed.ac.uk/project_documents.

Augenstein, D., Dawson, M., & Thielbbrger, P. (2018). The UNGPs in the European Union: The open coordination of business and human rights? *Business and Human Rights Journal, 3*(01), 1–22.

Bartels, L. (2014). *A model human rights clause for the EU's international trade agreements. German Institute for Human Rights and Misereor*. Retrieved from http://papers.ssrn.com/sol3/Papers.cfm?abstract_id=2405852.

Borowsky, M. (2010). Die Grundrechtecharta als normatives Fundament der Europäischen Union. In O. Leiße (Ed.), *Die Europäische Union nach dem Vertrag von Lissabon* (pp. 147–158). Wiesbaden: VS Verlag für Sozialwissenschaften.

Buhmann, K. (2011). Integrating human rights in emerging regulation of Corporate Social Responsibility: the EU case. *International Journal of Law in Context, 7*(02), 139–179.

Buhmann, K. (2018). Neglecting the proactive aspect of human rights due diligence? A critical appraisal of the eu's non-financial reporting directive as a pillar one avenue for promoting pillar two action. *Business and Human Rights Journal, 3*(1), 23–45.

CorA Netzwerk für Unternehmensverantwortung. (2014). Briefing Paper: Öffentliche Beschaffung mit der EU-Vergaberichtlinie 2014/24/EU. Retrieved from https://www.cora-netz.de/cora/wp-content/uploads/2015/07/CorA_Beschaffung-mit-EU-Richtlinie_2014.pdf.

Council of the European Union. (2016). council conclusions on business and human rights, 20 June 2016. *3477th Meeting of the Foreign Affairs Council, 10254/16*.

De Búrca, G. (2011). The road not taken: The European union as a global human rights actor. *The American Journal of International Law, 105*(4), 649–693.

De Schutter, O. (2005). The implementation of fundamental rights through the open method of coordination. In O. De Schutter & S. Deakin (Eds.), *Social Rights and Market Forces. Is the open coordination of employment and social policies the future of Social Europe?* (pp. 279–343). Brussels: Bruylant.

De Schutter, O. (2008). Corporate social responsibility European style. *European Law Journal, 14*(2), 203–236.

Bundestag, D. (2013). Antwort der Bundesregierung auf die Kleine Anfrage der Abgeordneten Josip Juratovic, [...] Vereinigungsfreiheit auch bei Tochterunternehmen deutscher Unternehmen sicherstellen, *17/12808*.

Directive 2014/23/EU of the European Parliament and of the Council of 26 February 2014 on the award of concession contracts. (2014). Official Journal of the European Union, L 94.

Directive 2014/24/EU of the European Parliament and of the Council of 26 February 2014 on public procurement and repealing Directive 2004/18/EC. (2014). Official Journal of the European Union, L 94.
Directive 2014/25/EU of the European Parliament and of the Council of 26 February 2014 on procurement by entities operating in the water, energy, transport and postal services sectors and repealing Directive 2004/17/EC. (2014). Official Journal of the European Union, L 94.
Directive 2014/95/EU of the European Parliament and of the Council of 22 October 2014 amending Directive 2013/34/EU as regards disclosure of non-financial and diversity information by certain large undertakings and groups. (2014). Official Journal of the European Union, L 330.
Dolowitz, D. P., & Marsh, D. (1996). Who Learns What from Whom: A Review of the Policy Transfer Literature. *Political Studies, 44*(2), 343–357.
Douglas-Scott, S. (2006). A tale of two courts: Luxumbourg, Strasbourg, and the growing European human rights acquis. *Common Market Law Review, 43*(3), 629–665.
Douglas-Scott, S. (2014). Opinion 2/13 on EU accession to the ECHR: a Christmas bombshell from the European Court of Justice. *U.K. Const. L. Blog*. Retrieved from http://ukconstitutionallaw.org.
European Coalition for Corporate Justice. (2014). Assessment of the EU Directive on the disclosure of non-financial information by certain large companies.
European Commission. (2001). Green Paper—Promoting a European framework for Corporate Social Responsibility, *COM(2001)*.
European Commission. (2010). Buying social: A guide to taking account of social considerations in public procurement. Brussels.
European Commission. (2011). Communication from the commission to the european parliament, the council, the european economic and social committee and the committee of the regions: A renewed EU strategy 2011–14 for corporate social responsibility, *COM(2011)*.
European Commission. (2015). commission staff working document on implementing the UN guiding principles on business and human rights—state of play. Brussels.
European Commission. (2016a). EU Public Procurement reform: Less bureaucracy, higher efficiency. An overview of the new EU procurement and concession rules introduced on 18 April 2016. Brussels. Retrieved from http://ec.europa.eu/DocsRoom/documents/16412/attachments/1/translations/.
European Commission. (2016b). Public procurement—Study on administrative capacity in the EU—Denmark Country Profile. Retrieved from https://ec.europa.eu/regional_policy/sources/policy/how/improving-investment/public-procurement/study/country_profile/dk.pdf.
European Commission. (2016c). Public procurement—Study on administrative capacity in the EU—France Country Profile. Retrieved from https://ec.europa.eu/regional_policy/sources/policy/how/improving-investment/public-procurement/study/country_profile/fr.pdf.
European Commission. (2016d). Public procurement—Study on administrative capacity in the EU—Germany Country Profile. Retrieved from https://ec.europa.eu/regional_policy/sources/policy/how/improving-investment/public-procurement/study/country_profile/de.pdf.
European Commission. (2016e). Public procurement—Study on administrative capacity in the EU—United Kingdom Country Profile. Retrieved from http://ec.europa.eu/regional_policy/sources/policy/how/improving-investment/public-procurement/study/country_profile/uk.pdf.
Fairbrass, J. (2011). Exploring corporate social responsibility policy in the EU: A discursive institutionalist analysis. *Journal of Common Market Studies, 49*(5), 949–970.
Falkner, G., Treib, O., Hartlapp, M., & Leiber, S. (2005). *Complying with Europe. EU Harmonisation and soft law in the member states*. New York: Cambridge University Press.
Friedman, M. (1970). The social responsibility of business is to increase its profits. *The New York Times Magazine*, (32), September 13.
Gatto, A. (2011). *Multinational enterprises and human rights: obligations under EU law and international law*. Cheltenham: Edward Elgar.
Haas, P. M. (1992). Introduction: Epistemic communities and international policy coordination. *International Organization, 46*(1), 1–35.

Hall, P. A., & Soskice, D. (2001a). An introduction to varieties of capitalism. In P. A. Hall & D. Soskice (Eds.), *Varieties of capitalism: The institutional foundations of comparative advantage* (pp. 1–68). Oxford: Oxford University Press.
Hall, P. A., & Soskice, D. (Eds.). (2001b). *Varieties of capitalism: The institutional foundations of comparative advantage*. Oxford: Oxford University Press.
Hebly, J. M., & Van Rooij, N. L. (2007). *European public procurement: Legislative history of the "Classic" Directive 2004/18/EC*. Alphen aan den Rijn: Kluwer Law International.
Heydenreich, C., Paasch, A., & Kusch, J. (2014). *Bericht 2014: Globales Wirtschaften und Menschenrechte—Deutschland auf dem Prüfstand*. Berlin.
Institute for Human Rights and Business. (2015). Protecting rights by purchasing right—the human rights provisions, opportunities and limitations under the 2014 EU Public Procurement Directive.
International Labour Organization (ILO). (2017). *Global Estimates of Modern Slavery: Forced labour and forced marriage*. Geneva.
Itschert, P., Passant, F., Chaplier, J., & Goyens, M. (2013). Letter to commissioner Tajani, subject: Legislative Proposal on non-financial reporting, 4 March 2013. Retrieved March 4, 2016, from http://www.eurosif.org/wp-content/uploads/2014/06/111.letter_comtajani_nfr_eccj_etuc_beuc_eurosif_march2013_en.pdf.
Kahlenborn, W., Moser, C., Frijdal, J., & Essig, M. (2011). *Strategic use of public procurement in Europe—Final Report to the European Commission MARKT/2010/02/C*. Berlin.
Kamminga, M. T. (1999). Holding multinational corporations accountable for human rights abuses: A challenge for the European community. In P. Alston (Ed.), *The EU and human rights* (pp. 553–569). New York: Oxford University Press.
Kinderman, D. (2008). The political economy of corporate responsibility in Germany, 1995–2008. *Mario Einaudi Center for International Studies, No 5-08*.
Kinderman, D. (2013). Corporate social responsibility in the EU, 1993-2013: Institutional ambiguity, economic crises, business legitimacy and bureaucratic politics. *Journal of Common Market Studies, 51*(4), 701–720.
Kinderman, D. (2015). The struggle over the EU Non-financial disclosure directive. *WSI-Mitteilungen, 8*(2015), 613–621.
Kusch, J. (2014). Hintergrundinformationen: Die EU Regulierung zur Offenlegung von nicht-finanziellen Informationen durch Unternehmen. *Germanwatch/ CorA AG Offenlegung*, (April 2013), 1–6.
Lowi, T. J. (1972). Four systems of policy, politics, and choice. *Public Administration Review, 32*(4), 298–310.
Majone, G. (1996). Regulating Europe. London: Routledge.
Methven O'Brian, C. (2016). The home state duty to regulate the human rights impacts of TNCs abroad: A case of extraterritorial overreach? *DIHR Matters of Concern Human Rights Research Papers*, (No.2016/4).
Monti, M. (2010). A New strategy for the single market—Report to the President of the European Commission José Manuel Barroso. Milan.
Ruggie, J. (2013). *Just business: Multinational corporations and human rights*. New York: W. W. Norton.
Sabatier, P. (1998). The advocacy coalition framework: revisions and relevance for Europe. *Journal of European Public Policy, 5*(1), 98–130.
Santoro, M. A. (2015). Business and human rights in historical perspective. *Journal of Human Rights, 14*(2), 155–161. Retrieved from https://doi.org/10.1080/14754835.2015.1025945.
Schmidt, C. P. (2013). *Grund- und Menschenrechte in Europa*. Baden-Baden: Nomos.
Schmitter, P. C. (1974). Still the century of corporatism? *The Review of Politics, 36*(1), 85–131.
Semple, A. (2014). The link to the subject-matter: A glass ceiling for sustainable public contracts? *University of Oslo as Part of the European Law Conference 2014, Forthcoming Volume Published by Cambridge University Press*, 1–18.
Siaroff, A. (1999). Corporatism in 24 industrial democracies: Meaning and measurement. *European Journal of Political Research, 36*(2), 175–205.

Spar, D. L. (1998). The spotlight and the bottom line: How multinationals export human rights. *Foreign Affairs, 77*(2), 7–12.

Spießhofer, B. (2014). Die neue europäische Richtlinie über die Offenlegung nichtfinanzieller Informationen—Paradigmenwechsel oder Papiertiger? *Neue Zeitschrift Für Gesellschaftsrecht, 1281*(33), 1281–1320.

Stobbe, H.-G. (2011). European Governance. Ein Beitrag zu ihrem normativen Fundament. In G. Simonis & H. Elbers (Eds.), *Externe EU-Governance* (pp. 55–82). VS Verlag für Sozialwissenschaften.

Stone, D. (2000). Non-governmental policy transfer: The strategies of independent policy institutes. *Governance, 13*(1), 45–70.

Streeck, W. (2010). E Pluribus Unum? Varieties and Commonalities of Capitalism. *MPIfG Discussion Paper, 10*(12), 419–455.

TEU [Lisbon]. Consolidated version of the treaty on European Union. Official Journal of the European Union, C 326.

TEU [Maastricht]. Consolidated version of the treaty on European Union, C 191 Official Journal of the European Union.

TFEU [Lisbon]. Consolidated Version Of The Treaty on the functioning of the European Union. Official Journal of the European Union, C 326.

Thomson, R. (2007). Time to comply: National responses to six eu labour market directives revisited. *West European Politics, 30*(5), 987–1008.

Thomson, R. (2009). Same effects in different worlds: the transposition of EU directives. *Journal of European Public Policy, 16*(1), 1–18.

United Nations. (2006). *Promotion and protection of human rights—interim report of the special representative of the secretary-general on the issue of human rights and transnational corporations and other business enterprises*. New York: Economic and Social Council.

United Nations. (2011). *Guiding principles on business and human rights*. New York: Office of the United Nations High Commissioner for Human Rights.

Verisk Maplecroft. (2014). Human Rights Risk Atlas 2014. Retrieved September 29, 2017, from https://maplecroft.com/portfolio/new-analysis/2013/12/04/70-increase-countries-identified-extreme-risk-human-rights-2008-bhuman-rights-risk-atlas-2014b/.

Weiler, J. H. H. (2004). Human rights, constitutionalism and integration. In E. O. Erikseon, J. E. Fossum, & A. J. Menéndez (Eds.), *Developing a constitution for Europe* (pp. 59–68). London: Routledge.

Weiler, J. H. H., Haltern, U., & Mayer, F. (1995). European democracy and its critique—Five Uneasy Pieces. *EUI Working Paper RSC*, (95).

Wensen, K. van, Broer, W., Klein, J., & Knopf, J. (2011). The State of play in sustainability reporting in the European Union.

Wood, S. (2009). The European union: A normative or normal power? *European Foreign Affairs Review, 14*(1), 113–128.

Zhelyazkova, A., & Torenvlied, R. (2011). The successful transposition of European provisions by member states: application to the Framework Equality Directive. *Journal of European Public Policy, 18*(5), 690–708.

Chapter 3
Theoretical Explanations for the Domestic Impact of EU Law

Studies on the transposition of EU directives belong to the more general research field of 'Europeanization', in which scholars examine the reciprocal exchanges between EU member states and the processes of European integration. As a subset of Europeanization, directive transposition studies seek to understand why and how EU member states comply with EU rules. For European studies, this question bears particular significance, because ultimately, the functioning of European integration depends on the compliance of member states. This chapter will approach theoretical explanations for the domestic impact of EU law by going from general explanations for institutional change and compliance to more specific explanations for directive transposition. First, however, the term compliance should be clarified. Jacobson and Brown-Weiss provide an apt definition, stating that "[c]ompliance refers to whether countries in fact adhere to the provision of the accord and to the implementing measures that they have instituted" (Jacobson & Brown-Weiss, 1995, p. 123).

What are the possible conceptual approaches that can be employed when studying cases of compliance in the EU context? From the literature review of compliance literature, I identify four possibilities. First, the concepts of International Relations (IR) and comparative politics literature can be applied to the case of the EU. Haas (1998) examines, in how far IR-approaches are suited to analyse directive transposition. In international relations research, scholars sought to explain states' observance of international agreements. Haas holds that state compliance with external rules mainly depends on two conditions, willingness, and capacity, both of which are determined by a large variety of factors. Haas concludes that compliance in the EU is largely determined by constructivist and institutional forces (ibid). A second approach to compliance with EU rules is classical implementation theory, which focuses on procedural and administrative factors when explaining compliance outcomes. Developed in the 1980s, implementation theory looked at compliance from a top-down administrative perspective and stressed the relevance of clear rules and efficient bureaucracies for successful compliance (Schwarze, Becker, & Pollak, 1993). Such straightforward assumptions attracted criticism of oversimplification from the early Europeanization scholars (Falkner, Treib, Hartlapp, & Leiber, 2005, p. 22).

P. Drahn, *Adoption of EU Business and Human Rights Policy*,
Contributions to Political Science, https://doi.org/10.1007/978-3-030-46935-1_3

Europeanization, the third and most prominent approach to analysing compliance with EU rules, emerged out of EU integration research, from which it expanded the perspective from the supranational level to the relationship between the EU and its member states (see Sect. 3.2 in this chapter). To formulate assumptions about the exchange and the outcomes of these exchanges, Europeanization largely relies on new institutionalism. The fourth approach to assess compliance in the EU context is policy transfer. This research field has its roots in the field of comparative politics and examines the exchange of policies and ideas between different national or international political systems. Policy transfer, as well as related concepts such as policy convergence (see Knill, 2005) and policy diffusion (see e.g. Starke, 2013), seek to understand how and why ideas travel between different polities. With regard to the EU, policy transfer has most prominently been applied by Bulmer and Padget (2004) and by Bulmer et al. (Bulmer, Dolowitz, Humphreys, & Padgett, 2007). Of those four approaches, I will focus my analysis on the Europeanization approach and the underlying assumptions of new institutionalist theory. In addition, policy transfer will be used in two respects. First, it is employed to capture the influence on international norms on the processes of directive transposition. Second, it further informs the understanding of voluntary compliance in the EU context.

To move from general explanations for compliance with EU rules to specific explanations for directive transposition, this chapter begins by presenting the main strands of new institutionalism and explains the leading assumptions that will be employed when analysing the empirical results of this study. Building on this theoretical foundation, Europeanization is explained both as a political phenomenon and as a research approach, putting a particular emphasis on the understandings of domestic political factors. Going further from general to particular, the third section of this chapter provides an overview of the literature on directive transposition, while sections four and five address two conceptual specificities of this book. Section four explains how policy transfer contributes to the theoretical design of this study. The fifth section addresses the issue of voluntary compliance and identifies gaps in the literature. Most importantly, I show that the ‘discretionary room’ in EU directives has not yet been used to measure the dependent variable and thereby measure member states’ policy commitment. I address this research gap in the final section of this chapter, where I present the analytical framework of this study. I explain how I use the discretionary room to build the DV, and how, following a deductive reasoning, I employ the relevant theoretical approaches to identify six independent variables. For these six IVs, I postulate hypotheses that will be tested in the second part of the empirical analysis.

3.1 New Institutionalist Theory

New institutionalism provides the theoretical basis for almost all Europeanization and directive transposition studies. Especially rational choice institutionalism, historical institutionalism, and sociological institutionalism, the three approaches I rely on in this book, have been widely applied by Europeanization scholars. In academic literature, Europeanization is usually not understood as a theory per se, but a research approach laden with different theoretical assumptions, which provides the framework to formulate assumptions about national adaptations to EU rules (e.g. Bulmer, 2007). However, to conceptually understand *why* transfer and adaptation processes take place requires to go beneath the surface of conceptual frameworks, which provide a lower level of specificity than theories.[1] As Elinor Ostrom explains:

> The development and use of a general framework helps identify the elements and relationships among these elements that one needs to consider for institutional analysis. Frameworks organize diagnostic and prescriptive inquiry. (Ostrom, 2007, p. 25)

Only theories "enable the analyst to specify which elements of the framework are particularly relevant to certain kinds of questions and to make general working assumptions about these elements" (ibid). Therefore, it is necessary to understand the underlying assumptions of new institutionalism.

Political scientists have devoted considerable attention to the role that institutions play in affecting human social, political and economic interactions. As Peters (1999) states, "political thinking has its roots in the analysis and design of institutions" (p. 3). Institutions can be defined as "formal rules, standard operating procedures, and governmental structures" (Graziano & Vink, 2013, p. 40) or simply "the rules of the game" (North, 1990, p. 3). March and Olsen (1998) go into more detail when they speak of institutions as "a relatively stable collection of practices and rules defining appropriate behaviour for specific groups of actors in specific situations" (March & Olsen, 1998, p. 948). Such practices and rules are "embedded in structures of meaning and schemes of interpretation" (ibid) and legitimize the identities of actors, provide for roles of appropriate behaviour, and make it possible that individuals who deviate from appropriate behaviour are sanctioned.

Historically, political science scholars "have tended to treat political institutions, particularly the state, as independent factors, important to the ordering and understanding of collective life" (March & Olsen, 1984, p. 735). This understanding of political institutions followed a functional logic and stressed hierarchical principles and bureaucratic coordination of state activities. In the period between the 1950s until the 1970s, this view has received less attention, as scholars focused less on institutions, but rather on the individual, whose behaviour was either based on socio-psychological features or rationality. Such societal factors were regarded as more important for shaping society than political institutions.[2] Against the backdrop of the successes of behaviouralism and rational choice, new institutionalism was first named and coined by March and Olsen (1984), who rediscovered the relevance of institutions. However, instead of restating the claims of the 'old institutionalism', the

[1] Ostrom (2007) distinguishes between three levels of specificity on which institutional analysis can be conducted: frameworks, theories, and models.

[2] March and Olsen (1984) explain that society was seen to influence politics more than the other way around: "It is assumed that class, geography, climate, ethnicity, language, culture, economic conditions, demography, technology, ideology, and religion all affect politics but are not significantly affected by politics" (p. 735).

two scholars formulated a critique of the behavioural and rational choice approaches that had been popular in the post-war period.[3] Based on this critique, March and Olsen stress the continued relevance of institutions, which is captured in new institutionalism. They write: "This new institutionalism emphasizes the relative autonomy of political institutions, possibilities for inefficiency in history, and the importance of symbolic action to an understanding of politics" (March & Olsen, 1984, p. 734). They recognize the impact of societal forces on political institutions, but at the same time, they underline the reciprocal influences between the two, arguing that "the state is not only affected by society but also affects it" (p. 738). As such, new institutionalism reconciles the focus on the individual that was propagated by behavioural and rational choice approaches with the recognition that 'institutions matter'. Institutions are put in relation to actors because "political struggles are mediated by prevailing institutional arrangements" (Bulmer, 1993, p. 355). Institutions provide the context and the structure in which actors operate and which therefore determine or at least influence their behaviour. At the same time, the renewed acknowledgement of institutions also stemmed from the recognition that social, political, and economic institutions had grown in size, complexity, and importance (March & Olsen, 1984).

This starting point by March and Olsen was taken up by other scholars who advanced these ideas into different strands of institutionalism. The large differences between the assumptions formulated by these strands, as well as their separate developments, have led to the conclusion that new institutionalism does not constitute a unified body of thought (Hall & Taylor, 1996). Three schools of thought have been identified early on as the most influential institutionalisms: rational choice institutionalism, historical institutionalism, and sociological institutionalism. Europeanization and compliance research have to varying degrees relied on all of these approaches. Rational choice institutionalism was the first institutionalism to arise when American scholars analysed policy stability in the US Congress, relying on the rational-choice approach (Pollack, 2009). This approach assumes that individuals presented with a number of alternatives will try to achieve the optimal outcome, by making the "consistent, value-maximizing choice within specified constraints" (Mastenbroek & Kaeding, 2006, p. 341). Under the assumptions of rational choice, "political behavior became a function of economic motivations and calculations" (Peters, 1999, p. 12). Given the emphasis on individual rational behaviour, the presumed relevance of institutions seems puzzling at first. If actors act according to their own, value-maximising calculations, what role do institutions play in explaining their behaviour? Rational choice institutionalists reconcile the individual with institutions, as they recognize that most political life takes place within institutions. B. Guy Peters explains the rational institutionalist understanding:

> [I]nstitutions are conceptualized as collections of rules and incentives that establish the conditions for bounded rationality, and therefore establish a 'political space' within which many interdependent political actors can function. (Peters, 1999, p. 44)

[3] Their critique centred around five issues: Contextualism, Reductionism, Utilitarianism, Functionalism, and Instrumentalism. For a more detailed discussion of this critique, see Peters (1999), p. 15.

Hence, the central argument of rational choice institutionalists is that political players act within the parameters of an institution which resemble the 'rules of the game'. As such, rational choice institutionalism is compatible with the notion of *bounded rationality*, which means that when a maximization of utility is not possible, actors try to find the optimal solution within the confines of institutions. Herbert A. Simon was the first to frame the concept of bounded rationality and was later joined by March and Olsen, as well as other authors such as Richard Cyert, who all sought to understand the constraints that limit fully rational behaviour (March, 1978). They argued that because human rationality is limited, individuals try to *satisfice* by meeting context-specific expectations that are embedded in cultural, socioeconomic, and political institutions (March & Olsen, 1989). Simon developed the idea of satisficing when describing decision making in business organizations, where he observed that a decision maker, for whom it is impossible to achieve perfect utility maximization, chooses another option that would meet the decision maker's level of aspiration, thereby abandoning the search for perfectly rational solutions (Simon, 1979). In the policy context, actors, therefore, seek to achieve optimal solutions within the confines of institutions, which also means that they accept this constraining influence (Peters, 1999). This understanding represents an advantage of the rational choice school over other institutionalisms because it yields an analytic connection between the individual and the institution (ibid). To explain how this connection informs our understanding of individual and collective behaviour, March and Olsen refer to the *logic of expected consequences* (March & Olsen, 1998). Particularly insightful is the how March and Olsen explain the role of this logic in politics:

> Within the consequentialist perspective, politics is seen as aggregating individual preferences into collective actions by some procedures of bargaining, negotiation, coalition formation, and exchange. (March & Olson, 1998, p. 949f)

In this respect, rational choice institutionalists expect actors to act in a highly strategic manner, where calculations are made about how other actors will behave. Concerning Europeanization research, rational choice institutionalism is closely connected with classical theories of European integration, because it stresses member states' political opportunities provided by the EU (Graziano & Vink, 2013).

Historical institutionalism, on the other hand, understands the relationship between institutions and individual actors in much broader terms. It stresses the "institutional organization of the polity or political economy as the principal factor structuring collective behaviour and generating distinctive outcomes" (Hall & Taylor, 1996, p. 937). Historical institutionalists thus underline the 'structuralism' that is inbuilt in institutions (ibid). In this school of thought, power, and the unequal distribution thereof receives more attention than in the other schools. They assume that institutions "give some groups or interests disproportionate access to the decision-making process; and [...] they tend to stress how some groups lose while others win" (ibid, p. 941). Moreover, historical institutionalism concerns itself, as the name suggests, with the role of the past in determining future policy outcomes. It assumes that "the policy choices made when an institution is being formed, or when a policy is initiated, will have a continuing and largely determinate influence over the policy far into the future" (Peters, 1999, p. 63). This 'path dependency' is due to the persistent nature of institutions and represents the central assumption of historical institutionalism. Of course, historical institutionalists also account for policy developments to break away from institutional legacies, but only under exceptional circumstances. Crises and military conflicts can represent such critical junctures, which lead to substantial change and put developments on a new path (Hall & Taylor, 1996). In the context of compliance with EU rules, such paths are analysed with respect to the relationships member states have built with the EU. In the context of Europeanization, historical institutionalism is therefore concerned with the "analysis of the sequences of domestic adaptations in connection to the evolution of European political discourses, strategies, institutions, and policies" (Graziano & Vink, 2013, p. 40).

The last of the classical three institutionalisms, sociological institutionalism, is rooted in the post-war successes of behaviouralism and underlines the impact of societal factors on institutions.[4] Rejecting the Weberian view of rational institutions, sociological institutionalists highlight the importance of culture, collective norms, and understandings. It is less outcome-oriented than its rational counterpart, as it is "somewhat more concerned with the process of creating values and cognitive frames within an organization than it is with the end state" (Peters, 1999, p. 105). In this field, scholars recognize that such rules can either be formal and take the form of political institutions such as the state or be informal, such as conventions and codes of behaviour (North, 1990, p. 3). In this respect, sociological institutionalists define institutions in much broader terms (Peters, 1999, p. 106). How are individuals and institutions linked in this field? Following the constructivist logic, it is argued that the dominant belief system prevalent in the institutions constitute the identity of the actors and determine their behaviour (Mastenbroek & Kaeding, 2006, p. 344). Peters makes this point more explicit:

> Institutions as systems of meaning do convey a sense of how their members should behave, whether that is the profit maximization of economic organizations or the altruism of religious and charitable organizations. The view that institutions must shape behavior is the dominant perspective within the sociological study of institutions, with emphasis on the manner in which individuals within organizations. become habituated to accepting the norms and values of their organization. (Peters, 1999, p. 107)

Concerning Europeanization, scholars applying sociological institutionalism argue that domestic actors are by the EU's institutions, thereby generating change that is less visible but might still prove powerful, especially in policy areas where the EU has only limited competence.

These three approaches to intuitionalism have been widely used in the field of European studies and have informed many of the assumptions made by Europeanization scholars. The focus of these approaches was "the analysis of the sequences of domestic adaptations in connection to the evolution of European political discourses,

[4]When March and Olsen initiated the debate on new institutionalism, their understanding leaned towards sociological understanding of institutions (Peters, 1999, p. 98).

strategies, institutions and policies" (Graziano & Vink, 2013, p. 40). How the interactions between the EU level affected the domestic level depends on the respective assumptions of each institutionalism. To a certain degree, rational choice institutionalism can be separated from sociological and historical institutionalism, as it focusses predominantly on interest-maximising behaviour, while the other two assume that institutions are, in different ways, 'sticky', and in principle difficult to change (Falkner et al., 2005, p. 16). In this study, I employ these three institutionalisms and test, if they are suited to explain the empirical results presented in the empirical chapters.

Notwithstanding, these three approaches are by no means the only variants of institutionalism employed in political science. Fritz Scharpf famously proposed the integrated framework of *Actor-Centered Institutionalism*, in which he combines rational and structural paradigms, which, as he claims, are conventionally regarded as mutually exclusive (Scharpf, 1997). *Empirical institutionalism* focuses solely on testing the theoretical institutional assumptions in the real world. Instead of formulating new assumptions, empirical institutionalism classifies different types of institutions and compares their impact on government performance (see Peters, 1999, pp. 78–96). A more recent addition to the institutionalist school was put forward by Schmidt (2008, 2010). Her *Discursive Institutionalism* brings together the other three theoretical schools, but puts an emphasis on ideas and discourse and understands itself as an "umbrella concept" (Schmidt, 2010, p. 3), which focuses on the role of ideas and the interactive processes through which ideas travel in public discourses. Schmidt differentiates between two kinds of processes (coordination and communication) and advocates a more dynamic understanding of institutions and institutional change than the 'traditional' institutionalisms.

However, I do not deem these approaches suitable to explain member state behaviour in response to EU rules, and therefore rely on the three classical institutionalisms and test their validity for explaining the empirical results. There are two reasons for this decision. First, the concepts and instruments that have been developed by Europeanization scholars, such as 'misfit' and 'facilitating factors', build almost exclusively on the classical three institutionalisms. Other variants of institutionalism are, judging from the research conducted for this book, not employed to compare compliance with EU law. Second, the three institutionalisms are not mutually exclusive for the explanation of institutional influences on policy outcomes. As Peters notes in this regard: "These approaches to institutions also should be seen as complementary [...], even if the partisans of one or the other may often claim pride of place" (Peters, 1999, p. 2). Thus, hypotheses that are formed on the basis of the three classical institutionalisms do not have to be competing but may well be complementary. For these two reasons, I rely on the classical three institutionalisms, which allows me to draw on the insights and concepts of the Europeanization approach, which are presented in the next section.

3.2 Europeanization and the Analysis of Directive Transpositions

3.2.1 *The Emergence of Europeanization*

The concept of Europeanization became prominent among European studies scholars in the 1990s, in part as a reaction to the intensification of European integration. For almost four decades, European integration research focussed on the question, why national governments are willing to pool part of their sovereignty in common European institutions. Scholars of European studies formulated theoretical assumptions that sought to explain how the ensuing European polity would develop. In the centre of this research was the debate between the 'Grand Theories' of European integration, most notably neo-functionalism as initially put forward by Haas (1958), and (liberal) intergovernmentalism, which was initially proposed by Hoffmann (1966) and then further developed by other scholars, most notably by Moravcsik and Schimmelfennig (2009). While intergovernmentalism saw the governments of the member states, seeking to advance their geopolitical and economic interests, as the main drivers of European integration, neo-functionalism stressed the central role of the supranational institutions, especially the ECJ and the European Commission. From different perspectives, these theoretical strands sought to identify relevant factors in the dynamics of the European integration process that would best explain the outcomes on the European level. During the 1990s, theoretical contributions had shifted focus to the question of what kind of polity European integration processes were bringing about. Studies on multi-level governance (see e.g. Bulmer, 1993; Jachtenfuchs & Kohler-Koch, 1996; Marks, 1993; Wessels, 1996) were concerned with the question of how the institutional order of the European Community could be understood, e.g. as a construct 'sui generis' or as a political system that can be compared to other political systems. From a different perspective, the fusion thesis, developed by Wessels (1992, 1997a, 1997b), portrays the EU's development as a process of cyclical but structural growth and differentiation. The quality of this process is a 'fusion' of the vertical multilevel constellations and of the horizontal EU-multi-institutional architecture (Wessels, 1997a).

This approach already entails an understanding of member states' adaptational processes in response to European integration, a subject on which more and more studies emerged in the second half of the 1990s (see e.g. Bulmer & Burch, 1998; Ladrech, 1994; Rometsch & Wessels, 1996). Instead of asking how and why member states shaped the European integration project, these studies asked how European integration impacted structures, procedures, and norms at home. This "Europeanization turn" (Graziano & Vink, 2013, p. 33) was in line with the trend prevalent at the time to study the domestic impacts of international institutions and norms. To explain the emergence of this field, some authors highlight the sequential relationship with classical integration research. Following that logic, classical integration research analyzing the establishment of European institutions was the first step, which was followed in a second step by Europeanization research, investigating the domestic impact of these institutions (Axt, Milososki, & Schwarz, 2007).[5] For some, it is thus no surprise that Europeanization research had its peak of publications at the end of the 1990s and early 2000s, at a time when the policies following the Maastricht treaty were increasingly taking effect (Graziano & Vink, 2013). Newer accounts of European integration have highlighted differentiation as a central characteristic of the EU and delineate a system of 'differentiated integration' (Schimmelfennig, Leuffen, & Rittberger, 2015).

To find the "missing link" (Goetz, 2000, p. 222) between this increased European output and domestic change, scholars of Europeanization have heavily relied on neo-institutionalist explanations (see e.g. Börzel, 1999; Börzel & Risse, 2000; Héritier, 2001; Olsen, 2002; Radaelli, 2000b, 2003), recognizing institutions are central agents in political systems that play a vital role in the implementation of European rules. As is shown below, historical institutionalism, rational-choice institutionalism, and sociological institutionalism have informed different assumptions about the logic behind domestic adaptational processes.

3.2.2 *Expounding the Concept*

Europeanization is a broad concept and in order to grasp the "many faces of Europeanization" (Olsen, 2002), the differences between definitions for Europeanization should be illustrated.[6] Graziano and Vink argue that the definitional debate is still in its ontological phase (Graziano & Vink, 2013, p. 37). The first definitions underlined the EU's impact on policy making in general. Ladrech (1994) described Europeanization as an "incremental process re-orienting the direction and shape of politics to the degree that EU political and economic dynamics become part of the organizational logic" (Ladrech, 1994, p. 69). Following this understanding, Europeanization is understood as *Vergemeinschaftung*, which then, as an independent variable, can have an impact on domestic processes (Börzel & Risse, 2000, p. 3). The definition by Risse et al. (2001) was more refined, but contained similar elements:

We define Europeanization as the emergence and development at the European level of distinct structures of governance, that is, of political, legal, and social institutions associated with political problem-solving that formalize interactions among the actors, and of policy-networks specializing in the creation of authoritative European rules. (Risse, Cowles, & Caporaso, 2001, p. 3)

[5]A different interpretation of the relationship between classical European integration research and Europeanization research was provided by Börzel (2005), who argued that theorizing Europeanization would turn around the explanatory logics of the classical integration paradigms (supranationalism and intergovernmentalism).

[6]Olsen distinguishes between five possible uses of Europeanization: the changes in external territorial boundaries, the development of institutions on the European level, the penetration of national and sub-national systems of governance, the export of forms of political organisation and governance beyond Europe and the political project of a united and strong Europe (Olsen, 2002, p. 3f).

Some authors found it difficult to clearly delineate this understanding of Europeanization from processes of European integration, and thus criticized that it would not be very innovative and would essentially not add anything new to the debate (see e.g. Axt et al., 2007; Graziano & Vink, 2013; Radaelli, 2004). Instead, other definitions increasingly highlighted a sequential understanding of Europeanization, where activity on the European level is followed by a domestic impact. In this respect, a short definition by Vink and Graziano became popular, where Europeanization is understood as "domestic adaptation to European regional integration" (Vink & Graziano, 2007, p. 7). An equally minimalist definition by Schimmelfennig and Sedelmeier (2005) is particularly well suited for analysing the adoption of EU law. It describes Europeanization as "a process in which states adopt EU rules" (Schimmelfennig & Sedelmeier, 2005, p. 7).

A more refined definition was formulated by Héritier (2001), who subdivides Europeanization into the following elements: "the European decisions, the process triggered by these decisions as well as the impacts of these processes on national policies, decision procedures and institutional structures." (Héritier, 2001, p. 3). An even more detailed and widely used definition was put forward by Radaelli:

> Europeanization consists of processes of a) construction, b) diffusion and c) institutionalisation of formal and informal rules, procedures, policy paradigms, styles, 'ways of doing things' and shared beliefs and norms which are first defined and consolidated in the EU policy process and then incorporated in the logic of domestic (national and subnational) discourse, political structures and public policies. (Radaelli, 2003, p. 30)

This definition highlights not only the impact on national and subnational levels of governance; it also underscores the variety of institutionalist and constructivist channels through which the adaptation can take place. It neglects the notion that *impact* on the domestic level has to be static or mechanistic and allows for both pull and push understandings of adaptation that can occur through formalized institutions as well as through informal discourses (Radaelli, 2004, p. 4). When the term Europeanization is used in this book, it will follow the understanding of this definition, because it highlights both the policy construction on the European level and a broad understanding of adaptation on the domestic level. Moreover, the definition by Radaelli (2003) takes into account different directions of influence.

With regard to the direction of influence in Europeanization, Radaelli (2004, p. 4) goes on by distinguishing between top-down and bottom-up Europeanization.[7] To him, top-down Europeanization research is more established, with the research design following a simple sequence (Fig. 3.1).

Such studies, which still account for most Europeanization research, are looking at "uni-directional changes and narrow impacts" (ibid) by analysing the implementation of European policies. On the other hand, Europeanization studies with a bottom-up perspective would start and end at the domestic level. Radaelli summarizes bottom-up research designs as follows:

[7] To show the main innovation of Europeanization research, his depiction he also mentions European integration research, where the direction of influence goes from the domestic to the European level.

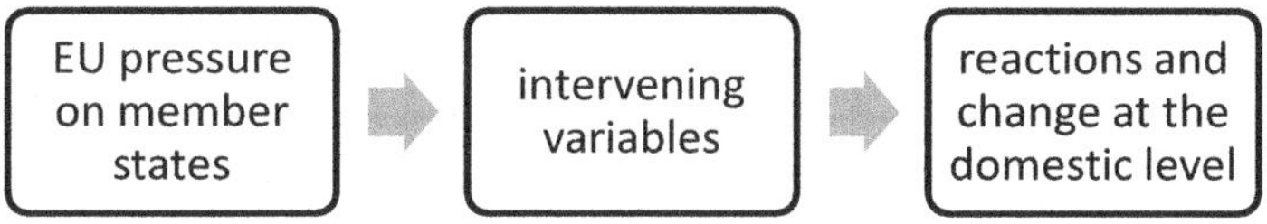

Fig. 3.1 Classical design of top-down Europeanization research

> [T]he starting point is a system of interaction at the domestic level. By using time and temporal causal sequences, a bottom-up approach checks if, when, and how the EU provides a change in any of the main components of the system of interaction. Finally, 'bottom-uppers' try to measure the consequences of all this in terms of change at the domestic level. (ibid)

This understanding of Europeanization comprises the view that Europeanization is a "two-way street" (Bomberg & Peterson, 2000, p. 7), because, while the EU impacts domestic policies, "[m]ember States also project themselves by seeking to shape the trajectory of European integration in ways that suit national interests" (ibid). Especially later Europeanization research acknowledged such feedback processes that include both 'uploading' and 'downloading' between different levels of governance (Börzel & Risse, 2000; Graziano & Vink, 2013), which some studies have even tried to combine (Lodge, 2006). Saurugger (2014, p. 125) calls this *Circular Europeanization*, stating under this definition Europeanization is understood "not as a linear process, but a circular one, which also includes European integration and the process's influence at the national level, which, in turn influences European integration anew" (ibid).

While such attempts have led to some degree of "conceptual confusion" (Graziano & Vink, 2013, p. 38), they underscore the fact that Europeanization is not an *explanans* (i.e. the solution that explains the dependent variable), but rather an *explanandum* (i.e. the phenomenon that needs to be explained) (Gualini, 2003; Radaelli, 2004). Indeed, a look at the various understandings of Europeanization reveals that they do not ascribe assumptions about political processes to Europeanization. In the research community, it is by now widely agreed that Europeanization as such is not a theory, but rather a phenomenon that needs to be understood, which then usually requires theoretical explanations[8] (Bulmer, 2007; Bulmer & Lequesne, 2013; Radaelli, 2004). From a researcher's perspective, Europeanization is an "approach that enables us to orchestrate exiting concepts and to contribute to cumulative research in political science" (Radaelli, 2004, p. 5). At the same time, Europeanization does not provide a sui generis analytical framework. Rather, it combines existing approaches to explain the phenomenon of Europeanization.[9] Thus, studying Europeanization holds enormous potential for providing insights about the consequences of European integration. Radaelli (2004) writes on this matter:

---

[8]Olsen (2002) takes a slightly different perspective, calling Europeanization an „attention–directing device and a starting point for further exploration" (Olsen, 2002, p. 24).

[9]Therefore, the research area has been criticized for pursuing methodological eclecticism (Axt et al., 2007, p. 145).

Fig. 3.2 Magnitude and direction of national change in response to EU rules

> The most original work on Europeanization has contributed to the emergence of new insights, original explanations, and interesting questions on three important issues: the understanding and analysis of 'domestic impact' of international politics, how to endogeneise international governance in models of domestic politics (in terms of research design), and the relationship between agency and change. (Radaelli, 2004, p. 2)[10]

Europeanization is therefore also the EU-related part of a broader research field that analyses the interplay between, on the one side, international organisations, regimes, and norms, and on the other side the domestic political sphere, consisting of polity, policies, and politics. It therefore touches upon some of the central issues of political integration and globalization. Olsen even argues that Europeanization was "conceptualized in a way that makes it (in principle) possible to compare European dynamics with the dynamics of other systems of governance" (Olsen, 2002, p. 2). In this book I address this connection between European influence and international influence, by formulating a Hypothesis (H5), which tests if international BHR obligations affected national directive transpositions.

To determine the degree of Europeanization is a central prerequisite for comparing domestic impacts. Researchers have produced several typologies to describe different degrees of Europeanization. Radaelli (2000b, p. 14) proposes a comprehensive categorization that covers the "magnitude of change and its direction" (ibid). It consists of four stages: retrenchment, inertia, absorption, and transformation. Inertia refers to a lack of change, either through delays or through outright resistance. In the EU, long periods of inertia are impossible to sustain because either political or economic pressure will lead to crises or abrupt change (ibid). Absorption refers to cases where states adapt to EU rules by relying on a combination of "resiliency and flexibility" (Radaelli, 2000b, p. 15). The category refers to instances, where member states abide by EU rules without changing the essential national structures in the area where the rules apply (Fig. 3.2).

Transformation, on the other hand, refers to cases where the change of rules of logics is fundamental and paradigmatic. "Paradigmatic change occurs when the fundamental logic of political behavior changes" (ibid). In cases of these "third order changes" (ibid), national policies are replaced by European ones and go into a fundamentally different direction. Radaelli also acknowledges that adaptation to European pressure does not necessarily have to go in only one direction. In cases of retrenchment, member states might deliberately adopt contrary measures, which he calls "negative Europeanization" (ibid). Other scholars have proposed variants

[10]Radaelli goes on arguing that due to these potential advancements, which are otherwise found in different research disciplines, "Europeanization has the merit of having brought European Studies into mainstream political science" (Radaelli, 2004, p. 2).

of this classification but are less comprehensive. For example, the categorization of Börzel and Risse (2000, p. 10) only distinguishes between three stages: absorption, accommodation, and transformation, and therefore neglects negative Europeanization. Radaelli's structure for measuring the domestic impact of the EU is thus more precise. Therefore, I will rely on this typology for the operationalisation of the dependent variable. Instead of the categories inertia, absorption, and transformation, I use *non-transposition*, *transposition*, and *over-transposition*. Moreover, as I explain in more detail in Chap. 4, I leave out retrenchment, but add *discretion-passed-on*, a specific category for directive transposition.

3.2.3 The Analysis of Directive Transpositions

One central aspect of Europeanization research deals with the implementation and transposition of EU directives. As directives are a crucial tool in EU secondary legislation, a large part of EU compliance research has focused on the transposition of EU directives. Unlike regulations, directives must be transposed by member states' laws as the result to be achieved. Directive transpositions are interesting cases to study in this respect because EU directives are neither purely supranational nor completely national (Ciavarini Azzi, 2000). They represent the will of the EU legislators but allow for a distinctive national interpretation. As such, directives give discretion to the member states as to how they want to transpose them. Because in some cases detailed provisions in the directives that are of concrete relevance for EU citizens have been implemented with delay, the European Court of Justice has ruled that under certain circumstances directives may also become directly applicable even before they have been transposed into national law (Ciavarini Azzi, 2000, p. 53).[11] However, in most cases, directives only take effect once member states adopt the transposition law and are therefore more flexible than regulations. Directives are usually not used when the aim is to impose narrow standardization measures, but when the Commission seeks to progressively harmonize national regulations (Ciavarini Azzi, 2000). When the Commission decides, if they are going to make a proposal for a regulation or a directive, the policy area plays a role. Some areas are predominantly governed by regulations, while others are dominated by directives.[12] Hence, it is not surprising that for example the non-financial reporting legislation analysed in this study was proposed as a directive because the Commission seeks to gradually acquaint member states and companies with reporting standards that are completely new in many member states and industries. The choice of a directive in the field of public procurement is not surprising either, but for different reasons. National procurement rules have existed for a long time in each country and vary greatly between member

[11] See for example the cases C-129/96 Inter-Environment Wallonie (1997) and C-144/04 Mangold v. Helm (2005).

[12] For example, regulations are regularly used in agricultural policy, while in environmental policy directives are more dominant (Töller, 2010, p. 427).

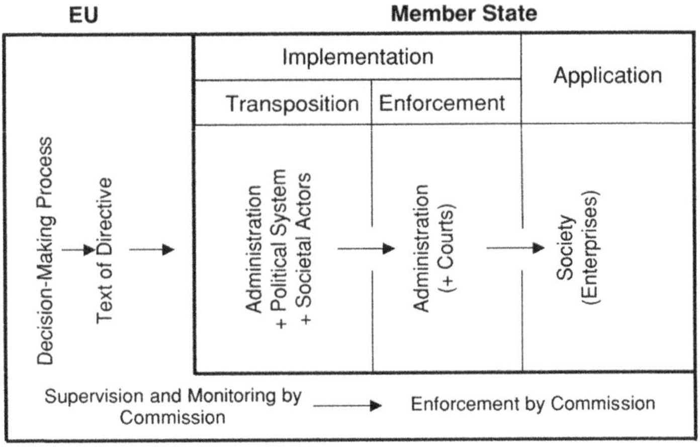

Fig. 3.3 Directives in the EU multi-level process

states and also between regions within member states. Therefore, harmonizing this area required flexibility that is only possible with a directive.

Researchers on EU directives have investigated all stages a directive undergoes between adoption and application. To avoid confusion, the terms used to describe the different stages should be clarified. *Transposition* refers to the adoption of a national law by the national government, often together with societal actors, whereby the directive provisions are converted into national law (Falkner et al., 2005). The national administration and national courts are then responsible for the *enforcement* of the directive. *Implementation* refers to the combination of transposition and enforcement (ibid). The *application* of the directive then takes place by either society, businesses or both (ibid) (Fig. 3.3).

Transposition studies have distinguished between these stages and have analysed them by looking at one of two dimensions: timeliness and correctness (Hartlapp & Falkner, 2009, p. 283). Regarding timeliness, authors usually look at three dates: the date the national legislation is adopted, the date it is published, and the date the law comes into force, which is usually regarded as most relevant (ibid). They seek to understand why member states comply with EU directives only after the deadline, or not at all (Börzel, 2001; Kaeding, 2006; Mastenbroek, 2003).

Most of these enquiries are quantitative large-N studies that want to detect transposition patterns for the EU as a whole, whereby the ground is laid for more in-depth qualitative studies (see Luetgert & Dannwolf, 2009). While the timeliness is often captured with quantitative research designs, the correctness of the transposition is more often studied with qualitative research designs. In the late 1990s and the early 2000s, many authors looked at correctness and timeliness of directive transposition in order to assess the member states' and also the EU's overall regulative capabilities. At a time when many member states were struggling with societal and economic challenges, scholars assessed the EU's ability to generate 'good' policy output to meet those challenges (see e.g. Ciavarni Azzi, 2000). In this respect, the timely and correct implementation of EU directives was seen as part of the EU's problem-solving capability (see e.g. Treib, 2003). Such studies have their roots in classical implementation theory, which focusses on procedural and administrative factors. They understand directive transposition as an apolitical process, the success of which only depends on the clarity and coherence of the directive and the speed and efficiency of the national administrations (Schwarze et al., 1993). In the context of discussions about 'better regulation', more recent studies are also focussing only on timeliness (see e.g. Kaeding, 2007). Especially quantitative transposition studies understand directive transposition largely as a technical process (e.g. Berglund, Gange, & Van Waarden, 2006; Steunenberg & Toshkov, 2009).[13] Haverland and Romeijn (2007) include administrative effectiveness as one of the domestic factors in their large-scale analysis of social directives in six member states. This research interest shows that the issue of administrative effectiveness should not be ignored when studying the transposition of directives, which is why I include the issue of administrative effectiveness as a control variable in my research design. Hypotheses H6 is formulated in a way to control for the fact that administrative inefficiency affected the transposition outcome.

3.2.4 The Concept of Misfit in Europeanization and Directive Transposition Research

To structure the processes of Europeanization and explain the differences in the degree of compliance between member states the concept of 'misfit' has gained most prominence.[14] As I explain below, I use two variants of the misfit to formulate the first two hypotheses of this research design (H1 and H2). Börzel and Risse describe misfit as the "incompatibility between European-level processes, policies and institutions [...] and domestic-level processes, policies and institutions" (2000, p. 1). The degree of incompatibility then determines the pressure on the member states when implementing the EU rules. The central hypothesis of the misfit thesis has been summarized by Börzel (1999):

> The greater the misfit between European and domestic institutional rules and procedures, the greater the potential changes in the distribution of resources among domestic actors and the greater the pressure for institutional adaptation. (p. 591)

The misfit thesis builds on the assumptions of historical institutionalism (see Sect. 3.1). Institutional arrangements that have existed for a long time are expected to be 'sticky' and therefore difficult to change (Mastenbroek & Kaeding, 2006; Treib,

---

[13] For a review of quantitative directive transposition studies, see Toshkov (2010).

[14] There are different names for these concepts in the literature. E.g. Mastenbroek and Kaeding (2006) use the term 'goodness of fit', while other authors have, mainly for linguistic reasons, replaced 'misfit' with 'mismatch'.

2004). The misfit is a central element in almost all Europeanization and compliance studies. The amount of attention the misfit received stems partly from the fact that especially earlier Europeanization studies attributed a lot of explanatory power to the concept (see e.g. Börzel & Risse, 2000; Knill & Lehmkuhl, 1999). Börzel and Risse (2000) gauged misfit to be the necessary condition to expect domestic change. Misfit alone, however, would not suffice. The domestic change would follow from the combination of misfit and mediating factors, which would function according to different logics, depending on the nature of the mediating factor (see below). More recent research on Europeanization and compliance studies still pay a lot of attention to the misfit, but at the same time, they call its explanatory power, at least as a single factor, increasingly into question. Scholars are more interested in how the misfit interacts with other factors (e.g. Falkner et al., 2005; Mastenbroek & Kaeding, 2006; Thatcher, 2004).

When it comes to the operationalization of misfit, Börzel and Risse distinguish between two types. The *policy misfit* refers to "equal compliance problems" (Börzel & Risse, 2000, p. 5), i.e. to the divergence between national and European policy requirements. *Institutional misfit* describes the discrepancy between EU rules, procedures and the collective understandings attached to them, and the domestic ones (ibid). For example, such misfit can arise when EU rules give national governments a privileged position vis-à-vis domestic actors, which in turn alters the balance of power between the national government and regional governments. In the literature, institutional misfit is considered to have less immediate effect, but rather a long-term incremental, but none the less powerful impact. Gerda Falkner employs a slightly different categorization in her research project on the 'worlds of compliance' (see below) (Falkner, 2003; Falkner et al., 2005). She distinguishes between *policy misfit*, *politics/polity misfit*, and *costs*. There are differences to Börzel and Risse's system with regard to the latter two categories. The politics/polity misfit includes institutional and procedural aspects as well as political ramifications institutional adaptation might entail. The category of costs refers to the economic consequences of implementing an EU rule, which "may fall on different units of the state, on semi-public and on private actors or companies" (Falkner et al., 2005, p. 4). While she admits that it is impossible to specify the exact costs of implementing a directive, she proposes to estimate different categories of costs (e.g. social security costs, administrative costs, wages) in order to determine, if the adaptational costs are high, medium, or low. Drawing on these considerations, I use the policy misfit and the institutional misfit in this study. As I explain in more detail in the last section of this chapter and in the research design in Chap. 4, these two types of misfit are employed as two individual variables that are operationalized separately.

In the literature on directive transposition, many theory-oriented studies have included the misfit in their research designs. Several scholars ascribe a great deal of validity to the misfit for explaining directive transposition outcomes. For example, Steunenberg and Toshkov (2009) find in their regression analysis of four directives that legal misfit is a significant factor and decreases the likelihood of transposition. Versluis (2003) identifies the misfit as an important factor to explain transposition delays. Some researches state that misfit only has an effect in combination with other factors (Steunenberg, 2005).

At the same time, a large number of scholars have called the misfit's explanatory power into doubt (Falkner & Treib, 2008; e.g. Falkner et al., 2005; Mastenbroek & Kaeding, 2006; Thatcher, 2004; Töller, 2010). Falkner et al. (2005) state that the misfit thesis is only a 'sometimes true theory'. In their study about the implementation of six social policy directives (see more detail below), they show that many factors that can lead to adaptation even in the case of a large misfit.[15] However, a control study analysing the same data disagrees with this conclusion and finds that a high misfit decreases the likelihood of compliance (see Thomson, 2007). One of the most fundamental critiques of the misfit hypothesis has been formulated by Mastenbroek and Kaeding (2006). They argue that "[t]he relationship between goodness of fit and the attitude towards an EU input is spurious, as both variables are contingent on domestic preferences or beliefs" (p. 347). They contend that "goodness of fit is an essentially apolitical concept" (p. 337) and state that more attention should be paid to 'political' variables, as misfit is not even relevant as a necessary condition for change. Similarly, Mastenbroek (2005) criticizes that the concept of misfit fails to account for the role of agency. While I support the call to take more domestic political variables into account, the outright rejection of the misfit hypothesis does not seem convincing. While it is possible that the relationship between misfit and transposition behaviour is spurious, this connection is not generalizable. First, it neglects the factor of time. Domestic preferences and beliefs may have changed between the period where they shaped domestic policies and institutions and the moment of directive transposition. Second, EU directives often confront a member state with new policy areas, such as BHR policy. The process of directive transposition might therefore be the first time that domestic preferences are articulated on this issue in a member state. Lastly, Mastenbroek and Kaeding (2006) reduce their understanding of misfit to the goodness of fit between policies. However, as I explained above, the literature has brought about several types of misfit, such as politics misfit, institutional misfit, and costs, which do not fit their critique of the misfit hypothesis.

As this short literature review on the misfit shows, there is no agreement among scholars of Europeanization and directive transposition on the viability of the misfit hypothesis. While the misfit has been criticised on many accounts, it remains a central aspect of directive transposition research and its impact is still investigated in newer directive transposition studies (e.g. Thomann, 2015; Zhelyazkova, 2013). In view of the numerous studies that find evidence for its impact on transposition outcomes, I argue that the misfit is too relevant to be ignored in any analysis of directive transposition. Assuming that policy makers take different kinds of adaptational efforts into account when transposing a directive, I formulate two misfit hypotheses, one investigating the influence of the policy misfit (H1), and one testing the effect of the institutional misfit (H2). At the same time, the literature review has suggested that the

[15]The factors identified are: decision-making structure with a small number of veto points, consensus-oriented decision-making culture, presence of supporting institutions, supportive interest groups, process of elite learning (Falkner et al., 2005, p. 16).

misfit alone is not enough to explain differences between transposition outcomes. Directive transposition studies should also account for agency by complementing the misfit with variables that take into consideration the impact of domestic politics. Therefore, as shown below, I also postulate hypotheses regarding the influence of domestic political factors.

3.2.5 The Roles of Facilitating Factors and Domestic Politics

Next to the concept of misfit, most Europeanization studies also apply the concept of facilitating factors.[16] According to Börzel (2005, p. 60) the presence of misfit, as the necessary condition, and facilitating factors, as the sufficient condition, leads to domestic adaptation in response to Europeanization. In order to unfold the interplay between misfit and facilitating factors, most Europeanization research has relied on institutionalist explanations. Building on the work of March and Olsen (1998), Börzel and Risse explain the application of rational choice institutionalism and sociological institutionalism to Europeanization. Following the former, those EU rules that have to be implemented by member states, equip both societal and political actors with new opportunities that they can use to their advantage. The "differential empowerment of actors resulting from a redistribution of resources at the domestic level" (Börzel & Risse, 2000, p. 2) can then lead to domestic change. This reasoning builds on the logic of expected consequences by March and Olsen (1998, p. 949), which follows rational choice institutionalism and assumes that two facilitating factors determine the degree of domestic adaptation. First, multiple veto points in the member states' national institutional structure can either empower or restrict actors that are instrumental for the domestic change. Actors evaluate possible consequences of their actions for their own or collective goals and make their choices accordingly (March & Olsen, 1998). Moreover, formal institutions can equip actors with ideational and material resources and therefore increase the likelihood of change. This view on institutional change recognizes the importance of political actors in the policy process. "[P]olitics is seen as aggregating individual preferences into collective actions by some procedures of bargaining, negotiation, coalition formation, and exchange" (ibid, p. 950).

Sociological institutionalism on the other hand would assume that "Europeanization leads to domestic change through a socialization and collective learning process resulting in norm internalization and the development of new identities" (Börzel & Risse, 2000, p. 2). This "logic of appropriateness" attaches more importance to identity than to interests. March and Olsen write: "Action involves evoking an identity or role and matching the obligations of that identity or role to a specific situation" (March & Olsen, 1998, p. 951). Fitting this constructivist thinking, the two facilitating factors are 'change agents' (or norm entrepreneurs) and political culture and other informal institutions (Börzel & Risse, 2000). However, veto players and change

[16] Mastenbroek and Kaeding (2006) prefer to use the term 'mediating factors'.

agents also have only limited explanatory power. (see Falkner, Hartlapp, & Treib, 2007, p. 401).

In the literature on directive transposition, scholars have extensively investigated the influence of domestic political factors. For example, Treib (2003, 2004), analysed the relevance of national party politics for the implementation of EU directives in the area of social policies. He found that party-political preferences are more relevant for the transposition outcome than misfit. Such approaches rely on the *parties-do-matter thesis* that has been developed and applied in the field of comparative politics (Castles, 1982; Schmidt, 1996). Other studies have considered domestic politics in broader terms. Steunenberg and Rhinehard (2010) find that a high number of veto players in domestic policy-making prolongs the transposition process. Mastenbroek and Kaeding (2006) also argue that domestic preferences and domestic beliefs should be at the centre of directive transposition studies. More recently, Thomann (2015) detected evidence for the domestic politics hypothesis. Her analysis of the transposition of veterinary drug directives comes to the conclusion that domestic interests explain transposition "in conjunction with institutions" (Thomann, 2015, p. 1384). Since I agree with the strong and convincing evidence for political parties' influence on transposition outcomes, I use the composition of the domestic government as an explanatory factor in the research design of this study. I test this factor with a Hypothesis (H3), which postulates that a governing party's stance on the necessity of state intervention in the economy will affect the transposition of the directives in the field of BHR policy.

When Thomann (2015) stresses the relevance of domestic parties, she also states that the scope of the domestic politics hypothesis is contingent on the flexibility of EU instruments and only applies to salient issues. Thereby, she touches upon another important issue in the directive transposition literature: political salience. Taking into account political salience builds on the idea of 'politics of attention' (Jones & Baumgartner, 2005), according to which political decision makers are confronted with abundant information but have limited time to process this information. Jones and Baumgartner (2005) state that "decision-makers filter signals through their attentiveness, assimilate information in a biased manner, and generally act as bounded rationalists" (p. 9). In this respect, rational behaviour is not confined by institutions, but by the scarcity of time or resources to deal with a particular policy issue. Similarly, Spendzharova and Versluis (2013) explain that treating political salience as an independent variable in directive transposition studies builds on the assumption that policymakers only have a limited amount of time and are unable to devote the appropriate attention to all issues on the agenda (Spendzharova & Versluis, 2013). Therefore, they will prioritize politically salient issues over less salient issues. "[S]alience refers to the relative importance attached to a certain issue in relation to other issues" (ibid, p. 1499). The concept of political salience has been used in a number of transposition studies.[17] When Knill and Lenschow (1998) analysed the implementation of environmental policies in the UK and Germany, they showed that

[17] In this study, the term political salience will be used instead of 'issue salience' because the former term is more specific as it underlines the relative importance in the political context.

less salient regulations are ignored. Versluis (2003) compared the salience between EU directives and found that inspections and enforcement was much weaker with the less salient directive. Spendzharova and Versluis (2013) analyse the impact of salience on the transposition of environmental directives and found that more salient directives were transposed faster. They also examine the combination with other factors and find that the effect of salience is stronger with an environmental directive if a green party is in power. The findings in the literature therefore point to a considerable effect of political salience on directive transposition, which was summarized by Knill (1997): "If political salience is low, we assume that perception of adaptation pressure shifts from a moderate to a low level" (p. 11).

Due to the irrefutable logic behind the assumed impact of political salience on directive transposition outcomes, I also employ this factor as an independent variable. However, using political salience in directive transposition studies without explaining the political context can become a problem. If we understand political salience as the "relative importance attached to a certain issue in relation to other issues" (Spendzharova & Versluis, 2013, p. 1499), the question arises *by whom* the relative importance is attached. Authors such as Versluis (2003), and Franklin and Wlezien (1997) have analysed the political salience in general public opinion, and used newspaper databases to operationalize salience. However, many policy issues that are salient to political decision-makers involved in directive transpositions are not brought up in newspaper articles. The wider public rarely pays attention to the transposition of EU directives. Still, political salience can play a role in the specific policy context. In this respect, I identify a gap in the literature, because, to my best knowledge, researchers on directive transposition have not addressed this issue. Therefore, as I explain in more detail in Sect. 3.5 of this chapter, I analyse political salience *within the policy subsystem* in which the directive transposition takes place.[18] However, due to this analytical specification, I cannot simply follow the above-mentioned hypothesis by Knill (1997). While low political salience could lead to a decrease in adaptation pressure, the opposite effect could also occur. Low salience within the policy subsystem could also free policy actors from constraints and thereby promote adaptation. For this reason, I formulate two competing Hypotheses (H4.1 and H4.2) in the analytical framework of this study (see Sect. 3.5).

Apart from these main factors, directive transposition studies have also taken into account other determinants. First, each study has factors that are specific to the directives, policy areas, or countries investigated. Naturally, directive or country-specific factors cannot be generalized for directive transposition research, but should nonetheless be taken into account where necessary (Luetgert & Dannwolf, 2009). Some policy areas, such as environmental policy, have received much attention, which is why policy specific determinants are well explored (see e.g. Jans & Squintani, 2009; Spendzharova & Versluis, 2013). This is not the case for the policy area

[18] As I explain in more detail below, I follow the understanding of Sabatier (1998), who states that a policy subsystem "consists of actors from a variety of public and private organizations who are actively concerned with a policy problem or issue [...] and who regularly seek to influence public policy in that domain (p. 99).

of BHR, which has not been the subject of directive transposition studies so far. This is because BHR is a new policy area that is still being developed on the EU level. As I explained in Chap. 2, I address this research gap by investigating the influence of two factors specific to the BHR policy area: the degree of corporatism in a country (H2) and international policy transfer (H5).

Two more factors have received considerable attention in the literature but are not employed in this study. First, the role of advocacy coalitions, which can be formed among business interest groups, civil society or other non-governmental actors, has been investigated (Kaeding, 2006).[19] As Radaelli argues, including the advocacy coalition framework in Europeanization studies is "suited for an analysis of the interplay between 'exogenous' EU policy and domestic 'endogenous' factors" (Radaelli, 2000b, p. 25). As I explain in more detail in Sect. 3.5, I do not employ this factor because I regard its influence to be covered by the other variables.

The behaviour of member states in the decision-making stage is the second factor that has been used in directive transposition studies (see e.g. Thomson, 2010). Zhelyazkova (2013) established a connection between a member state's position during Council negotiations and the subsequent transposition behaviour. I do not doubt this connection, but I regard this factor to be of low value as an independent variable for this study. My argument is similar to the misfit critique of Mastenbroek and Kaeding (2006) explained above. The constellation of factors that shape a government's behaviour in council negotiations is most likely the same during the transposition of a directive unless a major change of government or other politically significant events have taken place in the meantime. Therefore, covariance between a government's position during the directive negotiations and a government's position during the directive transposition is highly likely. Member states' behaviour during the decision-making stage can thus be a useful indicator to predict *how* a government is going to transpose a directive, but I regard this factor unsuitable to explain *why* a government transposed a directive in a certain way.

All these approaches highlight the variety of factors that can be taken into account when studying the transposition of directives. This review has shown that scholars were unable to identify one overriding factor that would dictate transposition performance in all EU member states (Falkner et al., 2007; Falkner & Treib, 2008; Toshkov, 2010). Instead, researchers agree that the individual combination of factors needs to be judged for each case. The assessment by Héritier and Knill is accurate when they state that

> the scope and direction of domestic regulatory changes in the context of European policy-making are dependent upon the distinctive constellation of regulatory, ideological and institutional factors at the national level (Héritier & Knill, 2000, p. 27).

For researchers of directive transpositions, the challenge is to identify the appropriate constellation of factors that has the highest chance of explaining the respective

---

[19] The term advocacy coalitions was framed by Sabatier (1988) and refers to alliances of actors with similar normative priorities and causal assumptions that try to influence policies within a policy subsystem.

transposition outcomes. For this study, I conclude that a combination of the misfit, political factors, administrative factors, and policy-specific factors is needed to explain the variation in transposition outcomes.

3.2.6 *The 'Worlds of Compliance' Typology*

Rather than trying to identify specific factors determining transposition outcomes, the 'worlds of compliance' typology by Falkner et al. (2005), which has received much attention among scholars of Europeanization, takes a country-specific perspective on directive transposition. The researchers analysed the implementation of six EU social directives in 15 EU member states and tried to detect patterns of compliance. They begin by stating that, according to their findings, existing theoretical approaches, including the misfit-thesis and the role of veto-players, have only limited explanatory power. About the misfit-thesis, the authors found that in many of their cases party political factors overruled a high misfit. For the veto-player argument the study found that the mere number of veto players did not, as a general pattern, affect the transposition of the directives. Instead of generally applicable conceptual explanations, the researchers sought to identify country-specific patterns of transposition. First, they found that each member state of the EU 15 has a "specific national culture of digesting adaptation requirements" (Falkner et al., 2005, p. 345). As such, this insight was not new in the directive transposition literature. Knill (1998), for example, also examined the influence of national administrative traditions. However, Falkner and her colleagues go on to detect three patterns of how member states handle the duty to comply with EU law: the world of observance, the world of domestic politics, and the world of neglect. Countries in the world of observance attach high political importance to compliance with EU rules, usually transpose on time, and have a culture of good compliance as a self-reinforcing social mechanism (Falkner et al., 2005, p. 322). The countries grouped in this category are Denmark, Finland, and Sweden. In the world of domestic politics, comprised of Austria, Belgium, Germany, Ireland, Italy, the Netherlands, Spain and the UK, compliance with EU rules is only one ambition among many domestic concerns. Following the rationalist logic, member states only comply if there is no major conflict with domestic political interest (ibid). In the world of neglect, non-compliance is the rule rather than the exception. Here, national bureaucracies try to advance their own goals when EU law is transposed (ibid). The countries in this category are France, Greece, Luxembourg, and Portugal.[20]

Falkner and her colleagues concede that their explanatory model is not as parsimonious as previous explanatory models, but they claim it to be closer to reality. They describe their approach as "a filter that decides which factors are relevant for different countries and what is the direction of their influence" (Falkner et al., 2007, p. 410). While their findings stem from an analysis of social policy directives, the

[20] In 2008, Falkner and Treib have expanded their analysis for the new EU member states and added a fourth category, the 'world of dead letters' (see Falkner & Treib, 2008).

authors expect the typology to apply to other EU policy areas as well (Falkner et al., 2007, p. 411). The 'worlds of compliance' typology has received much attention by Europeanization scholars but has also been subject to criticism. Most notably, Thomson (2009) used the same quantitative data as Falkner et al. (2005) and tested the typology. He called both the empirical robustness and the theoretical assumptions of the worlds of compliance typology into question.

Despite the considerable attention for the 'worlds of compliance', I will not include this typology in my research design, because it takes a different perspective. Whereas the approach by Falkner et al. (2005) takes a country-specific perspective, I take an issue-specific perspective. Nonetheless, the countries that I inspect in my analysis incidentally also cover the three 'worlds of compliance'. Therefore, I briefly address in the conclusion, in how far my empirical results match the typology.

3.3 Policy Transfer

The subject matter of this study, the varied EU directive transposition in the field of BHR regulation, can also be captured by employing a concept related to Europeanization: policy transfer. In this book, I will rely on this concept in two respects. First, as the conceptual foundation to formulate the hypothesis on international influence on national transpositions. Second, to contribute to the understanding of voluntarism in EU directive transposition. However, first, it is necessary to explain the concept of policy transfer in general and concerning the EU. From the perspective of an EU researcher, this concept provides the possibility of analysing not only processes within the EU but also offers a tool to take into account external learning, diffusion, and transfer processes. It deals with "the exchange of ideas, policies and policy instruments between different political systems across the world" (Bulmer, 2007, p. 4) and has its roots in the comparative politics literature (Dolowitz & Marsh, 1996, p. 344). Much of the early policy transfer literature looked at policy exchanges among US states, but over time, the focus shifted more and more towards the diffusion of policies among sovereign states (ibid). Increasing globalisation, the growing interdependence of national economies, the advance in communication technologies, and the heightened importance of supranational institutions led to a rising popularity of policy transfer as an analytical concept (Dolowitz & Marsh, 2000; Saurugger, 2014). According to the widely accepted definition by Dolowitz and Marsh, policy transfer can be understood as

> a process in which knowledge about policies, administrative arrangements, institutions etc. in one time and/or place is used in the development of policies, administrative arrangements and institutions in another time and/or place." (Dolowitz & Marsh, 1996, p. 344)

The early policy transfer studies mainly dealt with voluntary transfer, i.e. the process of how policymakers could learn from other policy environments. Starting in the 1990s, more studies also dealt with the processes of coercive transfer processes (ibid). However, the growing application and the widening of the concept contains risks of concept stretching and analytical confusion (Knill, 2005; Saurugger, 2014), which is why scholars have put considerable effort into delineating the concept of policy transfer from other concepts.[21]

Concerning the European Union, reasons for policy transfer as well as the forms of transfer are different. First, within the structural environment of the EU, it is less risky for policy actors to adopt foreign ideas. Radaelli (2000a) argues that the EU is a "massive transfer platform" (p. 26), where dominant countries and winning advocacy coalitions transfer policies to other countries. In this setup, the Commission, often in cooperation with other policy actors, enables these processes and acts as a "very active policy entrepreneur" (Radaelli, 2000a, p. 26). Taking into account the role of EU institutions in policy transfer processes in the EU, Bulmer et al. (2007) adapt the definition of policy transfer by Dolowitz and Marsh (1996). With respect to the EU, they speak of "a process by which ideas, policy, administrative arrangements or institutions in one political setting influence policy development in another political setting, mediated by the institutional system of the EU" (Bulmer et al., 2007, p. 19). They thus adopt an institutional perspective, maintaining that institutional mediation is a crucial variable for explaining policy transfer in the EU.

As was noted above, the first way in which this study uses policy transfer is to explain the international influence on the transposition of EU directives. In this respect, policy transfer is the suitable concept, because it tackles a central problem of Europeanization research, which is that Europeanization "does take European processes systematically as a point of departure for changes at the domestic level" (Saurugger, 2014, p. 136). In a highly globalized and interconnected world, convergence effects from international institutions and lessons from other countries affect policy-making as well, especially in policy processes that connect to international politics. As was explained in Chap. 2, the international debate that eventually led to the adoption of the UNGPs was a precondition for the adoption of the NFR-Directive in the EU. This leads to the assumption that the transposition of the directive by member states, which are themselves active members in the international community, would also be affected by international norms and processes, which can be captured with the concept of policy transfer. Hence, Hypothesis H5 poses the question, if international BHR obligations cause member states to transpose more voluntary BHR directive provisions.

In general, the effects of globalization on nation-states is vast, ever-changing, and complex. Hence, the literature on policy transfer has paid much attention to policy transfer effects of globalization. Following economic determinism, one debate has centred around the question if global capital mobility will lead to de-regulation and the dissolution of national social contracts (for an overview see Drezner, 2001). Another issue discussed in the literature was concerned with the role transnational policy networks played in promoting policy transfer, stressing the influence of values, norms, and culture (Legrand, 2015). Business and policy elites often set up transnational policy networks, thereby establishing connections to national policymaking. Especially non-governmental actors, such as foundations, think tanks and NGOs play

[21] For a more detailed description of the different terms, see the paper by Knill (2005).

an important role as networks, information brokers, advocacy groups and experts (Stone, 2000). Non-state actors operate as "policy transfer entrepreneurs" (Stone, 2012, p. 15) that use their intellectual authority and their expertise to stimulate 'soft transfer' by promoting certain forms of policy or normative standards and sell them as 'best practice'. Initiatives by industries or NGOs can also induce the transfer of soft law. For example, in the area of BHR regulation, the Global Reporting Initiative (GRI), even though voluntary in nature, established itself as a global reference standard.

International organizations such as the OECD, or the WTO develop strong normative assumptions about which policies should be transferred. For this, they have several instruments at their disposal, such as "benchmarking, peer review, checklists and 'facilitated coordination'" (Dunlop & Radaelli, 2013, p. 601). Organisations such as the World Bank and the International Monetary Fund have been criticized for imposing economic reforms on some members, which Stone labels as cases of "indirect coercion" (Stone, 2012, p. 12). Overall, it has become clear that policy transfer can originate from various international sources. How influential and through which channels the transfer operates then depends on the specific circumstances. From a broader perspective, Stone (2008) terms this environment a *global agora*, whose policy processes coexist side by side with the national policy processes. This global agora is a "public space of policymaking and administration, although it is one where authority is more diffuse, decision making is dispersed and sovereignty muddled" (Stone, 2008, p. 19). In a more recent contribution, Stone and Ladi (2015) even examine the development of a *transnational administration*, which they term as "regulation, management and implementation of global policies of a public nature by both private and public actors operating beyond the boundaries and jurisdictions of the state, but often in areas beneath the global level" (Stone & Ladi, 2015, p. 840).

Bulmer et al. (2007, p. 28f) address the impact of such global influences on policymaking in the EU. They differentiate between three ways in which globalization can influence transfer processes in the EU. First, it may strengthen the institutional resources of supranational EU actors, for example, when they advocate economic liberalization. Second, globalization could have a "'facilitating' effect on negotiated policy transfer in the EU" (ibid). Especially technological change can lead to an increasing consensus among industry interests from different EU member states, which makes realizing shared opportunities and mutual gains more likely. Third, it can lead to a reduction of the 'misfit', which was discussed in the section on Europeanization. Globalization, Bulmer et al. (2007) argue, can cause national economic and political actors to reassess their preferences and thereby diminish the misfit between EU policy and national preferences.

These remarks highlight the similarities between the concepts of policy transfer and Europeanization. This is also the case with regard to measuring the outcomes of transfer processes. The policy transfer literature also recognises that the outcomes of transfer processes are "not an all or nothing process" (Dolowitz & Marsh, 2000, p. 13). Bulmer and Padgett (2004) make out four types of transfer, which they adopted from Rose (1991) and Dolowitz and Marsh (2000): Copying, synthesis, influence, rejection. Dolowitz and Marsh's (2000) typology had also featured four categories but did not account for the possibility of a negative transfer outcome.[22]

Regarding the EU, Bulmer et al. (2007, p. 17) use the same typology, while the wording is slightly changed. They speak of emulation, the strongest form of transfer when they refer to cases where a complete policy model is borrowed. Synthesis is used to describe the combination of policy models, while influence refers to a weak and only inspirational form of transfer. The fourth category is abortive transfer, which refers to cases when veto players block the transfer. This categorization bears several similarities to the one presented for Europeanization (see Sect. 3.2.2) and underscores the possibility to include policy transfer into a Europeanization study. The second way in which policy transfer is used in this study is to inform the understanding of voluntary compliance with EU rules. First, it is necessary to discuss and explain voluntary compliance from a conceptual and empirical perspective.

3.4 Voluntary Compliance with EU Rules

The previous sections of this chapter have dealt with theoretical and empirical explanations to why and how EU member states comply with EU rules. However, not all regulation from Brussels is mandatory. Many EU guidelines, such as those disseminated through the Open Method of Coordination, are not legally binding for member states. The four EU directives analysed in this book also include 'discretion', which means that they contain non-mandatory provisions. In order to answer the research question of this study, namely why member states comply (differently) with such voluntary regulation, this sub-chapter will first approach the issue of voluntary compliance from a conceptual perspective. Secondly, I review the directive transposition literature that has included the 'discretionary room' in their research designs and identify research gaps.

3.4.1 Conceptual Approaches to Explaining Voluntary Compliance with EU Rules

The term voluntary compliance seems contradictory at first. Why would member states comply with EU rules, if they do not have to? In the Europeanization literature, Knill and Lehmkuhl (1999) explain voluntary compliance by relying on normative considerations. When they propose three types of integration, they state that next to positive and negative integration, *framing integration* refers to voluntary rules. In this type of integration, which they describe as the weakest mechanism, European policy alters beliefs and expectations of domestic actors. They rely on sociological institutionalism to explain this type of integration, stating that policies in this field

[22]The categories were copying, emulation, combinations, and inspiration.

follow a "cognitive logic" (Knill and Lehmkuhl, 1999, p. 11). The literature on policy transfer addresses voluntary compliance similarly. In their work on policy transfer in EU governance, Bulmer et al. (2007) identify patterns of EU governance. One of these patterns is *governance by hierarchy*, which refers to those policy areas where member states delegated some authority to supranational institutions and where policymakers rely on directives (Bulmer et al., 2007, p. 21ff).[23] Governance by hierarchy refers to policy-making using the 'community method' and therefore encompasses a range of coercive mechanisms. However, when it comes to secondary legislation, Bulmer et al. also include a 'softer' variant of hierarchical governance. This variant does not concern the negotiation of secondary legislation, which also follows the community method. Instead, 'soft' hierarchical governance occurs when secondary legislation, such as EU directives, is transposed and implemented by member states.[24] This governance pattern includes the discretion over how directives are transposed, which can be used by member states "to 'domesticate' the legislation" (Bulmer et al., 2007, p. 23). They argue that this 'soft' governance by hierarchy rests upon common political norms, solidarity, and the respect for executive and judicial supranationalism, which bestows on the EU "a kind of normative legitimacy" (ibid). From this, Bulmer et al. go on to expect top-down processes of emulation:

> We argue that the exercise of supranational authority, the availability of coercive instruments, and the high institutional density associated with hierarchical governance, will entail coercive forms of policy transfer, obliging member states to emulate EU 'models' (Bulmer et al., 2007, p. 23)

Following these observations, one could assume that voluntary directive provisions also entail a normative legitimacy. This can be understood as a normative logic, whereby voluntary rules in combination with the "availability of coercive instruments" (ibid) create an obligation, which induces member states to adopt non-mandatory requirements as part of an EU model.

Another possibility to explain why member states comply with EU rules can be found in the literature on corporate compliance with voluntary business regulation. If we follow the definition by Majone (1996), who understands regulation as "sustained and focused control exercised by a public agency, on the basis of a legislative

---

[23]The other two patterns are governance by negotiation and governance by facilitation. Governance by negotiation refers to transfer by consent and mainly alludes to policy making in the Council. Governance by facilitation refers to the coordinative form of policy making, where member states are not obliged to adopt a single European model and EU institutions merely act as "enables of exchange amongst member states" (Bulmer et al., 2007, p. 24), while diffusion takes place horizontally between member states. "In place of prescription it employs 'soft' or flexible rules alongside systems of benchmarking and performance monitoring to persuade national actors to reassess their policy practices" (ibid). The transfer operates mainly through diffusion and mimetic isomorphism (ibid). This mode of governance has been associated with the Open Method of Coordination (OMC), which has for example been applied in employment policy, education policy, and, to some degree, for the Lisbon strategy. Bulmer et al. (2007) ascribe only limited transfer potential to this mode of governance.

[24]Bulmer et al. state three reasons why in this situation transfer outcomes are likely to be weaker and under more domestic influence: (1) the discretion member states have when transposing the directives (2) softer and less precise legal sanctions, and (3) the oversight by delegated authority, which tends to be much more localized in policy terms (Bulmer et al., 2007, p. 23).

mandate, over activities that are generally regarded as desirable to society" (p. 9), regulation must entail control, which means that it must have a mandatory character. While Majone also speaks of the possibility of self-regulation by industries, such self-regulation rules are always created by private bodies, not by governments. The primary role of governments, on the other hand, is to produce binding regulations. As Lowi notes: "the most significant political fact about government is that government coerces" (Lowi, 1972, p. 299). With a focus on voluntary business regulation, Potoski and Prakash (2009) define voluntary regulation as "rule structures [...] that seek to persuade firms to incur nontrivial costs of producing positive externalities beyond what the law requires of them" (p. ix).[25]

Beyond mere persuasion, a common concept employed to explain voluntary regulation is the so-called *shadow of hierarchy* hypothesis. The central argument of this hypothesis is that voluntary regulation will be adopted if the government can credibly threaten that they would otherwise hierarchically adopt binding measures (Töller, 2017). While Töller argues that the shadow of hierarchy is "more a metaphor than a theory" (Töller, 2017, p. 72), she still argues that in combination with rational actors, the shadow of hierarchy can indeed explain voluntary compliance. Therefore, voluntary compliance can also be based on rational considerations.

However, the *shadow of hierarchy* concept is usually only applied to voluntary state regulation, such as national regulations governing business enterprises. However, it could be assumed that a similar mechanism also leads member states to comply with voluntary directive provisions. After all, the purpose of a directive is also to formulate "a goal that all EU countries *must* achieve" (European Commission, 2018, para. 1 emphasis added). Similar to national laws, most EU directives are regularly revised. Therefore, a voluntary provision in a directive could become mandatory after the next revision if member states ignored it. Hence, the regular revisions of EU directives, which are initiated by the Commission, can also create a 'threat' of binding measures. European legislators sometimes seek to pursue a specific goal by including a voluntary provision in a directive, which only becomes mandatory after the next revision. For example, early accounting legislation in the EU, which eventually led to the NFR-Directive, included voluntary sustainability requirements in order to acquaint companies with standards that would become mandatory at a later stage (Interview 12). From this perspective, member state compliance with voluntary directive provisions could also be explained from a rational perspective. However, the 'threat' to turn a voluntary provision into a mandatory one is less powerful, because as co-legislators in the Council, member states can influence the next version of a directive.

This brief review has shown that member state compliance with EU rules can be explained from a sociological perspective, relying on the idea of normative legitimacy, and from a rational perspective, applying the *shadow of hierarchy* hypothesis.

---

[25] A related concept is provided by Vogel (2010), who, writing about international governance, coined the term civil regulation. "Civil regulations employ private, nonstate, or market-based regulatory frameworks to govern multinational firms and global supply networks" (Vogel, 2010, p. 69).

For the empirical analysis in this study, I derive from these two mechanisms the assumption that member states will go beyond the required legal minimum when transposing EU directives. However, these mechanisms are not integrated into the research design of this study, because they focus on the question how voluntary compliance can be explained, but they do not make assumptions about how member states comply, or how differences in compliance can be accounted for.

3.4.2 *Observations from Studies on EU Directive Transposition*

After having discussed conceptual approaches to voluntarism, empirical insights should be taken into account as well. Discretion, commonly understood as the degree of leeway contained in directive provisions, has predominantly been used as an independent variable in directive transposition studies. The impact of discretion on transposition can be looked at from two perspectives. On the one hand, more discretion can make transposition easier, because national administrations have more flexibility to adapt to national preferences. On the other hand, more discretion can make transposition more difficult because the transposition process becomes more political and can involve more national coordination processes (Steunenberg & Toshkov, 2009). Versluis (2007) finds evidence for the latter, stating that discretion makes implementing EU policies easier. Other studies found that more discretion in a directive also leads to more successful compliance (Knill, 2001; Zhelyazkova & Torenvlied, 2011). On the other hand, Steunenberg and Toshkov (2009) find that discretion has a negative impact on the timeliness of the transposition. Similarly, Thomson et al. (2007) find that more discretion in a directive, in combination with member states' disagreement with the content, increases the likelihood of infringement procedures. Kaeding's (2006) study finds that a larger number of recitals in a directive leads to a slower transposition process.

One term frequently mentioned in relation to discretion is *gold-plating*. The term refers to cases where member states "go beyond the minimum requirements of European legislation" (Thomann, 2015, p. 1369). While this behaviour accounts for the diversity between member states, it is usually considered as damaging for the single market (ibid). Especially in the field of business regulations, gold-plating is associated with creating excessive regulation and a competitive disadvantage for member states (Morris, 2011). Therefore, some member states such as the UK and Germany have specifically adopted no-gold-plating policies, which, as Jans and Squintani (2009, p. 434) argue, aims at protecting domestic industries. Even the Commission has considered prohibiting gold-plating in order to avoid over-regulation (Müller Gómez & Wessels, 2016, p. 173). Many studies have investigated why some member states decide to gold-plate directive provisions beyond directive requirements (e.g. Jans & Squintani, 2009; Morris, 2011). At this point, it should be noted that gold-plating is a broad, not clearly demarcated term (Thomann, 2015, p. 1370) and cannot be equated with the transposition of voluntary directive provisions. While transposing voluntary provisions, or not making use of possible derogations is also covered by the term, gold-plating is used to refer to the adoption of requirements that were not mentioned in the directive (Jans & Squintani, 2009; Müller Gómez & Wessels, 2016, p. 173).

This differentiation is crucial for explaining another gap in the literature. Even though many studies deal with discretion and gold-plating, analyses that focus solely on the transposition of voluntary provisions have been missing so far. The closest study found is the one by Thomann (2015), who introduces the concept of *customization*. Taking a bottom-up perspective, she describes how directive transposition processes result in "tailor-made solutions in a multilevel system" (ibid, p. 1368). She calls this process customization, which "means the degree to which the domestic regulations complement the EU directive with more or stricter rules than required" (ibid, p. 1370). This concept is more precise than gold-plating because it specifically addresses the density and stringency of domestic regulations. However, it also does not clearly differentiate between the transposition of voluntary provisions and the adoption of rules beyond the scope of the directive. Therefore, this study is, to my best knowledge, the first to focus only on the transposition of voluntary provisions and uses the discretionary room as a measure to compare a member state's commitment in a certain policy area. I argue that this is a research gap that should be addressed because there is a difference between implementing measures that have been mentioned in the directive and those that have not. Even though not binding, voluntary provisions in directives still represent an intention of the EU legislators and should, therefore, be addressed by EU policy research.

3.5 Constructing the Analytical Framework

The previous sections delineated three major schools of new institutionalism and illustrated the diversity of approaches that Europeanization and policy transfer scholars have taken to conceptually assess compliance with EU law in general and with EU directives in particular. In this review, I have identified three gaps in the literature. First, of the many issue-specific investigations of compliance with EU directives, no study has so far analysed directive transposition in the policy area of BHR. Second, studies on directive transposition that analysed the effects of issue salience have only considered the salience for the wider public but did not focus on political salience within the policy subsystem. Third, the literature review has shown that studies taking into account discretion in directive transpositions have mostly used it as an independent variable to explain transposition outcomes. So far, there are no studies that use the 'discretionary room' in EU directives to measure the dependent variable and thereby assess member states' policy commitment in a policy area. In this book, I address these three research gaps and conduct a comparative directive transposition analysis in the policy area of BHR that employs the transposition of voluntary directive provisions as the dependent variable.

Furthermore, the literature review showed that it is futile to single out one factor that would explain directive transposition in general or even in particular policy fields. A study of directive transposition has to start from the realization that the degree of change in response to EU rules depends on "the distinctive constellation of regulatory, ideological and institutional factors at the national level" (Héritier & Knill, 2000, p. 27). From the account of Europeanization and directive transposition literature, I have concluded that a combination of misfit factors, political factors, administrative factors, and policy-specific factors is needed to explain the variation in transposition outcomes. Accordingly, I take a pluri-theoretical approach that builds on the theoretical deliberations that were outlined in the previous sections of this chapter and in Sect. 2.3 of the previous chapter. The assumptions and main arguments of the theory are translated into six independent variables to answer the research question of this book: How and why do EU member states differ regarding the degree to which they transpose non-binding provisions of Business and Human Rights regulation in EU directives? Hence, the research design follows deductive reasoning, inferring from the general considerations to the particular explanations.

The six independent variables are separated into three groups. The first two factors test two types of misfit, the policy misfit, and the institutional misfit, which build on the historical institutionalist assumption of 'sticky' institutions. The third and fourth IVs investigate the influence of domestic political factors. The variable government composition examines the position of the political party that formed the member state's government during the transposition. The relevance of political parties for directive transposition outcomes has been explained with the *parties-do-matter thesis* (Treib, 2003, 2004), and with the logic of expected consequences, which builds on rational choice institutionalism. The IV political salience within the policy subsystem is considered as the third factor, which builds on the assumption of bounded rationality and the 'politics of attention' (Jones & Baumgartner, 2005). The last two variables, policy transfer and administrative effectiveness, are labelled as 'control variables'. While on the one hand, the literature review has suggested that these factors are not pivotal for the transposition outcome, the indications for a possible influence are too strong to neglect these aspects. The policy transfer from international BHR obligations on the transposition process builds on the assumptions of sociological institutionalism. Finally, drawing on the findings of classical implementation theory, the last IV controls for the fact that administrative inefficiency in the national bureaucracies affected the transposition outcome. Figure 3.4 shows a schematic outline of the independent and dependent variables.

Naturally, the literature on directive transposition could justify the inclusion of other factors as well. Most notably, it could be asked why advocacy coalitions have been excluded from the research design. After all, interest groups play important roles in the national transposition processes and are highly active in the policy area of BHR. However, I do not include advocacy coalitions because the variables outlined above already cover their influence. First, the party-political setup of the domestic government covers this factor because the relevant advocacy coalitions in the area of BHR entertain strong relationships with the political parties that are ideologically close to their causes. Secondly, the political salience within the policy subsystem is

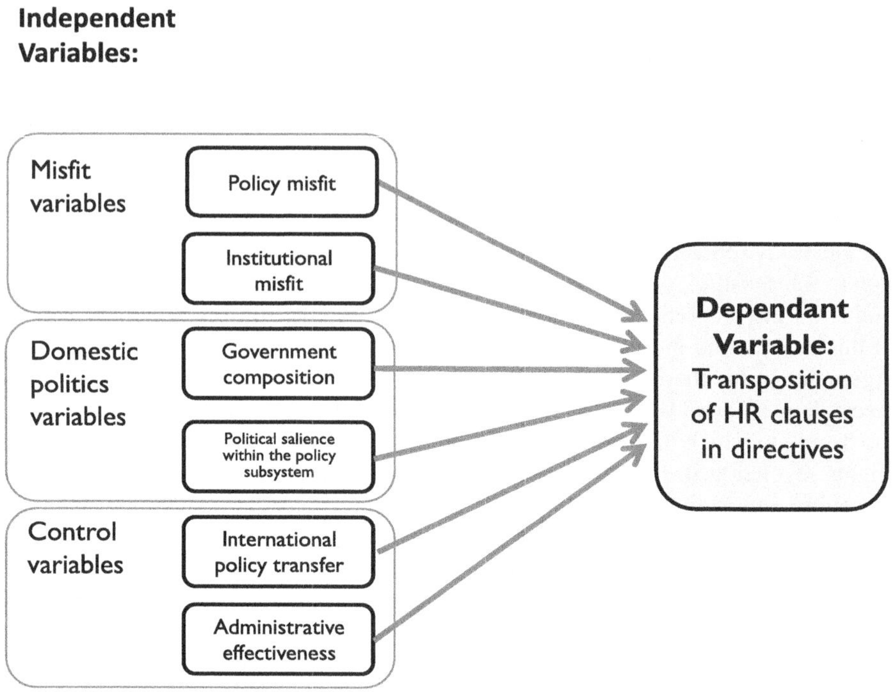

Fig. 3.4 Independent variables and dependent variable

related to this factor because any policy subsystem contains various interest groups. Lastly, the access that is provided to advocacy coalitions is highly dependent on the setup of the political economy. Corporatist states provide different access to (selected) interest groups than liberal market economies. Combining these three considerations, I argue that adding advocacy coalitions as a separate variable would only measure a symptom while not adding any insight concerning the structural and concrete power-political reasons behind a policy outcome. Therefore, I deliberately exclude advocacy coalitions from the research design.

The following sections will outline the analytical framework in more detail. First, I explain how the discretionary room of EU directives is used in order to determine the dependent variable in a way that allows for an evaluation of member states' commitment to human rights. Second, the derivation of the six dependent variables from theoretical approaches is explained in more detail. On this basis, I postulate hypotheses that are tested in Chap. 6. Finally, to place the policy effects of these factors in a broader context, the six variables are associated with two different logics of transposition.

3.5.1 *Using 'Discretion' to Build the Dependent Variable*

Directive transposition studies have so far treated discretion as an independent variable that influences the transposition result or the 'success' of compliance with EU directives (Knill, 2001; Steunenberg & Toshkov, 2009; Zhelyazkova & Torenvlied, 2011). This study takes a different approach and uses discretion to qualitatively measure the dependent variable by focussing on member states' usage of the 'discretionary room'. As was explained in Sect. 3.4.2, this is a largely underexplored area of EU directive transposition research so far. Only Thomann (2015) assesses in her study on the implementation of veterinary drug regulations how and why member states 'customized' their transpositions beyond the required minimum. In the present study, I use the discretionary room differently because I only consider transposition measures that respond to demands formulated in the directives. Consequently, this DV does not measure the gold-plating by member states, but the degree to which member states are willing to go beyond the required legal minimum. Naturally, I also verify if mandatory provisions were transposed.

The four directives in the area of BHR regulation chosen for this study contain several non-mandatory clauses. Many directive provisions give member states the option to transpose them, not to transpose them, or to leave the choice up to the actors that implement the provision.[26] In the directives that have been chosen for this empirical analysis, the human rights-related provisions regulate business conduct directly and indirectly. The NFR-Directive regulates business conduct directly, whereas the public procurement directives prescribe rules for contracting authorities, which are then passed on to businesses. The investigation of this policy area made clear that the business community does usually not welcome more stringent regulation.[27] Hence, I assume that the degree to which member states are willing to go beyond the minimally required human rights regulations reflects the government's commitment to human rights vis-à-vis the business community. Therefore, the disposition of a country to adopt stricter regulations, which potentially run counter to the interests of companies, is regarded as a stronger commitment to human rights in the BHR policy area.

3.5.2 *Determining Independent Variables and Formulating Hypotheses*

3.5.2.1 Policy Misfit

Misfit refers to the "incompatibility between European-level processes, policies and institutions [...] and domestic-level processes, policies and institutions" (Börzel &

[26] As is explained in Chap. 4, the actors implementing the directives are the contracting authorities (public procurement directives), and the business enterprises (NFR-Directive).

[27] The choice of the directives is explained in Sect. 4.2.

Risse, 2000, p. 1). It is the most common factor analysed in directive transposition research and is the first IV considered in this study. Even though several authors questioned its explanatory power as a single factor (e.g. Falkner et al., 2005; Mastenbroek & Kaeding, 2006; Thatcher, 2004), the misfit has proved to be a significant complementary factor in transposition studies (Steunenberg & Toshkov, 2009; Versluis, 2003). This is not surprising, because the logic behind the misfit hypothesis is sound: any member state whose national legislation contains large discrepancies to the EU directive is less likely to fully comply with all provisions than a member state whose national legislation is very similar to the rules in the directive.[28] The misfit thesis follows the assumptions of historical institutionalism, namely that long-established national rules are 'sticky' and difficult to change. Hence, this IV tests the supposition that national transposition laws are 'path-dependent' and follow alongside previously established lines.

In this study, I investigate two types of misfit, the policy misfit, and the institutional misfit (see below). The policy misfit refers to the incompatibility between the BHR provisions in the EU directives, and the laws and policies in the same policy area that were in place in the member states before the directives were adopted. The policy misfit hypothesis is formulated in a probabilistic manner, which means that the presence of an explanatory factor makes the outcome more likely. This hypothesis follows the logic of most directive transposition studies, which argue that a higher misfit makes a low transposition outcome more likely. Hence, I assume that new voluntary human rights regulations for businesses will be readily adopted if similar rules were already established in a member state. However, if such rules did not exist before, the willingness to adopt new externally prescribed directive requirements will be low. Then, member states are assumed to adopt the directives in a minimalistic fashion, which means that the voluntary provisions will be disregarded. Following this logic, I formulate the subsequent hypothesis:

> H1: The greater the policy misfit, the fewer voluntary BHR directive provisions are transposed by the member state.

Box 3.1 Hypothesis 1

3.5.2.2 Institutional Misfit

As I explained in Sect. 3.2.4, institutional misfit refers to the discrepancy between EU and domestic institutions, procedures, and the collective understandings attached to them. The institutional misfit does not cover the divergence between concrete policies but instead refers to long-established rules institutional arrangements that frame policymaking in a certain issue area. As I have laid down in previous chapters,

[28]The misfit thesis has been formulated in similar ways by a number of authors such as Duina and Blithe (1999, p. 499).

I argue that the degree of corporatism represents the institutional misfit in the BHR policy area. Siaroff (1999), describes the main features of corporatism as

> within an advanced industrial society and democratic polity, the co-ordinated, co-operative, and systematic management of the national economy by the state, centralised unions, and employers (these latter two co-operating directly in industry), presumably to the relative benefit of all three actors. (p. 177)

The assumed influence of corporatism on the transposition outcome is not derived from directive transposition literature but from the literature on comparative capitalism and BHR. Nonetheless, this study is not the first to use the institutional setup of a political economy in a directive transposition study. Thomson (2010) uses the degree of corporatism in a country as an independent variable and finds that corporatist countries show fewer problems with the correct transposition of a directive.

In the literature on corporate responsibility, scholars have established a connection between a country's degree of corporatism and the behaviour in the BHR policy area. The starting point for this connection is the literature on VoC. In this respect, the work by Hall and Soskice (2001) is one of the most comprehensive approaches to understand the differences between political economies in Europe.[29] Firms are at the centre of their analysis. They seek to rationally advance their interests by coordinating with a range of internal and external actors across several spheres (industrial relations, vocational training and education, corporate governance, inter-firm relations and employees) (ibid). In different countries, this process happens according to distinct modes of coordination, from which Hall and Soskice distinguish between two sorts of political economies: LMEs and CMEs (ibid). These modes of coordination are largely shaped by the corporatist arrangements, or the lack thereof, in the respective political economy. Among scholars of BHR, Kinderman (2008, 2009) has been most explicit in establishing a connection between the setup of the political economy and a government's behaviour in the field of corporate responsibility. He states that corporate responsibility is originally an "anglophone liberal market construct" (Kinderman, 2008, p. 5). In his analysis of the development of corporate responsibility in different countries he comes to the conclusion that corporate responsibility serves as a "substitute for institutionalized solidarity" (Kinderman, 2009, p. 5). He argues that after the policies of liberalization and privatization that took place in LMEs, corporate responsibility took over some functions formerly held by the state.[30] However, as the development of corporate responsibility in LMEs shows, these functions were assumed voluntarily. In CMEs on the other hand, corporatist arrangements institutionalize solidarity, which is why CMEs are regarded to be less compatible with voluntary forms of CSR (p. 44). Hence, it can be hypothesized that corporatist countries are more likely to rely on binding measures of BHR than non-corporatist countries. Accordingly, I formulate the following hypothesis:

---

[29]The VoC approach was not specifically designed to understand only European political economies, but it has been widely applied to European states, even in Chap. 6 of the initial publication (see Hall & Soskice, 2001, Chap. 6).

[30]Kinderman stresses that he regards this as an imperfect substitute.

H2: The higher the degree of corporatism, the more voluntary BHR directive provisions are transposed by the member state.

Box 3.2 Hypothesis 2

3.5.2.3 Government Composition

Studies of Europeanization and directive transposition have highlighted the importance of political parties for transposition outcomes (e.g. Mastenbroek & Kaeding, 2006; Treib, 2003; 2004). The IV 'government composition' tests, if the ideological preferences of the political party in power, or the combination of preferences in cases of a coalition government, affects the transposition outcome. The discussion of voluntary and mandatory regulation in BHR in Chap. 2 has highlighted preferences of the different party types. Generally, voluntary regulations are associated with conservative and market-liberal political parties, while parties from the left political spectrum (green parties, social democratic parties, and socialist parties) are associated with favouring state intervention through binding regulatory requirements. However, political science research on parties has developed more specific measures of a party's position on state intervention in the economy.[31] For this variable, I assume that a political party in favour of state intervention in the economy is more likely to support binding BHR regulations and vice versa. Therefore, I formulate the following hypothesis:

H3: The more the political parties that form the government in a member state are in favour of state intervention in the economy, the more voluntary BHR directive provisions are transposed.

Box 3.3 Hypothesis 3

3.5.2.4 Political Salience Within the Policy Subsystem

As I explained earlier in this chapter, the relative importance that is attached to an issue can affect the transposition of EU directives as well. Policymakers are confronted with an excess of information and cannot devote the same amount of attention to all policy issues. In their work on 'politics of attention', Jones and Baumgartner (2005) assume that political decision-makers act as bounded rationalists by acting strategically and prioritizing some issues over others. Directive transposition studies

[31] As I explain in chapter 4, I rely on the ECON_INTERVEN-indicator of the Chapel Hill Expert Survey (Version 2015.1).

have recognized the variation of political salience (e.g. Spendzharova & Versluis, 2013).

Similarly, I assume that in the coordination and negotiation processes for the directive transposition laws, policymakers treat politically salient issues differently than less salient issues. However, the literature on directive transposition has mostly investigated political salience by analysing how much attention a certain issue has received in the general public. However, the transpositions of the directives I analyse in this study, like most directive transpositions, did not receive wider public attention. Still, the relative importance can be a highly relevant factor and should be taken into account. Therefore, I investigate the relevance of political salience only *within the policy subsystem* of BHR. The concept of a policy subsystem was developed in relation to the advocacy coalition framework by Sabatier (1988). He states that

> [a] subsystem consists of actors from a variety of public and private organizations who are actively concerned with a policy problem or issue, such as agriculture, and who regularly seek to influence public policy in that domain. In most policy subsystems there will be numerous laws and policy initiatives at any given point in time. (Sabatier, 1998, p. 99)

He adds that a policy subsystem involves all levels of government and increasingly also international actors (ibid). In Chap. 2, I already highlighted which actors make up the policy subsystem of BHR. Actors within the policy subsystem of BHR include the parliamentarians and civil servants concerned with BHR legislation, labour unions, employers' associations, representatives of large companies, academics, representatives from international organizations, NGOs, and other civil society organizations.

The critical question with the development of this IV is, in which direction the political salience of an issue will influence the transposition outcome. Previous research that has analysed the impact of salience on the transposition of directives (e.g. Knill & Lenschow, 1998; Spendzharova & Versluis, 2013; Versluis, 2003)(found that the pressure to transpose correctly, to transpose on time, or to implement the directive provisions correctly was lower with less salient EU directives. Knill (1997) formulated this insight in a hypothesis: "If political salience is low, we assume that perception of adaptation pressure shifts from a moderate to a low level" (p. 11). For the present study, I cannot presume that the effect of political salience follows the same logic. While low political salience could decrease the pressure to transpose voluntary provisions, it could also have the opposite effect. Governmental or parliamentary actors might also feel liberated from business pressure and adopt more voluntary regulations. Therefore, I formulate two competing hypotheses for the effect of political salience within the policy subsystem on the transposition of voluntary directive provisions. The first corresponds with the hypothesis formulated by Knill (1997), the second tests the opposite relationship.

H4.1: If political salience of the directive transposition is low within the policy subsystem, fewer voluntary BHR directive provisions are transposed by the member state

H4.2: If political salience of the directive transposition is low within the policy subsystem, more voluntary BHR directive provisions are transposed by the member state

Box 3.4 Hypotheses 4.1 and 4.2

3.5.2.5 International Policy Transfer

One shortcoming of Europeanization research is that it "does take European processes systematically as a point of departure for changes at the domestic level" (Saurugger, 2014, p. 136). However, many policy areas tackled by the EU are strongly influenced by international policy processes. As Chap. 2 has shown, this is the case with EU BHR policy. The UNGPs were not only supported by the EU, but all EU member states also endorsed them, too. As members of the UN Human Rights Council, they adopted the UNGPs as a non-binding framework in June 2011. The UNGPs consist of 31 principles making recommendations to both businesses and governments. Especially the so-called 'operational principles' contain specific policy recommendations to all signatories of the UNGPs, such as recommendations in the areas of public procurement and non-financial reporting. The UNGPs are at the core of a corpus of international agreements that EU member states have committed to.[32] Relying on the sociological institutionalist 'logic of appropriateness', I assume for this IV, that policy transfer from these international agreements affected the national transpositions of EU BHR directives.[33]

However, the question arises, in which direction the UNGPs can be assumed to influence the national transpositions. To answer this question, it is necessary to take a closer look at the specific recommendations the UNGPs make about the dichotomy of voluntary and binding regulations, and about legislation on non-financial reporting and public procurement. The UNGPs say that states should consider "a smart mix of measures—national and international, mandatory and voluntary" (United Nations, 2011, p. 5). This alone does not indicate any preferences of voluntary or mandatory measures. However, the UNGPs continue to recommend various legally binding measures states could adopt in order to protect human rights. While the UNGPs recognize that international law does not oblige states to regulate the extraterritorial activities of states, they recommend adopting "direct extraterritorial legislation and enforcement" (United Nations, 2011, p. 4). Moreover, the text of the principles

[32]The other relevant agreements are the OECD Guidelines for Multinational Enterprises, the ISO 26000 social responsibility standard, and the ILO Tripartite Declaration.

[33]By using policy transfer as an IV, this study follows the suggestion of some scholars that have argued that in order to achieve more relevant results, policy transfer should rather be used as an independent variable than as a dependent one (Dolowitz & Marsh, 2000, 2012; Ellison, 2017).

stresses the need to enforce existing laws and ensure "greater clarity in some areas of law" (p. 5).

Regarding procurement legislation, they underline the importance of corporate law for shaping business behaviour in relation to human rights. The UNGPs also address the *state-business-nexus* and specifically mention public procurement. Principle 6 lays down that states should promote respect for human rights through procurement contracts. Human rights reporting receives even more attention in the UNGPs, demanding reporting elements that can now be found in the EU NFR-Directive. The UNGPs underline that "[f]inancial reporting requirements should clarify that human rights impacts in some instances may be 'material' or 'significant' to the economic performance of the business enterprise" (United Nations, 2011, p. 6). Moreover, the UNGPs call for reporting in sectors that have high human rights risks, for concrete topics and indicators, and for independent verification of the reports. In light of these recommendations, it becomes clear that the UNGPs are more in line with a mandatory interpretation of the EU directives than with a voluntary one. This assessment is substantiated by the fact that NGOs frequently use the UNGPs as an argument to convince government representatives to adopt binding human rights requirements.

Following the assumptions of sociological institutionalism, the hypotheses for this IV presumes that the international BHR agreements create a normative obligation, a 'logic of appropriateness', to transpose the voluntary provisions of the four EU directives considered in this study. This leads to the following hypothesis:

> H5: International BHR obligations cause member states to transpose more voluntary BHR directive provisions.

Box 3.5 Hypothesis 5

3.5.2.6 Administrative Effectiveness

Lastly, this study seeks to control for the possibility that an inefficient national administration affected the transposition outcome. Classical implementation theory stresses the relevance of bureaucratic efficiency and the existence of technical and legal capacities as a precondition for the successful implementation of EU law. From this perspective, a directive transposition is a mostly apolitical process in which efficient bureaucracies implement the rules that have been adopted by the European legislators. Cases of non-transposition or incomplete transposition will take place if administrative resources are insufficient or if coordination problems occur. Indeed, some directive transposition studies have shown that administrative inefficiencies and corruption can impede both timeliness and correctness of directive transposition (Ciavarini Azzi, 2000; Thomson, 2009). For directives in the area of BHR regulation, administrative effectiveness as an independent variable could be assumed to affect the degree to which voluntary provisions are adopted. National administrations that have insufficient resources or that have a negative track record of transposing directives on time would then only focus on the mandatory provisions. Being confronted with new policy requirements, national officials would focus on avoiding infringement proceedings by the European Commission and choose to devote administrative resources to the transposition of the legally required minimum. Consequently, the following hypothesis is formulated:

> H6: If the national administration of a member state is ineffective, the member state transposes fewer voluntary BHR directive provisions.

Box 3.6 Hypothesis 6

3.5.3 Two Logics of Directive Transposition

The formulated hypotheses are tested to explain the variation between directive transpositions in the policy area of BHR and thereby respond to the research question. However, apart from answering this specific research question, I also seek to draw conclusions that are relevant for directive transposition research in general. In this respect, I argue that the six explanatory factors can also be understood by the distinction between a functional transposition logic and a power-political transposition logic. The functional logic starts from the idea that the transposition of a directive is an administrative task that bureaucracies have to complete efficiently and according to established rules. Following this logic, procedural factors and institutions are more relevant for the transposition outcome than political factors. This logic is less centred on actors, but more on structure, which means that transposition results are more consistent and predictable. From the six variables described above, I associate the policy misfit, the institutional misfit, and the administrative effectiveness with this logic. The policy misfit fits the functional logic because it underscores the functional effect that results from the difference between the national laws and the EU directive.

For this reason, the misfit has been dubbed an "apolitical concept" (Mastenbroek & Kaeding, 2006, p. 337). Even though the misfit thesis also recognises the role of facilitating and constraining factors, the main assumption states that a larger misfit automatically leads to delayed or incorrect transposition results. The institutional misfit also follows a functional logic. The degree of corporatism affects, how a state systematically manages coordination and cooperation processes within a national economy. Within each system, the modes of coordination are highly institutionalized and not subject to short-term changes. Policymakers within each system are accustomed to these modes and adopt rules that fit each system. Government effectiveness also corresponds with the functional logics, as this factor stresses the relevance of efficient administrative and financial resources and the necessary expertise to achieve a 'correct' transposition outcome.

The power-political logic, on the other hand, is more actor-centred and stresses the importance of political factors. The preferences of national domestic actors and the influence they have in the policy process determine the transposition outcome. Unlike with the functional logic, the transposition according to the power-political logic is not a matter of principle, but rather a decision that is taken on a case-by-case basis. I associate the IVs government composition, political salience within the policy subsystem, and international policy transfer with this logic. The composition of the domestic government plays into the power-political logic, as it stresses the ideological influence of the political party that is in power during the transposition. Political salience within the policy subsystem also fits with the power-political logic, because in the end, political actors *decide*, which issues to prioritize over others. While international policy transfer has in some cases been associated with unintentional diffusion processes, the literature in this field widely regards policy transfer as a matter of choice. In this study, I also regard policy transfer from international BHR obligations to national transposition processes as a conscious and deliberate act by policymakers who, for political or ideological reasons, chose to adopt certain policy instruments. Therefore, I associate international policy transfer with the power-political transposition logic. Table 3.1 provides an overview of the six IVs, their theoretical foundations, their assumed impact, and the corresponding transposition logic.

The two transposition logics have the aim to classify the results of this study in a more generalizable manner. Qualitative studies with many units of analysis run the risk of delivering only very country-specific 'stories' that have little explanatory power outside the case analysed. Next to the conceptual conclusions that will be drawn in Chap. 7, the two transposition logics are instrumental in detecting and explaining patterns of transposition that can provide insights for directive transposition research in general. The following chapter puts the analytical framework presented in this section in more concrete terms. It specifies the methodological approach, accounts for the case selection, and operationalizes the variables presented above.

Table 3.1 Display of IVs with the assumed theoretical effects and associated transposition logics

	Independent variable	Theoretical/conceptual foundations	Assumed impact on transposition outcome	Transposition logic
Misfit variables	Policy misfit	Historical institutionalism	The smaller the policy misfit, the more voluntary provision are transposed	Functional
	Institutional misfit	Historical institutionalism, Varieties of capitalism, economic assumptions about the relationship between corporatism and BHR policy behaviour	Less corporatist countries transpose fewer voluntary provisions than more corporatist countries	Functional
Domestic politics variables	Governmental setup	Rational choice institutionalism (logic of expected consequences), Politics matter thesis	Political parties' position on state intervention in the economy influences transposition outcome	Power-political
	Political salience within the policy subsystem	Bounded rationality, 'politics of attention' (Jones & Baumgartner, 2005)	The degree of political salience within the policy subsystem affects the transposition outcome (direction not clearly established by the literature)	Power-political
Control variables	International policy transfer	Sociological institutionalism, and 'logic of appropriateness'	Policy transfer from international BHR agreements to national administrations leads to more transpositions of voluntary provision	Power-political
	Administrative efficiency	Classical implementation theory	Inefficient administrations transpose fewer voluntary provisions	Functional

References

Axt, H.-J., Milososki, A., & Schwarz, O. (2007). Europäisierung - ein weites Feld Literaturbericht und Forschungsfragen. *Politische Vierteljahresschrift, 48*(1), 136–149.

Berglund, S., Gange, I., & Van Waarden, F. (2006). Mass production of law. Routinization in the transposition of European directives: A sociological- institutionalist account. *Journal of European Public Policy, 13*(5), 692–716.

Bomberg, E., & Peterson, J. (2000). *Policy transfer and Europeanization: Passing the Heineken Test? Queens papers on Europeanization*. Retrieved from http://citeseerx.ist.psu.edu/viewdoc/summary?doi=10.1.1.530.7978.

Börzel, T. (1999). Towards convergence in Europe? Institutional adaptation to Europeanization in Germany and Spain. *Journal of Common Market Studies, 37*(4), 573–596.

Börzel, T. (2001). Non-compliance in the European Union: Pathology or statistical artefact? *Journal of European Public Policy, 8*(5), 803–824.

Börzel, T. (2005). Europeanization: How the European union interacts with its member states. In C. Lequesne & S. Bulmer (Eds.), *The member states of the European Union* (Vol. 1, pp. 45–69). New York: Oxford University Press.

Börzel, T., & Risse, T. (2000). When Europe hits home: Europeanization and domestic change. *European Integration Online Papers, 4*(15).

Bulmer, S. (1993). The governance of the European Union: A new institutionalist approach. *Journal of Public Policy, 13*(4), 351–380.

Bulmer, S. (2007). Theorizing Europeanization. *Europeanization: New research agendas* (pp. 46–58). Basingstoke: Palgrave Macmillan.

Bulmer, S., & Burch, M. (1998). Organizing for Europe: Whitehall, the British State and European Union. *Public Administration, 76*(4), 601–628.

Bulmer, S., Dolowitz, D., Humphreys, P., & Padgett, S. (2007). *Policy transfer in European Union governance: Regulating the utilities*. New York: Routledge.

Bulmer, S., & Lequesne, C. (2013). The European Union and its member states: An overview. In S. Bulmer & C. Lequesne (Eds.), *The member states of the European Union* (second, pp. 1–28). Oxford: Oxford University Press.

Bulmer, S., & Padgett, S. (2004). Policy transfer in the European Union: An institutionalist perspective. *British Journal of Political Science, 35,* 103–126.

Castles, F. G. (1982). *The impact of parties: Politics and policies in democratic capitalist states*. London and Beverly Hills, CA: Sage.

Ciavarini Azzi, G. (2000). The slow march of European Legislation: The implementation of directives. In K. Neunreither & A. Wiener (Eds.), *European integration after Amsterdam: Institutional dynamics and prospects for democracy* (p. 384). Oxford: Oxford University Press.

Dolowitz, D. P., & Marsh, D. (1996). Who learns what from whom: A review of the policy transfer literature. *Political Studies, 44*(2), 343–357.

Dolowitz, D. P., & Marsh, D. (2000). Learning from abroad: The role of policy transfer in contemporary policy-making. *Governance, 13*(1).

Dolowitz, D. P., & Marsh, D. (2012). The future of policy transfer research. *Political Studies Review, 10*(3), 339–345.

Drezner, D. W. (2001). Globalization and policy convergence. *International Studies Review, 3*(1), 53–78.

Duina, F., & Blithe, F. (1999). Nation-states and common markets: The institutional conditions for acceptance. *Review of International Political Economy, 6*(4), 494–530.

Dunlop, C. A., & Radaelli, C. M. (2013). Systematising policy learning: From Monolith to dimensions. *Political Studies, 61,* 599–619.

Ellison, N. (2017). Politics, power and policy transfer. *Journal of Asian Public Policy, 10*(1), 8–24.

European Commission. (2018). Regulations, Directives and other acts. Retrieved March 1, 2018, from https://europa.eu/european-union/eu-law/legal-acts_en#directives.

Falkner, G. (2003). Comparing Europeanisation effects: From metaphor to operationalisation. *European Integration Online Papers, 7*(13), 1–18.
Falkner, G., Hartlapp, M., & Treib, O. (2007). Worlds of compliance: Why leading approaches to European Union implementation are only "sometimes-true theories". *European Journal of Political Research, 46*(3), 395–416.
Falkner, G., & Treib, O. (2008). Three worlds of compliance or four? The EU-15 compared to new member states. *Journal of Common Market Studies, 46*(2), 293–313.
Falkner, G., Treib, O., Hartlapp, M., & Leiber, S. (2005). *Complying with Europe. EU harmonisation and soft law in the member states*. New York: Cambridge University Press.
Franklin, M. N., & Wlezien, C. (1997). The responsive public: Issue Salience, policy change, and preferences for European unification. *Journal of Theoretical Politics, 9*(3), 347–363.
Goetz, K. H. (2000). European integration and national executives: A cause in search of an effect? *West European Politics, 23*(4), 211–231.
Graziano, P. R., & Vink, M. P. (2013). The Europeanization turn in EU studies: Beyond heory. In S. Bulmer & C. Lequesne (Eds.), *The member states of the European Union* (second). Oxford: Oxford University Press.
Gualini, E. (2003). *Multi-level governance and institutional change—The Europeanization of regional policy in Italy*. Aldershot.
Haas, E. B. (1958). *The uniting of Europe: Political, social, and economic forces 1950–1957*. London: Stevens.
Haas, P. M. (1998). Compliance with EU Directives: Insights from international relations and comparative politics. *Journal of European Public Policy, 5*(1), 17–37.
Hall, P. A., & Soskice, D. (Eds.). (2001). *Varieties of capitalism: The institutional foundations of comparative advantage*. Oxford: Oxford University Press.
Hall, P. A., & Taylor, R. C. R. (1996). Political science and the three new institutionalisms. *Political Studies, 44*(5), 936–957.
Hartlapp, M., & Falkner, G. (2009). Problems of operationalization and data in EU compliance research. *European Union Politics, 10*(2), 281–304.
Haverland, M., & Romeijn, M. (2007). Do member states make European policies work? Analysing the EU transposition deficit. *European Forum, 85*(3), 757–778.
Héritier, A. (2001). Differential Europe. The European Union impact on national policymaking. In M. G. Cowles, J. A. Caporaso, & T. Risse (Eds.), *Transforming Europe. Europeanization and domestic change* (pp. 1–22). Lanham, MD: Rowman & Littlefield.
Héritier, A., & Knill, C. (2000). Differential responses to European Policies: A comparison. *Max-Planck Project Group Preprint, No. 2000/7.*
Hoffmann, S. (1966). Obstinate or obsolete? The fate of the nation-state and the case of Western Europe. *Daedalus, 93*(3), 862–915.
Jachtenfuchs, M., & Kohler-Koch, B. (1996). *Europäische integration*. Opladen: Leske und Budrich.
Jacobson, H., & Brown-Weiss, E. (1995). Compliance with international environmental accords. *Global Governance, 1*(1), 119–148.
Jans, J. H., & Squintani, L. (2009). "Gold plating" of European environmental measures? *Journal for European Environmental & Planning Law, 6*(4), 417–435.
Jones, B. D., & Baumgartner, F. R. (2005). *The politics of attention: How government prioritizes problems*. University of Chicago Press.
Kaeding, M. (2006). Determinants of transposition delay in the European Union. *Journal of Public Policy, 26*(03), 229.
Kaeding, M. (2007). *Better regulation in the European Union: Lost in translation or full steam ahead? The transposition of EU transport directives across member states*. Leiden: Leiden University Press.
Kinderman, D. (2008). *The political economy of corporate responsibility in Germany, 1995–2008*. Mario Einaudi Center for International Studies, No 5-08.
Kinderman, D. (2009). Why do some Countries get CSR sooner, and in greater quantity, than others? The political economy of corporate responsibility and the rise of market liberalism across the

OECD: 1977–2007. *Wissenschaftszentrum Berlin Für Sozialforschung*, (Discussion Paper SP III 2009-301).
Knill, C. (1997). Implementing European policies: The impact of national administrative traditions. *EUI Working Papers 97/56*.
Knill, C. (1998). European policies: The impact of national administrative traditions. *Journal of Public Policy, 18*(1), 1–28.
Knill, C. (2001). *The Europeanisation of national administrations: Patterns of institutional change and persistence*. New York: Cambridge University Press.
Knill, C. (2005). Introduction: Cross-national policy convergence: Concepts, approaches and explanatory factors. *Journal of European Public Policy, 12:5*(October), 764–774.
Knill, C., & Lehmkuhl, D. (1999). How Europe matters. Different mechanisms of Europeanization. *European Integration Online Papers, 3*(7), 1–19.
Knill, C., & Lenschow, A. (1998). Coping with Europe: The impact of British and German administrations on the implementation of EU environmental policy. *Journal of European Public Policy, 5*(4), 595–614.
Ladrech, R. (1994). Europeanization of domestic politics and institutions: The case of France. *Journal of Common Market Studies, 32*(1), 69–88.
Legrand, T. (2015). Transgovernmental policy networks in the anglosphere. *Public Administration, 93*(4), 973–991.
Lodge, M. (2006). The Europeanization of governance—top down, bottom up or both? In G. F. Schuppert (Ed.), *The Europeanisation of governance* (pp. 59–76). Baden-Baden.
Lowi, T. J. (1972). Four systems of policy, politics, and choice. *Public Administration Review, 32*(4), 298–310.
Luetgert, B., & Dannwolf, T. (2009). Mixing methods: A nested analysis of EU member state transposition patterns. *European Union Politics, 10*(3), 307–334.
Majone, G. (1996). Regulating Europe. London: Routledge.
March, J. G. (1978). Bounded rationality, ambiguity, and the engineering of choice. *The Bell Journal of Economics, 9*(2), 587–608.
March, J. G., & Olsen, J. P. (1984). The new institutionalism: Organizational factors in political life. *The American Political Science Review, 78*(3), 734–749.
March, J. G., & Olsen, J. P. (1989). *Rediscovering institutions: The organizational basis of politics*. New York: The Free Press.
March, J. G., & Olsen, J. P. (1998). Institutional dynamics of international political orders. *International Organization, 52*(4), 943–969.
Marks, G. (1993). Structural policy and multi-level governance in the European community. In A. Cafruny & G. G. Rosenthal (Eds.), *The state of the European community* (pp. 491–511). New York: Lynne Rienner.
Mastenbroek, E. (2003). Surviving the deadline: The transposition of EU Directives in the Netherlands. *European Union Politics, 4*(200312), 371–395.
Mastenbroek, E. (2005). EU compliance: Still a 'black hole'? *Journal of European Public Policy, 12*(6), 1103–1120.
Mastenbroek, E., & Kaeding, M. (2006). Europeanization beyond the goodness of fit: domestic politics in the forefront. *Comparative European Politics, 4*(4), 331–354.
Moravcsik, A., & Schimmelfennig, F. (2009). Lberal intergovernmentalism. In A. Wiener & T. Diez (Eds.), *European integration theory* (pp. 67–87). Oxford: Oxford University Press.
Morris, R. K. A. (2011). The application of the Habitats Directive in the UK: Compliance or gold plating? *Land Use Policy, 28*(1), 361–369.
Müller Gómez, J., & Wessels, W. (2016). *Die deutsche Verwaltung und die Europäische Union - Deutsche Beamte im EU-Mehrebenensystem*. Brühl: Bundesakademie für öffentliche Verwaltung im Bundesministerium des Innern.
North, D. C. (1990). *Institutions, institutional change, and economic performance*. New York: Cambridge University Press.

Olsen, J. P. (2002). The many faces of Europeanization. *Journal of Common Market Studies, 40*(5), 921–952.
Ostrom, E. (2007). Institutional rational choice: An assessment of the institutional analysis and development framework. In P. Sabatier (Ed.), *Theories of the policy process* (2nd ed., pp. 21–64). Westview Press.
Peters, B. G. (1999). *Institutional theory in political science: The "new institutionalism"*. London and New York: Pinter.
Pollack, M. (2009). The new institutionalisms and European integration. In A. Wiener & T. Diez (Eds.), *European integration theory* (pp. 125–143). Oxford/New York: Oxford University Press.
Potoski, M., & Prakash, A. (2009). *Voluntary programs: A club theory perspective*. MIT Press.
Radaelli, C. M. (2000a). Policy transfer in the European Union: Institutional isomorphism as a source of legitimacy. *Governance, 13*(1), 25–43.
Radaelli, C. M. (2000b). Whither Europeanization? Concept stretching and substantive change. *European Integration Online Papers, 4*(8).
Radaelli, C. M. (2003). The Europeanization of public policy. In K. Featherstone & C. M. Radaelli (Eds.), *The politics of Europeanization* (pp. 27–56). Oxford: Oxford University Press.
Radaelli, C. M. (2004). Europeanisation: Solution or problem? *European Integration Online Papers, 8*(16), 26.
Risse, T., Cowles, M. G., & Caporaso, J. A. (2001). Europeanization and domestic change: Introduction. In M. Green Cowles, J. A. Caporaso, & T. Risse (Eds.), *Transforming Europe: Europeanization and domestic change* (pp. 1–20). Ithaca: Cornell University Press.
Rometsch, D., & Wessels, W. (1996). *The European Union and member states: Towards institutional fusion?*. Manchester and New York: Manchester University Press.
Rose, R. (1991). What is lesson-drawing? *Journal of Public Policy, 11*(May), 3–30.
Sabatier, P. (1988). An advocacy coalition framework of policy change and the role of policy-oriented learning therein. *Policy Sciences, 21*(2/3), 129–168.
Sabatier, P. (1998). The advocacy coalition framework: Revisions and relevance for Europe. *Journal of European Public Policy, 5*(1), 98–130.
Saurugger, S. (2014). *Theoretical approaches to European integration*. Basingstoke: Palgrave Macmillan.
Scharpf, F. (1997). Actor-centered institutionalism. *Games real actors play: Actor-centered institutionalism in policy research* (pp. 36–50). Boulder: Westview Press.
Schimmelfennig, F., Leuffen, D., & Rittberger, B. (2015). The European Union as a system of differentiated integration: Interdependence, politicization and differentiation. *Journal of European Public Policy, 22*(6), 764–782.
Schimmelfennig, F., & Sedelmeier, U. (2005). Introduction: Conceptualizing the Europeanization of Central and Eastern Europe. In F. Schimmelfennig & U. Sedelmeier (Eds.), *The Europeanization of Central and Eastern Europe* (pp. 1–25). Ithaca and London.
Schmidt, M. (1996). When parties matter: A review of the possibilities and limits of partisan influence on public policy. *European Journal of Political Research, 30*(2), 155–183.
Schmidt, V. (2008). Discursive institutionalism: The explanatory power of ideas and discourse. *Annual Review of Political Science, 11*(1), 303–326.
Schmidt, V. (2010). Taking ideas and discourse seriously: Explaining change through discursive institutionalism as the fourth 'new institutionalism'. *European Political Science Review, 2*(01), 1.
Schwarze, J., Becker, U., & Pollak, C. (1993). *Die Implementation von Gemeinschaftsrecht: Untersuchungen zur Gesetzgebungs- und Verwaltungspolitik der Europäischen Gemeinschaft und ihrer Mitgliedstaaten*. Baden-Baden: Nomos.
Siaroff, A. (1999). Corporatism in 24 industrial democracies: Meaning and measurement. *European Journal of Political Research, 36*(2), 175–205.
Simon, H. A. (1979). Rational decision making in business organizations. *The American Economic Review, 69*(4), 493–513.

Spendzharova, A., & Versluis, E. (2013). Issue salience in the European policy process: What impact on transposition? *Journal of European Public Policy, 20*(10), 1499–1516.
Starke, P. (2013). Qualitative methods for the study of policy diffusion: Challenges and available solutions. *Policy Studies Journal, 41*(4), 561–582.
Steunenberg, B. (2005). Turning swift policymaking into deadlock and delay: National policy coordination and the transposition of EU directives. In *33rd Joint Sessions of Workshops of ECPR* (pp. 14–19).
Steunenberg, B., & Rhinard, M. (2010). The transposition of European law in EU member states: Between process and politics. *European Political Science Review, 2*(3), 495–520.
Steunenberg, B., & Toshkov, D. (2009). Comparing transposition in the 27 member states of the EU: The impact of discretion and legal fit. *Journal of European Public Policy, 16*(7), 951–970.
Stone, D. (2000). Non-governmental policy transfer: The strategies of independent policy institutes. *Governance, 13*(1), 45–70.
Stone, D. (2008). Global public policy, transnational policy communities and their needs. *The Policy Studies Journal, 36*(1), 19–38.
Stone, D. (2012). Transfer and translation of policy. *Policy Studies, 33*(6), 483–499.
Stone, D., & Ladi, S. (2015). Global public policy and transnational administration. *Public Administration, 93*(4), 839–855.
Thatcher, M. (2004). Winners and losers in Europeanisation: Reforming the national regulation of telecommunications. *West European Politics, 27*(2), 284–309.
Thomann, E. (2015). Customizing Europe: Transposition as bottom-up implementation. *Journal of European Public Policy, 22*(10), 1368–1387.
Thomson, R. (2007). Time to comply: National responses to six EU labour market directives revisited. *West European Politics, 30*(5), 987–1008.
Thomson, R. (2009). Same effects in different worlds: The transposition of EU directives. *Journal of European Public Policy, 16*(1), 1–18.
Thomson, R. (2010). Opposition through the back door in the transposition of EU directives. *European Union Politics, 11*(4), 577–596.
Thomson, R., Torenvlied, R., & Arregui, J. (2007). The paradox of compliance: Infringements and delays in transposing European Union directives. *British Journal of Political Science, 37*(4), 685–709.
Töller, A. E. (2010). Measuring and comparing the europeanization of national legislation: A research note. *Journal of Common Market Studies, 48*(2), 417–444.
Töller, A. E. (2017). Voluntary regulation by the pharmaceutical industry—which role for the shadow of hierarchy and social pressure? *European Policy Analysis, 3*(1), 48–80.
Toshkov, D. (2010). *Taking stock: A review of quantitative studies of transposition and implementation of EU law*. Institute for European Integration Research (November), 25–26.
Treib, O. (2003). Die Umsetzung von EU-Richtlinien im Zeichen der Parteipolitik: Eine akteurszentrierte Antwort auf die Misfit-These. *Politische Vierteljahresschrift, 44*(4), 506–528.
Treib, O. (2004). *Die Bedeutung der nationalen Parteipolitik für die Umsetzung europäischer Sozialrichtlinien*. Frankfurt/New York: Campus.
United Nations. (2011). *Guiding Principles on Business and Human Rights*. New York: Office of the United Nations High Commissioner for Human Rights.
Versluis, E. (2003). *Enforcement matters enforcement and compliance of European Directives in four member states*. Utrecht.
Versluis, E. (2007). Even rules, uneven practices: Opening the 'black box' of EU law in action. *West European Politics, 30*(1), 50–67.
Vink, M. P., & Graziano, P. R. (2007). Challenges of a new research agenda. In P. R. Graziano & M. P. Vink (Eds.), *Europeanization: New research agendas* (pp. 3–20). Basingstoke: Palgrave Macmillan.
Vogel, D. (2010). The private regulation of global corporate conduct. *Business and Society, 49*(1), 68–87.

Wessels, W. (1992). Staat und (westeuropäische) Integration. Die Fusionsthese. In M. Kreile (Ed.), *Die Integration Europas* (pp. 36–61). Wiesbaden: VS Verlag für Sozialwissenschaften.
Wessels, W. (1996). Verwaltung im EG-Mehrebenensystem: Auf dem Weg zur Megabürokratie? In *Europäische Integration* (pp. 165–192). Springer.
Wessels, W. (1997a). An ever closer fusion? A dynamic macropolitical view on integration processes. *Journal of Common Market Studies, 35*(2), 267–299.
Wessels, W. (1997b). Die Europäische Union der Zukunft—immer enger, weiter und … komplexer? Die Fusionsthese. In T. Jäger & M. Piepenschneider (Eds.), *Europa 2020: Szenarien politischer Entwicklungen* (pp. 45–79). Wiesbaden: VS Verlag für Sozialwissenschaften.
Zhelyazkova, A. (2013). Complying with EU directives' requirements: The link between EU decision-making and the correct transposition of EU provisions. *Journal of European Public Policy, 20*(5), 702–721.
Zhelyazkova, A., & Torenvlied, R. (2011). The successful transposition of European provisions by member states: Application to the Framework Equality Directive. *Journal of European Public Policy, 18*(5), 690–708.

Chapter 4
Research Design

4.1 Methodological Approach

The general phenomenon I single out for examination is the EU's commitment to human rights in relation to globally operating corporations. As discussed in chap. 2, the institutional and political commitment to human rights can be studied from a variety of angles in the EU multi-level system. To arrive at significant results about the general phenomenon it is, from a methodological perspective, useful to move down the 'ladder of generality' and identify a sub-type of the general phenomenon (George & Bennett, 2005). The three public procurement directives and the NFR-Directive are central legal instruments to promote respect for human rights by globally operating corporations in the EU. They represent suitable subjects of analysis because EU directives leave it up to the member states to adopt the specific laws by which they are transposed. The selected directives contain several non-binding provisions, which give member states the possibility to impose more restrictions (e.g. reporting requirements) on their businesses. From a theoretical perspective, as I explained in chap. 3, variation between the national transpositions could be expected. As a policy area, BHR is relatively new to the European and to most national stages. While the behaviour of EU institutions in the field of BHR has been subject to an increasing number of, mostly legal, analyses (see e.g. De Schutter, 2008; De Schutter, Ramasastry, Taylor, & Thompson, 2012; Taylor, 2013), there has been no study to analyse BHR regulation in the context of the transposition of directives. Therefore, I address the following research question:

> How and why do EU member states differ regarding the degree to which they transpose non-binding provisions of Business and Human Rights regulation in EU directives?

Box 4.1 Research question

P. Drahn, *Adoption of EU Business and Human Rights Policy*,
Contributions to Political Science, https://doi.org/10.1007/978-3-030-46935-1_4

The research design of this study is a qualitative comparison of the transposition of four EU directives in the policy area of BHR regulation. It follows the method of structured and focused comparison (George & Bennett, 2005). The structure is, most importantly, provided by the research question, which consists of two sub-questions, one descriptive and one causal question. To answer the descriptive question, I conduct a policy analysis of the national transposition laws. After identifying the relevant BHR provisions in the selected directives and categorizing them according to human rights relevance and degree of obligation, I examine the corresponding provisions in the national transposition laws. This allows for a structured comparison of the transposition outcomes. To approach the causal part of the research question I formulate hypotheses in chap. 3, on the basis of which I systematically compare six IVs. The focus of the research method stems from the decision to concentrate on four EU directives and four EU member states. Moreover, the focus follows from the limitation of variables. Policy-making in EU member states is highly complex, and it is impossible to account for all factors that have some degree of influence on the passing of a transposition law. However, it is the strength of qualitative research to focus on a small number of factors that have been identified, by relying on theoretical insights and previous empirical evidence, to have the largest validity for explaining the dependent variable.

The conceptual research objective of this comparative case study is theory testing. According to George and Bennett "[t]heory testing case studies assess the validity and scope conditions of single or competing theories" (2005, p. 75). As was explained in chap. 3, this study adopts a pluri-theoretical approach in order to conceptually assess the transposition processes and transposition outcomes.[1] The explanatory powers of rational choice institutionalism, sociological institutionalism, and historical institutionalism are examined by investigating the impact of the independent variables on the national transpositions. The theories that have been portrayed in the previous chapter have already been applied to compliance research or even the study of directive transposition before. What is then the added value of testing the theories in the study at hand? First, the theoretical approaches that were outlined are tested in a new and contentious policy area. This is not only relevant in order to grasp this area of activity from a political perspective. Moreover, testing previously established patterns and assumptions about relationships adds to the further development of theories. Each case study that examines a sub-type of a general phenomenon adds a "building block [...] which fills a 'space' in the overall theory or in a typological theory" (George & Bennett, 2005, p. 78). The policy area of BHR policy represents a suitable case in this respect. Not only has this recent policy field not yet been the subject of a directive transposition study. Furthermore, it is, as the previous chapters have shown, a policy area that prescribes binding social and human rights regulation, which are fields that are traditionally left within the competence of member states. The second reason for the added value concerns the method used to measure the dependent variable. As I showed in chap. 3, previous studies that test the 'classical' three institutionalisms sought to measure the 'correctness', success, or timeliness of

[1] The term 'pluri-theoretical approach' was adopted from Falkner et al. (2005).

directive transposition. Instead, in this study, I measure the commitment to human rights as reflected in the degree to which member states use the discretionary room provided for in the directives. This is an innovative approach for which the theories at hand have not yet been tested.

4.2 Selection of EU Directives

The four EU directives have been chosen as subjects of analysis because they are suited to measure the commitment to human rights by member states. They contain mandatory clauses, voluntary clauses, and clauses with mandatory and voluntary elements. They are therefore instrumental in evaluating the degree to which national governments are willing to impose regulatory prescriptions that are potentially unwanted by businesses, but that aim at promoting more socially responsible business conduct. At the same time, the four directives are central to the EU's efforts to implement the UNGPs, which is why the transposition results can, to a certain extent, be generalized for EU BHR policy. Not all directives considered are solely concerned with BHR regulation. As Toshkov (2010) and Thomann (2015) note, explanatory patterns are more likely to be detected for single policy issues, rather than for whole directives. The NFR-Directive has been the most recent example of BHR legislation that has become somewhat of a poster-child for European BHR regulation. It requires large European companies to disclose information about their policies and impacts on human rights and other social and environmental matters. The public procurement package consists of three directives regulating public procurement for different sectors. The Public Sector Directive (PSD) spells out the rules public institutions must follow before giving a contract to a supplier (i.e. public supply, services, and works contracts) when the value of the contract exceeds a certain threshold. The Utilities Directive (UD) is concerned with procurement regulations for the transport, water, energy, and postal sectors. The Concessions Directive (CD) foresees new rules for concessions exceeding the value of five million Euro. While the public procurement directives differ with respect to the sector they apply to, structure and regulatory provisions are very similar, which is why for each country the transposition of the three directives will be treated as one unit of analysis.

The NFR-Directive and the public procurement directives address the protection of human rights and the promotion of responsible business conduct differently. The NFR-Directive affects human rights standards directly because it imposes reporting obligations on companies. The procurement directives affect human rights standards indirectly because it only applies to public authorities, the so-called contracting authorities, which invite private companies to bid for public tenders. The directives spell out that the requirements specified in the tenders also include social and human rights standards. Moreover, procurement legislation becomes applicable to companies, only after it has been interpreted by contracting authorities. Therefore, to leave 'room for interpretation' in the legislation has different consequences for the implementation. For the NFR-Directive, leaving room for interpretation means giving more freedom to private companies. For the public procurement directives, the interpretation is done by local public authorities, which also have a democratic mandate. Third, setting higher standards in public procurement rules can directly raise costs for the government itself, which is not the case for the NFR-Directive.

The transposition of these four directives is assessed in four member states. Since the three public procurement directives are treated as one, the combination of the cases and the directives selected results in a total of eight units of analysis. The selection of the directives also determines the time frame for this study, which is set between February 2014 and August 2017. The four directives considered in this analysis were adopted in 2014 and had to be transposed by April 2016 and December 2016 respectively. However, France transposed the NFR-Directive only in August 2017, which is hence the end of the period of investigation.

4.3 Selection of Cases

To investigate differences in the transposition of these four directives, and to understand the differences, the case selection is a critical element of this research design. The cases selected should provide the necessary control and variation to tackle the research question and to be generalizable for other cases as well. Therefore, the selection of cases followed the logic of diverse cases. This selection strategy aims at "the achievement of maximum variance along relevant dimensions" (Gerring, 2007, p. 97). The approach has the objective to achieve large representativeness of the sample by choosing countries that show diversity in the dimensions that are relevant for the policy area in which the comparative analysis is conducted. This increases the chance that the results can be generalized for other countries that share characteristics in the dimension in question. Starke (2013) highlights the advantage of a case selection according to the most-diverse logic for compliance research:

> [The diverse case strategy] allows to contrast cases with high or low values on crucial variables and thereby assess different hypotheses by comparing theoretical predictions with empirical reality under different constellations of theoretical factors or explore new hypotheses by unearthing contrasting outcomes in different settings. (Starke, 2013, p. 570)

To find applicable cases, it is a valid approach to use previously established analytical frameworks (George & Bennett, 2005, p. 83). For this study, the cases were selected by trying to achieve variance on two dimensions: the positioning of the governments in the area of BHR and the institutional setup of the political economy. With respect to the relevance of concrete economic indicators, the variance between countries was intended to be kept to a minimum, as is explained below.

Since BHR is a relatively recent policy area, no comprehensive classification of the positioning of countries in BHR exists yet. However, Albareda et al. propose a typology of "models of government action in the development of CSR-endorsing public policies" (Albareda, Lozano, & Ysa, 2007, p. 401). As was discussed in more detail in chap. 2, in policy terms the concept of CSR is the broader predecessor of BHR, which is less specifically defined and also includes environmental measures. Still, the concepts are similar enough to use the typology by Albareda et al. to categorize member states. Based on the analysis of the CSR policies of 15 EU member states the authors propose four (and a half) models with regard to government behaviour on CSR: *partnership* (Denmark, Finland, the Netherlands, Sweden), *business in the community* (Ireland, UK), *sustainability and citizenship* (Germany, Austria, Belgium, Luxembourg, and as a sub-model 'regulatory' France), and *agora* (Italy, Spain, Greece, Portugal) (ibid).

In countries in the *partnership* group, CSR is understood as a common societal responsibility that requires the involvement of all social actors. Businesses, trade unions, and social organizations build a partnership and are jointly committed to the implementation of CSR policies. As this partnership is seen as a key tool to solve social problems, the government moderates this cooperation through CSR policies, which are seen as part of the regular framework for social practices. The countries in *business in the community*, UK, and Ireland have developed CSR policies in response to a deficit in social policies that resulted from economic crises. In these countries, companies integrate CSR measures into their business operations in order to contribute to the economic development in their communities. The government's role is not to prescribe this involvement but is limited to "'soft intervention' to promote and endorse corporate action in CSR areas" (Albareda et al., 2007, p. 402). In the countries in the group *sustainability and citizenship,* companies take their place as "citizens in civil society" (ibid, p. 403). Under this model companies are considered to have an obligation to maintain direct links with their local communities and take part in solving social problems together with other social groups. As the countries in this group are classical corporatist states, governments actively include companies and regard them as crucial agents for the promotion of social and environmental sustainability. This approach goes hand in hand with their model of a social market economy, which came under strain due to economic crises in the 1990s. The advent of CSR was therefore regarded as a way to sustain the model of the social market economy, while at the same time raising competitiveness. Unlike in the partnership model, debates and concrete measures on CSR were developed within companies. Albareda et al. describe France as a regulatory sub-version of the sustainability and citizenship model. In France, the government also formulates an obligation of companies to contribute to a sustainable societal development. But in the French case, the government, being rooted in a centralist tradition, takes an even more active role, which gives the impression as if the government has directed corporate sustainability activities. The agora model is used to describe the implementation and enforcement of CSR policies in the Mediterranean countries. In these countries CSR arrived later than in the other groups, largely only due to the CSR initiative of the Commission in 2001. As welfare states in these countries were less developed, CSR did not build on the social model as it was the case in the *partnership* and the *sustainability and citizenship* countries. The governments' role is less proactive but rather reduced to providing the public forum in which CSR activities are discussed.

The second dimension that I take into account for the case selection is the institutional setup of the political economy. Including this dimension is necessary in order to capture the difference between CSR and BHR. Whereas CSR, especially under the old definition, is used to describe various kinds of voluntary social and environmental activities by companies, BHR only focusses on human rights in global supply chains. Therefore, BHR affects an integral part of companies' business operations. How companies organize these operations differently, and which firm relations are important in organizing them, is captured by the typologies of political economies. The VoC-approach by Hall and Soskice (2001a) has become the most established typology in this respect. As was explained in more detail in Sect. 2.3.1, Hall and Soskice have formulated assumptions about the links between the institutional configurations in a political economy and a country's stance towards regulation. They state that LMEs, such as the UK, Ireland, Canada, and the US, are more likely to be in favour of de-regulation because this is favourable for domestic companies that coordinate their operations primarily through the market (ibid, p. 57). On the other hand, CMEs such as Germany, the Nordic states and the Benelux-countries are assumed to be more favourable to regulation, because deregulation would endanger the institutional advantages of their corporatist political economies. Several studies have either relied on the VoC-approach, or on other measures of corporatism to explain countries' position towards stricter business regulation (Falkner, Treib, Hartlapp, & Leiber, 2005; Kinderman, 2008, 2015; Thomson, 2007, 2009).

The focus of the case selection is to achieve variance on the positioning of the governments in the area of BHR and the institutional setup of the political economy. Economic factors, such as the integration of companies in global supply chains, should be held constant as much as possible. Naturally, it can be assumed that countries with a highly internationalized economy would behave differently in the area of BHR regulation than countries with closed national economies. However, it is not the aim of this study to investigate the impact of a country's economic performance on transposition behaviour. Therefore, the openness of a national economy is not a relevant dimension for the case selection.

After taking these factors into account, the UK, France, Germany, and Denmark are chosen as the four cases for the empirical analysis. All four countries have open national economies that are highly integrated into global supply chains. The OECD-indicator *import content of exports* shows that the integration of these four countries in global supply chains is relatively similar. The share of imported inputs in the overall exports is 21.9% in the UK, 25.4% in Germany, 26.3% in France, and 30.7% in Denmark (Organisation for Economic Co-operation and Development, 2018). As the import content of exports is considered as "a reliable measure of international 'backward linkages' in analyses of global value chains" (ibid, para 1), I do not assume that the degree of economic openness of the countries selected was a relevant factor for the transposition.

More importantly, I argue that these four countries are representative for four archetypes of government behaviour in BHR (see Table 4.1). Denmark represents the archetype *nordic sustainability consensus*, which also includes Sweden and Finland. This type refers to countries where a large coalition of societal actors naturally regards the prevention of human rights abuses through corporate conduct as their

Table 4.1 Spectrum of governmental approaches to BHR

	Variety of capitalism	Model of CSR	Archetypes for government behaviour in BHR
UK	Liberal market economy	Business in the community	Free-market facilitation
Germany	Coordinated market economy	Sustainability and citizenship	Corporatist sustainability
France	State-enhanced capitalism	Regulatory version of sustainability and citizenship	Regulated sustainability
Denmark	Coordinated market economy	Partnership	Nordic sustainability consensus

common responsibility. Firms, labour unions, and NGOs build networks to commonly establish non-market rules and coordinate mechanisms and standards that firms implement in their supply chains. The UK represents the archetype *free-market facilitation*, which also includes Ireland. Here, I assume that governments trust that the mechanisms of the free market will induce companies to actively prevent human rights violations in supply chains. In those countries, governments strongly support the 'business case' of BHR, which means that they expect global civil society to scrutinize and pressure globally operating businesses. Firms which organize their relationships hierarchically and through competitive arrangements are then expected to implement human rights due diligence measures by following a cost-benefit rationale.

Germany is one example of the *corporatist sustainability* archetype, which would also describe Austria and the Benelux-countries. These countries seek to integrate BHR policy in the social market model, as governments expect companies to take an active role in the development and implementation of BHR measures. Like in the nordic sustainability consensus, companies coordinate with other societal actors, but the initiative comes from within the firms, which seek to balance out their role in a corporatist system with the aim to enhance international competitiveness. Finally, France represents the archetype *regulated sustainability*. Similar to the corporate sustainability type, the government expects companies to take an active role because they are regarded as agents in the centralized French social model, which places a high value on the protection of human rights. However, the coordination of firms with the government and other societal actors takes place mainly through the personal connections between elites. This close elite coordination is expected to result in a higher regulatory density than in the corporate sustainability archetype. Following the logic of diverse cases, I expect that the focus on these four countries will make it possible to generalize the empirical results of this study for other countries in the archetypes. Thereby I seek to contribute to the understanding of national BHR policies in the EU because focussing on common types has "the greatest implications for theory-building or policy-making" (George & Bennett, 2005, p. 235).

4.4 Dependent and Independent Variables

This study employs a Y-centred research perspective, as the research question already suggests. Y-centred research perspectives assume variation on the DV and ask the questions: 'What led to Y' and 'how can the variance in Y be explained?' (Ganghof, 2005, p. 77). The DV in this research design is the transposition of mandatory and voluntary human rights clauses in the four EU directives outlined above. The discretionary leeway created by the voluntary provisions allows for a comparison of the degree to which member states are willing to impose regulation that either directly or indirectly affects their national businesses. To explain the variation in the DV between member states, six IVs were determined in chap. 3: policy misfit, institutional misfit, government composition, political salience within the policy subsystem, international policy transfer and administrative effectiveness. Like any Y-centred research design, this study looks at a larger number of IVs. From a methodological perspective, this can be problematic because qualitative studies in which the number of explanatory variables exceeds the number of cases become susceptible to over-determination. I take two measures to address this issue. First, not all possible outcomes are considered. If each independent variable has two or more values, the number of possible outcomes, the 'property space' would be so large that it would become difficult to qualitatively assess all possible outcomes. However, in qualitative studies the full property space is rarely considered, because "researchers are usually interested only in the types that are relatively common or that have the greatest implications for theory-building or policy-making" (George & Bennett, 2005, p. 235). Second, the explanatory relevance of each variable will initially only be assessed *within* each case. More general conclusions for all four countries, which could also be generalized for other member states, are only drawn in a second step. This approach follows similar methods of qualitative comparisons that used a larger number of IVs (Ganghof, 2005, p. 85).

As I explained in the previous chapter, the six variables are clustered into three groups. The first group contains two misfit variables, the policy misfit, and the institutional misfit. The second group of variables includes two 'political' factors: the composition of the domestic government and the political salience within the policy subsystem. The last group contains the variables international policy transfer and administrative effectiveness. As this is a qualitative research design, I do not claim that all IVs have the same relevance. I assume the two control variables to have less an effect on the outcome than the other four variables. Therefore, they are included as 'control variables'. While I expect them to be of low relevance, I seek to make sure that they did not significantly affect the transposition outcome, because the literature on BHR and directive transposition has shown that in some cases these factors were relevant (Fig. 4.1).

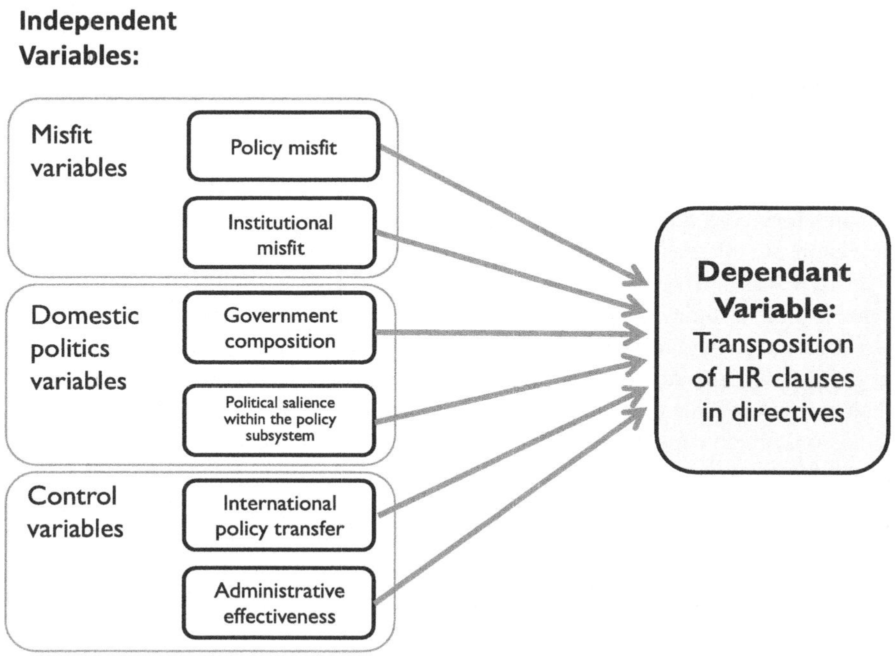

Fig. 4.1 Independent variables and dependent variable

4.5 Operationalization of the Dependent Variable

The DV does not measure the 'correctness' or the 'success' of the transposition, but the degree of commitment to human rights as reflected in the transposition of the four EU directives. The operationalization of this DV aims at making this commitment measurable.[2] For this purpose, I assess the degree to which mandatory and non-mandatory clauses in the four EU directives have been transposed.

The operationalization proceeds in three steps. The first step is to identify and evaluate the relevant provisions. The four directives differ regarding the share of provisions that deal with human rights. For the NFR-Directive human rights is, next to environmental concerns, one of the two main foci. The public procurement package addresses a wide variety of concerns, as it contains detailed regulations on modalities and procedures for public procurement tenders and concession contracts. In both cases, I only focus on the provisions that relate to human rights. For this analysis, a provision is understood as one clearly formulated legal requirement that is relevant for the respect of human rights and social concerns. This can either be a complete article in the directive, a numbered sub-section of an article, or just a sentence. Since I want to measure the commitment to human rights as reflected in the transposition, it

[2]Operationalization is defined as "the process through which (abstract) concepts are translated into (measurable) variables" (Harvey, 2013).

is necessary to rate the provisions according to their relevance for human rights. For this, I use three categories: low human rights relevance (coded as 1), medium human rights relevance (coded as 2), and high human rights relevance (coded as 3). In the analysis, I take into account all clauses that prescribe where and how human rights concerns and labour law shall be (mandatory) or can be (voluntary) considered. Often, the mandatory part and the voluntary part are combined in provisions that contain a mandatory core and a discretionary part (mandatory with discretion). For some provisions, I will consider the discretion to go beyond the legally required minimum, even if it was not specifically spelt out in the directive. While this might seem inconsistent, in some cases the political context of a provision implicitly includes the possibility to go beyond the required minimum. Not considering such cases would fail to grasp politically relevant transposition decisions. However, the consideration of such cases is explained in detail and underpinned with policy documents. Mandatory provisions are considered as well, even though the main focus of this analysis is put on the 'discretionary room'. While generally it can be expected that member states will transpose them, the non-transposition of mandatory provisions would reveal relevant insights of their policy preferences, too. All human rights-related provisions, regardless if voluntary or mandatory, will be allocated a human rights score.

In the second step of the operationalization, I analyse the national transposition laws and evaluate, if and how each provision has been transposed. Existing studies that have analysed the transposition in more details, such as those by Zhelyazkova and Torenvliedb (2011) and Zhelyazkova (2013), used binary coding (0 for non-transposition and 1 for transposition). However, such approaches are not suited to precisely assess transposition. Legal language in EU directives is not always straightforward, because it is the product of controversial negotiations. Many provisions contain complicated language that can be interpreted in different ways. Especially the transposition of voluntary regulation, i.e. provisions that use the subjunctive, cannot be assessed in a binary way because member states always have the option to simply copy the voluntary clause and pass on the decision to those who implement and apply the law. Therefore, my analytical framework uses a more fine-grained scheme. The starting point for this scheme is the categorization to measure Europeanization by Radaelli (2000, p. 14), which consists of four stages: retrenchment, inertia, absorption, and transformation.[3] I adapt this categorization to adequately capture the differences between the transpositions of directives which contain discretion. The first of Radaelli's categories, retrenchment, is not included in my typology, because there is no empirical evidence for retrenchment in provision-level transposition analyses. Moreover, it is highly unlikely that a member state will adopt a provision, which specifically achieves the opposite of a particular directive transposition. I adjust the other three categories and add one new category. As a result, I arrive at four categories: *non-transposition*, *transposition*, *discretion-passed-on*, and *over-transposition*. *Non-transposition* refers to cases where a full provision, voluntary or mandatory, was incorrectly or not at all transposed by the member state. *Transposition* refers to cases where everything a member state had to transpose, was

[3]For a detailed description of this typology, see Sect. 3.2.2.

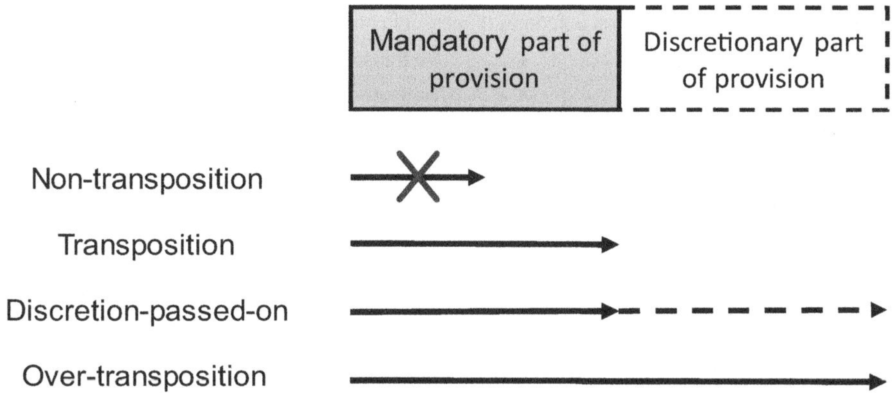

Fig. 4.2 Categories for transposition analysis

correctly transposed. *Discretion-passed-on* is a new category, which I introduce to capture the transposition of discretionary clauses. It refers to cases where the provision or parts of a provision are voluntary and where a member state leaves it up to the implementing authorities if they chose to apply the rules. For example, a member state may determine that a contracting authority is free to consider social requirements when awarding a procurement contract or not. By passing on the discretion to the implementing authority, a member state would go further than not transposing the measure, because an implementing authority would not violate the law if it awarded a procurement contract to a more expensive bidder that meets the social criteria. On the other hand, the member state did not want to go so far as to require the contracting authorities to take social concerns into account. If member states were to do this, it would fall in the fourth category, *over-transposition*. In such cases the member states would make full use of the discretion provided by the directive.[4] This analytical scheme deviates from those of other studies of directive transposition, but it corresponds best with the research question, because it addresses the issue of transposing discretion in EU directives (Fig. 4.2).

In the third step, human rights scores are assigned to the transposition results. If a directive provision is correctly transposed (*transposition*), the human rights score of this provision is allocated to the member state. In cases of non-transposition, no points are allocated to the transposing country. For *discretion-passed-on* the double human rights score is allocated to the member states. In cases of *over-transposition*, four times the human rights score is allocated to the member state. Consequently, the combination of human rights score can lead to twelve possible outcomes (see Table 4.2). This design assigns higher scores to member states that over-transpose than to member states that simply transpose or pass on the discretion. This is intended because the IV is designed to measure the commitment to human rights as reflected

[4]This category is not equivalent to 'gold plating'. As was explained in Sect. 3.4.2, gold-plating also refers to the adoption of requirements that have no direct connection to the directive.

Table 4.2 Possible transposition outcomes to measure commitment to human rights

Low human rights core (1)	+	No transposition	→	0
Low human rights core (1)	+	Transposition	→	1
Low human rights core (1)	+	Discretion-passed-on	→	2
Low human rights core (1)	+	Over-transposition	→	4
Medium human rights core (2)	+	No transposition	→	0
Medium human rights core (2)	+	Transposition	→	2
Medium human rights core (2)	+	Discretion-passed-on	→	4
Medium human rights core (2)	+	Over-transposition	→	8
High human rights core (3)	+	No transposition	→	0
High human rights core (3)	+	Transposition	→	3
High human rights core (3)	+	Discretion-passed-on	→	6
High human rights core (3)	+	Over-transposition	→	12

in the directive transposition. A research design that would aim to assess the 'correctness' of the transposition would not assign such high value to over-transposition but aim for a more balanced score ratio between cases of transposition and over-transposition. Research designs that measure the efficiency of the transposition, i.e. a transposition that seeks to avoid excessive regulation and bureaucratic rigidity, would probably seek to allocate negative scores to cases of over-transposition. But for the research design of this study, the aim is to estimate the degree to which member states are willing to commit themselves to the protection and promotion of human rights. To that aim, instances of over-transposition have to be allocated considerably higher values than normal transpositions, because over-transposition reflects the intention of a government to favour the promotion of human rights over (other) political or economic goals.

While the numerical human rights score is the most meaningful value for assessing the DV, the hypothesis testing becomes easier once the final transposition results for each directive are grouped into categories. To classify the human rights scores, three categories for the DV are used: high, medium, and low. Setting the right thresholds for these categories is a crucial element in every quantitative and qualitative research design. To ensure a neutral assessment of empirical results it is necessary to provide a sound qualitative justification of the thresholds used.

In this study, I use three yardsticks to set the thresholds: the legally required minimum to transpose the directive correctly, a transposition result where the discretion to implement voluntary rules is always passed on, and the maximum possible human rights score. Naturally, these scores differ between the public procurement directives and the NFR-Directive, because the number of human rights-related provisions is not the same. Therefore, the thresholds for high, medium, and low are different as well. As I explain in Sect. 5.2.1, I single out 17 core provisions that can be found in the PSD (PP 1, PP 2, etc.). As the PSD is the 'lead' directive, most of these provisions are identical in the CD and the UD. In total, the three public procurement directives contain 45 provisions that are of relevance for human rights. The provisions differ regarding the degree of obligation (mandatory, voluntary, mandatory with discretion). On this basis, the three yardsticks can be calculated. As Table 4.3 shows, a transposition of the legally required minimum arrives at a human rights score of 59. A transposition where the discretion to implement voluntary rules is always passed on leads to a human rights score of 206, and the maximum possible human rights score is 412. I use 206, the human rights score for 'discretion always passed on', as the middle of the scale to categorize the transposition outcomes. This is not the mathematical middle between the minimum score (59) and the maximum score (412), but a qualitatively chosen middle, because I regard a government's decision to pass on the discretion to the implementing actors as the middle ground between a minimum transposition and a maximum transposition.

On the basis of these three yardsticks I set the thresholds for a low, medium, and high human rights score. As Fig. 4.3 shows, the threshold between a low human rights score and a medium human rights score is set at 132.5, at the mean between the legally required minimum transposition and the transposition with discretion always passed on. The threshold between a medium human rights score and a high human rights score is set at 309, the mean between a transposition with discretion always passed on and the maximum possible transposition.

For the NFR-Directive, the calculation of thresholds between the categories follows the same logic. As I show in Sect. 5.2.2, the NFR-Directive consists of nine human rights-related provisions. Two of these provisions are completely voluntary, and the rest are mandatory with discretion. Table 4.4 shows the calculation of the yardsticks for the NFR-Directive, while Fig. 4.4 displays the thresholds on a scale.

A member state that only transposes the legally required minimum would receive a human rights score of 13. When the discretion to implement voluntary provisions is always passed on to the implementing actors, a member state would receive a human rights score of 34. The maximum possible transposition arrives at a human rights score of 68. Similar to the calculation above, this leads to the following yardsticks: All outcomes between 13 and 23.5 receive a low human rights score, all transpositions between 23.5 and 51 receive a medium human rights score, and all outcomes between 51 and 68 receive a high human rights score. In the empirical analysis of this book I use these thresholds first to categorize the transposition outcomes of the four member states, and second to test the hypotheses that were formulated in chap. 3.

4.6 Operationalization of the Independent Variables

4.6.1 Policy Misfit

As was explained in chap. 3, compliance studies have pursued different approaches when trying to operationalize the fit between EU and domestic rules. According to Börzel and Risse (2000) the misfit consists of policy misfit and institutional misfit.

Table 4.3 Calculation of yardsticks for the public procurement directives

Number	Directive	HR relevance	Degree of obligation	Legally required minimum transposition	Transposition with discretion always passed on	Maximum possible transposition
PP 1	PSD	1	Voluntary	0	2	4
	UD	1		0	2	4
	CS	1		0	2	4
PP 2	PSD	3	Mandatory with discretion	3	6	12
	UD	3		3	6	12
	CS	3		3	6	12
PP 3	PSD	3	Mandatory with discretion	3	6	12
	UD	3		3	6	12
	CS	3		3	6	12
PP 4	PSD	3	Voluntary	0	6	12
	UD	3		0	6	12
	CS	3		0	6	12
PP 5	PSD	2	Voluntary	0	4	8
	UD	2		0	4	8
	CS	2		0	4	8
PP 6	PSD	3	Mandatory with discretion	3	6	12
	UD	3		3	6	12
PP 7	PSD	1	Voluntary	1	2	4
	UD	1		1	2	4
PP 8	PSD	1	Voluntary	1	2	4
	UD	1		1	2	4
PP 9	PSD	3	Mandatory	3	6	12
	CS	3		3	6	12
PP 10	PSD	2	Mandatory with discretion	2	4	8
	UD	2	Voluntary	0	4	8
	CS	2	Mandatory with discretion	2	4	8
PP 11	PSD	3	Voluntary	0	6	12
	UD	3		0	6	12
	CS	3		0	6	12

(continued)

Table 4.3 (continued)

Number	Directive	HR relevance	Degree of obligation	Legally required minimum transposition	Transposition with discretion always passed on	Maximum possible transposition
PP 12	PSD	3	Mandatory	3	6	12
	UD	3		3	6	12
PP 13	PSD	1	Voluntary	0	2	4
	UD	1		0	2	4
	CS	1		0	2	4
PP 14	PSD	3	Mandatory with discretion	3	6	12
	UD	3		3	6	12
PP 15	PSD	2	Voluntary	0	4	8
	UD	2		0	4	8
	CS	2		0	4	8
PP 16	PSD	2	Voluntary	0	4	8
	UD	2		0	4	8
	CS	2		0	4	8
PP 17	PSD	3	Mandatory	3	6	12
	UD	3		3	6	12
	CS	3		3	6	12
Total human rights score				59	206	412

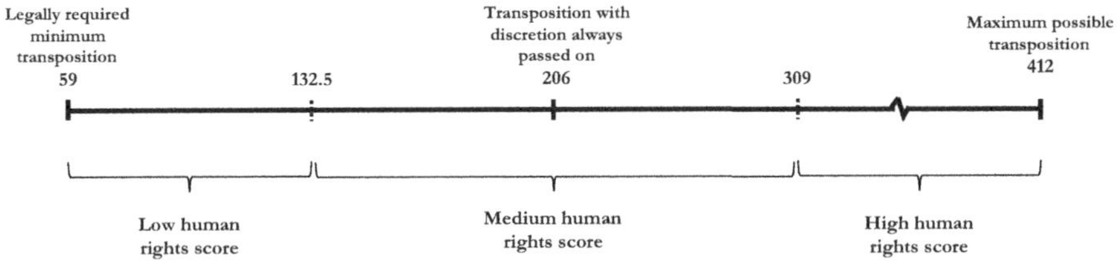

Fig. 4.3 Thresholds for categorizing human rights scores for the public procurement directives[6]

Gerda Falkner (2003) (Falkner et al., 2005) distinguishes between policy misfit, politics/polity misfit, and costs. In this research design, I use two variants of the misfit, the policy misfit, and the institutional misfit. The policy misfit refers to the difference between the requirements formulated in the directive provisions, and the laws and domestic-level laws and policy measures. The institutional misfit refers to the discrepancy between institutions and procedures conveyed in the EU directives and the domestic-level institutions and procedures (see next sub-section). The element of costs is excluded because, as was explained in Sect. 4.3, the cases were selected

Table 4.4 Calculation of yardsticks for the NFR-directive

Number	HR relevance	Degree of obligation	Legally required minimum transposition	Transposition with discretion always passed on	Maximum possible transposition
NFR 1	3	Mandatory with discretion	3	6	12
NFR 2	2	Mandatory with discretion	2	4	8
NFR 3	3	Mandatory with discretion	3	6	12
NFR 4	1	Mandatory with discretion	1	2	4
NFR 5	1	Mandatory with discretion	1	2	4
NFR 6	3	Voluntary	0	6	12
NFR 7	2	Mandatory with discretion	2	4	8
NFR 8	1	Voluntary	0	2	4
NFR 9	1	Mandatory with discretion	1	2	4
Total human rights score			13	34	68

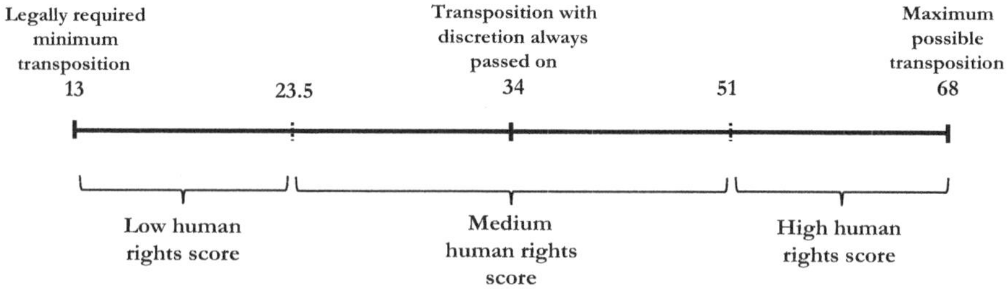

Fig. 4.4 Thresholds for categorizing human rights scores for the NFR-Directive

in order to hold this factor constant. The polity misfit, which for example Falkner (2003) includes in her research, can also be disregarded for this study. None of the provisions in the four directives analysed will force the member states considered in this study to make substantial changes to their polity.

To operationalize the policy misfit in any directive transposition study is a challenging task because directives often regulate intricate details of national regulation. While it is easy to discern that there is a policy misfit, it is more difficult to measure the exact difference between a national law and an EU directive in a way that would allow for a direct comparison between member states. In order to measure and compare the policy misfit, I use three categories. A large policy misfit will be attributed if the reporting requirements or the procurement rules that have to be adopted by the member state require completely new legal rules, and/or far-reaching qualitative innovations. A medium policy misfit refers to cases where the legal rules and qualitative innovations are not entirely new, because similar rules had in some form already existed before the transposition. A small policy misfit exists when the same or almost the same legal and policy requirements were in already in place under national law. As will be shown below, there is not only one way for a member state to fall into one of these categories. National laws are diverse and in the end, the determination of the misfit is it is a qualitative assessment. This is why chap. 6 will give detailed explanations for each categorization. Boxes 4.2 and 4.3 show how the categories are identified for the public procurement directives, and the NFR-Directive.

Low misfit:

Over-arching mandatory social clause in procurement law
or mandatory social regulation in one more than one procurement field or in one of the six procurement stages
or mandatory requirement for subcontractors or a clause that establishes legal liability of the contractor for the subcontractor (liability clause)

Medium misfit:

Set of voluntary social clauses in procurement law
or voluntary requirement for subcontractors (incl. liability clause)
or voluntary social regulation in one of the six procurement stages

High misfit:

Few voluntary provisions in procurement law
or no mention of social procurement rules.

Box 4.2 Operationalization of the policy misfit for the public procurement directives

Low misfit: Mandatory social reporting requirements
Medium misfit: Voluntary reporting requirements

High misfit: Few or no voluntary reporting requirements

Box 4.3 Operationalization of the policy misfit for the NFR-directive

4.6.2 Institutional Misfit

The institutional misfit refers to the discrepancy between institutions and procedures conveyed in the EU directives and the domestic-level institutions and procedures. For this study, I argue that the institutional misfit is determined by the setup of the political economy. Chaps. 2 and 3 already elucidated the connection between the institutional characteristics of a political economy and governments' behaviour in the field of BHR. I argue, drawing on the observations of VoC literature, that binding measures of corporate responsibility are more compatible with CMEs than with LMEs. The VoC-typology by Hall and Soskice (2001b) already gives us an indication of the positioning of the UK, France, Germany, and Denmark on the scale between CMEs and LMEs. However, I do not regard the VoC-typology by Hall and Soskice to be a suitable indicator for operationalization, because it does not provide an ordinal scale on which the four countries I analysed could be arrayed. Hall and Soskice focused on developing the typology by describing the archetypical varieties of political economies. While they did classify countries with regard to a number of central indicators such as employment protection, stock market capitalization, or trade union density, they did not present a combined measure. The classification of France shows this problem, as it is in an "ambiguous position" (Hall & Soskice, 2001a, p. 21) between liberal market economies and coordinated market economies. The typology of Hall and Soskice would not have allowed us to determine the political economy of France.

Therefore, I rely on the measure of corporatism developed by Siaroff (1999). He proposed a quantitative index of 24 industrialized democracies, which has found wide application in the literature. The advantages of Siaroff's classification is that he combines the insights of 23 other rankings of corporatism into one unified index. Scholars of Europeanization and directive transposition have heavily relied on this index (e.g. Kaeding, 2006; Thomson, 2009, 2010; Zhelyazkova & Torenvlied, 2011). Table 4.5 shows the Siaroff's classification of 24 countries. On a scale between 1 and 5, higher values indicate a higher level of corporatism, i.e. a higher level of institutional integration of unions and employer organizations in a country's policy-making processes.

Table 4.5 Siaroff's corporatism scores in 24 countries

Country	Corporatism scores mean (std. dev.)
Austria	5.000 (0.000)
Norway	4.864 (0.351)
Sweden	4.674 (0.556)
Netherlands	4.000 (0.989)
Denmark	*3.545 (0.999)*
Germany (West)	*3.543 (0.940)*
Switzerland	3.375 (1.286)
Finland	3.295 (1.043)
Iceland	3.000 (0.000)
Israel	3.000 (0.000)
Luxembourg	3.000 (0.000)
Japan	2.912 (1.603)
Belgium	2.841 (0.793)
Ireland	2.000 (1.015)
New Zealand	1.955 (0.907)
Australia	1.680 (0.873)
France	*1.674 (0.792)*
UK	*1.652 (0.818)*
Portugal	1.500 (1.000)
Italy	1.477 (0.748)
Spain	1.250 (0.500)
Canada	1.150 (0.489)
USA	1.150 (0.489)
Mean	2.648
Standard Deviation	1.234

4.6.3 Government Composition

Since it is unlikely that political parties will be neutral to the interpretation of the directive provisions, the influence of national parties are also taken into account. The operationalization of the government position is straightforward. I assess, which parties formed the government during the transposition of the directives. While other studies have taken this issue into consideration as well (see e.g. Treib, 2003, 2004), it is surprising how little attention it has received in directive transposition studies so far. As was explained in chap. 3, the assumption is that political parties from the political 'left' will lean towards the social market understanding of BHR, while the conservative parties are going to assume a more market-liberal view. In order to get a more precise assessment of the political positioning of the political parties that were involved in the transposition process, the Chapel Hill Expert Survey (CHES) will

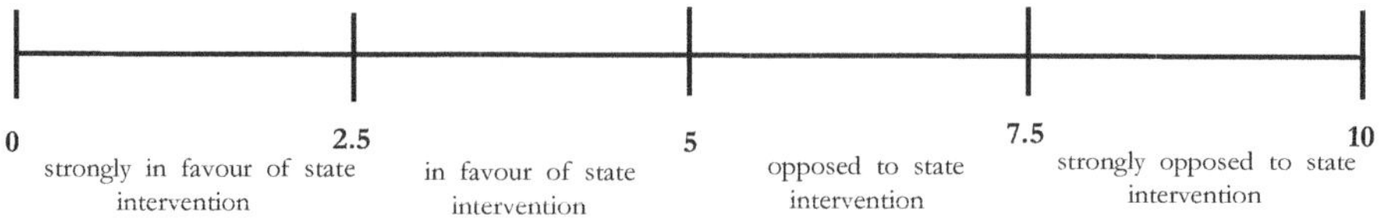

Fig. 4.5 Scale to measure the position of political parties on state intervention in the economy

be used. This survey, which exists since 1999, relies on interviews with experts that specialize in political parties and European integration.[7] The survey estimates "party positioning on European integration, ideology and policy issues for national parties in a variety of European countries" (CHES, 2017, para. 1). The dataset includes an indicator that measures the position of political parties on state intervention in the economy (ECON_INTERVEN). The CHES uses a 10-point scale, between 0 (fully in favour of state intervention) and 10 (fully opposed to state intervention). Using this data, I rank how the political parties that were in power during the transposition scored on this indicator. Values below 2.5 are regarded as strongly in favour of state intervention, values below 5 as in favour of state intervention. Scores between 5 and 7.5 are opposed to state intervention, and values above 7.5 are denominated as strongly opposed to state intervention. If two parties formed a coalition, the average score of the two parties will be used. To assess the positioning of a political party, data from 2014 is used (Fig. 4.5).

4.6.4 Political Salience Within the Policy Subsystem

Political salience refers to "the relative importance attached to a certain issue in relation to other issues" (Spendzharova & Versluis, 2013, p. 1499). Unlike previous studies that investigated the role of issue salience within the wider public, in this study I scrutinize the impact of political salience within the policy subsystem. Actors within the policy subsystem of BHR include the parliamentarians and civil servants concerned with BHR legislation, labour unions, employers' associations, representatives of large companies, academics, representatives from international organizations, NGOs, and other civil society organizations.

In order to operationalize this IV, I seek to find out how salient an issue was for the actors that constitute the national policy subsystem of BHR. Qualitative estimations of political salience have proven to be a reliable approach to capture all dimensions of political salience (Versluis, 2003). To qualitatively measure this variable, I rely on expert interviews and policy reports by actors in the policy subsystem. Other studies have also regarded expert interviews as the most precise source to evaluate the relative importance of a political issue (Spendzharova & Versluis, 2013). Public consultations national governments conduct for the transposition of the directive also

[7] In this study I use the 2014 Chapel Hill Expert Survey of July 2015 (Version 2015.1).

serve as indicators for political salience. Actors within the policy subsystem usually respond to such consultations if the issue is important to them. If such a consultation took place, the number and content of the responses can also give indications of the relative importance attached to the issue within the policy subsystem. The salience is only analysed with regard to the social and human rights aspects of the directives.

4.6.5 International Policy Transfer

The term policy transfer refers to the "exchange of ideas, policies and policy instruments between different political systems across the world" (Bulmer, 2007, p. 4). For this IV, policy transfer is understood as the intentional vertical exchange of policy instruments from international BHR agreements to the national governments that transpose the EU directives. As was noted, all EU member states have signed the UNGPs and have therefore made a commitment to human rights in the areas of public procurement and non-financial reporting. In addition, NGOs have petitioned member states in Brussels to take the UNGPs into account when transposing the directives. In Commission working groups that developed transposition guidelines, international NGOs, such as Shift, were present and argued for adhering to the UNGPs (Interview 9). While the UNGPs are clearly the most important international BHR agreement, other international agreements complement the UNGPs, most notable the OECD Guidelines for Multinational Enterprises, the ISO 26000 social responsibility standard, and the ILO Tripartite Declaration. Together, these agreements constitute the corpus of international BHR obligations to which the four EU member states in this analysis have subscribed. Therefore, I hypothesize that this international obligation affects the transposition of BHR provisions in the four EU directives. As stated in chap. 3, hypothesis H5 reads: International BHR obligations cause member states to transpose more voluntary BHR directive provisions.

The difficulty in testing this variable is to ascertain that policy transfer took place and that the international obligation *caused* member states to transpose more BHR provisions, given that there is no variation between member states. Policy transfer will only be recognized if the transfer has been confirmed by actors of the national governments or experts that were involved in the transposition process. For this purpose, I rely on three sources to determine if policy transfer took place: expert interviews, the official justifications for the transposition laws, and the documentation of the public consultations. If one of these three sources confirms that transposition of one or more directive provisions was decisively influenced by the government's commitment to comply with international BHR obligations, a case of policy transfer will be determined. The number of such cases will be added for each country and allow for a comparison of the policy transfer between the four cases.

4.6.6 Administrative Effectiveness

EU member states differ with regard to their administrative effectiveness. This is a factor that needs to be taken into consideration because transposing an EU directive requires substantial organisational and bureaucratic resources. The variable is taken into account in order to control for the fact that an inefficient national administration was responsible for the transposition result. Administrative effectiveness will be operationalized using the 'government effectiveness' indicator by the World Bank, one of the Worldwide Governance Indicators that was initially developed by Kaufmann et al. (Kaufmann, Kraay, & Mastruzzi, 2006). This is a well-established reference for measuring the effectiveness of a country's bureaucracy which covers more than 200 countries worldwide and which has been employed by other transposition studies as well (see e.g. Thomson, 2009). The indicator captures

> perceptions of the quality of public services, the quality of the civil service and the degree of its independence from political pressures, the quality of policy formulation and implementation, and the credibility of the government's commitment to such policies. (Kaufmann, Kraay, & Mastruzzi, 2011, p. 4)

The results for the indicators are presented in two ways, the *country score* that is displayed in standard normal units of the indicator ranging from around -2.5 to 2.5, and in the *percentile rank of the country*, which ranges from 0 (lowest) to 100 (highest) among all countries worldwide. Any country score below zero will be regarded as an inefficient administration. In addition, the country scores will be compared with the EU average. Furthermore, the percentile rank also allows for a comparison between the four cases. The newest available version of this indicator will be used, which was published in September 2017. In addition, the potential effect of administrative effectiveness will also be validated in expert interviews and the study of policy documents.

4.7 Data Collection

The main methods of data collection are qualitative document analysis and expert interviews. The primary sources considered are the four EU directives, the national laws that were adopted to transpose them, as well as policy reports, meeting transcripts, and other policy documents from EU institutions and national governments. Next to academic literature, secondary sources that are taken into account are reports from think tanks, NGOs, and other civil society institutions. Moreover, in order to better understand the transposition processes in each country, I conducted 18 semi-structured expert interviews with representatives from national governments, the European Commission, civil society, and other policy experts. Interviewees were first asked to describe their experience and interpretation of the transposition processes. Then, questions were posed to them about the influence of the above-mentioned factors on the transposition. How the information used from the interviews is cited depends on the preferences expressed by the interviewees. If the interviewees did not want that any information is associated with them, this study will only refer to 'interview evidence'. The interviews took place either in person or on the phone, depending on the preferences of the interviewee or on logistical circumstances. In some cases, the interviewees preferred to answer the questions in written form. A list of the interviews conducted can be found in Appendix I.

References

Albareda, L., Lozano, J. M., & Ysa, T. (2007). Public policies on corporate social responsibility: The role of governments in Europe. *Journal of Business Ethics, 74*(4), 391–407.

Börzel, T., & Risse, T. (2000). When Europe hits home: Europeanization and domestic change. *European Integration Online Papers, 4*(15).

Bulmer, S. (2007). Theorizing Europeanization. *Europeanization: New research agendas* (pp. 46–58). Basingstoke: Palgrave Macmillan.

CHES. (2017). Chesdata-1999–2014 chapel hill expert survey (CHES) trend file. Retrieved September 14, 2017, from https://www.chesdata.eu/our-surveys.

De Schutter, O. (2008). Corporate social responsibility European style. *European Law Journal, 14*(2), 203–236.

De Schutter, O., Ramasastry, A., Taylor, M. B., & Thompson, R. C. (2012). *Human rights due diligence: The role of states.* Retrieved from http://humanrightsinbusiness.eu/wp-content/uploads/2015/05/De-Schutter-et-al.-Human-Rights-Due-Diligence-The-Role-of-States.pdf.

Falkner, G. (2003). Comparing europeanisation effects: From metaphor to operationalisation. *European Integration Online Papers, 7*(13), 1–18.

Falkner, G., Treib, O., Hartlapp, M., & Leiber, S. (2005). *Complying with Europe. EU harmonisation and soft law in the member states.* New York: Cambridge University Press.

Ganghof, S. (2005). Vergleichen in qualitativer und quantitativer Politikwissenschaft: X-zentrierte versus Y-zentrierte Forschungsstrategien. In S. Kropp & M. Minkenberg (Eds.), *Vergleichen in der Politikwissenschaft* (pp. 76–93). Wiesbaden: VS Verlag für Sozialwissenschaften.

George, A., & Bennett, A. (2005). *Case studies and theory development in the social sciences.* Cambridge: MIT Press.

Gerring, J. (2007). *Case study research : principles and practices.* Cambridge University Press.

Hall, P. A., & Soskice, D. (2001a). An Introduction to Varieties of Capitalism. In P. A. Hall & D. Soskice (Eds.), *Varieties Of Capitalism: The Institutional Foundations of Comparative Advantage* (pp. 1–68). Oxford: Oxford University Press.

Hall, P. A., & Soskice, D. (Eds.). (2001b). *Varieties Of Capitalism: The Institutional Foundations of Comparative Advantage.* Oxford: Oxford University Press.

Harvey, L. (2013). Social research glossary. Retrieved September 8, 2017, from http://www.qualityresearchinternational.com/socialresearch/csr.htm.

Kaeding, M. (2006). Determinants of transposition delay in the European Union. *Journal of Public Policy, 26*(03), 229.

Kaufmann, D., Kraay, A., & Mastruzzi, M. (2006). Governance Matters VI: Governance Indicators for 1996–2006. *World Bank Policy Research Working Paper No. 4280.*

Kaufmann, D., Kraay, A., & Mastruzzi, M. (2011). The worldwide governance indicators: methodology and analytical issues. *Hague Journal on the Rule of Law, 3*(02), 220–246.

Kinderman, D. (2008). The political economy of corporate responsibility in Germany, 1995–2008. *Mario Einaudi Center for International Studies, No 5–08.*

Kinderman, D. (2015). Corporate social responsibility–Der Kampf um die EU-Richtlinie. *WSI-Mitteilungen, 2015/8.*

Organisation for Economic Co-operation and Development. (2018). Import content of exports. Retrieved January 15, 2018, from https://data.oecd.org/trade/import-content-of-exports.htm.

Radaelli, C. M. (2000). Whither Europeanization? Concept stretching and substantive change. *European Integration Online Papers, 4*(8).

Siaroff, A. (1999). Corporatism in 24 industrial democracies: Meaning and measurement. *European Journal of Political Research, 36*(2), 175–205.

Spendzharova, A., & Versluis, E. (2013). Issue salience in the European policy process: what impact on transposition? *Journal of European Public Policy, 20*(10), 1499–1516.

Starke, P. (2013). Qualitative methods for the study of policy diffusion: Challenges and available solutions. *Policy Studies Journal, 41*(4), 561–582.

Taylor, M. B. (2013). *Human rights due diligence: The Role of States-2013 progress report*. Retrieved from http://humanrightsinbusiness.eu/wp-content/uploads/2015/05/De-Schutter-et-al.-Human-Rights-Due-Diligence-The-Role-of-States.pdf.

Thomann, E. (2015). Customizing Europe: transposition as bottom-up implementation. *Journal of European Public Policy, 22*(10), 1368–1387.

Thomson, R. (2007). Time to comply: National responses to six EU labour market directives revisited. *West European Politics, 30*(5), 987–1008.

Thomson, R. (2009). Same effects in different worlds: the transposition of EU directives. *Journal of European Public Policy, 16*(1), 1–18.

Thomson, R. (2010). Opposition through the back door in the transposition of EU directives. *European Union Politics, 11*(4), 577–596.

Toshkov, D. (2010). Taking stock: a review of quantitative studies of transposition and implementation of EU law. *Institute for European Integration Research*, (November), 25–26.

Treib, O. (2003). Die Umsetzung von EU-Richtlinien im Zeichen der Parteipolitik: Eine akteurszentrierte Antwort auf die Misfit-These. *Politische Vierteljahresschrift, 44*(4), 506–528.

Treib, O. (2004). *Die Bedeutung der nationalen Parteipolitik für die Umsetzung europäischer Sozialrichtlinien*. Frankfurt/New York: Campus.

Versluis, E. (2003). *Enforcement matters enforcement and compliance of European directives in four member states*. Utrecht.

Zhelyazkova, A. (2013). Complying with EU directives' requirements: the link between EU decision-making and the correct transposition of EU provisions. *Journal of European Public Policy, 20*(5), 702–721.

Zhelyazkova, A., & Torenvlied, R. (2011). The successful transposition of European provisions by member states: application to the framework equality directive. *Journal of European Public Policy, 18*(5), 690–708.

Chapter 5
Empirical Analysis I: Transposition of the Directives

This chapter represents the first part of the empirical analysis and provides a detailed comparative account of the transpositions of the four directives in the UK, France, Denmark, and Germany. The first section analyses the transposition of the public procurement directives by analysing the human rights-related provisions in these directives. I explain and categorize the clauses with respect to their human rights relevance and their degree of obligation, as I laid down in the operationalization (Sect. 4.6). Then, I describe the transposition of the three directives in the four countries in a comparative manner. The result of the transposition and the human rights score are combined and result in a transposition score. The second section provides the analysis of the transposition of the non-financal reporting directive, which follows the same structure. A brief final section categorizes, visualizes, and compares the transposition results.

5.1 Transposition of the Public Procurement Directives

5.1.1 Human Rights Provisions in the Public Procurement Directives

Following the Commission's understanding, EU public procurement rules should open the public procurement market and ensure the free movement of goods, services, and labour within the EU and thereby make public procurement more transparent and competitive (European Commission, 2016a). In 2011, the Commission presented proposals to revise the 2004 directives of public sector procurement (2004/18/EC) and utilities procurement (2004/17/EC). In addition, the Commission proposed a new directive on the award of concession contracts. Apart from simplifying procurement rules and modernizing some practices, for example by gradually introducing new rules on e-procurement, the new directives also contained a strategic realignment. Taking note of the fact that the public sector is the biggest single spender in the EU, the

P. Drahn, *Adoption of EU Business and Human Rights Policy*,
Contributions to Political Science, https://doi.org/10.1007/978-3-030-46935-1_5

Commission sought to integrate public procurement into the overall political goals of the Juncker Commission, among others in order to create "a more innovative, green and socially-inclusive economy" (European Commission, 2016c, para. 1).[1]

In this context, the scope and strength of social and human rights-related provisions have been radically extended. The new directives replaced purely market-based approaches with a more qualitative perspective. For example, the old directives prescribed public suppliers to follow the principle of the 'lowest price only' when awarding a public contract, while human rights-related considerations could only be taken into account at the end of the procurement process (Institute for Human Rights and Business, 2015). This stands in contrast to the 2014 directives, which include several social and human rights-related provisions throughout the procurement process and contain one overarching 'social clause'. This "significant shift" (Institute for Human Rights and Business, 2015, p. 14) was not only initiated by the Commission but largely supported by the Council and the EP. However, as has been noted, many of the relevant provisions are to differing degrees discretionary on the transposition and implementation by the member states.

The three directives of the 'procurement package' are similar with respect to their aims and structure. The Public Sector Directive (PSD) is the 'lead directive' and serves as a model for the other two more specific directives. The main differences are due to their focus. The PSD applies to the procurement of general works, supplies, and services by central and sub-central government authorities. The Utilities Directive (UD) applies only to tenders in the area of water, energy, transport, and postal services, while the Concessions Directive (CD) applies only to the procurement of concession contracts.[2]

In total, the three public procurement directives contain 45 provisions that touch on human rights. For analytical purposes, I pool similar provisions from the PSD, CD, and UD, and arrive at 17 provisions. As was noted, the PSD is the 'lead' directive and the CD and the UD 'mirror' most clauses of the PSD. Moreover, I number the provisions (PP 1, PP 2, PP 3 etc.), which also makes them distinguishable from the provisions of the NFR-Directive (NFR 1, NFR 2, etc.). The following section describes the 17 provisions in the EU public procurement directives that I identify as being relevant for human rights.[3]

Studies have distinguished between two kinds of human rights provisions in the public procurement directives, cross-cutting provisions and provisions referring to specific phases of the procurement process. Cross-cutting provisions refer to the

---

[1]According to the EU Commission, public authorities spend € 1.9 trillion every year, which represents approximately 14% of the EU's GDP (European Commission, 2016a).

[2]Differences can also be found regarding the threshold above which the directives apply. The exact thresholds for each directive are published on the website of the European Commission (see European Commission, 2016d). Tenders below the threshold remain under national legislation, but still must follow general principles of EU law.

[3]For the legal analysis of the provisions that include human rights considerations, I partly drew on the Occasional Paper by the Institute for Human Rights and Business (2015), which provides an in depth legal analysis of the EU public procurement directives.

procurement process in general or to more than one phase of the process. The most important overarching provision is the 'social clause' (PP 1),[4] which requires that

> [m]ember States **shall take appropriate measures** to ensure that in the performance of public contracts economic operators comply with applicable obligations in the fields of environmental, **social and labour law established by Union law, national law, collective agreements or by the international environmental, social and labour law provisions listed in Appendix X**.[5] (PSD, Art 18(2), emphasis added)[6]

To assess, if this clause has been transposed or not is difficult because 'appropriate measures' are not defined. Therefore, this analysis is not going to try to determine if measures were appropriate or not. Instead, I only assess, if the respect for social and labour law obligations was laid down as a procurement principle or not. If legislators decide to include the social clause among national principles, they thereby emphasise its importance vis-à-vis the contracting authorities and the public. The transposition score should reflect this. In past procurement decisions, social criteria were often regarded as being 'external' to the procurement decisions and were, therefore, less relevant than, for example, attributes and price of procured items. If, however, social criteria are included in the principles of procurement, it is difficult to argue that social criteria are 'external' to the procurement (Interview 6).[7] In the assessment, this clause will, therefore, be denoted as voluntary. The clause which states that member states 'shall take appropriate measures' is not voluntary, but to include the social provision in the procurement principles is voluntary.

To attribute a human rights score to the social clause is not straightforward. On the one hand, it is the central human rights clause in the procurement directives. On the other hand, the effect on human rights is small, if the social clause is *only* listed under the procurement principles. The real effect on human rights only unfolds, once provisions that regulate specific phases of the procurement process demand adherence to the social clause. Therefore, the establishment of the social clause as a procurement principle alone is not regarded as highly relevant for the legal protection of human rights, which is why I assign this provision a human rights relevance of 1. When the obligations of the social clause apply to other stages of the procurement process, they are assigned higher human rights scores and will also be treated as mandatory, where appropriate (see below).

The second provision with human rights relevance in the public procurement directives, provision PP 2, states that the social clause should also apply to the subcontractors of the economic operators.[8] From a human rights perspective, this is

[4]While this provision is "cross-cutting" (European Commission, 2016b, p. 1), recital 40 of the directive states that the social criteria should be taken into consideration when applying the exclusion criteria and when awarding the contract (see below).

[5]Annex X of the PSD lists twelve international conventions in the area of international social and environmental law.

[6]The Social clauses in the CD (Article 30(3)) and the UD (Article 36(2)) have similar wordings.

[7]The German term 'vergabefremd' was used in the interview to describe issues being external to the procurement.

[8]Article 71(1) in the PSD, Article 42(1) in the CD and Article 88(1) in the UD.

highly relevant because most human rights violations take place at the lower end of the supply chain. Subcontractors are often located outside the EU, making this a provision with potentially extraterritorial reach (human rights score of 3). The formulation of the degree of obligation is not straightforward. The clause states that the observance of the social clause by subcontractors "is ensured through appropriate action" (PSD, Article 71(1)) by the member states. While the wording 'is ensured' is clearly mandatory, the formulation 'appropriate action' gives member states discretion of how to achieve this. For the assessment, I consider this provision as transposed, if the transposing laws unequivocally state that subcontractors must abide by the social clause. For the clause to be considered as fully transposed this must be stated as a matter of principle, and not only with respect to a specific aspect of phase of the procurement process. Article 71(6)[9] proposes two voluntary measures, how to hold subcontractors to account. First, if member states design rules for a joint liability of main contractor and subcontractor, they are invited to ensure the application of the social clause (PP 3). Second, it is proposed that member states apply the same exclusion criteria to the subcontractors that they are required to apply to the main contractors (PP 4). Naturally, the complete transposition of these provisions would have significant consequences for public procurement in the member state.

Regarding the issue of legal liability—a central problem in human rights violations in supply chains—the next provision (PP 5) gives member states much leeway. The PSD states that member states "may provide for more stringent liability rules under national law" (PSD, Article 71(7)) between contractors and subcontractors. Similar clauses can be found in Articles 42(5) in the CD, and Article 88(7) in the UD. Another provision, laid down in Article 63(1) of the PSD,[10] deals with the issue of compliance of 'other entities' with the selection and exclusion criteria (PP 6). It is stated that economic operators can rely on these other entities "regardless of the legal nature of the links which it has with them" (PSD, Article 63(1)). This clause is relevant because thereby the directive states that operators that are not subcontractors in the legal sense also have to abide by certain social standards. The core provision is mandatory and demands that contracting authorities must verify if these 'other entities' fulfil the relevant selection and exclusion criteria. If there are compulsory grounds for exclusion, the entities must be replaced. If there are non-compulsory grounds for exclusion, the entities may be replaced. Thus, the provision also contains discretion in this clause. The last overarching provisions in the directives address social labels and certifications. While under the directives, contracting authorities are not allowed to ask for one specific label in the tender, they can generally ask for labels as a means of proof for fulfilling technical specifications, award criteria or contract conditions (PP 7).[11] Furthermore, member states are given the possibility to use labels for

[9] Article 42(4) in the CD, and 88(6) in the UD.

[10] Article 79(1) in the UD, the CD does not contain a similar provision.

[11] Article 43(1) in the PSD, and Article 61(1) in the UD. The CD does not contain a similar provision.

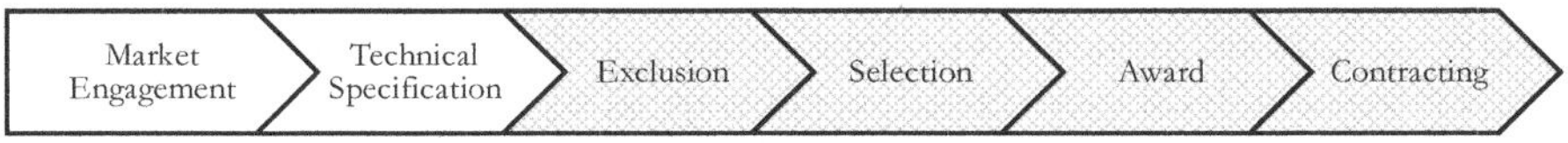

Fig. 5.1 Stages of the EU public procurement process

their "[o]fficial lists of approved economic operators" (PSD, Article 64) (PP 8).[12] Companies on that list can then be presumed to be suitable for the tender.

In addition to the cross-cutting provisions, there are human rights-related provisions that relate to the regular phases of public procurement processes in the EU: market engagement, technical specification, exclusion, selection, award, and contracting. During market engagement phase, when contracting authorities consult the market and inform economic operators about the procurement plans, there are no human rights provisions, because the directive does not regulate this step. In the technical specification phase, where contracting authorities define the characteristics of the material, product, or supply, the directives do not foresee any human rights clauses have either (Fig. 5.1).[13]

In the exclusion phase, human rights are addressed again. Article 57 of the PSD[14] lists both the compulsory and non-compulsory grounds for exclusion (PP 9). As a compulsory ground for exclusion, Article 57(1)f of the PSD[15] states that companies that have been convicted of child labour or other forms of human trafficking must be excluded from the procurement procedure. In addition, Article 57(2)[16] specifies that economic operators can be excluded if they are in breach of paying social security contributions (PP 10). The mandatory part[17] of the provision stipulates that when the breach was established by a judicial or administrative decision, the economic operator must be excluded. The discretionary part states that contracting authorities "may be required by Member States" (ibid) to exclude companies where they can "demonstrate by any appropriate means" (PSD, Article 57(2)) a breach of social

[12] Article 64(1)-(4) in the PSD and Article 62(1) in the UD. The CD does not contain an equivalent provision.

[13] Technical specifications phase contains provisions on accessibility for disabled people in public buildings and in other places. The relevant provision, (Article 42(1) and Annex VII in PSD, Article 60 and Appendix VIII in UD, and Article 36, Recitals 66 and 67 in CD) require member states that all procurement that is intended to be used by persons (general public, staff etc.) has to take into account the accessibility for disabled persons, provided the requirements relate to the specific goods, works or services in question. While these clauses clearly have a social component, they are only relevant in the domestic sector and do not apply to human rights in the international context.

[14] Article 38 in the CD.

[15] Recital 70 and Article 38(4)f in the CD. The UD does not contain a similar provision, but as the report of the Institute for Human Rights and Business (2015, p. 16) suggests, the issue is covered by the overarching social clause.

[16] Article 38(5) in the CD.

[17] Derogations are possible for reasons relating to public interest such as public health or protection of the environment. In this analysis, the provision will still be regarded as mandatory.

security obligations. In the UD, this complete provision is only listed in the Recitals,[18] which means that for this directive it is not mandatory.

Another human rights provision (PP 11) in the exclusion phase can be found in Article 57(4)a of the PSD,[19] which refers to the 'social clause'. This provision is a non-compulsory ground for exclusion, and it stipulates that contracting authorities may exclude bidders based on non-compliance with social or labour law obligations. Again, the authorities "may be required by Member States" (PSD, Article 57(4)a) to exclude such companies, which gives national legislators scope in their transposition. Article 69(3) of the PSD states that tenders that are "abnormally low" (PSD, Article 69(3)) because they do not comply with social or labour law obligations, have to be rejected by the contracting authority (PP 12).[20] Moreover, the 'social clause' as such can be used to exclude bidders on human rights grounds (see above). Here, the formulation that member states shall ensure that companies "comply with applicable obligations in the fields of environmental, social and labour law" (PSD, Art 18(2)) includes considerable flexibility for the national transposition.

In the next phase of the procurement process, the selection phase, contracting authorities create a short-list of capable companies that will be considered in the award stage. Article 58(1) of the PSD[21] states, "[s]election criteria may relate to (a) suitability to pursue the professional activity; (b) economic and financial standing; (c) technical and professional ability" (PSD, Article 58(1)). The means to provide evidence for the technical ability of the company are laid down further in Annex XII of the PSD.[22] Human rights are not specifically mentioned here, but when enquiring about the capabilities for managing the supply chain, member states could ask for responsible supply chain management (PP 13). Concerning professional abilities, contracting authorities could ask if the company employed human rights specialists or other workers who can ensure compliance with social standards.

The award phase is central to the procurement process because it affects the future performance of the economic operator during the time of the contract. Under the 2004 directives, it was also possible to award a contract based on the 'lowest price only', which could lead to situation where socially responsible, but more expensive companies were legally excluded from procurement contracts. The 2014 directives state that the tender should be awarded to the "most economically advantageous tender" (PSD, Article 67(1)) (MEAT),[23] a formulation that gives more room for interpretation. The contracting authorities can assess what they regard as economically advantageous. Next to cost-effectiveness, they "may include the best price-quality ratio, which shall be assessed on the basis of criteria, including [...] social aspects" (PSD, Article 67(2))

[18] Recitals 105 and 106.

[19] Article 38(7)(a) in the CD. There is no similar provision in UD, but it allows reference to criteria under the PSD (Article 80).

[20] Article 84(3) in the UD. The CD does not contain a similar provision.

[21] Article 38 in the CD and Article 80 in the UD.

[22] Article 62 UD. No similar provision in the CD.

[23] Article 82(1) in the UD. The CD does not contain an equivalent provision.

(PP 14).[24] The CD contains a weaker wording in this respect. Article 41(2) states that the award criteria "may include, inter alia, environmental, social or innovation-related criteria" (CD, Article 41(2)). For the other directives, the MEAT assessment includes references to the overarching social clause (PSD Article 56(1)b),[25] and to the principles of transparency, non-discrimination and equal treatment (PSD, Recital 90).[26] In addition, the directives stress that the list of social award criteria is "non-exhaustive" (PSD, Recital 92).[27] Therefore, member states have a large scope for including social requirements in the award phase of the procurement process, as long as the criteria applied remain linked to the subject matter of the contract.[28] This scope can go in both directions, because many provisions in the directives also stress, not without contradictions, the importance of cost-effectiveness.[29]

The last phase of the procurement process, the contracting phase, contains three possibilities to include human rights-related provisions in national laws. First, the recitals of the directives state that the contractual conditions "might also be intended [...] to comply in substance with fundamental International Labour Organisation (ILO) Conventions" (PSD, Recital 98, para 2) (PP 15).[30] Second, Article 70 of the PSD states that contract conditions "may include [...] social or employment-related considerations" (PSD, Article 70) (PP 16).[31] Third, Article 73 of the PSD (PP 17)[32] states that member states shall give contracting authorities the possibility to terminate a public contract during its term if the economic operator was convicted for child labour or human trafficking when the contract was signed (Article 57(1) of the PSD[33]).

As this overview has shown, the 2014 public procurement directives allow for ample applications of human rights provisions by member states. In comparison to the 2004 directives on public procurement, the directives, therefore, mark a significant adjustment toward a more socially sustainable EU procurement regime. At the same time, the discretionary room is substantial as well. As the overview in Table 5.1 shows, ten out of 17 provisions are voluntary, whereas four are mandatory with discretion,[34] and only three are completely mandatory. While many of the mandatory aspects of

[24] Article 82(2) in the UD.

[25] Article 76(6) in the UD.

[26] Recital 95 in the UD. There is no similar provision in the CD.

[27] Recital 97 in the UD. There is no comparable provision in the CD.

[28] As the International Institute for Human Rights and Business (2015, p. 21) notes, the case of Concordia Bus Finland (C-513/99) clarified that non-economic criteria, such as human rights criteria, can be used as long as the criteria remain linked to the subject matter of the contract, do not give contracting authorities unrestricted freedom of choice, are expressly mentioned in the tender, and comply with the EU's fundamental freedoms.

[29] See e.g. Recital 90 and Article 67(2) in the PSD, and Recital 97 in the UD.

[30] Recital 103 in the UD and recital 65 in the CD.

[31] Article 87 in the UD and recital 64 in the CD.

[32] Article 90 in the UD and Article 44 in the CD.

[33] Article 90(b) in the UD and Article 44(b) in the CD.

[34] Provision PP 10 is only mandatory with discretion for the PSD and the CD. For the UD, this provision is voluntary.

Table 5.1 Provisions with human rights relevance in the three EU public procurement directives

No.	Aim of provision	Human rights related provision	Recital or article number			Degree of obligation	HR relevance
			PSD	UD	CD		
PP 1	Establish the social clause as a procurement principle	Member states **shall take appropriate measures** to ensure that economic operators comply with applicable social and labour law obligations established by Union law, national law, collective agreements or by international environmental, social, and labour law provisions listed in Annex X, which contains central ILO Conventions	Article 18(2)	Article 36(2)	Article 30(3)	Voluntary (to set as procurement principle)	1
PP 2	Make social clause applicable to subcontractors	As the first provision on subcontracting, this provision states that member states **should take "appropriate action"** in order to ensure that subcontractors also ensure the obligations of the social clause	Article 71(1)	Article 88(1)	Article 42(1)	Mandatory with discretion	3

(continued)

Table 5.1 (continued)

No.	Aim of provision	Human rights related provision	Recital or article number			Degree of obligation	HR relevance
PP 3	Ensuring that the social clause also applies to subcontractors by establishing joint legal liability	**If** member states provide for mechanisms of joint liability between subcontractors, the mechanisms **should** comply with the social clause	Article 71(6)a)	Article 88(6)a)	Article 42(4)a)	Voluntary	3
PP 4	Require contracting authorities to verify if there are reasons to exclude subcontractors	Contracting authorities **may** be required to verify if there are reasons to exclude subcontractors. In case of compulsory grounds for exclusion subcontractors must be excluded. In case of non-compulsory grounds for exclusion, they may be excluded	Article 71(6)b)	Article 88(6)b)	Article 42(4)b)	Voluntary	3
PP 5	Extending rules on legal liability	Member states **may** provide for more stringent liability rules under national law	Article 71(7)	88(7)	Article 42(5)	Voluntary	2

(continued)

Table 5.1 (continued)

No.	Aim of provision	Human rights related provision	Recital or article number			Degree of obligation	HR relevance
PP 6	Compliance of other entities with selection and exclusion criteria	Contractors **shall verify** that other entities comply with selection and exclusion criteria and shall exclude the entities if there are compulsory grounds for exclusion. Possibility to require replacement also in cases where there are non-compulsory grounds for exclusion	Article 63(1)	Article 79(1)	No provision	Mandatory with discretion	3
PP 7	Giving contracting authorities the possibility to use labels to ensure social requirements	Contraction authorities **may**, in technical specifications, award criteria or contract performance conditions, require a specific label as means of proof that works, services, and supplies meet required characteristics	Article 43(1)	Article 61(1)	No provision	Voluntary	1
PP 8	Providing the possibility to use labels to prove operators suitability	Member states **may** use labels for their official lists of approved economic operators. Companies on that list are presumed suitable	Article 64(1)-(4)	Article 62(1)	No provision	Voluntary	1

(continued)

Table 5.1 (continued)

No.	Aim of provision	Human rights related provision	Recital or article number			Degree of obligation	HR relevance
PP 9	Excluding companies convicted of child labour or human trafficking	Contracting authorities **shall** exclude an economic operator if they have been convicted for child labour and other forms of trafficking in human beings	Article 57(1)f	No provision	Recital 70, Article 38(4)f	Mandatory	3
PP 10	Excluding companies convicted of not paying social security contributions	Economic operators **shall** be excluded when a breach of its obligations to pay of taxes or social security contributions has been established by a judicial or administrative decision. They **may** be excluded, where the contracting authority can demonstrate the breach by any appropriate means	Recital 101, Article 57(2)-(3)	Recitals 105 and 106	Recital 70, Article 38(5)-(6)	PSD and CD: mandatory with discretion, UD: voluntary	2
PP 11	Excluding companies in breach of social or labour law obligations	Contracting authorities **may** exclude or **may be required by member states** to exclude where contracting authorities can demonstrate a violation of social or labour laws (reference to the social clause)	Article 57(4)(a)	UD—Article 80 refers to the exclusion criteria of the PSD	Article 38(7)(a)	Voluntary	3

(continued)

Table 5.1 (continued)

No.	Aim of provision	Human rights related provision	Recital or article number			Degree of obligation	HR relevance
PP 12	Rejecting abnormally low bids due to non-compliance with social or labour law	Contracting authorities **shall reject the tender**, if the tender appears to be ‘abnormally low’, because it did not comply with the social clause	Article 69(3)	Recitals 55 and 108, Article 84(3)	No provision	Mandatory	3
PP 13	Including human rights when inquiring about technical capabilities	Selection criteria **may** relate to technical and professional abilities. Here human rights could be included, e.g. By including questions about responsible supply chain management or staff members tasked to ensure the respect for human rights	Article 58(1), Annex XII	Article 62 and 80	Article 38(1)-(2)	Voluntary	1
PP 14	Including social award criteria	The award of public contracts **shall** be based on the most economically advantageous tender. The assessment of the most economically advantageous tender **may** include the best price-quality ratio, which can also include social aspects. (reference to the social clause)	Article 67(2) and Article 56(1)b, Recital 92	Article 82(2), Recital 97	No provision	Mandatory with discretion	3

(continued)

Table 5.1 (continued)

No.	Aim of provision	Human rights related provision	Recital or article number			Degree of obligation	HR relevance
PP 15	Including compliance with ILO Conventions in the contract	The contractual conditions **might** also be intended to comply in substance with fundamental ILO Conventions	Recital 98	Recital 103	Recital 65	Voluntary	2
PP 16	Including social or employment conditions in contracts	Contract conditions **may include** […] social or employment-related considerations	Article 70	Article 87	Recital 64	Voluntary	2
PP 17	Exclusion grounds can apply after the contract has been signed	Member states **shall ensure that contracting authorities have the possibility** to terminate the contract after it has been signed if the contractor was violating the mandatory exclusion criteria (e.g. child labour and human trafficking)	Article 73	Article 90	Article 44	Mandatory	3

the provisions are of high relevance for human rights, these numbers still show that the effectiveness of the human rights provisions depends on the transposition by member states.

5.1.2 Comparative Transposition of the Three Public Procurement Directives

The four member states considered in this study have transposed the public procurement directives each in their own manner. Apart from the UK, the countries used the transposition as an opportunity to conduct a general reform of their national procurement systems. This section first accounts for the laws that were adopted to transpose the directives. Then, I analyse how each of the 17 provisions that have human rights relevance were transposed by the national laws.

The UK was the first EU member state to transpose the public procurement directives. Each directive was transposed with one Statutory Instrument. Statutory Instruments are delegated legislative measures, which can be adopted by the British government promptly, and which are usually used to transpose EU directives. For the directives on public contracts and utilities, they replaced the Statutory Instruments that had been adopted for the 2004 directives on public procurement. The PSD was transposed with the Public Contracts Regulations 2015, adopted in February 2015.[35] The UD was transposed with the Utilities Contracts Regulations 2016, adopted in March 2016.[36] For the CD, which had no predecessor, a new Statutory Instrument was adopted, the Concession Contracts Regulations 2016, also adopted in March 2016.[37] All transposing laws were adopted in time. The provisions of the Statutory Instruments follow mostly, with only few deviations, the numbering of the EU directives.

The French transposition was not accomplished with one law, but with a series of legal acts that were adopted successively. The comparatively complicated process also stems from the fact that with the new EU directives, the French public procurement legislation was reorganized. Before the 2014 directives, public procurement was divided into three types of contracts: public procurement contracts, public-private partnership contracts and concession contracts, each of which was regulated by a separate set of laws (Dentons, 2016, p. 8). These regulations were repealed when the laws transposing the EU directives came into effect in April 2016. Four laws transpose the public procurement package. The PSD and the UD are taken together and transposed with two laws, *Ordonnance no 2015-899 du 23 juillet 2015 relative aux marchés publics* (Ordonnance 2015-899) and *Décret no 2016-360 du 25 mars 2016 relatif aux marchés publics* (Décret 2016-360). The CD is transposed with the *Décret no 2016-86 du 1er février 2016 relatif aux contrats de concession* (Décret

[35] SI 2015 No. 102 Public Procurement.
[36] SI 2016 No. 274 Public Procurement.
[37] SI 2016 No. 273 Public Procurement.

2016-86) and *Ordonnance no 2016-65 du 29 janvier 2016 relative aux contrats de concession* (Ordonnance 2016-65).

The German government transposed the procurement package before the deadline by adopting five legal acts. The core of the new procurement rules, which applies to all three directives, is laid down in the Act against Restraints of Competition, the *Gesetz gegen Wettbewerbsbeschränkungen* (GWB). This law has been updated with the new part 4, which contains the transposing provisions for the EU public procurement package.[38] The more detailed rules have been transposed with four German regulations. The *Vergabeverordnung* (VgV), specifies the rules for services and supply contracts. Procurement rules for public works are governed by the *Vergabe- und Vertragsordnung für Bauleistungen* (VOB/A). The rules for utilities contracts are specified in the *Sektorenverordnung* (SektVO), while the award of concession contracts is subject to the *Konzessionsvergabeverordnung* (KonzVgV).

Before the 2014 public procurement directives, Danish governments did not transpose EU procurement rules with a regular transposition law. Instead, they merely passed a law, which stated that the EU procurement directives would directly become Danish law. The Danish Procurement Act of 2015 diverted from this practice and introduced a national Danish procurement regime that provides for national rules for procurement contracts below the national threshold (Kroman Reumert, 2016). However, this new regime applies only to the PSD, which was transposed with a new Contract Law (*Udbudsloven*), adopted on 19 November 2015. For tenders that are below the EU threshold but that have a clear cross-border interest, the Danish government adopted a separate executive, which is not relevant for this analysis.[39] Two governmental orders transposed the other two directives. Order No. 1624 of December 2015[40] transposed the UD and governmental order No. 1625 of December 2015 transposed the CD.[41] In both of these orders, the first article states that the rules of the respective EU directive apply. This follows the former Danish practice, whereby the provisions from the EU directives directly become Danish law. Unless stated otherwise, the Danish transpositions of the UD and the CD are thus identical to the provisions in the EU directives. What does this mean for the assessment of these transpositions? In these cases, I consider all mandatory provisions as transposed. Voluntary provisions that state the possibility to oblige contracting authorities are considered as cases of *discretion-passed-on*. Voluntary provisions that address member states (e.g. 'member states *may* do X ...') are considered as not transposed.

---

[38]With the *Gesetz zur Modernisierung des Vergaberechts (Vergaberechtsmodernisierungsgesetz—VergRModG)*, adopted on 17 February 2016.

[39]The *Law Bekendtgørelse om annoncering af offentlige indkøb under tærskelværdierne med klar grænseoverskridende interesse og om anvendelsen af elektroniske kommunikationsmidler i udbud efter udbudslovens afsnit II og III* was published on 17 December 2015 (Number: 1643).

[40]*Bekendtgørelse Om fremgangsma˚derne ved indga˚else af kontrakter inden for vandog energiforsyning, transport samt posttjenester*, adopted on 15 December 2015.

[41]*Bekendtgørelse Om tildeling af koncessionskontrakter*, adopted 15 December 2015.

5.1.2.1 PP 1: The Social Clause as a Procurement Principle

The social clause is the central human rights-related provision in the EU public procurement directives, as it requires member states to take appropriate measures to ensure that economic operators comply with central social and labour law obligations. The EU PSD lists the social clause, Article 18(2), under the principles of procurement. In the UK transposition law, the corresponding article on procurement principles in the UK Public Contracts Regulations makes no mentions of social law but stresses only the market-based principles of non-discrimination and fair competition. The same can be observed in the cases of the UK transposing laws of the CD and the UD, where the relevant articles[42] do not contain a social clause. In all British transposition laws, the social clause is only included with regard to specific phases of the procurement process (see below), but not under the procurement principles. Therefore, I do not regard the social clause to be transposed as a procurement principle in the UK transposition law.

In the French laws, the social clause is not explicitly mentioned in Article 1 of Ordonnance 2015-899, which specifies the procurement principles.[43] Both the Décret 2016-360, transposing the UD, and Ordonnance 2016-65, transposing the CD do not establish the social clause as a procurement principle either.[44] Therefore, I do not regard this provision as transposed for all three French transposition laws.

In the German transposition laws, procurement principles are laid down in § 97 of the GWB, where, under point (3), it is stated that social aspects will be considered. Due to the reference to social aspects in the procurement principles, the clause is regarded as transposed for Germany. The Danish transposition is similar to the French. The social clause is not mentioned as a general principle of procurement, but only with regard to the provisions on non-compulsory grounds for exclusion (PP 11), abnormally low offers (PP 12), and awards of contracts (PP 14). Therefore, following the reasoning laid down above, the provision is considered as not transposed. The situation for the UD and the CD is different. Since for these two directives all EU provisions directly become Danish law, the social clause becomes a procurement principle for concession and utility contracts, which is why I regard the provisions as transposed.

---

[42]Regulations 8 and 30–35 in the SI 2016 No. 273 and Reg. 36 in the SI 2016 No. 274.

[43]Articles 30 and 38 of Ordonnance 2015-899 state that the nature and scope of the demand for a public tender as well as the conditions for executing the procurement may take social concerns into account.

[44]Décret 2016-360 does not mention the social clause as a general principal either, it only contains the wording in Article 60, which deals with abnormally low tenders (see below). With respect to the CD, Ordonnance 2016–65 states in Articles 27 and 33 that, like Ordonnance 2015-899, the nature and scope of the demand for a concession contract as well as the conditions for executing the concessions contract may take social concerns into account.

5.1.2.2 PP 2: Application of Social Clause for Subcontractors

The EU procurement directives also extended the application of the social clause to subcontractors of the economic operators, as Article 71(1)[45] of the PSD states. This possibility is highly relevant from a human rights perspective because it would enable member states to extend their national human rights legislation extraterritorially. In the UK transposition laws, the provisions that deal with subcontracting[46] do not mention the social clause. Since social concerns are not at all mentioned in the provisions that deal with subcontracting, I consider this clause as not transposed for the UK.

The French transposition of this clause is more complicated. The articles concerned with subcontracting in Décret 2016-360 (Article 133–Article 137) and Ordonnance 2015-899 (Article 62–Article 63) do not contain direct references to the social clause. The only social provisions regarding sub-contractors deal with abnormally low tenders. Article 60 of Décret 2016-360 states that main contractors must justify abnormally low tenders, adding that with respect to the public sector, cases where the main contractor "plans to subcontract" (Article 60I, Décret 2016-360) are included. This is clarified in the applicable Article 62 of Ordonnance 2015-899, which states that if the price for the subcontractor seems abnormally low, the economic operator should deliver precisions and justifications. If the contracting authority still deems the price for subcontracting to be abnormally low, it must either reject the offer or not accept the subcontracting. As Article 60 of Décret 2016-360 states, social and labour concerns can also be taken into account. Therefore, instead of establishing a direct legal link between subcontractors and the social clause, the French legislation merely considers cases in which the subcontracted part of the contract is abnormally low. For the analytical assessment, this transposition poses a challenge. On the one hand, the assessment of the abnormally low offer should take into account social and labour regulations "in force at the place where the performance is executed" (Article 60, Décret 2016-360). At the same time, a subcontract does not necessarily have to be abnormally low, for there to be social or labour concerns. However, the requirement of the directive was to 'take appropriate action' and the French legislator clearly sought to include social concerns in subcontracts by addressing abnormally low tenders. Therefore, I regard this provision as transposed. For the CD, the assessment is simpler. The matter of subcontracting is mentioned in none of the transposing laws, which means that the provision can be regarded as not transposed.

The German GWB addresses the application of the social clause for subcontractors in the procurement principles as well. § 97(4) stipulates that the above mentioned § 97(3), which transposes the social clause, also applies to sub-contractors.[47] Since

---

[45]Article 42(1) in the CD and Article 88(1) in the UD.

[46]Reg. 71 in the Public Contracts Regulations, Reg. 42 in the Concession Contracts Regulations and Reg. 87 in the Utilities Contracts Regulations.

[47]Moreover, § 36(4) of the VgV also contains a provision requiring subcontractors to respect social concerns.

the more specific regulations do not entail any further connections between subcontracting and the social clause, I regard this provision as transposed, too. The Danish transposition is similar to the French case. The provision under § 169 para. 3 addresses abnormally low tenders (see PP 12) and includes subcontractors as well. It states that offers, which are abnormally low because subcontractors have breached the social clause, must be rejected. Thereby, following the same reasoning as in the French transposition, I consider this clause as transposed.

5.1.2.3 PP 3: Legal Liability Between Contractors and Subcontractors

As was mentioned in Sect. 5.1, Article 71(6) of the PSD[48] lists two voluntary measures of how the application of the social clause can be ensured. The first proposes to include the social clause in mechanisms of joint liability between contractors and subcontractors if member states provide for them. This clause, which exists in all three directives, is not transposed in any of the UK laws. The same can be observed regarding the French transposition. The French laws, including those transposing the CD, contain no provisions laying down joint liability between contractors and subcontractors. The German transposing laws mention a joint legal liability between main contractors and subcontractors only with regard to the economic and financial capability. A further-reaching legal liability that would become relevant in the case of human rights abuses is not provided for. Therefore, the German transposition laws do not transpose this provision either. The same can be observed for the Danish transposition laws, which do not address the legal liability between contractors and subcontractors. For the Danish transposition of the UD and the CD the provision is also not considered transposed, even though the directive provisions directly apply to Danish law. The mere possibility to provide for joint liability between contractors and subcontractors, as mentioned in these directives, does not create such liability under Danish law.

5.1.2.4 PP 4: Verification of Subcontractors

The second voluntary measure mentioned by Article 71(6) of the PSD[49] recommends that member states may require contracting authorities to verify if there are compulsory or non-compulsory grounds for the exclusion of subcontractors. If member states include such a provision, compulsory grounds for exclusion (e.g. conviction for child labour) *must* lead to a replacement of the subcontractor, while non-compulsory grounds for exclusion (e.g. breach of the social clause) *may* lead to a replacement. This provision is transposed word-by-word in all three British transposing laws,[50]

[48] Article 88(6) in the UD and Article 42(4) in the CD.

[49] Article 88(6) in the UD and Article 42(4) in the CD.

[50] Regulation 71(8) in the Public Contracts Regulations, Regulation 42(7) in the Concession Contracts Regulations and Regulation 87(8) in the Utilities Contracts Regulations.

which means that the discretion, namely if verification is required, and if merely compulsory or also non-compulsory grounds for exclusions should be taken into consideration, is being passed on to the contracting authorities. The French transposition law, however, does not transpose this provision at all. Apart from considering abnormally low tenders (see above), the four transposing laws do not impose any more conditions on subcontracting. The German transposition, on the other hand, does address this issue. In the German VgV, § 36(5) states that contracting authorities must verify if there are mandatory or non-mandatory grounds for exclusion. The provision goes on to say that if there are mandatory grounds for exclusion, the subcontractor *must* be replaced, while in the case of non-mandatory grounds for exclusion the subcontractor *may* be replaced. The provision to require contracting authorities to verify if there are grounds to exclude subcontractors is voluntary, which is why the German mandatory requirement of § 36(5) VgV is a case of over-transposition. The Danish law also addresses the verification of subcontractors in § 177 of the *Udbudsloven*. Para. 5 of this article is almost identical to the respective provision in the PSD, which means that verification of subcontractors is optional for contracting authorities. However, if the verification takes place and grounds for exclusion have been established, the subcontractor must be excluded, regardless if the grounds for exclusion are mandatory (e.g. child labour) or voluntary (e.g. breach of the social clause). This transposition goes further than the minimum required by the Directive, which is why I consider this as a case of over-transposition.[51] For the CD, the provision is addressed by § 5 of order no. 1625, which includes an identical clause.

5.1.2.5 PP 5: More Stringent Liability Rules for Subcontractors

The issue of legal liability of subcontractors is addressed again with Article 71(7) in the Public Contracts Directive, which mentions the option for member states to provide for more stringent liability requirements.[52] The UK Public Contracts Regulation stresses under Regulation 71(2)[53] that providing information about the subcontractor does not affect the liability of the main contractor, but the liability is not strengthened. Therefore, for the UK this voluntary provision is considered to be not transposed. Regarding the French transposition of this provision, none of the four French transposing laws mentions any strengthening of legal liability. Article 62 of Ordonnance 2015-899 only states that a contractor can subcontract "under its responsibility" (Article 62, Ordonnance 2015-899), but does not go further to extend the liability. The same can be said for the German and Danish transposition laws, which do not mention a strengthening of legal liability.

[51] The same applies to the transposition of the UD. Executive order No. 1624 refers in § 10 to Udbudsloven § 177 para. 5.

[52] Articles 42(5) in the CD, and 88(7) in the UD.

[53] Reg. 42(2) in the Concessions Contracts Regulations and Reg. 87(2) in the Utilities Contracts Regulations.

5.1.2.6 PP 6: Compliance of 'Other Entities'

Article 63(1) of the PSD[54] goes beyond subcontractors and regulates the compliance of other entities on which economic operators might rely. The provision is mandatory and prescribes to verify the compliance with the selection and exclusion criteria, but it contains discretion regarding the question when other entities must be replaced. Similar to provision PP 4, they stipulate that member states must require the replacement, if there are compulsory grounds for exclusion (e.g. conviction for child labour), while the replacement is optional if there are non-compulsory reasons for exclusion (e.g. breach of the social clause). The UK transposition takes, once again, a copy-out approach to this provision. Regulation 63(4) is an almost word-by-word transposition of the mandatory requirement to verify 'other entities'. Regulation 63(5) states that the replacement of other entities is mandatory if there are compulsory grounds for exclusion, while in cases of non-mandatory grounds for exclusion, the decision is left to the contracting authority. Therefore, the UK's transposition of this clause is a case of discretion-passed-on. In the French transposition laws, Article 48 II refers to the issue of other entities. The clause merely states that economic operators can require that such 'other entities' and the economic operator are jointly responsible. The verification requirement, however, is not transposed. For the German transposition, the same article in the VgV applies (§ 36(5) VgV) as for the verifications of subcontractors (see PP 4). Therefore, this provision is regarded as transposed. Denmark also aligns the transposition of this clause with the verification of subcontractors. § 144 para. 4-5 in *Udbudsloven* also states that the contracting authority must verify if the 'other entities' comply with the exclusion criteria. If grounds for exclusion are found, replacement is mandatory, regardless if the grounds for exclusion are compulsory or non-compulsory. Like provision PP 4, this is a case of Danish over-transposition.

5.1.2.7 PP 7: Use of Social Labels

The next cross-cutting clause is a voluntary provision that concerns the use of labels. The directives state in Article 43(1)[55] that labels can be used to ensure social requirements when contracting authorities buy works, supplies or services. In the UK transposition laws, Regulations 43 and 61 in the Public Contracts and Utilities Regulations contain almost word-by-word transpositions of this clause. Since the UK law leaves it up to the contracting authorities to decide if they wish to use labels, this is a case of discretion-passed-on. The situation is similar for the French transposition. In Décret 2016-360, Article 10 contains a word-by-word transposition, hence this is also a case of discretion-passed-on. The German transposition is similar, because § 34 VgV, § 7a EU(6) VOB/A, and § 31 SektVO respectively state that contracting authorities can rely on labels. In the Danish law, § 46 also refers to the use of labels. Even

[54] Article 79(1) in the UD. The CD does not contain a similar clause.

[55] Article 61(1) in the UD. The CD does not deal with labels.

though social labels are not mentioned, the wording allows for any labels that meet the technical criteria. Therefore, this is also a case of discretion-passed-on.

5.1.2.8 PP 8: Use of Official Lists of Approved Economic Operators

As the last overarching provision of the public procurement directives, Article 64(1)-(4) in the PSD[56] states that member states may use labels for their official lists of approved economic operators. In the UK transposition, this clause was transposed similar to Article 43(1) on the use of labels and is also regarded as a case of discretion-passed-on. The same verdict applies to France and Germany. The French law passes the discretion on with Article 54 of Décret 2016-360, while the German law does the same with § 48(8) in the Vg, § 6bEU in the VOB/A and § 31 in the SektVO. The Danish laws do not transpose this provision because the *Udbudsloven* § 156 merely states that the responsible minister may establish rules on the use of lists.

5.1.2.9 PP 9: Exclusion Because of Child Labour and Human Trafficking

Regarding the exclusion phase, the EU directives state that economic operators shall be excluded if they have been convicted of child labour and other forms of human trafficking. This provision, which does not exist in the UD, is mandatory without discretion.[57] It is part of the compulsory grounds for exclusion the directive refers to in other situations. In the UK transposition laws,[58] the applicable regulations simply refer back to the original articles in the EU directives, and thereby transpose them correctly. The French transposition laws transpose this clause, too. The provision is transposed with Article 45 of ordonnance 2015-899 for the PSD and the UD and with Article 39 of ordonnance 2016-65 for the CD. In the German GWB, § 123(1) mentions only human trafficking, but not child labour, which is why this provision is not regarded as transposed. The Danish legislators transposed this provision with § 135 para. 1 (6) of the *Udbudsloven*. For the CD, § 3 of executive order 1625 refers back to this article, thereby also transposing this provision.

5.1.2.10 PP 10: Exclusion for not Paying Social Security Contributions

The provision in the directives which regulates the exclusion of corporations that did not pay social security contributions has one mandatory and one non-mandatory

---

[56] Article 62(1) in the UD.

[57] Article 57(3) states that derogations are possible for reasons of public health or where exclusion would be disproportionate. For this study, this exemption clause will not be considered as discretion.

[58] Regulation 57(1) in the Public Contracts Regulations and Regulation 38(8) in the Concessions Contracts Regulations.

part. It is obligatory that contracting authorities exclude economic operators, where a judicial or administrative decision has confirmed that social security contributions have not been paid. Alternatively, member states may determine that it would be sufficient to exclude an economic operator if the contracting authority determined the non-payment of social security obligations "by any appropriate means" (Article 57(2), PSD). The UK regulations transpose this clause, once again, almost word-by-word, leaving it up to the contracting authorities to exclude companies that did not pay taxes or social security contributions, but which have not (yet) been confirmed by a judicial or administrative decision. The provision in the UD, which is not mandatory because it is only mentioned in the recitals, is not transposed by the UK Utilities Contracts Regulations. Therefore, I regard the provisions as transposed in the British case. The French laws transpose this clause as well, but also make use of the non-mandatory part. Article 45 2° of Ordonnance 2015-899 states that all companies that did not pay social security obligations are to be excluded, without requiring a judicial or administrative decision. For the provision in the CD[59] the same transposition is achieved with Article 39 2° of Ordonnance 2016-65. Therefore, the French laws for this clause are considered as cases of over-transposition. The same can also be detected in the German laws. In the GWB, § 123(4) clearly states that the exclusion is mandatory in both cases, which is why this provision can be regarded as over-transposed. The Danish transposition law handles this provision differently because they do not differentiate between the kind of verdict, but between the amounts of contributions that have not been paid. § 135 para. 3 of the *Udbudsloven* states that companies that have DKK 100,000 or more in unpaid taxes or social security contribution must be excluded. § 137 (7) of the same law states that for amounts below DKK 100,000, the contracting authority may decide if the company should be excluded. Both provisions speak of situations where taxes or contributions have not been paid under Danish law or the law of the country where the company is established, which suggests that a judicial or administrative decision has confirmed the non-payment. The voluntary part of the EU provision, which refers to proof by any appropriate means, is not addressed. To decide if the mandatory part of the provision is transposed is difficult because not all cases of non-payment are strictly sanctioned. However, since the threshold was set very low, I consider the provision as transposed.[60]

5.1.2.11 PP 11: Exclusion for Violating the Social Clause

A highly relevant human rights provision in the procurement directives concerns the possibility of public authorities to exclude economic operators if they have violated the social clause. This provision is non-compulsory, as it only suggests that

[59]Recital 70 and Article 38(5)-(6).

[60]The same applies to the transposition of the CD. Order No. 1624 § 10 and order 1625 § 3 refer to § 135 para. 3 and § 137 (7) *Udbudsloven*. The transposition of the same clause in the UD is considered as discretion-passed-on, because the directive provision is voluntary.

> [c]ontracting authorities **may exclude or may be required by Member States to exclude** from participation in a procurement procedure any economic operator [...] where the contracting authority can demonstrate by any appropriate means a violation of [the social clause]. (PSD, Article 57(4), emphasis added)[61]

Once more, the UK regulations[62] transpose the provision almost literally, passing on the discretion to the contracting authorities. In the French transposition laws, the grounds for exclusion are determined in Article 45 of Ordonnance 2015-899 for the PSD, and in Article 39 in Ordonnance 2016-65 for the CD. None of these articles mentions the social clause. Therefore the French transposition laws do not transpose this provision. The German laws pass on the discretion to the contracting authorities. The violation of social and labour laws is only listed in § 124 of the GWB, the provision listing optional grounds for exclusion. In the Danish *Udbudsloven*, § 137 addresses exclusions for violating the social clause, which contains a copy of the text of the social clause. The provision is listed under the voluntary grounds for exclusion, thereby also passing on the discretion to the contracting authorities.[63]

5.1.2.12 PP 12: Rejection of Abnormally Low Tenders

The last exclusion clause,[64] also a compulsory ground for exclusion, sets down that tenders which are 'abnormally low' because they did comply with the social clause, must be rejected. This requirement is correctly transposed by the UK laws in Regulation 69(5) of the Public Contracts Regulations and with Regulation 84(5) of the Utilities Contracts Regulations. The French laws also correctly transpose this clause with Article 62 in Ordonnance 899 and Article 60 in Décret 2016-360. The same can be said for the German transposition because § 60 in the VgV, § 16d EU(1) in the VOB/A, and § 54 in the SektVO transpose this clause correctly. A correct transposition can also be observed under Danish law. In the *Udbudsloven*, § 169 contains a copy of the text of the social clause and states that exclusion is mandatory if offers are abnormally low because violations of the social clause have occurred.

5.1.2.13 PP 13: Inclusion of Human Rights in Selection Criteria

When contracting authorities select a short-list of capable companies, they take into consideration technical and professional abilities.[65] In this respect, member states

---

[61] Article 80 in the UD (with reference to the exclusion criteria of the PSD), and Article 38(7)(a) in the CD.

[62] Regulation 57(8) in the Public Contracts Regulations, Regulation 80 in the Utilities Contracts Regulations, and Regulation 38(16)(a) in the Concessions Contracts Regulations.

[63] The same applies to the transposition of the UD and the CD. Order 1624 § 10 and in order 1625 § 3 refer to § 137 *Udbudsloven*.

[64] Article 69(3) in the PSD, and Article 84(3) in the UD. The CD does not contain a similar clause.

[65] Article 58(1) in the PSD, Articles 62 an 80 in the UD, and Article 38 (1)-(2) in the CD.

can include human rights-related criteria, for example, those that relate to responsible supply chain management or specially trained staff members. However, none of the transposing laws in the four countries considered make use of this option.

5.1.2.14 PP 14: Possibility to Include Social Award Criteria

The award phase, arguably the most important procurement phase, contains one critical human rights-related provision, which has one mandatory and one discretionary part. Article 67(2) of the PSD[66] requires that procurement awards must be based on the most economically advantageous tender. In assessing what constitutes the most economically advantageous tender, social aspects may be taken into account, which gives member states discretion for the transposition. The CD does not contain provisions on the most economically advantageous tender. The applicable regulations[67] in the UK laws include only literal transpositions, which, again, pass on the discretion to the contracting authorities. The French laws do not copy the directive text but arrive at the same conclusion with their provision. Article 62 of Décret 2016-360 determines that the most economically advantageous tender can either be based solely on price or cost, or on a plurality of criteria, which can also include social aspects. Thus, the choice is left to the French contracting authorities. Under German law, § 127 GWB specifies that contracts should be awarded to the most economically advantageous tender, which should be based on the best price-quality ratio. The provision then states that when determining this ratio, social aspects can be taken into consideration. This is confirmed in § 58 VgV, § 16d EU VOB/A, and § 52 SektVO. Therefore, the discretion to include social award criteria is passed on.[68] The Danish transposition also passes on the discretion to the contracting authorities. §159 para. 7 of the *Udbudsloven*, which regulates the procedure of awarding contracts, copies the wording of the social clause, and leaves it optional if these social criteria are applied. § 162 para. 3 on the award criteria again states that social criteria may be considered.

5.1.2.15 PP 15: Inclusion of ILO Conventions in the Contract

The first provision that addresses human rights-related considerations in the contracting phase can be found in Recital 98 of the PSD,[69] which suggests including in the contractual conditions the intention to comply in substance with fundamental

[66] Article 82 in the UD. The CD does not contain a similar provision.

[67] Regulation 67(3) in the Public Contracts Regulations and Regulation 82 in the Utilities Contracts Regulation.

[68] Interestingly, § 152 of the GWB provides the possibility to consider social aspects in the award of concession contracts, even though the CD does not require or suggest this. However, this will not be considered by this analysis.

[69] Recital 103 in the UD, and Recital 65 in the CD.

ILO Conventions. This is a voluntary provision since recitals are *per se* not binding. The French, British, and German transposition do not make use of this option. The Danish transposition law, on the other hand, does include a reference to ILO Conventions. As was noted with regard to provision PP 14, the provision on social award criteria (§ 159 para. 7) includes the text of the social clause. The social clause refers to Appendix X of the NFR-Directive, which includes a list of the central ILO conventions. Therefore, the Danish law suggests to the contracting authorities to take ILO conventions into account, whereby this provision is considered as a case of discretion-passed-on.

5.1.2.16 PP 16: Inclusion of Social or Employment Conditions in Contracts

As a second human rights-related provision in the contracting phase, Article 70 of the PSD[70] specifies that contract conditions may also include social or employment-related considerations. The UK regulations transpose this provision for the PSD and the UD in a literal fashion,[71] passing on the discretion to the contracting authorities. For the CD, where the clause is only listed in the recitals, the provision is not transposed by the UK laws. Under French law, Article 38 of Ordonnance 2015-899 transposes this word by word, thus leaving it up to the contracting authorities if they wish to include it. Regarding the provision in the CD,[72] Article 33 of Ordonnance 2016-65 transposes the provision similarly. The German law transposes this voluntary provision for all directives with § 128(2) of the GWB, giving contracting authorities the possibility to incorporate social or employment-related clauses in the contracts, also passing on the discretion. The Danish *Udbudsloven* also takes up the possibility of this clause. § 176 states that the terms of the contract may include social considerations, thereby passing on the discretion to the contracting authorities.

5.1.2.17 PP 17: Application of Exclusion Criteria After the Contract Has Been Signed

The last human rights-related provision of the public procurement directives addresses the respect for human rights after the procurement contract has been signed. Article 57(1)f of the PSD[73] stipulates that economic operators convicted of child labour or human trafficking shall be excluded (see PP 9). Member states are required to provide contracting authorities with the possibility to apply this clause

[70] Article 87 in the UD and Recital 64 in the CD.

[71] Regulation 70 in the Public Contracts Regulations and Regulation 86 in the Utilities Contracts Regulation.

[72] Recital 64.

[73] See Article 57(1)f of the PSD, and 38(4)f in the CD. There are no similar provision in the UD.

also after the contract has been signed, as Article 73 of the PSD states.[74] Under UK law, this mandatory provision is transposed in Regulation 73 of the Public Contracts Regulations, Regulation 89 of the Utilities Contracts Regulations, and Regulation 44 of the Concession Contracts Regulations. All three state that the exclusion criteria can also be applied after the contract has been signed. The French laws transpose this provision with Article 49 of Ordonnance 2015-899, which states that contracting authorities can terminate the contract if such offences are revealed after the contract has been signed. Similarly, Article 43 of Ordonnance 2016-65 transposes the provision in the CD.[75] The German laws foresee under § 133(1) of the GWB that contracts can be cancelled after they have been signed if, at the time of the awarding of the contract, grounds for exclusion under § 123(1)-(4) existed. However, since § 123 only deals with human trafficking and does not include child labour, this provision cannot be considered to be transposed completely. The Danish law transposes this provision in a straightforward manner. § 147 para. 3 in the *Udbudsloven*,[76] which deals with changing selected candidates, refers to the compulsory grounds for exclusion (§ 135), which also includes provisions on child labour and human trafficking.

5.1.3 Overview of Transposition Results

The comparison between the transpositions of the UK, France, Germany, and Denmark shows not only different overall transposition scores, but it also reveals different approaches to how the directives have been transposed into national law. Table 5.2 gives an overview of the transposition outcomes for all four countries.

Based on the transposition outcomes I determined above, I calculate a human rights score for each country. As I explain in Chap. 4, a country receives more points on the human rights scale, if more voluntary provisions were transposed. If a directive provision is correctly transposed, the human rights value of this provision is allocated to the member state. In cases of non-transposition, no points are allocated. For discretion-passed-on countries receive the double human rights score and in cases of over-transposition, four times the human rights score is allocated to the member state. Table 5.3 shows the transposition outcome in combination with the human rights score.

Tables 5.2 and 5.3 show the differences between the four national transpositions of the public procurement directives. The UK chose a pragmatic transposition approach, having the highest number of cases where the discretion was passed on to the contracting authorities. None of the provisions was over-transposed, whereby the UK stuck to the British tradition to transpose only the required minimum of EU rules. For the most part, British legislators copied the directive provisions without making

[74] Article 90 in the UD and Article 44 in the CD.

[75] Recital 70 and Article 38(4) f.

[76] Section 16 in the Danish executive order No. 1624 on utilities, and § 7(2) in the executive order No. 1625 on concessions.

Table 5.2 Transposition outcomes for the public procurement directives

Number	Directive	Name of provision	Degree of obligation	UK	France	Germany	Denmark
PP 1	PSD	Social clause as a procurement principle	Voluntary (to set as procurement principle)	No transposition	No transposition	Over-transposition	No transposition
	UD			No transposition	No transposition	Over-transposition	Over-transposition
	CS			No transposition	No transposition	Over-transposition	Over-transposition
PP 2	PSD	Application of social clause for subcontractors	Mandatory with discretion	No transposition	Transposition	Transposition	Transposition
	UD			No transposition	Transposition	Transposition	Transposition
	CS			No transposition	No transposition	Transposition	Transposition
PP 3	PSD	Legal liability between contractors and subcontractors	Voluntary	No transposition	No transposition	No transposition	No transposition
	UD			No transposition	No transposition	No transposition	No transposition
	CS			No transposition	No transposition	No transposition	No transposition
PP 4	PSD	Verification of subcontractors	Voluntary	Discretion passed on	No transposition	Over-transposition	Over-transposition
	UD			Discretion passed on	No transposition	Over-transposition	Over-transposition
	CS			Discretion passed on	No transposition	Over-transposition	Over-transposition
PP 5	PSD	More stringent liability rules for subcontractors	Voluntary	No transposition	No transposition	No transposition	No transposition
	UD			No transposition	No transposition	No transposition	No transposition
	CS			No transposition	No transposition	No transposition	No transposition
PP 6	PSD	Compliance of 'other entities'	Mandatory with discretion	Discretion passed on	No transposition	Transposition	Over-transposition
	UD			Discretion passed on	No transposition	Transposition	Transposition

(continued)

Table 5.2 (continued)

Number	Directive	Name of provision	Degree of obligation	UK	France	Germany	Denmark
PP 7	PSD	Use of social labels	Voluntary	Discretion passed on	Discretion passed on	Discretion passed on	Discretion passed on
	UD			Discretion passed on	Discretion passed on	Discretion passed on	Discretion passed on
PP 8	PSD	Use of official lists of approved economic operators	Voluntary	Discretion passed on	Discretion passed on	Discretion passed on	No transposition
	UD			Discretion passed on	Discretion passed on	Discretion passed on	Discretion passed on
PP 9	PSD	Exclusion because of child labour and human trafficking	Mandatory	Transposition	Transposition	No transposition	Transposition
	CS			Transposition	Transposition	No transposition	Transposition
PP 10	PSD	Exclusion for not paying social security contributions	Mandatory with discr.	Discretion passed on	Over-transposition	Over-transposition	Transposition
	UD		Voluntary	No transposition	Over-transposition	Over-transposition	Discretion passed on
	CS		Mandatory with discr.	Discretion passed on	Over-transposition	Over-transposition	Transposition
PP 11	PSD	Exclusion for violating the social clause	Voluntary	Discretion passed on	No transposition	Discretion passed on	Discretion passed on

(continued)

Table 5.2 (continued)

Number	Directive	Name of provision	Degree of obligation	UK	France	Germany	Denmark
	UD			Discretion passed on	No transposition	Discretion passed on	Discretion passed on
	CS			Discretion passed on	No transposition	Discretion passed on	Discretion passed on
PP 12	PSD	Rejection of abnormally low tenders	Mandatory	Transposition	Transposition	Transposition	Transposition
	UD			Transposition	Transposition	Transposition	Transposition
PP 13	PSD	Inclusion of human rights in selection criteria	Voluntary	No transposition	No transposition	No transposition	No transposition
	UD			No transposition	No transposition	No transposition	No transposition
	CS			No transposition	No transposition	No transposition	No transposition
PP 14	PSD	Possibility to include social award criteria	Mandatory with discretion	Discretion passed on	Discretion passed on	Discretion passed on	Discretion passed on
	UD			Discretion passed on	Discretion passed on	Discretion passed on	Transposition
PP 15	PSD	Inclusion of ILO Conventions in the contract	Voluntary	No transposition	No transposition	No transposition	Discretion passed on
	UD			No transposition	No transposition	No transposition	Discretion passed on

(continued)

Table 5.2 (continued)

Number	Directive	Name of provision	Degree of obligation	UK	France	Germany	Denmark
	CS			No transposition	No transposition	No transposition	Discretion passed on
PP 16	PSD	Inclusion of social or employment conditions in contracts	Voluntary	Discretion passed on	Discretion passed on	Discretion passed on	Discretion passed on
	UD			Discretion passed on	Discretion passed on	Discretion passed on	Discretion passed on
	CS			No transposition	Discretion passed on	Discretion passed on	Discretion passed on
PP 17	PSD	Application of exclusion criteria after contract has been signed	Mandatory	Transposition	Transposition	No transposition	Transposition
	UD			Transposition	Transposition	No transposition	Transposition
	CS			Transposition	Transposition	No transposition	Transposition

Table 5.3 Transposition outcomes and human rights scores for the public procurement directives

Number	Directive	HR relevance	UK		France		Germany		Denmark	
			Transposition outcome	HR score	Transposition outcome	HR score	Transposition outcome	HR score	Transposition outcome	HR score
PP 1	PSD	1	No transposition	0	No transposition	0	Over-transposition	4	No transposition	0
	UD	1	No transposition	0	No transposition	0	Over-transposition	4	Over-transposition	4
	CS	1	No transposition	0	No transposition	0	Over-transposition	4	Over-transposition	4
PP 2	PSD	3	No transposition	0	Transposition	3	Transposition	3	Transposition	3
	UD	3	No transposition	0	Transposition	3	Transposition	3	Transposition	3
	CS	3	No transposition	0	No transposition	0	Transposition	3	Transposition	3
PP 3	PSD	3	No transposition	0	No transposition	0	No transposition	0	No transposition	0
	UD	3	No transposition	0	No transposition	0	No transposition	0	No transposition	0
	CS	3	No transposition	0	No transposition	0	No transposition	0	No transposition	0
PP 4	PSD	3	Discr. passed on	6	No transposition	0	Over-transposition	12	Over-transposition	12
	UD	3	Discr. passed on	6	No transposition	0	Over-transposition	12	Over-transposition	12

(continued)

Table 5.3 (continued)

Number	Directive	HR relevance	UK		France		Germany		Denmark	
			Transposition outcome	HR score	Transposition outcome	HR score	Transposition outcome	HR score	Transposition outcome	HR score
	CS	3	Discr. passed on	6	No transposition	0	Over-transposition	12	Over-transposition	12
PP 5	PSD	2	No transposition	0	No transposition	0	No transposition	0	No transposition	0
	UD	2	No transposition	0	No transposition	0	No transposition	0	No transposition	0
	CS	2	No transposition	0	No transposition	0	No transposition	0	No transposition	0
PP 6	PSD	3	Discr. passed on	6	No transposition	0	Transposition	3	Over-transposition	12
	UD	3	Discr. passed on	6	No transposition	0	Transposition	3	Transposition	3
PP 7	PSD	1	Discr. passed on	2	Discr. passed on	2	Discr. passed on	2	Discr. passed on	2
	UD	1	Discr. passed on	2	Discr. passed on	2	Discr. passed on	2	Discr. passed on	2
PP 8	PSD	1	Discr. passed on	2	Discr. passed on	2	Discr. passed on	2	No transposition	0
	UD	1	Discr. passed on	2	Discr. passed on	2	Discr. passed on	2	Discr. passed on	2

(continued)

Table 5.3 (continued)

Number	Directive	HR relevance	UK		France		Germany		Denmark	
			Transposition outcome	HR score	Transposition outcome	HR score	Transposition outcome	HR score	Transposition outcome	HR score
PP 9	PSD	3	Transposition	3	Transposition	3	No transposition	3	Transposition	3
	CS	3	Transposition	3	Transposition	3	No transposition	3	Transposition	3
PP 10	PSD	2	Discr. passed on	4	Over-transposition	8	Over-transposition	8	Transposition	2
	UD	2	No transposition	0	Over-transposition	8	Over-transposition	8	Discr. passed on	4
	CS	2	Discr. passed on	4	Over-transposition	8	Over-transposition	8	Transposition	2
PP 11	PSD	3	Discr. passed on	6	No transposition	0	Discr. passed on	6	Discr. passed on	6
	UD	3	Discr. passed on	6	No transposition	0	Discr. passed on	6	Discr. passed on	6
	CS	3	Discr. passed on	6	No transposition	0	Discr. passed on	6	Discr. passed on	6
PP 12	PSD	3	Transposition	3	Transposition	3	Transposition	3	Transposition	3
	UD	3	Transposition	3	Transposition	3	Transposition	3	Transposition	3
PP 13	PSD	1	No transposition	0	No transposition	0	No transposition	1	No transposition	0
	UD	1	No transposition	0	No transposition	0	No transposition	1	No transposition	0

(continued)

Table 5.3 (continued)

Number	Directive	HR relevance	UK		France		Germany		Denmark	
			Transposition outcome	HR score	Transposition outcome	HR score	Transposition outcome	HR score	Transposition outcome	HR score
	CS	1	No transposition	0	No transposition	0	No transposition	1	No transposition	0
PP 14	PSD	3	Discr. passed on	6	Discr. passed on	6	Discr. passed on	6	Discr. passed on	6
	UD	3	Discr. passed on	6	Discr. passed on	6	Discr. passed on	6	Transposition	3
PP 15	PSD	2	No transposition	0	No transposition	0	No transposition	6	Discr. passed on	4
	UD	2	No transposition	0	No transposition	0	No transposition	0	Discr. passed on	4
	CS	2	No transposition	0	No transposition	0	No transposition	0	Discr. passed on	4
PP 16	PSD	2	Discr. passed on	4	Discr. passed on	4	Discr. passed on	0	Discr. passed on	4
	UD	2	Discr. passed on	4	Discr. passed on	4	Discr. passed on	4	Discr. passed on	4
	CS	2	No transposition	0	Discr. passed on	4	Discr. passed on	4	Discr. passed on	4
PP 17	PSD	3	Transposition	3	Transposition	3	No transposition	4	Transposition	3
	UD	3	Transposition	3	Transposition	3	No transposition	0	Transposition	3
	CS	3	Transposition	3	Transposition	3	No transposition	0	Transposition	3
Human rights score				105		83		158		154

many changes. In a questionnaire conducted by the Italian Council presidency, the UK government openly described the approach: "Our general approach to transposing the Directive was to copy out its provisions so that we did not alter or add to the substance of its mainly mandatory provisions" (Italian Presidency, 2014, p. 144).

The French transposition of the public procurement directives is very surprising. Even in comparison to the minimalistic British transposition, French legislators paid little attention to the social aspects in the public procurement directives. Especially the restrained transposition of the social clause is notable. The social clause was not determined as a procurement principle (PP 1), and not mentioned under the exclusion criteria (PP 11). For two out of three procurement directives (PSD and UD) the French transposition law did, on the other hand, provide for rules to apply the social clause to subcontractors (PP 2). For the CD, this provision was not transposed. In addition, the French laws stressed the directive requirement whereby tenders that are abnormally low because a violation of the social clause has been confirmed have to be rejected. Still, France has the highest number of provisions that were not transposed at all. Over-transpositions were only used for the three provisions whereby companies can be excluded for not paying social security contributions (PP 10). In comparison with the other three member states, the tool to pass on the discretion was used least.

Germany has transposed the directives in a more balanced manner. Only 17 provisions were disregarded and seven regularly transposed. Moreover, Germany has over-transposed nine provisions, more than the other four countries. Most relevantly, Germany has established the social clause, whereby social law, labour law, and central ILO conventions have to be respected, as a principle of procurement (PP 1). The German government also put in place verification (PP 4) and exclusion (PP 10) requirements that go beyond the legally required minimum. Denmark has transposed the directives in an even more far-reaching manner. It has the lowest number of non-transpositions and almost as many cases of discretion-passed-on. Partly due to the practice of directly applying EU directives, Denmark over-transposed six provisions (Table 5.4).

Germany and Denmark have by far the highest human rights scores. These high results can partly be explained with the fact that both countries over-transposed voluntary provisions with a high human rights relevance (PP 4 and PP 6 in Denmark, PP 4, and PP 10 in Germany). The low human rights score by the UK is due to the copy-out approach. The UK has the highest number of cases, where the decision

Table 5.4 Human rights score and transpositions by type for the public procurement directives

	UK	France	Germany	Denmark
Total human rights score	105	83	158	154
Transpositions ordered by type				
Non-transpositions	20	24	17	11
Transpositions	7	9	7	14
Discretion-passed-on	18	9	12	14
Over-transposition	0	3	9	6

was passed on to the contracting authorities. At the same time, a large number of provisions was ignored. France's human rights score is almost half the German score, which is mostly explained by the large number of provisions the French laws ignored. A more detailed discussion of these outcomes follows in the last section of this chapter.

5.2 Transposition of the Non-financial Reporting Directive

5.2.1 Human Rights Provisions in the Non-financial Reporting Directive

The NFR-Directive requires large companies that have more than 500 employees to report on their social, human rights, and environmental impacts and state the risks their company activities pose for third parties. The relevance of the directive stems not only from these binding requirements but also from the fact that it aims at indirectly pushing companies towards more human rights due diligence and increasing transparency vis-à-vis economic stakeholders and civil society. In this respect, the voluntary provisions and the provisions that are mandatory with discretion play an important role. Legal scholars and civil society representatives criticised that the large number of voluntary provisions could decrease the regulatory function of the directive (Spießhofer, 2014). However, from a researcher's perspective, the large 'room for manoeuvre' makes it possible to comparatively assess the commitment to human rights in this area. Before being able to assess the member states' commitments, I outline the human rights-related provisions of the NFR-Directive. The overview in this sub-section highlights the relevant provisions, provides a structure for analysis, and explains where the directive allows for scope in the transposition.[77]

The NFR-Directive focuses only on corporate reporting in the areas of human rights and the environment and contains only nine articles. All regulatory provisions are contained in Article 1, which is formulated as a list of amendments to the Accounting Directive. Most importantly, it states:

> Large undertakings which are public-interest entities exceeding [...] the average number of 500 employees during the financial year shall include in the management report a non-financial statement containing information to the extent necessary for an understanding of the undertaking's development, performance, position and impact of its activity, relating to, **as a minimum, environmental, social and employee matters, respect for human rights**, anti-corruption and bribery matters [...]. (NFR-Directive, Article 1(1), emphasis added)

The so-called public-interest-entities include large listed companies such as credit institutions, insurance companies and other companies that are defined by member

[77]To understand and analyse the NFR-Directive from a legal perspective, an internal briefing note of the European Coalition for Corporate Justice (ECCJ) from January 2016, which was provided by the organization's director after the expert interview, was very helpful (see Appendix II).

states as such.[78] The directive specifies that the management reports of such companies have to include a short description of the company's business model and a report of the policies the company pursues in social and human rights matters. The directive then provides a list of elements that must be included in the non-financial reports. These elements are the company's due diligence processes, the outcomes of the policies a company has undertaken, social and human rights risks related to the company's operations, and how the company manages those risks. In addition, "non-financial key performance indicators" (NFR-Directive, Article 1(1)1e) that are relevant for the company's business operations have to be part of the reports. Such indicators can refer to social issues but could also include other areas.[79] Moreover, the directive sets out that when a company does not pursue any social or human rights policies, it must state in the report reasons for not doing so. These provisions make up the core of the NFR-Directive.

Since this one article contains various mandatory and voluntary requirements, it is necessary to break it down into issue-specific provisions, which serves as a structure for the transposition analysis.[80] Nine provisions have been identified (NFR 1, NFR 2, etc.), to each of which I allocate a human rights score (between 1 and 3). The first (NFR 1) is the provision requiring listed companies with more than 500 employees to publish a non-financial report. The directive explicitly only includes listed companies with more than 500 employees, which means that unlisted companies, state-owned companies, small and medium sized enterprises (SMEs), and specialized companies operating in high-risk sectors are excluded from the mandatory scope of the directive. In this analysis I will treat this provision as mandatory with discretion, even though the directive does not specifically state that smaller companies or unlisted companies can be excluded as well. The reason is that the scope of the NFR-Directive was the most controversially debated subject during the negotiation and the transposition of the directive. The initial Commission proposal recommended applying the clause to all companies with more than 500 employees, not only public listed companies, which would have included three times as many companies (Kinderman, 2015, p. 5).[81] Various NGOs argued against reducing the scope, both on the European and on the national level, and four member states[82] published a statement after the adoption of the directive in which they called for a wider scope. In view of this background, I regard the possibility to widen the scope when transposing the directive as implicit. From a human rights perspective, this provision is central. The mandatory reporting obligation is the key element of the directive and

---

[78] Article 2(1) of the Accounting Directive provides for a more detailed definition of 'public-interest entities'.

[79] Key Performance indicators are a standard accounting tools to measure the performance of companies. Non-financial indicators can include social and human rights issues but can also refer to other areas such as intellectual capital or customer satisfaction.

[80] Because the directive consists only of one article, these provisions do not necessarily correspond with articles or sub-articles.

[81] According to Kinderman (2015), the initial proposal would have applied to approximately 18.000 companies, while the final version of the NFR-Directive only applies to 6.000 companies.

[82] Belgium, France, Denmark, and Slovenia.

the discretionary part, the possibility to extend the scope, can have large implications for human rights reporting for business if transposed (human rights score of 3).

Provision NFR 2 relates to the question of how the impact of a company is defined in the transposition law. This relates to the fact that the directive provides for a new definition of the concept of *materiality*. Whereas in accounting this concept was traditionally only used to measure the economic significance of financial statements, the NFR-Directive departs from this understanding by specifying that risks to human rights and the environment, i.e. not business risks per se, can also be *material*. The directive only states that a company should publish information on the "impact of its activity, relating to, as a minimum, environmental, social and employee matters, [and] respect for human rights [...]" (NFR-Directive, Article 1(1)1.). The transposition by member states should prescribe to disclose the impact of a company's activity, but there is discretion as to how national law defines this impact. Recitals 3 and 8 of the directive give some more detailed indications in this respect. Recital 8 states that companies should publish

> [...] adequate information in relation to matters that stand out as being most likely to bring about the materialisation of principal risks of severe impacts, along with those that have already materialized. The severity of such impacts should be judged by their scale and gravity. (NFR-Directive, Recital 8)

This more specific understanding of impact could be taken up by the national transposition laws. From a human rights perspective, the definition of impact is moderately relevant (human rights score of 2).

The third provision (NFR 3) refers to the reporting on risks, the key human rights provision (human rights score of 3). The directive states that companies must provide information relating to social, employment, and human rights matters including

> the **principal risks** related to those matters linked to the undertaking's operations including, **where relevant and proportionate, its business relationships**, products or services which are likely to cause adverse impacts in those areas, and how the undertaking manages those risks. (NFR-Directive, Article 1(1)1d, emphasis added)

The directive does not provide for a definition of what constitutes "principal risks" (NFR-Directive, Article 1(1)1d). National transposition could clarify this. Recital 8 could be used as a reference in this respect since it states that risks may arise from a business' "operations, and, where relevant and proportionate, its products, services and business relationships, including its supply and subcontracting chains" (NFR-Directive, Recital 8). A key part of this provision is the reference to business relationships and supply chains. The phrase "where relevant and proportionate" (NFR-Directive, Article 1(1)1d) provides much discretion as to when supply chain risks must be included.

The fourth provision in the NFR-Directive refers to the use of non-financial key performance indicators (KPIs). The inclusion of such indicators is mandatory in the directive, but it is not specified, which indicators should be used. Thus, member states can choose, if they want to make more detailed regulations or leave the choice of indicators up to the businesses, which would mean that companies would be able to choose indicators most favourable to them. Both the choice to specify and the choice of the indicator can be of relevance to human rights. In comparison to the other provisions, I regard this provision to be of moderate human rights relevance (human rights score of 1).

Provision NFR 5 follows the so-called *comply or explain* principle (McGuire-Woods, 2015). It states that "[w]here the undertaking does not pursue policies in relation to one or more of those matters, the non-financial statement shall provide a clear and reasoned explanation for not doing so" (NFR-Directive, Article 1(1)1 para 2). The exception formulated in this provision does not define policies further and gives member states room for interpretation in the transposition. From a human rights perspective, this provision is only moderately important (human rights score of 1). More relevant is provision NFR 6 (human rights score of 3), which stipulates that member states may allow companies to omit certain information in "exceptional cases" (NFR-Directive, Article 1(1)), where the disclosure of the information would damage the commercial position of the company. This *safe harbour clause* is voluntary and could make it much easier to avoid the reporting obligations if member states decided to transpose this clause. If they do, there is leeway in how this exception is formulated, because the directive does not define it any further. As this provision provides for an exception to a human rights law, the measurement of the human rights score is inverse. Ergo, countries will be allocated three points if they do *not* transpose the provision. By the same token, I consider this a case of over-transposition if member states do not transpose this provision.

Provision NFR 7 states that member states must oblige companies covered under the directive to use a reporting framework. However, member states can choose between national, Union-based, and international frameworks, which differ considerably. As Spießhofer (2014, p. 1285) notes, the large differences between the reporting standards could lead to considerable heterogeneity in the reporting between member states. Recital 9 makes several suggestions of European and international frameworks member states could rely on.[83] Using only national frameworks could potentially diminish the reporting standard and the comparability of the report. This can have consequences for the company's impact on human rights, which is why this provision is of moderate human rights relevance (human rights score of 2).

Article 1(1)4, NFR 8, stipulates that member states can allow enterprises to publish the report separately from the general management report and up to six months after the balance sheet date. This gives companies the possibility to publish the report at a time convenient for the company. Moreover, if non-financial statements are published as part of the general management report, it is more likely that the policies are integrated into the overall strategy of the company. Therefore, this voluntary provision provides a possibility for member states to potentially weaken human rights reporting. Thus, similar to provision NFR 6, member states will be allocated points on the human rights score for *not* transposing this provision. From a human rights perspective, this provision is of moderate relevance (human rights score of 1).

[83] The recital refers to the (European) Eco-Management and Audit Scheme (EMAS), the UN Guiding Principles, the OECD Guidelines for Multinational Enterprises, and the ILO's Tripartite Declaration.

The last (Article 1(1)5–6) underlines member states' obligation to ensure that statutory auditors or audit firms make sure if the non-financial report has been provided. Member states may require that an independent assurance services provider must verify the report.[84] In relation to this, Recital 10 stipulates that member states are invited to implement effective national procedures to guarantee that companies publish non-financial reports as demanded in the directive. Under national law, such procedures should be made available to everyone with a "legitimate interest" (Recital 10, NFR-Directive). The voluntary wording and the placement of this provision in the non-binding recitals give member states large scope for transposition.

The account (see Table 5.5) has shown the discretionary room of the NFR-Directive. Of the nine directive provisions with human rights relevance, only one is completely mandatory, while six are mandatory with discretion, and two are completely voluntary. Similar to the public procurement directives, the effectiveness of this directive is conditional on the transposition by member states.

5.2.2 *Comparative Transposition of the Non-financial Reporting Directive*

The UK transposed the NFR-Directive with the Companies, Partnership and Groups Regulations on 19 December 2016.[85] Even though the transposing law was adopted ten days after the transposition deadline of 6 December 2016, the UK was still one of the early adopters. These regulations are an amendment to the Companies Act 2006, which already contained some non-financial reporting requirements.[86] The transposition of the NFR-Directive is provided for in Regulation 4, which contains two sections. Section 414CA on non-financial information statements and Section 414CB on the contents of the non-financial information statements. France transposed the NFR-Directive the latest of the four countries. The last transposition law was adopted on 9 August 2017, more than half a year after the transposition deadline of 6 December 2016. Interview evidence suggests that the political turbulences in the last phase of the Hollande presidency and the change of government were responsible for this delay (Interview 14). Following the transposition, the infringement procedure, which had been initiated by the Commission, was suspended.[87] Formally, France adopted three legal acts in order to transpose the NFR-Directive, but only Ordonnance 2017-1180 and Décret 2017-1265 translate relevant provisions of the directive into French

---

[84]Article 1(1)6.

[85]SI 2016 No. 1245 Companies Partnership, The Companies, Partnership and Groups (Accounts and Non-Financial Reporting) Regulations 2016.

[86]See Section on British misfit in chapter 6 for further information.

[87]On 24 January 2017, the Commission had opened infringement procedure with a formal notice according to Article 258 TFEU (infringement number 20170096).

Table 5.5 Overview of human rights-related provisions in the NFR-Directive

Number	Element	Aim of provision	Recital or Article	Degree of obligation	HR score
NFR 1	Non-financial statement and scope of reporting requirement	Listed companies with more than 500 employees must publish a non-financial report that includes among others social matters, employee matters, and respect for human rights	Article 1(1)	Mandatory with discretion	3
NFR 2	Definition of materiality	Member states have discretion as to how they define the impact of a company's activity on human rights	Article 1(1), recitals 3 and 8	Mandatory with discretion	2
NFR 3	Reporting on risks	Reports must include risks related to human rights and to social and employee matters	Article 1(1)1d, recital 8	Mandatory with discretion	3
NFR 4	Key performance indicators	Member states can choose if they want to adopt more detailed regulation in non-financial key performance indicators	Article 1(1)1e	Mandatory with discretion	1
NFR 5	Comply or explain provision on policies	If companies do not pursue human rights related policies, they have to provide reasons for not doing so. Member states can define what they mean by policies	Article 1(1)1	Mandatory with discretion	1

(continued)

Table 5.5 (continued)

Number	Element	Aim of provision	Recital or Article	Degree of obligation	HR score
NFR 6	Safe harbour clause	Member states can include the possibility to exclude *commercially sensitive* information in exceptional cases	Article 1(1)	Voluntary	3
NFR 7	Choice of reporting framework	Member states can prescribe which reporting framework the reports should be based on. The choice of the framework (national, Union-based, international) can affect the quality of the framework. Recital 9 lists a number of possible frameworks	Article 1(1), recital 9	Mandatory with discretion	2
NFR 8	Possibility for separate and later published reports	Member states can allow companies to publish a report separate from the management report. This can be up to six months after the balance sheet date	Article 1(1)4	Voluntary	1
NFR 9	Ensure that the non-financial report has been provided	Member states must ensure that statutory auditors or audit firms check if the non-financial report has been provided. They may require that an independent assurance services provider must verify the report	Article 1(1)5-6	Mandatory with discretion	1

legislation.[88] Ordonnance 2017-1180 contains the main requirement to publish a non-financial report, while Décret 2017-1265 defines the thresholds for the scope of the directive and implements the more specific requirements in the French commercial code.[89]

The German transposition law missed the deadline by four months. While a draft law prepared by the responsible Federal Ministry of Justice and Consumer Protection was made available to the public already in March 2016, the transposition law was only adopted one year later and was published and entered into force on 11 April 2017.[90] The German transposition law[91] is an amendment to the German Commercial Code (*Handelsgesetzbuch*). Article 1 contains all relevant paragraphs that transpose the directive. The Danish parliament adopted the law transposing the NFR-Directive[92] already in May 2015, which became law in January 2016. The law is an amendment to the Danish Financial Statements Act, which already contained non-financial reporting requirements before the adoption of the NFR-Directive. § 1(130) adds the new § 99 a to the Danish Financial Statements Act, which contains the transposition of the directive. Next, I present the national transpositions for each directive provision.

5.2.2.1 NFR 1: Non-financial Statement and Scope of the Reporting Requirement

The first provision states that member states must oblige listed companies with more than 500 employees to publish a non-financial statement. While this part is mandatory, member states can choose to extend the scope. For the UK, the Companies, Partnership and Groups Regulations state in Section 414CA(1-9) that large British companies that have more than 500 employees have to publish a non-financial statement.[93] Hence, the provision is transposed, but the scope is not widened. The French

---

[88] Ordonnance n° 2017-1180 du 19 juillet 2017 relative à la publication d'informations non financières par certaines grandes entreprises et certains groupes d'entreprises and Décret n° 2017-1265 du 9 août 2017 pris pour l'application de l'ordonnance n° 2017-1180 du 19 juillet 2017 relative à la publication d'informations non financières par certaines grandes entreprises et certains groupes d'entreprises.

[89] The third law presented as transposing the directive merely announces the adoption of the ordonnance. Article 216 of law 2017-86 (LOI n° 2017-86 du 27 janvier 2017 relative à l'égalité et à la citoyenneté), adopted on 27 January announces the ordonnance.

[90] Articles 2 and 4 of the transposition law will only enter into force in 2019, as will be explained further below.

[91] Law on strengthening non-financial company reporting in management reports (CSR-directive transposition law) *(Gesetz zur Stärkung der nichtfinanziellen Berichterstattung der Unternehmen in ihren Lage- und Konzernlageberichten (CSR-Richtlinie-Umsetzungsgesetz) vom 11. April 2017).*

[92] Lov om ændring af årsregnskabsloven og forskellige andre love.

[93] More specifically the Contracts Regulations state that the reporting obligations are relevant for any traded company, banking company, authorised insurance company, or a company carrying on insurance market activity.

laws transpose this clause similarly. The scope of the non-financial reporting requirements is specified in Article 1 of Décret 2017-1265, which states that only large companies with more than 500 employees have to publish a non-financial statement. The same can be observed with regard to the German transposition. The newly inserted § 289b merely states that listed corporations (*Kapitalgesellschaften*) that have more than 500 employees must publish a non-financial statement.

The Danish transposition differs substantially from the other three countries regarding this provision. The first sentence of § 99a specifies that the reporting requirements apply to all large companies, which is a much wider scope than large public interest entities. Specifically, the scope of the reporting requirement was widened to also include companies that have less than 500 employees and those of a different accounting class.[94] According to the Danish Business Authority (2015, p. 1), the scope of the directive would have applied to 50 Danish companies, while the extended scope applies to 1050 companies. However, for those companies that fall under the extended scope, the requirements only became binding after 1 January 2018, while for those companies covered by the directive, the requirement already took effect on 1 January 2016. Still, this extension of the scope has significant consequences for Danish companies. Therefore, this is a clear case of over-transposition.

5.2.2.2 NFR 2: Definition of Materiality

The second provision of the NFR-Directive gives member states leeway as to how they define the impact of a company's activity on human rights. More specifically, member states can specify, if they include human rights risks in their understanding of materiality. The British law transposes this clause in a minimalistic fashion, because the wording in Section 414CB is almost identical to the wording in the directive, without specifying the materiality any further. Similarly, neither the French, nor the Danish, or German transposition laws provide for more detailed definitions of materiality.[95]

[94]The requirements of the directive would only apply to all companies that are subject to accounting class D and have 500 or more employees. The Danish transposition law also applies to companies that fall into accounting class D and have less than 500 employees, and to companies that are subject to accounting class C (Danish Business Authority, 2015, p. 6).

[95]It should be noted that the German CSR Law uses the wording of Recital 7 to give a more detailed account of the areas in which it applies. For example, where law stipulates that the non-financial statement should include employee matters, it also lists possible measures, such as gender equality, workplace safety or the core ILO conventions. While these clarifications do not further the understanding of impact, they could make reporting in these areas more substantial.

5.2.2.3 NFR 3: Reporting on Risks

The third provision of the NFR-Directives requires member states to oblige companies to report on principal risks regarding social, employee, and human rights matters. As the directive does not specify these risks any further, member states have the possibility but are not obliged, to provide for a more detailed definition of principal risks. This is a key provision to assess member states commitment to human rights because reporting on human rights risks often depends on the degree of detail. For the British transposition, the same pattern can be observed as with the previous two transpositions. The wording in Section 414CB 1(d) on risks is an almost literal transposition of the directive text. The French transposition legislation, on the other hand, is very specific in this respect. Article 2 of Décret 2017-1265 lists several areas in which companies have to provide detailed information. These areas include, among others, details on employees, health and safety conditions in the workplace, workers' representation, training, and equality. The list also includes a separate section on subcontractors, which specifically stresses, among others, the respect for human rights, the promotion and observance of the core ILO conventions, freedom of association, the right to collective bargaining, the elimination of forced labour, the elimination of child labour, and other actions that further human rights. These detailed reporting obligations constitute a very detailed specification of principal risks. Therefore, I regard this as a case of over-transposition.

The German interpretation of risks is the opposite of the French. The language follows the wording of the directive and is even narrower in some respects. While the directive states that the non-financial report should include "principal risks [...] which are likely to cause adverse impacts" (NFR-Directive, Article 1(1)1(d)), the German CSR Law speaks of "principal risks, [...] which are **very** likely to have **grave** negative consequences" (German CSR Law, Article 1, §289c, emphasis added). Such small changes in the wording are an indication that the scope of risks that must be reported was supposed to be kept as small as possible. The Danish transposition of this clause is along the lines of the UK transposition. The relevant provision is an almost literal transposition of the directive text.

5.2.2.4 NFR 4: Key Performance Indicators

The provision dealing with key performance indicators is addressed in the UK law. It includes a specification of non-financial indicators as "factors by reference to which the development, performance, or position of the company's business, or the impact of the company's activity, can be measured effectively" (Partnership and Groups Regulations, Regulation 4, 414CB(3)). This definition does not refer to human rights and is regarded as transposed. The French law also provides for a simple transposition of this clause by stating in Article 2 of Décret 2017-1265 that the results of the measures taken by companies should include key performance indicators. Neither the German nor the Danish transposition laws use the possibility to go into more detail concerning the description of key performance indicators either.

5.2.2.5 NFR 5: 'Comply or Explain' Provision on Human Rights and Other Policies

Regarding the 'comply or explain' provision, none of the four member states goes beyond copying the text of the directive. While the UK transposition in Section 414 CB(4) is once again a word-by-word transposition of the 'comply or explain' paragraph in the EU directive, the French,[96] German, and Danish[97] wordings are very close the original directive text as well.

5.2.2.6 NFR 6: Safe Harbour Clause

Regarding provision NFR 6, the *safe harbour clause,* whereby member states may allow companies to leave out sensitive information, the UK sticks to the copy-out-approach. The wording is almost identical to the wording in the directive. In addition, the safe harbour clause was put at the end of the section and specifically underlines that the possibility to exclude information to protect commercial interests applies to the whole section. As this provision, which is an exception to a human rights clause,[98] is clearly transposed, the UK will be allocated zero points on the human rights score (inverse allocation). The opposite can be observed regarding the French transposition because the respective laws do not give large companies the possibility to hold back information the company deems sensitive. In France, the reporting obligations are mandatory without exception, which is why this provision is considered as over-transposed. The German CSR Law, on the other hand, makes use of the possibility to foresee a safe harbour clause, which gives companies the option to leave out non-financial information on matters that are impending or being negotiated if the publication would be commercially damaging. The respective provision[99] contains a wording very similar to the one in the directive. The Danish transposition is similar to the French and stands in contrast to the one of the UK and Germany, as the safe harbour clause is not transposed. This means companies must publish the information required under the directive, even if the information could be prejudicial to its commercial position.

5.2.2.7 NFR 7: Choice of Reporting Framework

This provision states that member states must require companies covered by the directive to use a reporting framework, but they can choose between national, Union-based, and international frameworks, which differ considerably. All four countries transpose this provision but do not specify any further which reporting frameworks companies

---

[96] Article 2 of Décret 2017-1265.

[97] Section 99a (3).

[98] Which means it can potentially weaken human rights reporting.

[99] Section 289e in the German CSR Law.

should rely on. Section 414CB (6) in the UK Companies, Partnership and Groups Regulations does not make any further prescriptions in this respect. The relevant clause merely states that if companies chose to use a national, international, or EU-based reporting framework, they should specify which one they use.[100] Therefore, the discretion as to which framework should be used is passed on to the companies. The same can be observed regarding the French transposition. Article 3 of Décret 2017-1265 states that companies are free to choose which reporting framework they want to rely on, they only have to state their choice. The German and Danish laws equally leave the choice, which reporting framework to use, up to the companies to decide.

5.2.2.8 NFR 8: Time and Place of Report Publication

Provision NFR 8, laid down in Article 1(1)4 of the NFR-Directive, states that member states can allow large companies to publish the report separately from the general management report and up to six months after the balance sheet date. This gives companies the possibility to publish the report at a time they deem suitable. At this point, the UK departs from the minimalistic transposition approach because the possibility to give member states more flexibility is not taken up. Article 1 of Section 414CA clearly states that the non-financial statement must be part of the strategic report of a company. Thus, one point will be allocated to the UK's human rights score (inverse allocation). The French transposition laws do not provide for the flexibility of a separate report either. Article 1 of Ordonnance 2017-1180 states that the non-financial report has to be integrated into the annual management report.

Regarding the question, if the non-financial reports should be published as part of the management report or as a separate report, the German law again gives companies much flexibility. Following § 289b (3), the non-financial information can be declared in a separate report and it must be published at the latest four months after the balance sheet date. The draft version of the German transposition law still included a period of six months, the maximum possible under the directive. But the final law shortened this period from six to four months.[101] Still, I regard this provision as transposed, because the German legislators wanted to give companies a large amount of flexibility. German companies were given the possibility to publish the non-financial reports separate from the general management report and have four months to do so. The Danish law, on the other hand, does not make use of the possibility to provide for a separate report. As § 99 a (4) of the Danish transposition law states, the non-financial report must either be part of the general management report or be in direct relation to it.[102]

---

[100] Section 414CB(6).

[101] This decision will be discussed further in chapter 6.

[102] This means that the report can either be published as a supplement to management report or be published online. In both cases, the management report must make a reference to the non-financial report.

5.2.2.9 NFR 9: Verification of the Non-financial Report

The last human rights-related provision of the NFR-Directive[103] underlines member states' obligation to ensure that statutory auditors or audit firms confirm that the non-financial report has been provided. Member states may require that an independent assurance services provider must verify the report.[104] With this provision, the UK returns to the minimalistic transposition style. As the non-financial statement must be part of a company's strategic report, the Financial Reporting Council, the British (semi-public) regulating authority in the accounting sector, is monitoring the compliance of companies with the non-financial reporting obligations. The verification of an independent assurance service provider is not provided for in the transposing law. The French laws are stricter in this respect. Article 1 of Ordonnance 2017-1180 states that an independent third-party body must verify the non-financial report according to specific modalities. Thereby, I regard this provision as over-transposed.

Under German law, the mandatory part of this provision, which states that an auditor must check if the report has been provided, is transposed with Article 1(12). The voluntary part of this provision, namely the option that an independent auditor verifies the content of the report, is also transposed, but with one limitation. Article 2, which states that companies that voluntarily allow independent auditors to verify the information of their non-financial statements, does not take effect until 1 January 2019. This means that voluntary and independent verification reports of social risks or human rights risks are not made public until late 2019. However, the possibility is still provided under the German law, even though companies that are willing to increase transparency are given more time to adapt. The Danish legislation transposes this provision, too, but the discretionary room is not used. While the regulations state that the auditors should not only check the existence of the non-financial report but also compare if it aligns with the information provided in the financial report, the Danish law does not go so far as to provide for the option to have the non-financial report verified by an independent assurance provider.

5.2.3 Overview of Transposition Results

The comparison between the transposition outcomes paints a clear picture. France and Denmark transposed the NFR-Directive in a very extensive manner, while Germany and the UK followed a restrictive approach. This can be observed both for the general transposition approach and for the transposition of provisions that are of high relevance for human rights. The main clause, the non-financial reporting requirement, was transposed by all member states, but only Denmark chose to extend the scope. The second clause that is highly relevant from a human rights perspective is the reporting on risks (NFR 3). Here only France over-transposed the provision, while

[103] Article 1(1)5–6 in the NFR-Directive.

[104] Article 1(1)6 in the NFR-Directive.

the other member states stuck to the wording of the directive. The so-called safe harbour clause (NFR 6) is also important from a human rights perspective, as it gives member states the possibility to allow companies to exclude sensitive information. Germany and the UK made use of the possibility, while France and Denmark do not allow for such exceptions. For four clauses, the discretionary room was disregarded by all four member states. Provisions NFR 2, NFR 4, NFR 5, and NFR 7 have all been transposed in a minimalistic manner. Table 5.6 gives an overview of the transposition outcomes.

The UK stuck to the same minimalistic approach it also pursued with the public procurement directives. The only exception is the British transposition of provision NFR 8, where the UK did not stick to the absolute minimum. Here the UK required companies to include the non-financial report into the general management report, even though the directive allowed for more flexibility about where and when to publish the report. Apart from this clause, the UK transposition is almost a perfect copy of the directive text. Since the wording of the directive contains a large number of non-binding clauses, the British legislation established a voluntarist reporting framework. The German transposition is almost identical to the British. The only difference is that with regard to provision NFR 9, the German law foresees that the possibility to provide for independent verification, even though this provision will only come into effect on 1 January 2019. Apart from this clause, Germany provides for an equally voluntarist transposition.

France made the most use of this discretionary room provided for in the directives. Two provisions were over-transposed and the possibility to insert a safe harbour clause (NFR 6) was not used. These three French interpretations of the directive are the main reason for the high human rights score (40). Next to the over-transpositions, France transposed four provisions regularly and passed on the discretion for provision NFR 7. Noteworthy is also the fact that the French legislation requires that all non-financial reports have to be verified by an independent third-party body. The result is a very rigid reporting framework. The Danish transposition resulted in a human rights score almost as high as the French one. Most notably, the Danish legislation extended the scope of the reporting obligation to include also companies with less than 500 employees, provided that they are in specific accounting classes. This is a substantial difference to the minimum required by the directive and explains part of the high Danish human rights score. The other essential element of the high score is the fact that Denmark, like France, did not make it possible for companies to exclude sensitive information under special circumstances. With the rest of the provisions, Denmark chose a very pragmatic approach and opted for a simple transposition. The transposition of provisions NFR 2 to NFR 5, NFR 7, and NFR 9 followed a copy-out approach. The minimalistic transposition of NFR 9 led to the fact that Denmark has a slightly lower human rights score than France (Table 5.7).

Table 5.6 Transposition outcomes for the NFR-Directive

No.	Name of provision		UK		France		Germany		Denmark	
NFR 1	Non-financial statement and scope of the reporting requirement (HR score: 3)	Mandatory with discretion	Transposition	3	Transposition	3	Transposition	3	Over-transposition	12
NFR 2	Definition of materiality (HR score: 2)	Mandatory with discretion	Transposition	2	Transposition	2	Transposition	2	Transposition	2
NFR 3	Reporting on risks (HR score: 3)	Mandatory with discretion	Transposition	3	Over-transposition	12	Transposition	3	Transposition	3
NFR 4	Key performance indicators (HR score: 1)	Mandatory with discretion	Transposition	1	Transposition	1	Transposition	1	Transposition	1
NFR 5	Comply or explain' provision on human rights and other policies (HR score: 1)	Mandatory with discretion	Transposition	1	Transposition	1	Transposition	1	Transposition	1
NFR 6	Safe harbour clause (hr score: 3)	Voluntary	Transposition	0	No transposition	12	Transposition	0	No transposition	12

(continued)

Table 5.6 (continued)

No.	Name of provision		UK		France		Germany		Denmark	
NFR 7	Choice of reporting framework (hr score: 2)	Mandatory with discretion	Discretion passed on	4	Discretion passed on	4	Discretion passed on	4	Discretion passed on	4
NFR 8	Allow for separate and later published reports (hr score: 1)	Voluntary	No transposition	1	No transposition	1	Transposition	0	No transposition	1
NFR 9	Ensure that the non-financial report has been provided (hr score: 1)	Mandatory with discretion	Transposition	1	Over-transposition	4	Discretion passed on	2	Transposition	1
Overall human rights score				16		40		16		37

Table 5.7 Human rights score and transpositions by type for the NFR-directive

	UK	France	Germany	Denmark
Total human rights score	16	40	16	37
Transpositions ordered by type				
Non-transpositions	1	2	0	2
Transpositions	7	4	7	5
Discretion-passed-on	1	1	2	1
Over-transposition	0	2	0	1

5.3 Account of Transposition Variation

The previous sections have provided a detailed analysis of the transpositions of the public procurement package and the NFR-Directive. In this brief section, I seek to visualize, categorize, and compare the transposition outcomes. At the beginnings of Sects. 5.1 and 5.2, I outlined the human rights-related provisions in the public procurement directives and the NFR-Directive. These overviews showed the extent to which the directives rely on voluntary rules. When combining the individual provisions of all four directives, 31 out of 54 provisions are voluntary (57%), while 16 (30%) are mandatory with discretion. Only seven provisions (13%) are solely mandatory. These numbers underline the importance of national transposition for the effectiveness of the directives.

Figures 5.2 and 5.3 show the transpositions of the public procurement directives and the NFR-Directive by type. While it becomes clear that each country chose a distinctive approach for each directive, there are some similarities between the public procurement directives and the NFR-Directive. The UK did not over-transpose

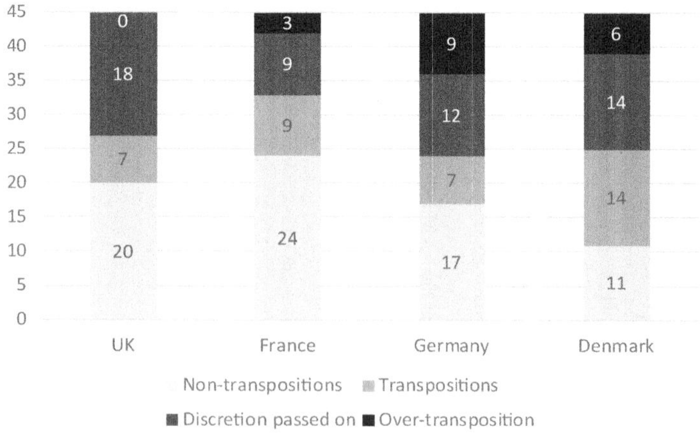

Fig. 5.2 Transposition of public procurement directives by type

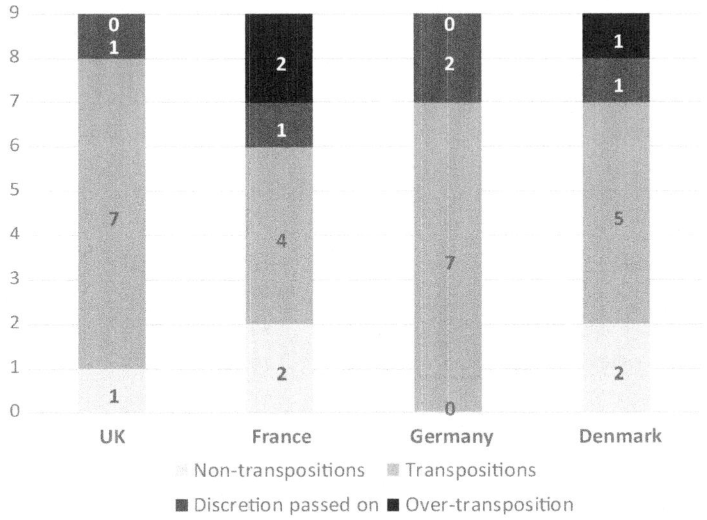

Fig. 5.3 Transposition of NFR-Directive by type

any of the voluntary provisions in the four directives analysed. The British transposition of the NFR-Directive is the most minimalistic of all transposition outcomes, whereas the British transposition of the public procurement directives is more balanced because for more than one-third of the provisions the discretion was passed on to the contracting authorities. The French transpositions used all four transposition types in both cases. It is notable that for the public procurement directives, the French government ignored more voluntary provisions (24) than all other countries. For Germany, the results show large differences between the two transpositions. While for the public procurement directives Germany relied on all four transposition types, the transposition of the NFR-Directive consists only of regular transpositions and two cases of discretion-passed-on. Denmark, on the other hand, shows more consistency between the two transpositions. It relied on over-transpositions in both cases and ignored fewer provisions than the other three countries.

While these results indicate the transposition style chosen by the member states, the human rights score is more significant for the interpretation (see Table 5.8). In the description of the research design in Sect. 4.5, I explained how the human rights scores are sorted into three categories: high, medium, and low. Using this categorization, the UK receives a low human rights score for all directives, while Denmark receives a medium score for all directives. France has a low score on the public procurement directives, and a medium score on the NFR-Directive, while Germany has a medium score on the public procurement directive and a low score on the NFR-Directive.

It is notable that none of the member states received a high human rights score. In part, this is due to the choice of the thresholds, which I describe in Sect. 4.5. The analytical frame was designed to be objective in assessing all voluntary provisions

Table 5.8 Overview of transposition results for all directives

	UK	France	Germany	Denmark
Public procurement directives				
Human rights score	Low (105)	Low (83)	Medium (158)	Medium (154)
Human rights score/provision	2.33	1.84	3.51	3.42
NFR-directive				
Human rights score	Low (16)	Medium (40)	Low (16)	Medium (37)
Human rights score/provision	1.78	4.44	1.78	4.11
Average human rights score/provision	2.06	3.14	2.64	3.77

so that it can also be employed for in other studies that analyse the transposition of the procurement directives and the NFR-Directive for other EU member states. While none of the four member states' transposition came close to the maximum human rights score, there is still considerable variation between the transposition results, which becomes more apparent when calculating the human rights score per provision for each member state. As Table 5.8 shows, the UK's human rights score per provision is almost half of the German score. For the NFR-Directive, both France and Denmark have more than twice the human rights score of the UK and Germany. The calculation of the human rights score per provision also allows us to combine the results of the public procurement directives and the NFR-Directive. On average and across all directives, Denmark received the highest score (3.77 points) on the human rights scale, while the UK received the lowest (2.06). France (3.14) and Germany (2.64) range in between the two.

This chapter has delivered a comprehensive transposition analysis for the UK, France, Germany, and Denmark. The results have revealed a large variation between the four transposition approaches. The next chapter will seek to account for this variation by testing the hypotheses formulated in Chap. 4 and explaining the transposition processes in the four countries.

References

Bekendtgørelse om fremgangsmåderne ved indgåelse af kontrakter inden for vand- og energiforsyning, transport samt posttjenester (Executive Order on the procedures for the award of contracts for water and energy supply, transport and postal services). (2015). Retsinformation, 1624, 1–4.

Bekendtgørelse om tildeling af koncessionskontrakter (Executive Order on the award of concession contracts). (2015). Retsinformation, 1625.

Danish Business Authority. (2015). Implementation in Denmark of EU Directive 2014/95/EU on the disclosure of non-financial information. Retrieved October 5, 2016, from http://csrgov.dk/file/557863/implementation-of-eu-directive.pdf.

Décret no 2016-360 du 25 mars 2016 relatif aux marchés publics. (2016). Journal Officiel de La République Française.

Décret no 2016-86 du 1er février 2016 relatif aux contrats de concession. (2016). Journal Officiel de La République Française.

Décret n° 2017-1265 du 9 août 2017 pris pour l'application de l'ordonnance n° 2017-1180 du 19 juillet 2017 relative à la publication d'informations non financières par certaines grandes entreprises et certains groupes d'entreprises. (2017). Journal Officiel de La République Française, ECOT171131.

Dentons. (2016). *A few questions about Implementation of the EU public procurement directives*. London. Retrieved from https://www.dentons.com/en/insights/guides-reports-and-whitepapers/2016/june/9/implementation-of-the-eu-public-procurement-directives.

Directive 2014/23/EU of the European Parliament and of the Council of 26 February 2014 on the award of concession contracts. (2014). Official Journal of the European Union, L 94.

Directive 2014/24/EU of the European Parliament and of the Council of 26 February 2014 on public procurement and repealing Directive 2004/18/EC. (2014). Official Journal of the European Union, L 94.

Directive 2014/25/EU of the European Parliament and of the Council of 26 February 2014 on procurement by entities operating in the water, energy, transport and postal services sectors and repealing Directive 2004/17/EC. (2014). Official Journal of the European Union, L 94.

Directive 2014/95/EU of the European Parliament and of the Council of 22 October 2014 amending Directive 2013/34/EU as regards disclosure of non-financial and diversity information by certain large undertakings and groups. (2014). Official Journal of the European Union, L 330.

European Commission. (2016a). EU Public Procurement reform: Less bureaucracy, higher efficiency. An overview of the new EU procurement and concession rules introduced on 18 April 2016. Brussels. Retrieved from http://ec.europa.eu/DocsRoom/documents/16412/attachments/1/translations/.

European Commission. (2016b). Public Procurement Reform Fact sheet No 8: Social Aspects of the New Rules. Brussels. Retrieved from http://ec.europa.eu/DocsRoom/documents/15526/attachments/1/translations/en/renditions/pdf.

European Commission. (2016c). Public procurement strategy. Retrieved December 5, 2016, from https://ec.europa.eu/growth/single-market/public-procurement/strategy_en.

European Commission. (2016d). Thresholds. Retrieved December 6, 2016, from https://ec.europa.eu/growth/single-market/public-procurement/rules-implementation/thresholds_en.

Gesetz zur Modernisierung des Vergaberechts (Vergaberechtsmodernisierungsgesetz–VergRModG). (2016). Bundesgesetzblatt, Teil I(8), 203–232.

Gesetz zur Stärkung der nichtfinanziellen Berichterstattung der Unternehmen in ihren Lage- und Konzernlageberichten. (2017). Bundesgesetzblatt, Teil I(20), 802–814.

Institute for Human Rights and Business. (2015). Protecting rights by purchasing right—the human rights provisions, opportunities and limitations under the 2014 EU Public Procurement Directive.

Italian Presidency. (2014). *Comparative Survey of the Transposition of the New EU Public Procurement Package*.

Kinderman, D. (2015). The struggle over the EU non-financial disclosure directive. *WSI-Mitteilungen, 8*(2015), 613–621.

Kroman Reumert. (2016). Procurement Law: New Danish Public Procurement Act as of 1 January 2016. Retrieved February 16, 2017, from https://en.kromannreumert.com/News/2016/01/Procurement-law-New-Danish-Public-Procurement-Act-as-of-1-january-2016.

Lov om ændring af årsregnskabsloven og forskellige andre love (Act amending the Danish Financial Statements Act and various other laws). (2015). Retsinformation, 738.

McGuireWoods. (2015). Legal Alert: The New EU Accounting Directive and (Non-) Financial Reporting Obligations. Retrieved January 12, 2017, from https://www.mcguirewoods.com/Client-Resources/Alerts/2015/2/New-EU-Accounting-Directive.aspx.

Ordonnance no 2016-65 du 29 janvier 2016 relative aux contrats de concession. (2016). Journal Officiel de La République Française.

Ordonnance no 2015-899 du 23 juillet 2015 relative aux marchés publics. (2016). Journal Officiel de La République Française, EINM150610.

Ordonnance no 2017-1180 du 19 juillet 2017 relative à la publication d'informations non financières par certaines grandes entreprises et certains groupes d'entreprises. (2017). Journal Officiel de La République Française.

Public Procurement, England and Wales Public Procurement, Northern Ireland: The Concessions Contracts Regulations 2016. (2016). Statutory Instruments, 273.

Public Procurement, England and Wales Public Procurement, Northern Ireland: The Utilities Contracts Regulations 2016. (2016). Statutory Instruments, 274.

Public Procurement: Public Contracts Regulations 2015. (2015). Statutory Instruments, 102.

Spießhofer, B. (2014). Die neue europäische Richtlinie über die Offenlegung nichtfinanzieller Informationen—Paradigmenwechsel oder Papiertiger? *Neue Zeitschrift Für Gesellschaftsrecht, 1281*(33), 1281–1320.

The Companies, Partnerships and Groups (Accounts and Non- Financial Reporting) Regulations 2016. (2016). Statutory Instruments, 1245.

Udbudsloven (Contract law). (2015). Retsinformation, 1564.

Vergabe- und Vertragsordnung für Bauleistungen Teil A (VOB/A) Hinweise für die VOB/A 2016. (2016). Bundesanzeiger, 1–71.

Verordnung über die Vergabe von öffentlichen Aufträgen im Bereich des Verkehrs, der Trinkwasserversorgung und der Energieversorgung (Sektorenverordnung–SektVO). (2016). Bundesgesetzblatt, Teil I(16).

Verordnung über die Vergabe von Konzessionen (Konzessionsvergabeverordnung–KonzVgV). (2016). Bundesgesetzblatt, Teil I(16).

Verordnung zur Modernisierung des Vergaberechts (Vergaberechtsmodernisierungsverordnung–VergRModVO). (2016). Bundesgesetzblatt, Teil I(16).

Chapter 6
Empirical Analysis II: Explanation of Transposition Variation

While the previous chapter showed how the directive transpositions differed between the four member states, this chapter contains the second part of the empirical analysis and explains how the differences can be explained. It is structured in four sections. To provide the analytical background for the hypotheses testing, the first section provides a brief overview of the political and administrative settings in which the transpositions took place. The second and third sections test the hypotheses formulated in Chap. 4 for the public procurement directives and the NFR-Directives respectively. The last section changes the perspective and explains the transposition processes in each country, thereby putting the results into the national policy-making context. This section, therefore, follows the demand by Lowi (1972), who writes that "one can say little new about the politics of regulation without introducing the general policy context" (p. 299). Therefore, in this section insights from the hypotheses testing are combined with empirical evidence from expert interviews and the analysis of policy documents. While the testing of the IVs allows for an understanding of the potential impact of single factors, a qualitative account of the transposition context permits to understand the interplay between different factors and therefore deliver a comprehensive picture of the transposition in each member state.

6.1 Country Transposition Background

6.1.1 United Kingdom

The UK is the archetypical majoritarian model of democracy, which is why this kind of political system is also called the 'Westminster model' of democracy (Lijphart, 1999). Due to the first-past-the-post-system, where only the candidate with the most votes is elected, British politics is dominated by two political parties, one of which

P. Drahn, *Adoption of EU Business and Human Rights Policy*,
Contributions to Political Science, https://doi.org/10.1007/978-3-030-46935-1_6

usually forms the government. For the last decades, these two parties were the Conservative Party and the Labour Party, which conform with the traditional left-right-spectrum and mainly disagree on the direction of socio-economic policies (Lijphart, 1999, p. 14). Smaller parties like the Liberal Democrats or other regional parties are usually not large enough to be the overall winners of elections. While coalition governments were rare in post-world-war Britain, the outcome of the general election in 2010 led to a coalition government of the Conservative party and the Liberal Democrats, which was still in power when the law transposing the PSD was adopted in February 2015. During the transpositions of the other legislative acts analysed in this book, a one-party Conservative government under prime minister David Cameron was in power.

In the British parliamentary system of government, the cabinet of ministers is formally dependent on the confidence of parliament because the House of Commons could remove a cabinet from office. In the political reality, however, the cabinet is usually dominant over the parliament because it is composed of the leaders of the majority party (ibid). The prime minister has, in comparison to other heads of government in the EU, a powerful role in national politics (King, 1994, p. 210f). In EU policy matters, the prime minister (and his/her personal advisor on EU matters) has traditionally played the most important role (Armstrong & Bulmer, 1996, p. 265). This role has grown in recent years, partly due to political ambition and partly due to the increasing importance the European Council for coordinating the direction of EU policy-making (Allen, 2013, p. 120). Nonetheless, cabinet ministers can enjoy a considerable degree of autonomy over their portfolio in EU policy questions. The British parliament only takes a subordinate role in shaping details of legislation and usually does not significantly affect the autonomy of individual departments (King, 1994). Especially in details of policymaking, single departments negotiate and represent interests on their own (Allen, 2013, p. 121; Armstrong & Bulmer, 1996). For the transposition of the NFR-Directive, the department for Secretary of State for Business, Energy and Industrial Strategy was responsible for the transposition of the directive, which was headed by the conservative politician Greg Clark.[1] The transposition of the public procurement directives was overseen by the Crown Commercial Service, which is an executive agency that reports directly to the Cabinet Office.

When it comes to the transposition of EU directives, the UK traditionally has a track record of a good performer (Allen, 2013; Wessels & Rometsch, 1996, p. 332). Efficient civil service and a centralized administration usually result in a timely and reliable transposition and implementation of EU directives. In addition, the UK relies to a large degree on delegated legislation in the form of Statutory Instruments when transposing directives (Wessels & Rometsch, 1996). While the British parliament can reject Statutory Instruments, the government's dominance over the House of Commons makes such instances rare (Treib, 2004, p. 106). Moreover, the adoption of Statutory Instruments is much faster than the regular legislative process (ibid).

[1] Until July 2016, the ministry was named Department for Business Innovation and Skills and was headed by Sajid Javid (Conservative Party).

As was noted in Sect. 5.2.2, the UK transposed all four directives considered in this study with Statutory Instruments.

Despite the focus on efficient transposition processes, the UK has one of the most rigorous parliamentary scrutiny systems for directive transpositions in the EU (Allen, 2013). The European Scrutiny Committee investigates all legislative proposals by the Commission and estimates legal and political implications. Ministerial departments have to provide regulatory impact assessments on each proposal, which creates pressures early in the transposition process to take potential negative implications into account. Interest groups and stakeholders, which the government seeks to involve in the transposition and implementation of EU law, also use this information. Next to several informal channels through which interest groups try to influence governmental departments, public consultation processes are the main means of participation. Such consultations were also conducted for the public procurement directives (see Cabinet Office, 2014, 2015) and the NFR-Directive (see UK Department for Business Innovation and Skills, 2016). The government invited stakeholders to comment on a specific set of questions. Summaries of the responses, and the government's responses to them, were then made available to the public. A variety of actors responded to the consultation processes. The most responses to the NFR-Directive and the human rights-related clauses of the public procurement directives came from two sides: civil society organizations such as Amnesty International, CORE, and Shift on the one hand, and large corporations and business associations such as the Confederation of British Industry on the other hand.

Despite these procedures, the government still retains a large degree of authority over the transposition process (Armstrong & Bulmer, 1996; Treib, 2004). This general estimate was also confirmed for the transpositions relevant in this dissertation (Interview 7). While the views of interest groups, and the views of parliament, and here especially the caveat that high costs of EU legislation should be avoided, were taken into account, the British government enjoys a larger degree of autonomy in transposing EU directives than most other EU governments.

The UK's transposition of the four directives analysed in this study cannot be analysed without taking note of recent political events. On 23 June 2016, the majority of participants in a national referendum voted to leave the EU. By that time, the public procurement directives had already been transposed. The NFR-directive was only transposed six months later. Interview evidence and public communication by the British government show that the vote had little immediate impact on the transposition process. It did not affect how the government approached the transposition processes or decided on the transposition outcomes (Interview 7). Moreover, the UK parliament already stated that laws transposing the public procurement directives and the NFR-directives will be part of the Great Repeal Bill (British Parliament, 2017). Nonetheless, the political climate was dominated by the campaigns surrounding the referendum and the discussions that ensued after the vote. I will consider this factor, when relevant, in the following analysis.

6.1.2 France

France has a semi-presidential system in which executive power is shared between the directly elected president and the government, consisting of a prime minister and the ministers. While the government is appointed by the president of the republic, it is also responsible to the deputies of the National Assembly, who are directly elected every five years. In effect, the president has only control over legislation, as long as he controls a majority in the National Assembly. Once the president loses his influence over parliament, the system of government effectively changes from a presidential system to a parliamentary system (Lijphart, 1999, p. 121). Traditionally, a classical left-right-spectrum characterized the landscape of political parties in France, in which the most relevant differences occur along the socioeconomic dimension. This characteristic was stronger in France than in many other member states, where, for example, the religious dimension played a larger role (Lijphart, 1999, p. 79ff). Governments in France were usually formed either by the *Parti Socialiste*, often supported by smaller parties from the centre-left coalition, or by one of the centre-right predecessor parties of what is now called *Les Républicains*. The first disruption to this party system was brought about by the electoral successes of the far-right *Front National*, whose candidates were able to qualify for the last round of the presidential elections twice. The traditional party system was altered more significantly when the centrist, pro-European, and social-liberal party of incumbent president Emmanuel Macron, *La République En Marche!* (LREM), won a large majority in the 2017 parliamentary elections. During the transposition of the public procurement directives, the government was still formed by the *Parti Socialiste*, the party of then-president François Hollande. The transposition law for the NFR-Directive was passed in August 2017, under the LREM-government, but most legislative preparations had already been finalized by the previous government (Interview 14).

The French president is the primary actor in France's policy towards the EU. He defines the main objectives of his country's European politics, turns the scale in case there is disagreement within the government about the position in EU negotiations, and represents the country in the European Council (Rozenberg, 2013). However, in the day-to-day policy decisions, the Prime Minister is central to French EU policy-making, as he executes the president's decisions and devises the French position in the Council. He coordinates inter-ministerial coordination in the *Secrétariat général du Comité interministériel* and has direct responsibility for the *Secrétariat général des affaires européennes* (SGAE), the agency that manages EU affairs and leads the intergovernmental negotiations (ibid). The Prime Minister also structures and dominates the process of transposing EU directives, while the French parliament plays a minor role in this respect. While both the Senate and the National Assembly have parliamentary committees that hold hearings on EU matters and scrutinize EU legislation, the real-world impact on France's EU policies is described to be limited and "[e]xamples of parliamentary influence in the European field are hard to find" (Rozenberg, 2013, p. 70). Paradoxically, the national parliament of one of the most relevant EU member states shows a low level of Europeanization and its members exhibit little motivation to shape the country's EU policies.

The policy-making role of the French prime minister in overseeing transposition processes can affect transpositions in two ways. On the one hand, a hierarchical ministerial bureaucracy, few veto players, and effective coordination among ministries through the *Secrétariat général du Comité interministériel* can enable an efficient transposition process (Lequesne, 1996). On the other hand, transposition processes have been found to be obstructed, if the content of the directive runs counter to the political priorities of the current government (Falkner, Treib, Hartlapp, & Leiber, 2005; Knill & Lehmkuhl, 2002).

The transposition of the EU public procurement directives was prepared by a working group organized by *France Stratégie*, a strategic body attached to the prime minister's office. The transposition itself was organized by the ministry for economy, which published an analysis of the regulatory and economic impact of the transposition and conducted a public consultation (Ministère de l'économie de l'industrie et du numérique, 2014).[2] The transposition of the NFR-Directive was organized by the *Direction Générale du Trésor*, which is an administrative body attached to both the ministry of economy and the ministry of foreign affairs and which consults the minister of the economy on matters of economic policy. With half of the staff located in embassies or international organizations, it is especially focused on French international economic activity and economic matters in the EU and in international organizations. Equally, a public consultation was conducted to include the views of stakeholders on the transposition (Direction Générale du Trésor, 2017). In both transposition processes, the French CSR platform (*Plateforme RSE*) was actively involved by the government (France Stratégie, 2015). This body, which had been installed by the French prime minister in June 2013, has the aim to foster dialogue among key stakeholders about French policies in the field of CSR (France Stratégie, 2018). As it brings together businesses, labour unions, civil society organizations, CSR researchers, and public institutions, the French CSR platform serves as a good representation of the BHR policy subsystem in France. Another relevant actor is the *Mouvement des Entreprises de France* (MEDEF), which is the largest employer organization in France and which represented the strongest voice of the business community in the transposition processes.

6.1.3 Germany

Germany is a parliamentary democracy that also conforms with the Lijphart's consensus style of democracy. The German Bundestag elects the chancellor and his or her federal government is dependent on the parliament's support. Horizontally, the

[2]The public consultation on the transposition of the procurement directives took place between 5 November and 4 December 2015. The position papers and the outcomes of the consultation were not published and could therefore not be used for this analysis.

executive and the legislative are not strictly separated because the leaders of the coalition that forms the government control the political groups that hold the majority in the Bundestag. While the German parliament is a central actor in the German political system, it is strictly speaking not a veto player in its own right in German policy-making (Ismayr, 2004; Treib, 2004).

The general political direction is shaped by agreements and meetings between the lead figures of the coalition partners, the German chancellor and the leaders of the other parties that form the governing coalition. This means that chancellor's authority over policy-making power is usually constrained by the coalition partner, which therefore acts as a veto player in the German political system (Ismayr, 2004). More concrete political decisions are taken collectively in the weekly meetings of the cabinet, usually without relying on formal voting procedures. Civil servants prepare these decisions in cabinet committees and working groups and therefore exert a large degree of influence on the day-to-day policy-making. According to the *Ressortprinzip*, ministries enjoy a large degree of autonomy over their portfolio. Decision making in German politics is characterized by the necessity to coordinate between a large number of actors. Beichelt (2013) summarizes the core elements of German decision making as "party dominance, coalition government, a working parliament based on a largely non-political administration and, last not lease, federal bicameralism" (p. 94).

Especially Germany's federal structure represents a central difference to the other countries analysed in this study. Parts of the legislative competencies lie with the federal level, while the regional governments are tasked with the implementation and enforcement of the federal laws. While both the Bundestag and the Bundesrat, the legislative body which represents the 16 *Länder* (German federal states), have the right to initiate legislation, most legislative processes are started by specific divisions within the German ministries (Ismayr, 2004, p. 460). Coordinative processes among the ministries shape the legislative process from the beginning (*Ressortabstimmung*) and are conducted on several administrative levels. The political 'colour' of a ministry, the party affiliation of the respective minister, plays a crucial role in these coordination processes.

Like with the other countries considered in this book, the left-right-spectrum traditionally characterizes the party landscape. Next to the socio-economic dimension, which is most relevant, the religious dimension plays a larger, though decreasing, role than in France, Denmark, and the UK (Lijphart, 1999, p. 80). Since the foundation of the Federal Republic, German chancellors have come only from two political parties, the *Social Democratic Party* (SPD), and the *Christian Democratic Union* (CDU), which forms a 'Union' with its regional sister party from Bavaria, the *Christian Social Union* (CSU). The market-liberal *Free Democratic Party* (FDP), the *Alliance 90/The Greens*, the party *The Left*, and more recently the far-right *Alternative for Germany* complement the German party landscape. During the transposition of the public procurement directives and the NFR-Directive, the government was formed by a 'Grand Coalition' between the CDU/CSU and the SPD.

The German chancellor and the chancellor's office shape the general direction of Germany's policy towards the EU. This position was strengthened further during the Eurozone crisis when the European Council assumed the role of the central crisis management body. Apart from this central role, German EU policy-making is less centralized than in the other three countries analysed and characterized by plenty of coordination processes between a large number of actors. In addition to the cabinet meetings, two committees are crucial for the inter-ministerial coordination: the monthly meetings of the heads of the EU departments of the ministries (Europa-Abteilungsleiter), and the monthly meetings of the state secretaries for European questions (Müller Gómez & Wessels, 2016, p. 228f). Two ministries take more elevated, cross-departmental roles in German EU policy-making. The German Foreign Office holds a central coordinating role because it is formally responsible for policy coherence, it runs the German representation in Brussels, and it is responsible for coordinating the instructions (*Weisungsabstimmung*) the Federal government sends to the COREPER II-meetings in Brussels (Müller Gómez & Wessels, 2016, p. 212f). The Federal Ministry for Economic Affairs is the second ministry with cross-departmental functions, as it coordinates the instructions sent to COREPER I-meetings, heads central coordinative meetings and organizes the transposition of directives (ibid). The Chancellor's office also holds a coordinative and supervisory role, but usually only interferes in cases of inter-ministerial conflict, or when a concrete political matter is directly relevant for the meetings of the chancellor (ibid). While the chancellor's office has much fewer resources than the other ministries, its role has still been elevated by the increased significance of the European Council. Much coordination is also necessary because national ministers retain a large degree of influence on EU policy issues that fall within their sphere of competence. Formally, the *Ressortprinzip* allows ministers to decide themselves how they vote in the Council, even though coalition agreements make such instances a rare occurrence.

This large degree of ministerial autonomy is also retained during the transposition processes of EU directives. The same division that was tasked with the negotiation of EU directives in the Council, usually also initiates the legislative processes for the transposition laws (Müller Gómez & Wessels, 2016, p. 171). Central questions to the transposition, such as the determination of departmental competencies, and the inclusion of regional and federal actors, are already tackled before the formal process begins (ibid). The central coordination of all German directive transpositions is supervised by the Federal Ministry for Economic Affairs, which also manages a central database EURICO (EU-Richtlinien-Controlling), in which all directives are listed that Germany has to transpose. However, the division within the responsible ministry that has been given the functional competence for the directive, and which already handled the negotiation, plays the most central role in the transposition process. It develops the transposition schedule and involves other departments in its own and in other ministries (ibid).

For the public procurement directives, the Federal Ministry for Economic Affairs was in charge of the transposition process, while the Federal Ministry of Justice and Consumer Protection led the transposition of the NFR-Directive. At the time, both ministries were under the leadership of the SPD. Unlike in Denmark or the UK, transposition laws are not delegated acts but are usually adopted following regular legislative procedures. Interest groups, most notably labour unions, and employers' unions, are usually involved in these processes through informal procedures. Public consultation procedures have only occurred more recently and have been used in the transposition processes for the public procurement directives and the NFR-Directive. A wide variety of interest groups participated in these processes and responded to the draft laws that were published by the respective ministries.

6.1.4 Denmark

Denmark is a parliamentary democracy with an electoral system based on proportional representation. It belongs to the Scandinavian 'consensual democracies', which have, even more than in other proportional systems of representation, a particular culture of consensus and conciliation (Lijphart, 1999, p. 250). As a parliamentary system of government, the directly elected, unicameral, Danish parliament, the *Folketing*, elects the prime minister and controls the government. As in most EU member states, the classical left-right-spectrum also dominates the landscape of political parties in Denmark, where the most relevant differentiations occur along the socioeconomic dimension (Lijphart, 1999, p. 80). Denmark's multi-party system has a low electoral threshold of only two per cent of the national vote.[3] Therefore, a large number of parties gain parliamentary mandates.[4] Coalitions of two or more parties usually form governments. Since minority governments are a regular occurrence in Danish politics, opposition parties have a large degree of influence of a government's policies, which, again, underlines the relevance of the consensual governance style. Danish prime ministers have in recent years usually been members of one of the three strongest political parties, the conservative-liberal Social Democrats (*Venstre*), Conservative People's Party, and the Danish Social Liberal Party. During the transposition of the NFR-Directive, the minority government of the social democratic prime minister Helle Thorning-Schmidt was in power. This government also prepared the transposition of the public procurement directives, even though the transposition law was passed by the minority government formed by the conservative-liberal *Venstre* party. However, reportedly only a few changes were made by the new government (Interview 15).

Decision-making processes in EU matters in Denmark are marked by a centralized and efficient national bureaucracy (Pedersen, 1996, p. 199). The coordination within government is organized between special committees, which are technical bodies that mirror the DGs in the European Commission, the EU committee, and the cabinet committee on EU affairs (Von Dosenrode, 2014, p. 53f). As the highest committee on EU affairs, the EU Committee is made up of senior civil servants who are tasked with solving conflicts among the special committees, filter politically relevant issues for

[3] Apart from passing the two-percent-threshold, it is also possible for parties to win seats directly in one of the ten constituencies, or by obtaining a critical number of votes in two of the three electoral provinces (Danish Parliament, 2011).

[4] At the time of writing, twelve parties have members in the Folketing.

the ministerial level, and monitor the EU's general development (ibid). In the cabinet committee on EU affairs, ministers agree on the positions taken in the Council. However, since ministers are traditionally granted autonomy within their portfolio, only issues that are politically highly relevant are discussed at this level. In accordance with the consensus-centred style of policy-making, the Danish government seeks to include the views of several bodies in EU decision-making, such as interest groups, as well as the opposition parties in the Committee for EU affairs (Bursens, 2002). Especially the Danish parliament is highly involved in EU decision making processes, both through a formal procedure in the EU Committee and through informal networks (Von Dosenrode, 2014). In these processes, the government seeks to receive the backing of the parliamentary majority, which often involves the incorporation of the opposition (ibid). This style conforms with the governance style of 'corporative democracy', where horizontal divisions between executive and legislative powers are not clearly demarcated (Pedersen, 1996, p. 198).

The transposition of EU directives is supervised by the Minister of Foreign Affairs, who was already involved in the negotiation of the directive and can, therefore, anticipate possible problems during the transposition process (Bursens, 2002). The Danish parliament is often less involved in the transposition process, as might be expected in this consensus model. Because the Folketing was already highly involved in the negotiation process of an EU directive, members of parliament often regard the transposition process itself as a technical and legal process, which can be left to civil servants (Bursens, 2002, p. 186). Furthermore, the Danish government often relies on delegated legislation, which does not require the same parliamentary involvement as regular legislative acts. Because the same civil servants that were involved in the negotiation of a directive and coordinated this process with parliament are also tasked with the transposition processes, deputies trust that the position that was coordinated is not altered in the transposition process (ibid).

The coordination of the transposition processes of the public procurement directives and the NFR-Directive was supervised by the Danish Business Authority, which is part of the Danish Ministry of Industry, Business and Financial Affairs. The public procurement directives were coordinated by the Danish Competition and Consumer Authority, a government agency under the same ministry. This agency did not conduct a public consultation but formed a committee that included the main corporatist stakeholders, including regional authorities, employee representatives and trade unions (Interview 15). NGOs were not invited to the non-public committee meetings (Interview 8). This committee developed a transposition proposal which was agreed unanimously and then proposed to the minister. For the transposition of the NFR-Directive, an open and publicly broadcasted hearing was held in the Danish parliament, which was attended by all relevant stakeholders, including the trade unions, business representatives and NGOs.

6.2 Testing Hypotheses for the Public Procurement Directives

6.2.1 Policy Misfit

The first factor I test in the second part of this empirical analysis is the policy misfit between the EU procurement legislation and the national laws. As I explained in Chap. 4, the degree of policy misfit is expressed in three categories: high, medium, and low. The following section applies this framework to the procurement legislation in the four member states. For reasons of simplicity and comparability, I determine one combined misfit for all three public procurement directives. I will also address cases, where social procurement rules apply to only one of the three directives.

The use of social requirements in public procurement was acknowledged in EU member states and in the EU already before the new public procurement directives had been adopted in 2014. By the time of the adoption of the directive, most member states had adopted national action plans on sustainable procurement. While these plans mostly focussed on green public procurement, they usually also mentioned sustainable public procurement in some form. From the countries considered in this study, only Germany did not have such an action plan, which owes to its complex federal procurement system (Kahlenborn, Moser, Frijdal, & Essig, 2011, p. 5f). Moreover, the possibility to include social concerns in procurement rules was, as a voluntary provision, already mentioned in Article 26 of the 2004 procurement directive (2004/18/EC).[5] However, the situation before the adoption of the 2014 directives was far from uniform, as the description below shows.

6.2.1.1 United Kingdom

Before the UK was tasked with transposing the EU public procurement directives, UK law[6] already stressed that obligations under the ECHR also apply to public procurement. While the UK had ratified the ILO Convention 94 on labour clauses in public contracts, the British government denounced it in 1982 in a move to reduce employment regulation. However, the UK Human Rights Act 1998 makes it unlawful for any 'public authority' to act in conflict with human rights enshrined in the ECHR (Human Rights Act, 1998, p. §6). Beyond this basic legal requirement, the UK procurement law before the transposition of the directive was governed by the Public Contracts Regulation 2006, which was the transposition law for the previous EU public procurement directives (2004/18/EC and 2004/17/EC). The Public Contracts

[5] Apart from the 2004 public procurement directives, a number of EU legal documents also encourage the use of social criteria in public procurement (see Kahlenborn et al. 2011, p. 9f).

[6] As was mentioned in Chap. 4, Scotland has adopted separate laws to transpose the EU public procurement directives, which will not be considered in this study.

Regulation 2006 provided the voluntary option to include social concerns in the conditions for the performance of contracts. This, however, was only a word-by-word transposition of Article 26 of Directive 2004/18/EC. In the Sustainable Procurement National Action Plan of 2006, the UK established a roadmap for more sustainable procurement practices. While this plan was focused on green public procurement, it also familiarized procurement authorities and companies with sustainable procurement practices and encouraged the consideration of social concerns in public tenders, but did not involve any binding legislation (see DEFRA, 2006). In 2010, the UK adopted the Government Timber Procurement Policy that included criteria to ensure basic labour rights of forest workers (Kahlenborn et al., 2011, p. 15). In 2012, the UK passed the Public Services (Social Value) Act 2012, which included a non-binding clause whereby public procurement authorities should consider how the procurement might improve the social well-being in the relevant area.

Beyond that, the British law did not mention social concerns as either mandatory or voluntary grounds for excluding companies or subcontractors. Instead, the UK procurement laws gave much freedom to contracting authorities in how they handle procurement, in line with the tradition of a public procurement policy focused on cost-effectiveness. Therefore, when applying the framework for analysing the policy misfit, I determine a medium policy misfit between the provisions in the EU procurement directives and the UK law. UK governments embraced sustainable procurement earlier than most other EU member states by adopting strategies and action plans but refrained from binding SRPP rules. The farthest-reaching act to ensure socially fair procurement practices was the Social Value Act of 2012, which was of non-binding nature.

6.2.1.2 France

In France, SRPP is pursued as part of an integrated national sustainable procurement strategy that is monitored annually. Social procurement is pursued together with green procurement in one policy instrument, the National Action Plan for Sustainable Public Procurement (PNAAPD). The first version of this plan was adopted in 2007.[7] For the first time, it promoted social aspects in the technical specifications and mentions as possible reference standards the SA8000 and ISO 26000 standards (European Commission, 2015, p. 2; Kahlenborn et al., 2011, p. 34). The Grenelle 1 Law of 2009 formulates clear objectives to achieve sustainable procurement for certain product groups. As another voluntary provision, a recommendation to respect ILO Core Labour Standards was inserted in the official public procurement guidelines in 2010 (Kahlenborn et al., 2011, p. 6). Besides these voluntary clauses, the French procurement law also includes binding requirements. The French education law, adopted in 2008, required that all school purchases must be in compliance with the ILO Convention against child labour (ibid, p. 11). In addition, France is also one of the

[7]In 2015 a second action plan was adopted to take into account the changes of the EU public procurement directives.

few EU member states that ratified the ILO Convention 94 on labour clauses in public contracts, which translates into an obligation to include social clauses in national procurement contracts.[8] As such, the French law contained several mandatory elements that existed next to the numerous voluntary clauses. Therefore, I ascertain a low policy misfit for France.

6.2.1.3 Germany

Due to its complicated federal procurement system, the German government had refrained from adopting a national action plan on sustainable public procurement (Kahlenborn et al., 2011, p. 11). After a reform of the procurement law in 2009, the German law provided contacting authorities with the possibility to include social criteria in all phases of the procurement law. The GWB (*Gesetz gegen Wettbewerbsbeschränkungen*) states under Article 97 (4) that social criteria such as the ILO core labour standards can be taken into consideration for those procurement contracts that lie above the EU threshold.[9] The law does not apply for those public tenders beneath the threshold. Here German budget law and the laws of the Länder apply. However, contracting authorities were often given more leeway with tenders below the threshold, which provided them with more possibilities to include social criteria in their tenders (Deutscher Städtetag, 2010, p. 12). For example, the Länder Bavaria and Baden-Wuerttemberg adopted laws that required bidders to declare that they are respecting ILO labour standards (Deutscher Städtetag, 2010, p. 22). In addition, several guidelines have been developed that help local authorities with the integration of social criteria (ibid). As such the German procurement law gave contracting authorities the possibility to include social provisions into public tenders and therefore meets the criteria for a medium policy misfit.

6.2.1.4 Denmark

Denmark has undertaken steps to include social clauses in public procurement for more than 20 years. Similar to its leadership role in green procurement, Denmark is also one of the leading countries in the EU and worldwide with regard to the legal integration of human rights concerns in their procurement systems (Kahlenborn et al., 2011, p. 14). Since Denmark has ratified the ILO Convention 94 on labour clauses, Danish authorities at the national level legally required to integrate labour clauses in procurement contracts, whereas this provision is voluntary at the municipal level (ibid, p. 34). With regard to the use of the social clauses, national contracting authorities rely on the 'comply or explain' approach (European Commission, 2016, p. 59). Social procurement is one of the strategic goals of Denmark's procurement strategy and was highlighted in Denmark's National Action Plan on Business and

---

[8]Regions and municipalities are not bound by ILO Convention 94.

[9]Germany has not ratified the ILO Convention 94 on labour clauses in public contracts.

Human Rights (Danish Business Authority, 2014). As of 2013, all suppliers that sign a contract with Denmark's central purchasing body, are requested to do human rights due diligence based on the OECD Guidelines for Multinational Corporations (International Learning Lab on Public Procurement and Human Rights, 2016, p. 42). To promote social procurement standards further, the Danish government launched an online tool, 'The Responsible Purchaser'.[10] Overall, Denmark has a considerable legal basis for socially responsible procurement, which includes some mandatory elements at the national level. As such, the policy misfit for Denmark can be classified as medium.

This stock-taking of the misfit in the four countries has revealed the differences between national procurement legislations. A high misfit could not be determined in any of the cases. The UK, Germany, and Denmark have a medium misfit, while France has a low policy misfit. If we combine the misfit scores with the transposition outcomes, the hypothesis formulated for the misfit can be confirmed for Denmark and Germany, as in both cases a medium misfit corresponds with a medium transposition outcome. The British medium misfit does not give a clear indication to explain the transposition outcome; here, further evidence is needed as well. The only case where the hypothesis could be clearly rejected is France, as it has a low misfit, but the opposite transposition result. The transposition result contradicts the misfit, which is why the hypothesis can be clearly rejected.

Policy misfit (public procurement directives)

H1: The greater the policy misfit, the fewer voluntary BHR directive provisions are transposed by the member state

Country	Policy misfit	Transposition score	Hypothesis test
UK	Medium	Low (105)	No indication
France	Low	Low (83)	Rejected
Germany	Medium	Medium (158)	Confirmed
Denmark	Medium	Medium (154)	Confirmed

Box 6.1 Test of hypothesis 1 for the public procurement directives

6.2.2 *Institutional Misfit*

The previous chapters have provided a detailed explanation for the connections between the institutional characteristics of a political economy and the governmental behaviour of a country in the field of BHR. Therefore, I decided to use the institutional setup of a political economy as a measure for the institutional misfit. As a starting point, I relied on the Varieties of Capitalism literature to give an indication

[10]Den Ansvarlige Indkøber (Responsible purchasing) can be assessed at: http://csr-indkob.dk/.

of the institutional setup of the political economy. Hall and Soskice classify the UK as a LMEs, Germany and Denmark as CMEs, and France as country in a more "ambiguous position" between the two (Hall & Soskice, 2001, pp. 19f, 21). As explained in Sect. 4.6.2, I rely on the quantitative index of corporatism by Siaroff (1999) to have a more detailed measure of the degree to which unions and employers are integrated into decision-making processes within a country. On Siaroff's scale between 1 and 5, where higher values indicate a higher level of corporatism, Denmark has a score of 3.545, which is the highest score of the four countries considered. Germany's score is almost identically high (3.543). Both France and the UK are found at the lower end of the scale. France has a score of 1.674 and the UK a score of 1.652.

The match between the degree of corporatism and the transposition outcome is striking. The hypothesis can be confirmed in all four cases. The two countries with low degrees of corporatism, UK, and France, also show low transposition outcomes. Both Germany and Denmark have high degrees of corporatism and have medium transposition scores. While for these two countries a high transposition score could also have been expected from the degree of corporatism, they rank fifth and sixth on Siaroff's ranking, I still regard the hypothesis as confirmed.

Institutional misfit (public procurement directives)

H2: The higher the degree of corporatism, the more voluntary BHR directive provisions are transposed by the member state

Country	**Degree of corporatism**	**Transposition score**	**Hypothesis test**
UK	1.652	Low (105)	Confirmed
France	1.674	Low (83)	Confirmed
Germany	3.543	Medium (158)	Confirmed
Denmark	3.545	Medium (154)	Confirmed

Box 6.2 Test of hypothesis 2 for the public procurement directives

6.2.3 Government Composition

The next IV, government composition, is operationalized using the indicator ECON_INTERVEN from the Chapel Hill Expert Survey (CHES), as I explained in Sect. 4.6.3. The indicator measures the position of political parties on state intervention in the economy on a scale from 0 (fully in favour of state intervention) to 10 (fully opposed to state intervention). To assess the positioning of a political party, data from 2014 is used (CHES, 2017). In the UK, the Conservative party formed the British government during the transposition of the public procurement directives. The Conservative party has a score of 7.42 on the Econ_interven-variable, which signals a low preference for economic interventionism. On the scale, this score is almost as high as the threshold to strong opposition to state intervention (7.5). The

French socialist party, which was in power in France during the transposition of the public procurement directives, has a score of 3.82, and show the higher willingness for the state intervening in economic affairs. In Germany, the Christian Democratic Union (score of 5.3) formed a coalition with the Social Democratic Party (score of 3.1). The average of these two scores is 4.12. In Denmark, the conservative-liberal *Venstre* party formed a minority government during the transposition of the public procurement directive.[11] The party has a score of 6.4, which represents a modest opposition to state intervention.

The score of the four countries and the hypotheses tests are displayed in Box 6.3. The results show that the hypothesis concerning the governing parties can be confirmed for Germany and the UK. In the UK, the opposition the government intervention matches the low transposition outcome. Of the four cases considered, the UK Conservative party shows the strongest opposition to government intervention in the economy, which is also shown by the ECON_INTERVEN-score of 7.42, which is close the 7.5-threshold to 'strongly opposed'. In Germany, the fact that the political parties that are generally in favour of government intervention is in accordance with the medium transposition outcome. In Denmark and France, the hypotheses about the political parties can both be rejected.

Composition of the domestic government (public procurement directives)

H3: The more the political parties that form the government in a member state are in favour of state intervention in the economy, the more voluntary BHR directive provisions are transposed

Country	Governing party's/parties' position on state intervention in the economy	Transposition score	Hypothesis test
UK	Opposed (7.42)	Low (105)	Confirmed
France	In favour (3.82)	Low (83)	Rejected
Germany	In favour (4.12)	Medium (158)	Confirmed
Denmark	Opposed (6.4)	Medium (154)	Rejected

Box 6.3 Test of hypothesis 3 for the public procurement directives

6.2.4 Political Salience Within the Policy Subsystem

In the UK, the importance of the human rights-related clauses in the public procurement directives was low compared to other issues. Evidence to support this assessment can be found in the consultation documents published by the British government (Cabinet Office, 2014, 2015). During the consultation process, which was conducted in 2014, the general interest in the transposition of the public procurement directives was large (204 responses), but there are no indications for a

[11] The party's minority government was tolerated by a far-right, a liberal, and a conservative party.

high salience of the human rights-related clauses. When the UK government asked stakeholders, if they would prefer the awards to be based on the Most Economically Advantageous Tender (MEAT) or on the lowest price only (see provision PP 14), the question did not receive much attention. "Most respondents did not comment on this area specifically but supported the proposed regulations overall and the flexibilities offered by it" (Cabinet Office, 2015, p. 23). The transposition of the social clause was also addressed in the consultation. Here, the consultation documents claim that "compelling arguments against regulation have been made by a significant number of stakeholders" (Cabinet Office, 2014, p. 22). In addition, it is stated that out of 204 responses to the public consultations, only five demanded that binding regulatory measures are adopted instead of voluntary measures (p. 29). In addition, the assessment that political salience of the human rights clauses in public procurement is low was supported by interview evidence (Interview 7).

In France, a general overhaul of the public procurement legislation accompanied the transposition of the public procurement directives. Next to the ambition to make public procurement more socially responsible, the aim was also to simplify procurement rules and to raise the competitiveness between contractors (France Stratégie, 2015). In the national CSR platform, key actors within the policy subsystem debated both the reform in general, as well as aspects of socially (and environmentally) responsible public procurement (France Stratégie, 2015; Interview 16). Surprisingly, the fact that the EU directives provide a large discretion as to how the human rights-related provisions are transposed, was only of low importance in these discussions. Gérard Brunaud, a French policy expert on responsible procurement, stated in an expert interview: "the question of human rights has never been at the heart of the debates on transposition on public procurement" (Interview 16, own translation). While NGOs alluded to the human rights-related provisions, most actors within the policy subsystem did not establish the connection between the procurement directives and human rights. While this behaviour could also be explained with a focus on competitiveness, Brunaud states that many actors regard human rights as an important cultural achievement of France but did not associate it with the effect that public procurement can have on global supply chains. Given these considerations, I determine a low political salience of the human rights-related directive provisions within the policy subsystem.

In Germany, the general interest in the new procurement legislation was high because the transposition of the procurement directives was combined with a general overhaul of the German procurement legislation.[12] The high interest in the procurement reform was reflected in 77 responses to the public consultation that was conducted in 2015.[13] However, only four of the position papers address possible

[12]Before the reform, relevant parts of procurement legislation were decided by committees, which were composed of state representatives and representatives of contractors. The procurement reform changed this and 'elevated' relevant procurement rules to the level of a legal decree (Rechtsverordnung). The only exception to this was the construction sector.

[13]Unlike the British government, the German government did not publish any responses to the public consultation, but only stakeholders' position papers.

implications of the new procurement rules for human rights.[14] Half of these statements came from NGOs and labour unions that argued for a stricter interpretation of the human rights-related provisions, while the other half, representatives from the industry, proposed to rely on few and voluntary requirements. In the parliamentary process, the Green party, which was in the opposition, addressed some human rights concerns during a plenary debate and through press statements and a motion for a resolution (Deutscher Bundestag, 2015b). While some issues, such as the question if child labour was listed among the mandatory grounds for exclusion, were subject to larger discussions among stakeholders, the transposition of the human rights clauses did not raise a lot of attention. Therefore, a low political salience within the policy subsystem is determined for the German transposition of the procurement directives.

In Denmark, the human rights-related provision of the public procurement directives did not show a high degree of political salience within the policy subsystem. The transposition of the PSD was the first EU procurement directive that was transposed with a Danish transposition law, while the CD and the UD, like previous procurement directives, directly became national law. However, especially in comparison with the transposition of the NFR-Directive, public interest and debates among stakeholders were much less pronounced. Interview evidence suggests that the Danish government did not want to focus on the human rights-related provisions in the directive but centred the procurement reform on the issue of budget cuts (Interviews 8, 11). The government did not conduct a consultation process open for everyone but formed a special committee, which should work out proposals for the transposition laws. While representatives from labour unions and employers' associations were part of this committee, the Danish 92-Group, a coalition of 25 NGOs that advocated for a strong inclusion of human rights in the procurement directives, was excluded (Interview 8). Since policy debates were contained to this committee (Interview 15), the central actor within the policy subsystem that would have promoted the question of human rights-related regulation was kept out. According to expert interviews, domestic concerns about streamlined and cost-efficient procurement processes were prioritized over the inclusion of human rights clauses (Interviews 8, 11). As a consequence, a low political salience within the policy subsystem is also determined in this case.

If we use these insights to test the two hypotheses formulated in relation to political salience, we find evidence to support Hypothesis H4.1 for both France and the UK. In both cases the political salience and the transposition outcome were low. The cases of Germany and Denmark appear to support Hypothesis H4.2, which assumes a connection between a low political salience within the policy subsystem and a high transposition outcome. The confirmation of the hypothesis is less substantial since the transposition outcome is only medium. Given these results, we cannot yet make a clear statement about the direction of the effect political salience has on the transposition outcome.

---

[14]The position papers that were found to comprehensively address human rights-related provisions were those from the German Corporate Accountability Network (CorA), the German Trade Union Confederation (DGB), the Chambers of Commerce and Industry (DIHK), and the Federation of German Construction Industry.

Political Salience within the policy subsystem (public procurement)				
H4.1: If political salience of the directive transposition is low within the policy subsystem, fewer voluntary BHR directive provisions are transposed by the member state H4.2: If political salience of the directive transposition is low within the policy subsystem, more voluntary BHR directive provisions are transposed by the member state				
Country	**Political salience within the policy subsystem**	**Transposition score**	**Hypothesis test**	
			H4.1	H4.2
UK	Low	Low (105)	Confirmed	Rejected
France	Low	Low (83)	Confirmed	Rejected
Germany	Low	Medium (158)	Rejected	Confirmed
Denmark	Low	Medium (154)	Rejected	Confirmed

Box 6.4 Test of hypotheses 4.1 and 4.2 for the public procurement directives

6.2.5 International Policy Transfer

In general terms, the UK is highly committed to the UNGPs and underlines the fact that it was the first country in the world to adopt a national action plan on BHR after the UNGPs had been adopted. With regard to the transposition of the EU public procurement directives, however, no evidence was found that would indicate a strong influence of international norms on the transposition process. In the reports documenting the public consultation, no references were made to abide by the UNGPs or the relevant ILO conventions. On the contrary, in a short handbook by the Crown Commercial Service for public sector buyers the UK government openly propagated that "[t]here are also new obligations in the Regulations that require procurers to take certain actions to ensure compliance with various international laws" (Crown Commercial Service, 2015, p. 4). This corresponds with the non-transposition of the clauses in the directives where member states could have included references to international obligations (PP 1, PP 15).

In France, no evidence of policy transfer from the international level on the transposition process could be found either. In the documentation of the transposition process, public authorities made no references to the importance to abide by international agreements through the transposition. A note that was published together with the transposition laws lists all international agreements based on which abnormally low offers can be rejected (PP 12).[15] This list contains the same agreements published under Annex X of the PSD. Beyond the stipulations in the directive, instruments from the international level were not transferred to the French transposition law. A similar assessment can be made with regard to Germany, where international agreements

[15]JORF n° 0074 du 27 mars 2016, texte n° 64, Avis relatif à la liste des dispositions internationales en matière de droit environnemental, social et du travail permettant de rejeter une offre comme anormalement basse en matière de marchés publics.

that refer to the importance of human rights due diligence in public procurement did not play a relevant role. In the official justification for the transposition law by the ruling parties, the UN Guiding Principles are not mentioned. The document only states that the new social criteria also create incentives for companies, to comply with international corporate accountability standards, such as ILO core conventions (Deutscher Bundestag, 2015a). However, this mentioning is combined with the note that the ILO Convention is listed in Annex X of the PSD. Beyond the international agreements mentioned in the EU directives, no references to international agreements are made in the official papers documenting the transposition (Deutscher Bundestag, 2015a, 2015c). In an expert interview, when a representative of the German government was asked about the influence of international norms on the transposition process, he answered that it did, because "Article 18(2) [the social clause] is a result of the discussions on the international level" (Interview 6, own translation). This confirms the assessment, that international agreements were only relevant to the transposition, in so far as they were explicitly mentioned in the EU directives. In the committee discussions in the German parliament obligations from international BHR agreements did not play a significant role either (Interview 18). International NGOs, advocates for international BHR agreements in national policy subsystems, influenced the transposition processes largely through the Green party, which was in the opposition and had little influence on the transposition outcome (ibid). In sum, no signs of international policy transfer could be found for Germany.

Similar to the previous three member states, the Danish transposition was also not affected by international policy transfer. How the EU procurement directives were transposed was largely considered a domestic affair (Interviews 6, 8). In public communication about the transposition law, the Danish government did not establish the connection between the international human rights frameworks and the Danish transposition of the EU directives. A press statement published by the Ministry of Industry, Business, and Financial Affairs put the focus on clarity simplification of the procurement rules and underlined the budget savings that would ensue from the reform (Danish Ministry of Industry Business and Financial Affairs (Erhvervsministeriet), 2015). References to the social requirements of the directives and their relation to international human rights standards were not made. The low significance of international norms in the transposition process is further underlined by the fact that internationally connected NGOs and human rights institutions were not closely engaged in the transposition process.

International policy transfer (public procurement)			
H5: International BHR obligations cause member states to transpose more voluntary BHR directive provisions			
Country	**Policy transfer**	**Transposition score**	**Hypothesis test**
UK	No transfer	Low (105)	Rejected
France	No transfer	Low (83)	Rejected
Germany	No transfer	Medium (158)	Rejected
Denmark	No transfer	Medium (154)	Rejected

Box 6.5 Test of hypothesis 5 for the public procurement directives

6.2.6 Administrative Effectiveness

The last hypothesis that is tested refers to the IV administrative effectiveness. This hypothesis is tested in order to control for the fact that inefficient national administrations were responsible for the transposition result. This variable is operationalized with the 'government effectiveness' indicator that was developed by the World Bank and that was initially developed by Kaufmann, Kraay, & Mastruzzi (2006). The World Bank provides the results for this indicator in two ways, in the standard normal units of the value of the indicator, ranging from −2.5 to 2.5, and in percentile rank terms, which ranges from 0 (lowest) to 100 (highest) among countries worldwide.[16] The results show that all four countries score high on administrative effectiveness (see Table 6.1). Of the four countries, only France shows slightly lower scores than the other three. All four countries show well above zero and above the EU average (1.14 in 2016, 1.15 in 2015 and 2014).

Interview evidence and policy documents did also not give any indication of inefficient national administrations having affected the transposition processes. Hence, the possibility that administrative ineffectiveness affected the transposition process can be ruled out and the hypothesis can be disregarded.

[16]The Worldwide governance indicators include 214 countries.

Table 6.1 Results for the government effectiveness indicator

Indicator	Country	Year	Number of sources	Governance (−2.5 to + 2.5)	Percentile rank	Standard error
Government effectiveness	Denmark	2014	7	1.82	97.12	0.23
	Denmark	2015	7	1.85	97.6	0.23
	Denmark	2016	7	1.89	99.04	0.22
	France	2014	7	1.4	88.94	0.23
	France	2015	7	1.44	88.46	0.23
	France	2016	7	1.41	89.9	0.22
	Germany	2014	7	1.73	94.71	0.23
	Germany	2015	7	1.74	93.75	0.23
	Germany	2016	7	1.74	94.23	0.22
	United Kingdom	2014	7	1.63	92.79	0.23
	United Kingdom	2015	7	1.74	94.23	0.23
	United Kingdom	2016	7	1.61	92.79	0.22

6.3 Testing Hypotheses for the Non-financial Reporting Directive

6.3.1 Policy Misfit

Similar to the public procurement directive, EU legislation in sustainability reporting has also existed before the adoption of the NFR-Directive. The EU Accounts Modernization Directive (2003/51/EC) as well as a 2006 update (2006/46/EC) already included provisions that mention the possibility for companies to consider environmental and social matters. Due to these suggestions, the idea to include social concerns into non-financial reports was not entirely new to member states. Some countries have adopted farther-reaching regulations, creating their own mix of voluntary and mandatory requirements, which creates variation in the policy misfit. The following operationalization of the policy misfit gives an account of the mandatory and voluntary sustainability reporting requirements that are relevant for the protection of human rights.[17]

[17]To a large extent the information for this review stems from a 2011 report on the state of play in sustainability reporting that was produced for the European Commission (see Wensen et al., 2011).

6.3.1.1 United Kingdom

The most relevant element in the British policy misfit is the Companies Act of 2006. It requires all companies not considered to be small to publish a strategic report, which should explain principal risks to the company. For quoted companies, next to reporting on environmental matters, the strategic report also has to include information on employee and social matters. The relevant sections in the UK Companies Act bear a striking resemblance to the NFR-Directive, both concerning structure and content.[18] These similarities can be attributed to the fact that the UK government managed to include elements of the UK reporting requirements in the directive during the Council negotiations (Interview 9). Like the NFR-Directive, the UK Companies Act had required a non-financial statement, including KPIs. This statement had to comprise of basic company information, human rights issues, and a description of principal risks. The wording used in the Companies Act, stating that information had to be provided "to the extent necessary for an understanding of the development, performance or position of the company's business" (UK Companies Act, 2016, Sections 414C(4) and (7)), was adopted almost word-by-word in the text of the directive. However, there are a number of relevant differences between the Companies Act and the NFR-Directive. The non-financial statements in the Companies Act are mandatory but are applied on a 'comply or state' basis. That means companies that do not wish to publish information, have to state that they are not publishing a non-financial statement. The NFR-Directive, on the other hand, follows the 'comply or explain' approach, which means that companies either have to comply with the requirements or publish a detailed explanation if they do not comply. Other differences are the scope of the reporting requirements, the references to reporting frameworks, and the specificity of the required human rights-related information. Unlike the Companies Act, the EU NFR-Directive requires to include policies, due diligence processes, and outcome of those policies in the reports (UK Department for Business Innovation and Skills, 2016, p. 14f).

In addition to the UK Companies Act, the UK Corporate Governance Code and the UK Stewardship Code are two complementary instruments that aim at promoting good practice and accountability. The UK Corporate Governance Code applies to listed companies, while the UK Stewardship Code applies to institutional investors. The latter foresees that investors follow certain principles when investing in companies, which can also include social concerns. Both the UK Governance Code and the Stewardship Code are also applied on a 'comply or explain' basis.

In sum, the mix of voluntary and mandatory elements in UK law shows that the government has taken several steps to encourage social reporting. While some reporting requirements are formulated to be mandatory, exceptions are usually made possible if companies do not wish to report or deem the reporting harmful for the business activities, for example through 'comply or state' mechanisms. While there are striking similarities between the UK regulatory framework and the NFR-Directive,

[18] Section 414C of the 2006 UK Companies Act.

the focus on voluntarism is evident. The UK government holds the view that "imposing new burdens on business could adversely affect competitiveness and stifle innovation" (Wensen, Broer, Klein, & Knopf, 2011, p. 60). In sum, the mix between a regulatory framework similar to the NFR-Directive and the focus on voluntarism leads to a medium policy misfit.

6.3.1.2 France

In the EU, France was the first country to introduce legally binding sustainability reporting requirements. Already in 1977, all companies with more than 300 employees had to publish a *bilan social* whereby the companies had to show that they complied with labour law. While this law did not foresee any sanctions in cases of non-compliance, it acquainted French companies with social reporting. This obligation was updated in 2001 with the New Economic Regulation Act (Nouvelle Loi Économique), which encouraged companies with the largest market capitalizations to address social (and environmental) concerns that arise in their global operations in the companies' annual reports. The law was expanded in 2009 and 2012 with the Grenelle I and Grenelle II laws, which I already mentioned concerning the misfit in the public procurement directives. Following these updates, the New Economic Regulation Act specified 40 indicators the reports should include, which are similar to the indicators by the Global Reporting Initiative (GRI). The crucial Article 225 of the Grenelle II law was adopted in 2010 and implemented in 2012.[19] Subsequently, the non-financial reports, which must contain environmental, social, and governance information, have to be sanctioned by the Board of Directors and then verified by a third-party. The legally binding obligations of the Grenelle II Law bear already substantial similarities to the NFR-Directive and was called the "strongest governmental mandate yet in support of sustainability reporting" (Neumayr, 2013, para. 2). The similarities to the NFR-Directive are not accidental because the text of this provision served as a blueprint for the directive (EY, 2015).

Moreover, shortly before transposing the NFR-Directive, France adopted a law that establishes reporting requirements, which in some respects even go beyond the NFR-Directive. After long political negotiations and a ruling by the French constitutional court, the corporate duty of vigilance law came into effect in March 2017.[20] Following this law, the largest French corporations have to develop and publish so-called 'vigilance plans' that show how these companies seek to identify and prevent human rights violations in their business operations and in the operations of suppliers and subcontractors. All in all, the long-standing history of sustainability reporting in France has led to a comprehensive reporting framework that contains

[19]Loi 2010-788, adopted on12 July 2010.

[20]Loi 2017-399 relative au devoir de vigilance des sociétés mères et des entreprises donneuses d'ordre publiée au Journal Officiel du 28 mars 2017.

several legally binding reporting obligations that are similar to the obligations under the non-financial reporting directive. Hence, the policy misfit for France is regarded as low.

6.3.1.3 Germany

Under German law, non-financial reporting was not entirely unknown either before the transposition of the NFR-Directive. Since 2004, the German Handelsgesetzbuch (HGB),[21] foresees that large joint stock companies, those that have more than 250 employees and surpass certain financial thresholds, credit institutions, and insurance companies have to report non-financial performance indicators insofar as they are necessary to understand the business operations (Spießhofer, 2014, p. 1282).[22] This information should be part of a company's annual report and has the purpose to provide a more accurate idea about the 'situation' of the company (Hecker, 2015, p. 6). While the reporting obligation is mandatory, there is no definition of non-financial indicators. The German HGB provides information on environmental measures or information about employee matters as examples (ibid). In addition, the German accounting standards committee published guidelines on how to interpret non-financial indicators, which stated as examples customer concerns, environmental concerns, employee concerns, research and development indicators, and social reputation of the company (ibid). This interpretation does not suggest taking human rights into account and represents a minimal transposition of the EU accounting directives of 2003. In short, before the transposition of the NFR-Directive, there was no legal obligation whatsoever, to report on social consequences or human rights impacts. However, Germany has promoted several voluntary initiatives. Commissioned by the German government, the council for sustainable development (Rat für Nachhaltige Entwicklung), developed a sustainability codex (Deutscher Nachhaltigkeitskodex). This codex shares several commonalities with the NFR-Directive (see Hecker, 2015), but is only a voluntary offering without any regulatory character. The codex contains a database where companies can upload their reports, which then serves as a comparison tool for German sustainability reporting.

Overall, the only mandatory reporting obligations Germany had before the transposition of the NFR-Directive did not specify what the non-financial indicators should include. Examples provided did not suggest the use of human rights-related indicators. Human rights were only considered with respect to voluntary tools. Therefore, the policy misfit for Germany is regarded as high.

---

[21] See §§ 289 para 3, 315 para 1 (4), 340a para 1, 341a para 1 HGB, as altered by the 2004 reform of the German accounting law (Bilanzrechtsreformgesetz).

[22] More precisely, the definition of large joint stock companies following § 267 para. 3 HGB states that two out of three conditions have to be met to qualify as a large joint stock company: more than 250 employees, a balance sheet total of more than 19,250,000 €, and a total revenue of 38,500,000 €.

6.3.1.4 Denmark

In 2001, the Danish government first included non-financial reporting into the Danish Financial Statements Act. Thereby, Denmark was one of the first EU member states to implement the Commission's recommendations on reporting requirements (Wensen et al., 2011, p. 62). In 2008, the Danish Financial Statements Act was amended to include CSR reporting obligations that were part of the National Action Plan for Corporate Social Responsibility adopted the same year. This means that large companies have to report what kind of CSR policies they are pursuing and what the impact of these policies is. If they do not have any CSR policy, this must be stated, too. After another amendment in 2012, the reporting obligations explicitly required companies to account for policies that ensure the respect for human rights in a company's business operations, even if these policies are not part of the companies official CSR efforts. This rule applied to all Danish companies that have more than 250 employees and that are above a certain financial threshold.[23] Similar requirements were adopted for institutional investors, mutual funds, and other listed financial companies.[24] However, both for the regular companies and for financial institutions, the 'comply or state' approach applies, which means that if companies do not report on CSR, they have to state that they do not pursue any policies. This is different to the 'comply or explain' approach, which was for example used by the UK and was eventually also part of the NFR-Directive, whereby a company has to provide a detailed explanation for not pursuing any CSR measures.

In addition to the Danish Financial Statements Act, the Danish government also pursues two initiatives that have voluntary implications for companies. The 'CSR Compass' of the Danish Ministry of Economic and Business Affairs assists companies with the integration of reporting into their supply chain management. The Communication Compass is a government-commissioned online tool that helps companies to report on CSR. Overall, Denmark is one of the first governments to strategically pursue a CSR policy and acquainted their companies early with human rights-related reporting requirements. At the same time, reporting remained voluntary and always followed the 'comply or state' approach. Therefore, when examining the legislation prior to the transposition of the non-financial reporting directive, the misfit for Denmark is considered to be medium.

Box 6.6 shows an overview of the misfit results for the NFR-Directive and the outcomes of the hypotheses tests. The results show that the misfit hypothesis can be confirmed for France and Germany. The German case is the best match between policy misfit and transposition score since Germany has a high misfit and transposed only a few voluntary directive provisions. The misfit hypothesis also holds for France, which had only low adaptational pressure and transposed comparatively many human rights provisions. The UK had a reporting framework with several similarities to the NFR-Directive but still showed only a minimalistic directive transposition. As such,

---

[23] Firms that have assets worth more than 19 million Euro or revenues of more than 38 million Euro.

[24] This requirement was not part of the Danish Financial Statements Act, but was implemented with executive orders from the Danish Financial Supervisory Authority.

the misfit hypothesis does not give a clear indication for the British case. In Denmark, a medium misfit matches a medium transposition score, but this result does not give a strong indication, in how far the misfit was relevant for the transposition outcome.

Policy misfit (NFR-Directive)			
H1: The greater the policy misfit, the fewer voluntary BHR directive provisions are transposed by the member state			
Country	**Policy misfit**	**Transposition score**	**Hypothesis test**
UK	Medium	Low (16)	No indication
France	Low	Medium (40)	Confirmed
Germany	High	Low (16)	Confirmed
Denmark	Medium	Medium (37)	Confirmed

Box 6.6 Test of hypothesis 1 for the NFR-Directive

6.3.2 Institutional Misfit

The degree of corporatism, the indicator I employ to operationalize the institutional misfit, was already specified in the previous section on the hypothesis testing for the public procurement directives. Box 6.7 shows the combination of the country scores on Siaroff's (1999) indicator on corporatism, with the transposition results for the NFR-Directive (scale between 1 and 5; higher values indicate a higher level of corporatism). Hypothesis H2 can clearly be confirmed for the UK and Denmark. The UK is the clearest case, as a low degree of corporatism matches the low transposition score. From the high degree of corporatism in Denmark, a high transposition score could have been expected. Still, due to the medium transposition score, I assess the hypothesis as confirmed, even though the validity is lower than for the UK. For Germany, the hypothesis can be clearly rejected, as the high degree of corporatism contradicts the low transposition outcome. For France, the hypothesis can also be rejected, even though the significance of this result is lower than for Germany.

Institutional misfit (NFR-Directive)			
H2: The higher the degree of corporatism, the more voluntary BHR directive provisions are transposed by the member state			
Country	**Degree of corporatism**	**Transposition score**	**Hypothesis test**
UK	1.652	Low (16)	Confirmed
France	1.674	Medium (40)	Rejected

(continued)

(continued)

Germany	3.543	Low (16)	Rejected
Denmark	3.545	Medium (37)	Confirmed

Box 6.7 Test of hypothesis 2 for the NFR-Directive

6.3.3 Government Composition

When the NFR-Directive was adopted, the British government was formed by the Conservative party. The indicator ECON_INTERVEN from the Chapel Hill Expert Survey (CHES), which measures the position of political parties on state intervention in the economy on a scale from 0 (fully in favour of state intervention) to 10 (fully opposed to state intervention) shows a score of 7.42 for the Conservative party. For the French case, the data on party positioning is not available. In August 2017, when the transposition law for the NFR-Directive was adopted, the French government was formed by the *La République En Marche!*, which was founded in April 2016. Hence, the CHES has no data on this party. While it could be assumed that the score would be more in sceptical of state intervention than the French socialist party, this score will be left blank.

For the UK, Hypothesis H3 can again be confirmed. Similar to the situation for the public procurement directives, the government was formed by the Conservatives, which are opposed to state intervention in the economy (7.42). In Germany, the government was also the same for the NFR-Directive as for the public procurement directives. The coalition of the CDU (score of 5.3) with the SPD (score of 3.1) leads to an average score of 4.12. However, unlike with the public procurement directives, the transposition outcome for the NFR-Directive shows a low score. Therefore, Hypothesis H3 can clearly be rejected for the German transposition of the NFR-Directive. In Denmark, the transposition law was adopted already in May 2015, which is why the government was still formed by a coalition of the Danish Social Democrats (score of 3.3) and the Danish Social Liberal Party (score of 4.89). Taken together, this leads to a score of 4.09, which signals a modest tendency to be in favour of state intervention in the economy. This score matches the medium transposition outcome, which is why the hypothesis can also be confirmed for Denmark.

Government composition (NFR-Directive)

H3: The more the political parties that form the government in a member state are in favour of state intervention in the economy, the more voluntary BHR directive provisions are transposed

Country	**Governing party's/parties' position on state intervention in the economy**	**Transposition score**	**Hypothesis test**
UK	Opposed (7.42)	Low (16)	Confirmed

(continued)

(continued)

France	No value	Medium (40)	–
Germany	In favour (4.12)	Low (16)	Rejected
Denmark	In favour (4.09)	Medium (37)	Confirmed

Box 6.8 Test of hypothesis 3 for the NFR-Directive

6.3.4 Political Salience Within the Policy Subsystem

For the transposition of the NFR-Directive, the UK government conducted a public consultation. In total, 76 responses were received, a considerably lower outcome than for the public procurement directives. The overall public attention to the transposition was not described as very high (Interview 7). Two issues raised some controversy among in the consultation of the government with stakeholders, the question if a non-financial report should be allowed to be published separately from the overall management report and the question of the scope of the UK reporting requirements. While these two matters were debated among NGOs and business representatives, and eventually solved during the consultation process, it did not raise the level of attention to the transposition (Interview 7; see also Sect. 6.4). This was also due to the ongoing Brexit discussions: "In the context of lots of things going on, it wasn't a huge political priority" (Interview 7). In sum, the transposition of the directive was not highly politically salient within the policy subsystem. Insights from the interviews suggested that the only attempts to 'gold-plate' the directive would have raised the level of attention (Interview 9).

In France, the NFR-Directive has received a lot of attention among the stakeholders involved. However, this attention was not the result of a high degree of political contention. France already had far-reaching non-financial reporting requirements in place, which is why, apart from some contested issues (see Sect. 6.4.2), the transposition process was not very contested (Interview 14). Instead, the government and key stakeholders were keen on transferring French national reporting requirements to the EU level. In Germany, the transposition of the NFR-Directive received a considerable amount of attention from actors within the policy subsystem. In the public consultation process, the Federal Ministry of Justice and Consumer Protection received 55 position papers. While the public procurement directives received more position papers in general, only four addressed the human rights-related provisions. In the case of the NFR-Directive, all 55 position papers addressed demands that were relevant for the reporting of human rights-related issues.[25] The stakeholders that were involved in the process represent a wide variety of actors. Pro- and anti-regulation

[25] Some position papers only addressed environmental concerns. However, the concrete demands that were formulated addressed reporting obligations, such as scope or verification by independent auditors, which would also affect the human rights-related regulations.

positions papers were relatively balanced out.[26] In addition to the large interest in the consultation process, the transposition law received widespread attention in the media. NGOs ran public campaigns to agitate for stricter reporting requirements, often referring to the collapse of the Rana Plaza textile factory in Bangladesh in April 2014. At the same time, representatives from employers and industry were, for their part, engaged in a campaign against stricter reporting requirements, arguing that excessive regulatory requirements would be a burden on business. Organisations from both sides, such as the UPJ-network for corporate responsibility and the Federation of German Industries (BDI), organized conferences about the general issue of CSR, during which whole segments were only devoted to the transposition of the NFR-Directive. In sum, I can determine a high political salience within the policy subsystem for the German transposition of the NFR-Directive.

In Denmark, the transposition of the NFR-Directive was a politically salient issue within the policy subsystem. As was noted, a governing coalition of the Danish social democrats and the Danish liberal democrats adopted the transposition law. The mere fact that this government planned to over-transpose an EU Directive caused much discussion. In the opposition, the conservative party criticised the over-transposition in terms of the scope (NFR 1) and considered repealing it once they took over the government briefly after the transposition law had been passed, arguing it caused too high administrative burdens for companies (Interview 8). In addition to the different views in the Danish parliament, business representatives on one side and a coalition of trade unions and NGOs on the other side tried to influence the government (ibid). While there was a general consensus among stakeholders that Danish businesses should operate in a sustainable way, the question of over-transposition gave rise to political contestation that took place in the consultation procedure in public communication. Overall, the directive transposition can be described as very politically salient within the policy subsystem. This assessment shared by all experts interviewed about Denmark (Interviews 8, 10, 11).

Given the results of the IV political salience within the policy subsystem, the first of the two competing hypotheses, H4.1, appears to have higher validity. The case of the UK supports this hypothesis, as a low salience within the policy subsystem matches a low transposition outcome. In France and Denmark, the transposition of the NFR-Directive showed high political importance within the policy subsystem, and in both countries the transposition outcome is medium. While the result is less significant than for France, the hypothesis can still be confirmed. The only case that clearly contradicts Hypothesis H4.1 is Germany. Here a high political salience within the policy subsystem is combined with a low transposition outcome. Therefore, for Germany Hypothesis H4.2 can be confirmed.

---

[26]The 55 position papers were distributed as follows: 24 from business or industry representatives, 22 from NGOs and other civil society organisations, 6 from representatives of auditors and tax accountants, 2 from lawyers' associations, and 1 from a labour union.

Political Salience within the policy subsystem (NFR-Directive)				
H4.1: If political salience of the directive transposition is low within the policy subsystem, fewer voluntary BHR directive provisions are transposed by the member state H4.2: If political salience of the directive transposition is low within the policy subsystem, more voluntary BHR directive provisions are transposed by the member state				
Country	**Political salience within the policy subsystem**	**Transposition score**	**Hypothesis test**	
			H4.1	H4.2
UK	Low	Low (16)	Confirmed	Rejected
France	High	Medium (40)	Confirmed	Rejected
Germany	High	Low (16)	Rejected	Confirmed
Denmark	High	Medium (37)	Confirmed	Rejected

Box 6.9 Test of hypotheses 4.1 and 4.2 for the NFR-Directive

6.3.5 *International Policy Transfer*

In the UK, the commitment to international norms did not play a relevant role in the process of transposing the NFR-Directive. Neither the government's answers to the consultation process nor the explanatory memorandum (UK Department for Business Enterprise and Industrial Strategy, 2016), which justified the transposition, referred to the UNGPs or to any other international BHR frameworks.[27,28] However, according to interview evidence, NGOs stressed the importance of the UNGPs and other frameworks during the transposition process (Interview 9). They were present during meetings the European Commission had organized after the adoption of the directive, in order to develop reporting guidelines. Moreover, NGOs were very active in the UK consultation process. An NGO representative who used the UNGPs to argue for a farther-reaching transposition, commented on the impact of international norms: "It gives civil society a tool to push government further" (Interview 7). However, the argument of international norms did not have enough leverage to change the government position. When asked about the impact of international agreements, one interviewee stated that the political decision by the UK government appeared to be irrevocable, stating that "they were literally not going to go beyond anything that was in the directive". In sum, the hypothesis that the UK's international BHR obligations had influenced how the government used the discretionary room can be rejected.

[27]The UK public consultation on the NFR-Directive was conducted between 16 February and 15 April 2016.

[28]The only reference to international frameworks was made in the impact assessment, which was published before the consultation process (UK Department for Business Innovation and Skills, 2014). Here it was stated that NGOs active in the field of human rights will benefit from the option that firms can refer to international reporting frameworks.

In France, international policy transfer did not influence the transposition process either. Document analysis and interview evidence suggest that the French transposition was largely aligned with previously existing French reporting requirements. Instead of incorporating international policy instruments in the French transposition law, the French government attempted the opposite and sought to export the domestic rules to the EU level. In the German transposition, international policy transfer was also not found. In the official justification for the law, references to international agreements were only made with regard to the provision NFR 7, which states that member states can choose between reporting frameworks. The justification for the law then put forward the reporting frameworks that are mentioned in Recital 9 of the NFR-Directive as examples of frameworks that can be used. In the politicized transposition process, NGOs repeatedly used international agreements to argue for a stricter interpretation of the directive. However, these attempts to influence the legislation did not find expression in the transposition law. Apart from those mentioned in the directive, international agreements were not incorporated in the legislation. Thus, the hypothesised effect that Germany's commitment to international BHR agreements would influence the transposition outcome could not be confirmed either. On the contrary, with regard to provision NFR 8, the ministry official from the department that coordinated the transposition within the German Federal Ministry of Justice and Consumer Protection used international frameworks to justify more voluntarism. She argued that since some companies had already adjusted to different international reporting frameworks, which also have diverging reporting cycles, it would be counter-productive to prescribe one reporting framework for all (Interview 13).

The Danish case is the only one where a policy transfer from international agreements on the national transposition could be identified. Both the analysis of policy documents and insights from the expert interviews show that compliance with international norms has been a relevant driving force behind the development of CSR in Denmark (Interviews 8, 10, and 11). In a hearing note from the Danish Ministry of Economic and Business Affairs on the NFR-Directive, the government states that "[t]he bill also aims to adapt the legislation to the international development in the accounting area" (Danish Ministry of Economic and Business Affairs, 2015, p. 1; own translation). In addition, interview evidence suggests that the commitment to the UNGPs and the OECD Guidelines for Multinational Enterprises were a central argument by the government to defend the over-transposition of provision NFR 1, the scope of the reporting requirement, vis-à-vis the business community (Interview 11). In addition, interviewees suggested that the ambition to abide by international norms also affected the transpositions of the safe harbour clause (NFR 6), and how the reports have to be published (NFR 8) (Interviews 8 and 11). The logic behind these influences was also communicated in the interviews and in government documents. The argument is that Denmark, being a small and open economy, depends on international norms to level the playing field. Moreover, compliance with high international sustainability standards gives Danish companies a competitive advantage in the global economy (Interviews 8, 10, 11). The influence of international norms on the transposition process is also in accordance with the Danish common practice, to comply with international human rights obligations through national laws (International Learning Lab on Public Procurement and Human Rights, 2016). Therefore, the policy transfer hypothesis can be confirmed for Denmark, while it is rejected for the UK, France, and Germany.

International policy transfer (NFR-Directive)			
H5: International BHR obligations cause member states to transpose more voluntary BHR directive provisions			
Country	**Policy transfer**	**Transposition score**	**Hypothesis test**
UK	No transfer	Low (16)	Rejected
France	No transfer	Medium (40)	Rejected
Germany	No transfer	Low (16)	Rejected
Denmark	Transfer	Medium (37)	Confirmed

Box 6.10 Test of hypothesis 5 for the NFR-Directive

6.3.6 Administrative Effectiveness

The results for administrative effectiveness are the same as for the public procurement directives. The 'government effectiveness' indicator of the World Bank shows a high degree of administrative effectiveness for all four member states. The only indication for a case where administrative performance could have played a role is the transposition of the NFR-Directive in France, which was significantly delayed. The last transposition law was adopted on 9 August 2017, more than half a year after the transposition deadline which was on 6 December 2016. However, interview evidence suggests that political reasons caused this delay. Michel Capron, a French expert on the NFR-Directive, explained that due to political turbulences in the last phase of the Hollande presidency, most notably the departure from the government by the minister of the economy Macron and the resignation of prime minister Valls, many legislative dossiers were postponed (Interview 14). After the new LREM!-government had formed, it took some time to pick up these legislative issues (ibid). In sum, administrative ineffectiveness did not cause the French transposition delay and did also not affect the transposition outcomes in the other countries. Hence, Hypothesis H6 can be disregarded.

6.4 Explaining Transposition Processes

In the previous section, I have tested the hypotheses that have been formulated in Chap. 3. Table 6.2 provides an overview off all hypotheses tests and shows that no hypothesis could be confirmed for all cases. The most hypotheses could be confirmed

Table 6.2 Overview of all hypothesis tests

Hypotheses		UK		France		Germany		Denmark	
		PP	NFR	PP	NFR	PP	NFR	PP	NFR
H1	The greater the policy misfit, the fewer voluntary BHR directive provisions are transposed by the member state	No indication	No indication	Rejected	Confirmed	Confirmed	Confirmed	Confirmed	Confirmed
H2	The higher the degree of corporatism, the more voluntary BHR directive provisions are transposed by the member state	Confirmed	Confirmed	Confirmed	Rejected	Confirmed	Rejected	Confirmed	Confirmed
H3	The more the political parties that form the government in a member state are in favour of state intervention in the economy, the more voluntary BHR directive provisions are transposed	Confirmed	Confirmed	Rejected	–	Confirmed	Rejected	Rejected	Confirmed
H4.1	If political salience of the directive transposition is low within the policy subsystem, less voluntary BHR directive provisions are transposed by the member state	Confirmed	Confirmed	Confirmed	Confirmed	Rejected	Rejected	Rejected	Confirmed
H4.2	If political salience of the directive transposition is low within the policy subsystem, more voluntary BHR directive provisions are transposed by the member state	Rejected	Rejected	Rejected	Rejected	Confirmed	Confirmed	Confirmed	Rejected

(continued)

Table 6.2 (continued)

Hypotheses		UK		France		Germany		Denmark	
		PP	NFR	PP	NFR	PP	NFR	PP	NFR
H5	International BHR obligations cause member states to transpose more voluntary BHR directive provisions	Rejected	Rejected	Rejected	Rejected	Rejected	Rejected	Rejected	Confirmed
H6	If the national administration of a member state is ineffective, the member state transposes fewer voluntary BHR directive provisions	Not applicable	Not applicable	Not applicable	Not applicable	Not applicable	Not applicable	Not applicable	Not applicable

for the institutional misfit hypothesis (H2), which tests the connection between the degree of corporatism and the transposition outcome. This confirms the observation made in the theoretical chapter, that transposition outcomes cannot be explained by one factor alone, but by a combination of factors. To understand how combinations of factors led to the individual transposition outcomes in the four countries analysed, this section explains the country-specific transposition processes.

6.4.1 United Kingdom

In the UK, the transposition processes for both the public procurement directives and the NFR-Directives were both conducted in a quick and transparent fashion.[29] Extensive documentation of the consultation processes, as well as documents on impact assessments and explanatory memoranda, give insights into the political context. With the public procurement directives, the UK followed a copy-out approach, as was shown in Chap. 5. Both the hypothesis testing and the contextual evidence provided by the interviews and the transposition documents paint a straightforward picture of the transposition process. The Conservative party that was in power during the transposition pursued a free-market, non-interventionist policy. The consultation documents clearly show this:

> We consider administrative measures are appropriate because they represent a reasonable balance between reflecting the requirements of the Directive and maintaining a suitably flexible approach. Imposing duties through regulations will remove that flexibility. (Cabinet Office, 2015, p. 29)

This position by the conservative government is consistent with the UK's low score on Siaroff's index of corporatism and the lack of policy transfer. The low degree of political salience within the policy subsystem, not least induced by the Brexit discussions, reportedly also promoted the low transposition outcome. However, the UK government knew that due to strong parliamentary scrutiny processes and a vigilant press, cases of over-transposition could change the level of public attention to the transposition process. The only factor whose expectations do not match the transposition outcome is the policy misfit. Before transposition, UK procurement law already consisted of several social regulations, which is why the efforts to adopt farther-reaching regulation would have been small. However, the political decision of the government not to intervene in the economy and not to 'gold-plate' overrode this factor.

The transposition of the NFR-Directive can be explained along similar lines. The low degree of corporatism, as well as the irrelevance of policy transfer and the low political salience within the policy subsystem, coincide with the low transposition outcome. Again, the medium policy misfit does not match the low transposition outcome. While adopting stricter reporting requirements would have required only a

[29] In an Email, an NGO representative described the transposition process of the public procurement directives as 'rushed'.

small legislative 'jump', political concerns of over-regulating businesses prevented this (Interview 9). An analysis of the transposition process shows that the political priorities of the government were most relevant for the transposition outcome. The option to go further than the required minimum in the legislation was officially not on the table, "but in the political context it was not completely unexpected" (Interview 7).

On the contrary, the government's options that were communicated in the public consultation concerning the scope of the directive were not between transposition and over-transposition, but between transposition and 'retrenchment'. This was due to the fact that the UK laws and the NFR-Directive have different accounting principles. Previous UK reporting requirements referred only to 'quoted' companies, a uniquely British classification of companies. According to these, less stringent, requirements, all medium and large companies had to publish strategic reports. The NFR-Directive, on the other hand, refers to public interest entities, a different classification, but only those that have more than 500 employees. In the public consultation, the first option proposed by the government was to transpose the directive requirements in addition to the existing laws, i.e. keeping the British reporting requirements and adding the EU reporting requirement. The second option was to reduce the scope of the previously existing laws and apply only the rules of the NFR-Directive, which would effectively have resulted in 'retrenchment', as overall reporting requirements would have been reduced in response to EU legislation. In the end, the government decided to use the first option. During the consultation process, which was described to have been very active and constructive, most respondents preferred that option (Department for Business Energy & Industrial Strategy, 2016; Interview 7).[30] One of the options for UK implementation was to extend the scope of the NFR-Directive also to those companies that are subject to the UK Companies Act (Interview 9). This would have reduced complexity the most because the same rules would have applied to all British companies subject to non-financial reporting requirements (ibid). However, the responsible ministry decided against this option (ibid).

This account shows that the variables considered in this analysis are suitable to explain the transposition outcome in the UK. However, two other factors that are specific to the UK need to be taken into account as well. First, the Brexit vote took place between the transposition of the public procurement directives and the transposition of the NFR-Directive. Interview evidence suggests that the UK government would not have transposed the directives differently if the Brexit vote had turned out differently.[31] However, the Brexit vote was reported to have influenced the fact that political salience for both directives was low (Interview 7). The second issue is the British 'no-gold-plating-rule'. In interviews and in policy documents, this rule was repeatedly mentioned. However, interviewees made clear that the strict insistence on this rule was a political priority of the conservative government and that it would

[30]The breakdown between sectors of the 76 responses: 16 from civil society, 10 from companies, 2 from investors, 21 from representative bodies, 9 from consultancies, 9 from accountants, 6 from individuals and 2 from academics (Department for Business Energy & Industrial Strategy, 2016).

[31]The British parliament already announced that the UK transposition laws of the public procurement directives and the NFR-directives will be transposed in UK law by means of the Great Repeal Bill (UK Parliament, 2017).

have been possible to 'gold plate' if it was politically desired by the government. A government comment explaining the decision not to make procurement decisions based on the MEAT-criterion mandatory exemplifies this stance:

> Taking account of the range of views and reflecting on the majority preference of stakeholders involved in the earlier feedback on the policy choice of MEAT versus lowest price, we conclude that there is not a sufficiently strong evidence base to justify gold-plating through banning use of the lowest price award criterion. However, there is sufficient opinion to warrant addressing the matter clearly in guidance, and stress the importance of MEAT criteria when awarding contracts where service quality is paramount e.g. services to the person. (Cabinet Office, 2015, p. 24)

In view of these comments, I argue that the no-gold-plating-rule does not affect the validity of the empirical findings that were presented.

6.4.2 *France*

The French case is less straightforward because the two transposition outcomes are completely different. While for the NFR-Directive, France has the highest human rights score of the four member states considered, it has the lowest score in the transposition of the public procurement directives. Many human rights-related provisions in the procurement directives were ignored and the social clause was neither established as a procurement principle (PP 1), nor as a mandatory requirement for exclusion (PP 11). This outcome is particularly surprising since the independent variables that were tested are mostly similar for both transpositions. During the transposition of the public procurement directives, the French socialist party was still in power, which is in principle in favour of state intervention in the economy. Moreover, as the low policy misfit indicates, France had already adopted comprehensive social procurement rules and is a signatory of the ILO Convention 94 on labour clauses in public contracts. So why did France transpose the public procurement directives in such a minimalistic manner?

A relevant aspect is the fact that the transposition of the public procurement directives was accompanied by a general overhaul of French public procurement legislation, which aimed at simplifying procurement rules and strengthening competitiveness in the procurement process (France Stratégie, 2015). Part of this reform was the law 2015-990 for growth, the activity, and the equality of the economic opportunities, initiated by then-minister of the economy Emmanuel Macron ('Loi Macron').[32] In times of budgetary constraints, this reform also aimed at reducing costs by simplifying procurement procedures, decreasing the regulatory burden for bidding companies, and making public tenders more attractive to small and medium-sized enterprises. In light of this reform, the political preference was put on reducing administrative efforts for companies. Interview evidence suggests that in this political climate the socialist government, usually in support of regulating the economy,

[32] LOI n° 2015-990 du 6 août 2015 pour la croissance, l'activité et l'égalité des chances économiques.

was more susceptible to lobby influences. Gérard Brunaud, a French policy expert on sustainable procurement and member of the national CSR platform, commented on this matter:

> No doubt an effective lobbying of some professional federations, very reluctant to the social clause from the beginning, and the MEDEF [the largest employer federation in France] were supported by slightly hasty and ill-founded 'analyses', such as the statements of Mr. Tirole and Mr. Saussier of the Council of Economic Analysis, as well as a specific remark in the report of Senator Bourquin, all of whom believed the insertion of the social clause to be a 'risk to competitiveness'. (Interview 16, own translation)

In addition, Brunaud hints that "certain members of the cabinet" (ibid) showed little support for the social clause.

Interestingly, the lack of a consensus culture in France also seemed to have played a role in the low transposition outcome for the public procurement directive. In the national CSR platform (*Plateform RSE*), which is organized by the government and which provides a good representation of the policy subsystem, actors were divided if a stronger wording on human rights-related exclusion criteria (PP 11) should be recommended or not (France Stratégie, 2015, p. 3f). Some members recommended to clarify the legal language in this respect and, interestingly, proposed to link exclusion criteria with the French legislation on non-financial reporting. Other members objected and stressed that the respective provisions should focus on encouraging CSR (ibid). The example of the discussion on the transposition of provision PP 11 shows that such conflicts within the policy subsystem did not lead to compromises, but to inaction:

> As often in France, the general approaches expressed themselves in ideological terms and did not really seek the consensus, leaving the public authorities to decide in the end, which is sometimes contradictory or inappropriate. (Interview 16, own translation)

Still, these clarifications do not explain, why the transposition outcome of the public procurement directives differed substantially from the transposition outcome of the NFR-Directive. The transposition took place only one year later, and misfit and institutional misfit were similar for both directives. If anything, the new government of LREM! was even more focussed on competitiveness.

According to the findings gathered from policy documents and expert interviews, the degree of political salience within the policy subsystem was the crucial factor that explains the differences between the two transposition outcomes. The question of how the social clause procurement directive should be transposed was discussed among the central policy actors, but it never received the same level of relative importance as the human rights clauses in the NFR-Directive. Within the policy subsystem, "the question of human rights has never been at the heart of the debates on transposition on public procurement" (Interview 16). Policy documents recognized the social clause of the procurement directive but did not pay attention to *how* the social provisions were transposed (Ministère de l'économie de l'industrie et du numérique, 2014). The low political salience of human rights clauses in the procurement directives within the policy subsystem is also related to the fact that France updated the National Action Plan for Sustainable Public Procurement in 2015. This comprehensive plan includes a number of concrete national sustainability targets. For example, it aspires that by 2020, 25% of all public tenders should contain a social clause (Ministère de l'écologie du Dévéloppement durable et de l'Énergie, 2015). In the shadow of this ambitious national plan, the transposition of the public procurement directives received only little attention. Under these conditions, the low misfit seemed to have the contrary effect than hypothesized. Interview evidence suggests that in the absence of public pressure, socially responsible public procurement was regarded as already well-established, which is why a simplification of public procurement rules was prioritized over a far-reaching transposition of the social clauses.

With the transposition of the NFR-Directive, the constellation of factors was similar in many respects, but the transposition outcome was different. Here, a higher political salience was attached to the human rights-related clauses by the actors within the policy subsystem, which then caused the misfit and the composition of the domestic government to have opposite effects on the transposition outcome. Labour unions and NGOs, as well as employers' associations, were highly active during the negotiations of the directive and the transposition process (Interview 14). Both coalitions took part in the public consultation process and their impact can be observed in the medium transposition outcome.[33] Still, the government also listened to industry demands by not increasing the scope of the reporting requirements regarding provision NFR 1(ibid). In the consultation procedure, stakeholders could state their preference among four options, three of which would have over-transposed the provision.[34] In the end, the government decided to keep administrative burdens low and to implement the option that transposes only the minimum required by the directive.

With regard to the 'safe harbour clause' (NFR 6), the government sided with NGO demands since it did not provide for the possibility to omit sensible information in exceptional cases (ibid). Apart from these issues, the transposition was not contended among the key stakeholders (ibid). The main reason for this is the low misfit in combination with the fact that French government, in unison with key actors within the policy subsystem, sought to transfer the French reporting requirements to the EU level and exporting them to the other member states (ibid). During Council negotiations, France was the strongest supporter of stricter reporting requirements in the directive. In a response to a consultation of the European Commission about the NFR-Directive, the French government argued for a reporting framework "as comprehensive as possible" (Gouvernement Français, 2016, p. 20, own translation). However, the French initiative to adopt stricter reporting requirements was, mainly

[33]The consultation took place between 23 June and 25 July 2016.

[34]The four options provided were: Option 1: all companies with a balance sheet above 20 million Euros and all PIEs with a total revenue of more than 40 million Euros; Option 2: all companies with a balance sheet of more than 100 million Euros, and all PIEs with a balance sheet between 20 million and 100 million and a total revenue between 40 million and 100 million Euros; Option 3: all companies with a balance sheet and entities that are subject to a simplified regime with a balance sheet of more than 20 million and a total revenue of more than 40 million Euros; Option 4: all companies with a balance sheet of more than 20 million Euros and a total revenue of more than 40 million Euros.

due to German resistance, not very successful (Kinderman, 2015). However, due to the position of the French government, MEDEF, the largest French employers' association, also supported a stricter NFR directive, even though they had previously been opposed to strict reporting obligations on the national level (Kinderman, 2016, p. 35). They supported more stringent reporting requirements in the EU to 'level the playing field' in the EU (ibid). The MEDEF thereby met context-specific expectations that were provided by political institutions and changed their position towards the NFR-Directive, which can be interpreted as *satisficing* behaviour. In the French discourse among observers of the transposition process, the directive was regarded as an export of the French model to the EU level. In a legal commentary on the transposition of the NFR-Directive was titled "Europe in tune with France" (EY, 2015). In view of this transposition environment, the public expectation was that France would transpose the directive in an extensive manner, anything else would have been a surprise.

This account shows how the different degrees of political salience affected the effect of the misfit on the transposition outcome. A similar effect could be noted with regard to the influence of the party-political formation of the domestic government. In the transposition of the public procurement directive, the socialist orientation of the French government was reported to have had little influence on the transposition (Interview 16). This situation was different for the NFR-Directive. Corporate sustainability had a higher political priority for president Hollande, as it had also been one of his election promises during the 2012 presidential campaign. This priority did not change any more, when in the final stage of the transposition process the government changed from a Socialist to an LREM!-government, as the text of the law had largely been finalized (Interview 14). In addition, the minister of economy and finance, who was responsible for the law at the time, was Emmanuel Macron, who would later become president.

The political salience within the policy subsystem is thus the central factor to understand the divergence between France's transposition of the public procurement directives and NFR-Directive. Of the two competing hypotheses formulated for political salience, Hypothesis 4.1, which states that low political salience leads to a low transposition outcome can be confirmed for both transpositions.

6.4.3 Germany

The German transposition outcomes are equally diverse. The analysis shows that the German transposition of the public procurement directives and the transposition of the NFR-Directive differ both with regard to the outcome and the process of the transposition. With the public procurement directives, the government aimed at a transposition that balanced prescriptive with voluntary measures. On the one hand, the transposition integrated some binding human rights provisions, for example by listing the social clause as a procurement principle (PP 1) and by adopting stricter verification requirements for subcontractors (PP 4). With many other provisions, the decision if social concerns should be taken into account was left to the contracting authorities. This approach was taken with the provision to include social concerns in the award criteria (PP 14), and the provision to include social criteria in contract conditions (PP 16).

The analysis has identified two factors that hold explanatory power for the transposition of the public procurement directives. First, the high degree of corporatism matches the transposition outcome. The transposition approach and its outcome are consistent with the idea of institutionalized solidarity that is common among CMEs. In the consultation process, industry representatives warned about the 'additional burden' stricter sustainability requirements put for the economy. On the other hand, the German Trade Union Confederation (DGB) and NGOs stressed the relevance of social standards, minimum wages, and the ratification of ILO Convention 94. This involvement was reflected in the transposition outcome. The views of companies that eventually have to abide by the procurement rules when they bid for public tenders were taken into account. At the same time, the transposition outcome reflected the input from labour unions, the classical 'social partners', and NGOs. The second factor that explains the transposition outcome is the stance of the political parties in government during the transposition. The coalition of the CDU (score on state intervention in the economy of 5.3) and the SPD (score of 5.3) led to a government moderately in favour of state intervention (average scores of 4.12). Interview evidence showed that in the process of inter-ministerial coordination, the political positions of the two parties were mirrored by the ministries, who aligned their positions in several coordination rounds, while always keeping in mind the governing coalition (Interviews 6, 18).[35] When the transposition law was proposed to the German parliament, further discussions ensued, also triggered by the Green Party, during which it was discussed, if some of the voluntary grounds for exclusion should be made mandatory. In the end, the compromise from the inter-ministerial coordination was adopted by the Bundestag without major changes, also because "going further would not have been possible with this party constellation" (Interview 6). In this respect, the party affiliation also affected the degree to which voluntary provisions could be transposed. Moreover, the deputies from the Green Party advocated for a farther-reaching transposition, most notably by demanding that a violation of the social clause would become a mandatory ground for exclusion (Interview 18). Due to these observations, I disagree with the assessment made by Beichelt (2013), who stated that in Germany [t]he transposition of EU legislation […] is usually deprived of open party competition" (p. 95).

The transposition of the NFR-Directive differed from the transposition of the public procurement directives both with regard to outcome and process. The outcome shows the minimalistic transposition approach taken by the German government. Of the nine directive provisions, none were over-transposed. Only in two cases was the discretion to apply stricter reporting requirements left to companies (NFR 7

[35] The federal ministries of the interior and finance favoured the position of the CDU, the ministries of labour, economics and foreign affairs took the position of the SPD. The ministry of economics portrayed itself as the broker in between (Interview 6).

and NFR 9). The minimalistic transposition is reflected in the low human rights score of 16, the same as the UK's. This result is rather surprising. From the high degree of corporatism, one would expect a different transposition outcome. Similarly, the position toward state intervention in the economy of the parties in power is in favour (score of 4.12), which equally does not match the hypothesis. The fact that no policy transfer could be reported also does not give any indication that would explain the outcome further. How, then, can the difference between the transposition outcomes of the procurement directives and the NFR-Directive be explained? Why did the governing coalition opt for a balanced transposition outcome with the public procurement directives, and a one-sided outcome with the NFR-Directive? Both directives introduce human rights-related regulations that the CDU/CSU regarded as rather 'alien' in the respective field of application (Interviews 6, 13). In both cases, the consultation process received a balanced consultation outcome from stakeholders.

From the evidence gathered I argue that the central factor for explaining the different transposition outcomes lies in the different degrees of political salience within the policy subsystem. Hypothesis H4.2, which postulates that low political salience leads to a low transposition score and vice versa, is best suited to explain the divergence between the transposition outcomes. In the case of the public procurement directives, the importance attached to the human rights clauses was low. More attention was paid to the fact that the transposition law was accompanied by a profound reform bill, which regulated procurement areas that were previously governed by specialized procurement committees (Interview 6). According to interview evidence, this facilitated a sober and fact-based transposition process (Interview 18). The transposition process was described to have been characterized by a constructive consensus culture and the aim was to achieve a balanced compromise (Interview 6), which is reflected in the transposition score. The transposition process of the NFR-Directive was described to have been more confrontational. Pro-regulatory actors (NGOs, labour unions) and anti-regulatory actors (employers' unions, large corporations) within the policy subsystem attached a high degree of political importance to the transposition. Interview evidence revealed that senior representatives from employers' associations and the chambers of commerce advocated a minimalistic transposition on a ministerial level (Interview 1). Four issues attest to the more politicized atmosphere of the transposition process of the NFR-Directive.[36] First, the high misfit was used by the advocacy coalition that favoured a minimalistic transposition as an argument to underscore that such a high regulatory 'jump' would be prejudicial for businesses. Second, the interpretation of the department within the leading ministry of Justice affected the transposition. The accounting department coordinated the transposition.[37] Due to the novelty of non-financial reporting legislation, the department interpreted the directive in a restrictive manner (Interview 1). According to an NGO representative, the

[36]The difference political salience also became evident during the research process. Ministry officials that worked on the public procurement directives showed a much larger willingness to speak openly about the political preferences of the actors involved than those officials tasked with the transposition of the NFR-Directive.

[37]The department that coordinated the transposition was Referat III A 3 (Rechnungslegung; Publizität; Recht der Abschlussprüfung) (Interview 13).

first draft of the law would have been substantially different, had the department for international law been in charge of the transposition process (ibid). The importance of this allocation for the transposition outcome was also stressed by another interviewee (Interview 4). Third, the commitment of the German Federal Government to transpose EU directives 'one-to-one' was repeatedly used as an argument for a minimalist transposition (Interview 13), while it was only rarely mentioned in interviews about the public procurement directives.

Lastly, in the coordination process for the transposition of the NFR-Directive between the two parties forming the governing coalition, the CSU/CSU, the larger political group, exerted a larger sway over the transposition outcome than in the transposition of the public procurement directives. The co-rapporteur from the SPD for the NFR transposition law stated that the SPD would have preferred a transposition outcome with a wider scope but was not able to assert this position (Deutscher Bundestag, 2017). The co-rapporteur from the CDU, on the other hand, repeatedly stressed the importance of minimal administrative burdens for companies. When asked about the relevance of rules that aim at fair supply chains, he stated: "The market regulates those things. Companies that do not take care of their supply chains cannot survive in global markets" (Interview 4, own translation). He again stressed the low importance the CDU/CSU assigned to binding human rights-related reporting obligations when he explained the reasons for the delayed transposition. During the parliamentary debate, he stated that the transposition was delayed because in his political group it was decided that the legislative schedule should not be changed for a law that puts additional burdens on the economy (Deutscher Bundestag, 2017). The transposition outcome shows that this view has prevailed in the transposition process.

Overall, it can be summarized that in the transposition of the NFR-Directive, the higher political salience within the policy subsystem induced the low transposition outcome. Hypothesis H4.2 can be confirmed for Germany and is backed up by interview evidence. This finding suggests that in the German BHR policy subsystem, a lower political salience is conducive to adopting more voluntary human rights-related provisions. A higher political salience appears to enable anti-regulatory actors and thereby lead to a low transposition score.

6.4.4 Denmark

Unlike France and Germany, Denmark shows a consistent transposition outcome. In both cases, Denmark adopted several voluntary human rights-related provisions. Of the four countries analysed in this study, Denmark has the highest average human right score per directive provision. The interesting aspect of the Danish case is that two completely different transposition processes lead to similar transposition outcomes, as the testing of the hypotheses has shown. Regarding the public procurement directives, the only clear indication for the transposition outcome is the high degree of corporatism. The medium misfit between previously existing procurement legislation and the EU directives and the absence of international policy transfer and political salience within the policy subsystem do not provide answers for the transposition outcome. The composition of the domestic government would even suggest the opposite transposition outcome, as the liberal-conservative coalition that was in power at the time is, according to CHES data, opposed to government intervention in the economy. To understand the transposition outcome, it is, therefore, necessary to take a closer look at the transposition context.

When starting the transposition of the procurement directives, the Danish government under the minority leadership of the liberal-conservative party did not conduct an open consultation process but suggest a closed transposition committee to which key stakeholders, such as labour unions and employers' representatives, were invited.[38] However, the most important advocate for human rights-related procurement criteria, the Danish 92-Group, was excluded from this committee, which was reported to have been the most relevant forum in the transposition process (Interviews 8, 11). The government's focus when transposing the EU public procurement directives was to reduce public expenditures and to simplify procurement procedures, which also becomes clear when analysing the government's communication about the directive (Danish Ministry of Industry Business and Financial Affairs, 2015; Interview 8). The allocation of competences and coordination between ministries also gives an indication of the low importance the government attached to the transposition of the social clauses. The transposition process was coordinated by the public procurement division ministry in the Danish Competition and Consumer Authority. Interview evidence suggests that the officials within this department were not familiar with CSR-related legislation and regarded the transposition of the directive largely as a technical process (Interview 11). Reportedly, the Danish Business Authority, which is the leading governmental body in all CSR-related matters, tried to influence the interpretation of the social clauses in the procurement legislation but remained largely external to the process (Interview 11). NGO demands to turn more of the voluntary requirements in the directive into mandatory requirements were dismissed by the government by referring to the government's role to merely guide contracting authorities. The government announced to reform its public procurement tool 'The Responsible Purchaser' to promote responsible procurement further.[39] Due to the low political salience of the directive transposition process, interest groups both from the business side and NGOs were reported to not have had a large degree of influence on the process. An NGO representative stated in an expert interview that because of budgetary concerns the government was politically determined to transpose the directive by relying on a simple transposition that follows a copy-out-approach. As a matter of principle, the government was not open to changing this approach, because

[38]The Danish government was reported to have sent the draft law to NGO representatives after a first draft law had been finalized. However, an NGO representative stated that the time provided to respond was very short and that the comments were thought to have had little effect (Interview 8).

[39]Den Ansvarlige Indkøber (Responsible purchasing) can be assessed at: http://csr-indkob.dk/.

"this was not a matter of left or right" (Interview 8). Despite this approach, Denmark still received a medium transposition score. Even though representatives from Amnesty International and the Danish Institute for Human Rights were not satisfied with the transposition outcome (Interviews 8, 11), the Danish outcome is still the second-highest among the four countries considered. This can mainly be attributed to the consensus culture within the transposition committee. According to a representative of the Danish government, all decisions within the committee were taken unanimously, which led to relatively balanced outcomes. In addition, the Danish government followed a copy-out-approach with the Utilities and Concessions Directives, whereby many human rights-related decisions were automatically passed on to the contracting authorities.

The transposition of the NFR-Directive followed a completely different process. Here all of the five explanatory variables that were tested hold explanatory power for the transposition outcome. The medium misfit was repeatedly described as having played an important role in negotiations on the scope of the reporting requirement (Interviews 8, 10, 11). The high degree of corporatism and the social-democratic government, principally in favour of state intervention in the economy, also match this transposition outcome. In addition, the Danish transposition of the NFR-Directive is the only case in this analysis, for which policy transfer from the international level on the transposition process could be determined. The high transposition outcome can, therefore, confirm the policy transfer hypothesis.

Party politics did not play a significant role in affecting transposition outcomes. While the conservative party was reported to have been initially reluctant to accept over-transposing the NFR-Directive, they eventually agreed to the fervent demands from pro-regulatory actors within the policy subsystem (Interview 8). Regarding the public procurement directives, an interviewee stated that the outcome would not have been different if the government had been formed by another party (Interview 15).

From the evidence gathered, the differences between the two transposition processes can be summed up in three points. The first and highly relevant aspect refers again to the different degrees of political salience within the policy subsystem. The interviews made clear that the human rights-related provisions received a lot of attention from actors within the policy subsystem in the transposition of the NFR-Directive, and only little attention in the transposition of the public procurement directives (Interviews 8, 11). In the policy debates, for example during the hearings in the Danish parliament, the transposition of the NFR-Directive was connected to Denmark's national CSR agenda. The high activity of stakeholders in the legislative process and the degree of attention devoted to the plan to increase the scope of the directive put pressure on the social-democratic government to meet the expectations of voters, labour unions, and NGOs. Moreover, the government put a priority on abiding by international rules. As was stated in the description of the international policy transfer, Danish governments have traditionally been keen to abide by international standards, because as a small and open economy, Danish businesses depend on an international level playing field. A study on sustainability reporting analysed this behaviour in 2011:

> By providing the possibility of basing the disclosure of sustainability information on international instruments, Denmark has explicitly refrained from developing its own national standards, but rather relies on instruments such as the Global Compact. (Wensen et al., 2011, p. 62)

The evidence suggests that this approach was continued with the transposition of the NFR-Directive, which also included the expectation that the compliance with high international sustainability standards would give Danish companies a competitive advantage in the global economy (Interviews 8, 10, 11). However, this connection to international BHR instruments was not made regarding the public procurement directives. The differences between the effects of the political salience within the policy subsystem are captured by the two hypotheses. Hypothesis H4.2, according to which low political salience induces a high transposition outcome, can be confirmed for the transposition of the public procurement directive. Hypothesis H4.1, which postulates that a high political salience leads to a high transposition outcome, can be confirmed for Denmark's transposition of the NFR-Directive

A second, and related, difference between the two transposition processes was that the Danish government was much closer involved in the negotiation of the NFR-Directive than it was the case with the public procurement directives. The Danish government tried to advocate the Danish model of non-financial reporting on the EU level and indeed the first Commission proposal was, next to French and British influences, inspired by the Danish model (Interview 8). As was stated in the description of the Danish misfit, the most relevant differences were the dissimilar understandings of materiality and the difference between the 'comply or state' approach under the old Danish requirements and the 'comply or explain' approach of the NFR-Directive. The directive as it was adopted in the end was regarded as a Danish success, and, similar to France, it was portrayed as the EU following the Danish model. The high compatibility of the NFR-Directive with the previous Danish reporting also facilitated a farther-reaching transposition because it was regarded as important that Denmark remains a front-runner in CSR (Interview 10). Another aspect were the practical considerations that resulted from the medium misfit. In the first draft law, the government did not propose to extend the scope of the directive. This would have meant that Danish companies that have less than 500 employees and fall under accounting classes C or D would have been required to abide by the old Danish reporting requirements, while companies that have more than 500 employees would have been required to report according to the new EU requirements. Various stakeholders argued that it was impractical for the businesses to create two separate tracks of reporting, which is why in the end the government decided to reduce complexity by creating one accounting standard with a larger scope.[40] Interview evidence suggests the lobbying of the Danish labour unions were, in the end, decisive for this decision.

[40]Due to this change, the new requirements applied to 1050 companies and not to 50 companies, as would have been the case if the scope had not been extended. However, it was determined that for those companies that fall under the extended scope, the new requirements will only take effect on 1 January 2018, while for those companies covered by the directive the requirement took effect on 1 January 2016.

A last major difference between the transposition processes in public procurement and the NFR-Directive was the administrative coordination. For the NFR-Directive the Danish Business Authority was in charge, the central government body responsible for the Danish CSR agenda (see Danish Business Authority, 2015). This department has the declared goal to keep Denmark as one of the global frontrunners in CSR and was in open dialogue with NGOs and the Danish Institute for Human Rights (Interview 11).

This chapter has provided a detailed account of the reasons behind the transposition outcomes that were presented in Chap. 5. It tested the hypotheses that were formulated in Chap. 4 in order to understand the influence single factors had on the transposition outcome. In the last section, these single factors were put in the political context for each country. In the concluding chapter of this book, the insights from this analysis will be discussed in order to work out theoretical and political conclusions.

References

Allen, D. (2013). The United Kingdom: Towards isolation and a parting of the ways? In S. Bulmer & C. Lequesne (Eds.), *The member states of the European Union*. Oxford: Oxford University Press.

Armstrong, K., & Bulmer, S. (1996). United Kingdom. In D. Rometsch & W. Wessels (Eds.), *The European Union and member states: Towards institutional fusion?*. Manchester and New York: Manchester University Press.

Beichelt, T. (2013). Germany: In Search of a new balance. In Bulmer & C. Lequesne (Eds.), *The member states of the European Union*. Oxford: Oxford University Press.

British Parliament. (2017). The implications of Brexit. Retrieved December 5, 2017, from https://publications.parliament.uk/pa/jt201617/jtselect/jtrights/443/44310.htm#_idTextAnchor087.

Bursens, P. (2002). Why Denmark and Belgium have different implementation records: On transposition laggards and leaders in the EU. *Scandinavian Political Studies, 25*(2), 173–195.

Cabinet Office. (2014). *Consultation document UK transposition of new EU Procurement Directives—Public contracts regulations 2015*. London. Retrieved from https://www.gov.uk/government/uploads/system/uploads/attachment_data/file/356492/Consultation_Document_UK_Transposition_of_new_EU_Procurement_Directives_Public_Contracts_Regulations_2015.pdf.

Cabinet Office. (2015). *Government response to the consultation on UK transposition of new EU Procurement Directives public contracts regulations 2015*. London. Retrieved from https://www.gov.uk/government/uploads/system/uploads/attachment_data/file/400242/Government_Response_to_the_Consultation_on_UK_Transposition_of_new_EU_Procurement_Directives_Public_Contracts_Regulations_2015.pdf.

CHES. (2017). Chesdata—1999–2014 Chapel Hill Expert Survey (CHES) trend file. Retrieved September 14, 2017, from https://www.chesdata.eu/our-surveys.

Crown Commercial Service. (2015). The public contracts regulations 2015—Guidance on social and environmental aspects, 1–10. Retrieved from https://www.gov.uk/government/uploads/system/uploads/attachment_data/file/430313/public-contracts-regulations-guidance.pdf.

Danish Business Authority. (2014). Danish national action plan—Implementation of the UN guiding principles on business and human rights, 2013/14:9.

Danish Business Authority. (2015). Implementation in Denmark of EU Directive 2014/95/EU on the disclosure of non-financial information. Retrieved October 5, 2016, from http://csrgov.dk/file/557863/implementation-of-eu-directive.pdf.

Danish Ministry of Industry Business and Financial Affairs (Erhvervsministeriet). (2015). Pressemeddelelse: Folketinget vedtager Danmarks første udbudslov. Copenhagen. Retrieved from http://em.dk/nyheder/2015/15-11-19-udbudslov.

Danish Ministry of Economic and Business Affairs. (2015). Høringsnotat vedrørende forslag til lov om ændring af årsregnskabs- loven, selskabsloven, lov om erhvervsdrivende fonde, lov om visse erhvervsdrivende virksomheder og lov om værdipapirhandel m.v. Copenhagen. Retrieved from http://www.ft.dk/samling/20141/lovforslag/L117/bilag/1/1490261/index.htm

Danish Parliament. (2011). *The Parliamentary Electoral System in Denmark: Guide to Danish Electorial System*. Copenhagen. Retrieved from http://elections.im.dk.

DEFRA. (2006). *Procuring the future—Sustainable procurement national action plan: Recommendations from the sustainable procurement task force sustainable*. Department for Environment Food and Rural Affairs. Retrieved from https://www.gov.uk/government/uploads/system/uploads/attachment_data/file/69417/pb11710-procuring-the-future-060607.pdf.

Department for Business Energy & Industrial Strategy. (2016). Government response to the consultation on implementation of the EU non-financial reporting directive (2014/95/EU), (November). Retrieved from https://www.gov.uk/government/consultations/non-financial-reporting-directive-uk-implementation.

Deutscher Bundestag. (2015a). Beschlussempfehlung und Bericht: Entwurf eines Gesetzes zur Modernisierung des Vergaberechts (Vergaberechtsmodernisierungsgesetz – VergRModG), 18/7086.

Deutscher Bundestag. (2015b). Entschließungsantrag der Abgeordneten Brigitte Pothmer, Katharina Dröge [...] zu der dritten Beratung des Gesetzentwurfs der Bundesregierung – Drucksachen 18/6281, 18/7086 – Entwurf eines Gesetzes zur Modernisierung des Vergaberechts, 18/7091, 12–15.

Deutscher Bundestag. (2015c). Gesetzentwurf der Bundesregierung Entwurf eines Gesetzes zur Modernisierung des Vergaberechts (Vergaberechtsmodernisierungsgesetz – VergRModG), 18/6281.

Deutscher Bundestag. (2017). Ausweitung der Berichts-pflichten für Unter-nehmen beschlossen. Retrieved November 14, 2017, from https://www.bundestag.de/dokumente/textarchiv/2017/kw10-de-berichtspflichten-unternehmen-csr/493972.

Deutscher Städtetag. (2010). Die Berücksichtigung sozialer Belange im Vergaberecht.

Direction Générale du Trésor. (2017). Consultation sur le projet de transposition de la directive 2014/95/UE relative à la publication d'informations extra-financières par les entreprises. Retrieved September 5, 2017, from https://www.tresor.economie.gouv.fr/Ressources/15700_consultation-sur-le-projet-de-transposition-de-la-directive-201495-ue.

Directive 2014/23/EU of the European Parliament and of the Council of 26 February 2014 on the award of concession contracts. (2014). Official Journal of the European Union, L 94.

Directive 2014/24/EU of the European Parliament and of the Council of 26 February 2014 on public procurement and repealing Directive 2004/18/EC. (2014). Official Journal of the European Union, L 94.

Directive 2014/25/EU of the European Parliament and of the Council of 26 February 2014 on procurement by entities operating in the water, energy, transport and postal services sectors and repealing Directive 2004/17/EC. (2014). Official Journal of the European Union, L 94.

Directive 2014/95/EU of the European Parliament and of the Council of 22 October 2014 amending Directive 2013/34/EU as regards disclosure of non-financial and diversity information by certain large undertakings and groups. (2014). Official Journal of the European Union, L 330.

European Commission. (2015). Study on "Strategic use of public procurement in promoting green, social and innovation policies"—France In-depth Country Report.

European Commission. (2016). Public procurement—Study on administrative capacity in the EU—Denmark Country Profile. Retrieved from http://ec.europa.eu/regional_policy/en/policy/how/improving-investment/public-procurement/study/#28.

EY. (2015). Directive sur la publication d'informations non financières—L'Europe au diapason de la France. Retrieved from https://webforms.ey.com/Publication/vwLUAssets/EY-Plaquette-CaS-Directive/$FILE/EY-Plaquette-CaS-Directive.pdf.

Falkner, G., Treib, O., Hartlapp, M., & Leiber, S. (2005). *Complying with Europe. EU harmonisation and soft law in the member states*. New York: Cambridge University Press.

France Stratégie. (2015). Avis du GT ad hoc achats publics responsables pour la transposition de la directive européenne "marchés publics". *Commissariat General à La Strategie et à La Prospective*, 1–8.

France Stratégie. (2018). Plateforme RSE. Retrieved March 27, 2018, from http://www.strategie.gouv.fr/chantiers/plateforme-rse.

Gouvernement Français. (2016). Rapport du Gouvernement Relatif à l'application par les entreprises des dispositions de l'article L.225-102-1 du code de commerce et du décret "Grenelle II" - Septembre 2016.

Hall, P. A., & Soskice, D. (2001). An introduction to varieties of capitalism. In P. A. Hall & D. Soskice (Eds.), *Varieties of capitalism: The institutional foundations of comparative advantage* (pp. 1–68). Oxford: Oxford University Press.

Hecker, A. (2015). *Untersuchung zur Umsetzung der „CSR-Richtlinie" in Deutschland unter Berücksichtigung der Initiative „Deutscher Nachhaltigkeitskodex"*. Düsseldorf.

Human Rights Act. (1998). *The national archives*, (c. 42). Retrieved from http://www.legislation.gov.uk/ukpga/1998/42/section/6.

International Learning Lab on Public Procurement and Human Rights. (2016). *Public procurement and human rights: A survey of twenty jurisdictions*.

Ismayr, W. (2004). Das politische System Deutschlands. In W. Ismayr (Ed.), *Die politischen Systeme Westeuropas*. Leske and Budrich: Opladen.

Kahlenborn, W., Moser, C., Frijdal, J., & Essig, M. (2011). *Strategic use of public procurement in Europe —Final report to the European Commission MARKT/2010/02/C*. Berlin.

Kaufmann, D., Kraay, A., & Mastruzzi, M. (2006). *Governance Matters VI: Governance Indicators for 1996–2006* (World Bank Policy Research Working Paper No. 4280).

Kinderman, D. (2015). Corporate Social Responsibility—Der Kampf um die EU-Richtlinie. *WSI-Mitteilungen, 2015/8*.

Kinderman, D. (2016). Time for a reality check: Is business willing to support a smart mix of complementary regulation in private governance? *Policy and Society, 35*(1), 29–42.

King, A. (1994). Ministerial autonomy in Britain. In M. Laver & K. A. Shepsle (Eds.), *Cabinet ministers and parliamentary government*. Cambridge: Cambridge University Press.

Knill, C., & Lehmkuhl, D. (2002). The national impact of European Union regulatory policy: Three Europeanization mechanisms. *European Journal of Political Research, 41*(2), 255–280.

Lequesne, C. (1996). France. In D. Rometsch & W. Wessels (Eds.), *The European Union and member states: Towards institutional fusion*? Manchester and New York: Manchester University Press.

Lijphart, A. (1999). *Patterns of democracy: Government forms and performance in thirty-six countries*. New Haven: Yale University Press.

Lowi, T. J. (1972). Four systems of policy, politics, and choice. *Public Administration Review, 32*(4), 298–310.

Ministère de l'écologie du Dévéloppement durable et de l'Énergie. (2015). *Plan national d'action pour les achats publics durables 2015 – 2020*. Paris.

Ministère de l'économie de l'industrie et du numérique. (2014). *Fiche d'impact projet d'ordonnance relative aux marchés publics*. Paris.

Müller Gómez, J., & Wessels, W. (2016). *Die deutsche Verwaltung und die Europäische Union - Deutsche Beamte im EU-Mehrebenensystem*. Brühl: Bundesakademie für öffentliche Verwaltung im Bundesministerium des Innern.

Neumayr, E. (2013). The Grenelle II act in France: A milestone towards integrated reporting. Retrieved July 5, 2016, from https://blogs.oracle.com/sustainability/the-grenelle-ii-act-in-france:-a-milestone-towards-integrated-reporting.

Pedersen, T. (1996). Denmark. In D. Rometsch & W. Wessels (Eds.), *The European Union and member states: Towards institutional fusion?*. Manchester and New York: Manchester University Press.

Rozenberg, O. (2013). France: Genuine Europeanization of Monnet for nothing. In S. Bulmer & C. Lequesne (Eds.), *The member states of the European Union*. Oxford: Oxford University Press.
Siaroff, A. (1999). Corporatism in 24 industrial democracies: Meaning and measurement. *European Journal of Political Research, 36*(2), 175–205.
Spießhofer, B. (2014). Die neue europäische Richtlinie über die Offenlegung nichtfinanzieller Informationen - Paradigmenwechsel oder Papiertiger? *Neue Zeitschrift Für Gesellschaftsrecht, 1281*(33), 1281–1320.
Treib, O. (2004). *Die Bedeutung der nationalen Parteipolitik für die Umsetzung europäischer Sozialrichtlinien*. Frankfurt/New York: Campus.
UK Department for Business Innovation and Skills. (2014). Non-financial Reporting: Impact Assessment. Retrieved May 14, 2017, from https://www.gov.uk/government/consultations/non-financial-reporting-directive-uk-implementation
UK Department for Business Enterprise and Industrial Strategy. (2016). Explanatory Memorandum to the Companies, Partnerships and Groups (Accounts and Non- Financial Reporting) Regulations 2016, (No. 1245), 1–12.
UK Department for Business Innovation and Skills. (2016). The Non-financial Reporting Directive: A call for views on effective reporting alongside proposals to implement EU requirements.
UK Parliament. (2017). The Implications of Brexit. Retrieved December 5, 2017, from https://publications.parliament.uk/pa/jt201617/jtselect/jtrights/443/44310.htm#_idTextAnchor087
Von Dosenrode, S. (2014). Denmark: The testing of a hesitant membership. In K. Hanf & B. Soetendorp (Eds.), *Adapting to European integration: Small states and the European Union*. Routledge.
Wensen, K. van, Broer, W., Klein, J., & Knopf, J. (2011). The state of play in sustainability reporting in the European Union.
Wessels, W., & Rometsch, D. (1996). Conclusion: European Union and national institutions. In D. Rometsch & W. Wessels (Eds.), *The European Union and member states: Towards institutional fusion?*. Manchester and New York: Manchester University Press.
Worldbank. (2017). The Worldwide Governance indicators. Retrieved September 7, 2017, from http://info.worldbank.org/governance/wgi/index.aspx#home.

Chapter 7
Conclusion

The previous chapters have provided a comprehensive account of the EU's BHR policy and conducted a comparative analysis of the transpositions of four EU directives in this policy area in four EU member states.[1] The objective of this book was to determine and explain the differences in the willingness of EU member states to oblige and incentivize globally operating companies to respect human rights in global supply chains. As a 'regulatory state' (Majone, 1996), the EU shapes the regulatory framework of TNCs domiciled in the EU and has, therefore, the potential to mitigate the widening gap between global markets and the limited capacity of some states to ensure the respect for human rights. In the developing field of EU BHR policy, many human rights-related requirements are formulated as voluntary rules and therefore depend on the member states' willingness to go beyond the required legal minimum. Among the limited studies of EU BHR policy so far, this study is the first to use the 'discretionary room' within EU directives as a yardstick to measure member states' disposition to adopt stricter human rights regulations vis-à-vis their national businesses. Accordingly, I formulated the following research question: How and why do EU member states differ regarding the degree to which they transpose non-binding provisions of Business and Human Rights regulation in EU directives?

To approach this research question, the introductory chapter stated the academic and political relevance of this research project and gave an overview of the structure. Chapter 2 provided a comprehensive account of the development and features of the EU BHR policy area, which was instigated by the political decision to implement the UNGPs. I argued that this policy area rests on two pillars: the EU human rights regime and EU CSR policy, both of which contain inherent contradictions which in turn also affect EU BHR policy. Regarding the EU's human rights regime, scholars have noted an 'implementation gap' between the commitment to human rights,

[1] The four EU member states considered are the UK, France, Germany, and Denmark. This study analyses and compares, how these countries transpose four EU directives, namely the Public Sector Directive (PSD), the Concessions Directive (CD), the Utilities Directive (UD), and the Non-Financial Reporting Directive (NFR-Directive) into national law.

P. Drahn, *Adoption of EU Business and Human Rights Policy*,
Contributions to Political Science, https://doi.org/10.1007/978-3-030-46935-1_7

which is both legally enshrined and actively communicated, and the concrete execution of human rights policy. EU CSR policy, on the other hand, is characterized by an inherent ambiguity between two competing interpretations, one stressing voluntary incentives and the other underlining mandatory regulation. This ambiguity also shapes EU BHR policy, which to a large degree formalized the status quo ante. Member states' interpretation of this question, which I address in this study, is, therefore, a decisive element of the future development of EU BHR policy. I characterize EU BHR policy as a regulative policy area that was transferred from the UN level to the EU level and discuss the links between a country's degree of corporatism and its willingness to regulate business conduct. After outlining current legislative acts and other policy measures in the area of EU BHR policy, I singled out the three EU public procurement directives, the Public Sector Directive (2014/24/EU), the Utilities Directive (2014/25/EU), and the Concessions Directive (2014/23/EU), as well as the NFR-Directive (2014/95/EU) as central and representative elements of this policy area.

Chapter 3 established the theoretical background of this study. It first explained the three main approaches of new institutionalist theory that deliver conceptual explanations to institutional change. Building on this theoretical foundation, I provided definitions and explanations of Europeanization both as a political phenomenon and as a research approach. I reviewed the literature on EU directive transposition and identified several factors that are relevant for the empirical analysis. Next, I provided a concise account of the concept of policy transfer, which addresses a problem of Europeanization, namely that it "does take European processes systematically as a point of departure for changes at the domestic level" (Saurugger, 2014b, p. 136). By explaining the similarities in the concrete applications of policy transfer and Europeanization, I underlined the compatibility of the two, and provide the basis for integrating policy transfer into my empirical analysis. Section 3.5 approached the issue of voluntary compliance within the EU from a conceptual perspective and discussed mechanisms that are suited to explain member states' willingness to comply with voluntary EU rules. In the last section of Chap. 3, I built the analytical framework for the empirical analysis. Drawing on previously gathered insights from the literature on Europeanization and directive transposition, as well as on the policy-specific links between corporatism and BHR, I formulated hypotheses to test the impact of six explanatory factors: policy misfit, institutional misfit, government composition, political salience within the policy subsystem, international policy transfer, and administrative effectiveness.

Chapter 4 delineated the research design of this study, first by outlining the methodological approach and by substantiating directive selection and country selection. Then, I explained how the six factors that were identified in the previous chapter are operationalized into measurable variables. For the operationalization of the DV, I developed a novel analytical framework that captures four possible ways in which EU member states can deal with directive provisions: non-transposition, transposition, discretion-passed-on, and over-transposition. For each country, I calculated a transposition score that measures the degree to which the transposition reflects a commitment to human rights. Chapters 5 and 6 contain the empirical analysis of this book. Chapter 5 comprises the first part of the empirical analysis by comparing how the UK, France, Germany, and Denmark transposed the 45 human rights-related provisions in the EU public procurement directives and the nine human rights-related provisions in the NFR-Directive. In Chap. 6, I explained the national policy contexts in which the transpositions took place and tested the hypotheses that were postulated in Chap. 3. Finally, relying on the analysis of policy documents and 18 expert interviews, I put the results of the hypothesis-testing back into the national policy contexts and delineate the respective transposition processes. Drawing theoretical and political conclusions from the insights gathered in these two chapters requires a nuanced discussion of the empirical results that takes into account both country-specific and cross-country transposition patterns.

7.1 Discussion of Empirical Results

The detailed account of the human-rights-related provisions showed the extent to which the four EU directives rely on voluntary rules. When combining the individual provisions of all four directives, 31 out of 54 provisions are voluntary (57%), while 16 (30%) are mandatory with discretion. Only seven provisions (13%) are completely mandatory. This large degree of discretion underlines the importance of national transposition for the effectiveness of the directives. On average and across the four countries, the transposition analysis shows that in several cases member states chose to turn voluntary provisions into mandatory ones. However, member states mostly relied on the possibility to either ignore discretionary clauses or to pass on the discretion to implementing actors. How and with respect to which provisions member states made use of these options varied greatly between the transpositions of the UK, France, Germany, and Denmark.

7.1.1 Country-Specific Transposition Patterns

The results for the UK and Denmark broadly correspond with the assumptions formulated when explaining the four archetypes of government behaviour in BHR in Sect. 4.3. The outcomes for France and Germany are much less intuitive. They show divergent transposition patterns that partly contradict initial assumptions and need further clarification. The results showed large divergences both with respect to total transposition scores and regarding the transposition tools member states relied on. This sub-section describes country-specific transposition patterns and draws wider conclusions for the four archetypes described in Chap. 3.

7.1.1.1 United Kingdom

The UK transposed all four EU directives in a minimalistic fashion. For the public procurement directives, the UK received 105 out of 412 possible points on the transposition scale. Of the 45 human rights-related provisions 20 were ignored and in 18 cases the discretion of how to implement the provisions was passed on to the contracting authorities. The British transposition of the NFR-Directive follows along similar lines, leading to a human rights score of 16 out of 68 possible points. Apart from requiring UK companies to include non-financial reports in their general management reports, the UK did not render any voluntary provisions mandatory and established thereby a heavily voluntarist reporting framework. Due to the political priority to achieve a minimalistic transposition, many provisions were simply copied from the EU directives. Voluntary provisions were often copied as well and thereby passed on to the implementing authorities. As a consequence, the UK provides more flexibility to apply human rights-related regulations and has a larger score on the NFR-Directive than France, where many voluntary provisions were ignored completely (see below). Nonetheless, on average and across all four directives, the UK received the lowest human rights score per directive provision (2.06) of the four countries considered in this study.

Similar to the transposition results, the transposition processes in the UK also show a large intra-country consistency. For all four directives, the British government conducted fast and transparent transposition processes that were both marked by low degrees of political salience within the policy subsystem. Interview evidence revealed that the levels of low salience can in part be attributed to the public debates on the Brexit-vote. But the interviews with actors within the British BHR policy subsystem also showed that directive transpositions are generally regarded as largely technical processes in which attempts to interpret voluntary provisions beyond the legal minimum were regarded as futile because it would not be politically desired. In light of vigorous scrutiny processes by the British Parliament and a Eurosceptic media landscape, the British government seems to have been aware that anything but a minimalistic transposition of the directive would have provoked opposition from anti-regulatory actors within the policy subsystem. From this perspective, a 'shadow of politicization' played a significant role during the British transposition processes.

Of the six IVs that were tested, the institutional misfit and the composition of the domestic government hold the greatest explanatory power for the British transposition result. Especially the low score on Siaroff's (1999) measure or corporatism, typical for a LME, matches the focus on a flexible approach towards BHR regulation. This is consistent with the market-liberal position of the Conservative party that formed the government during the transposition process. From a theoretical perspective, the evidence gathered about the UK's transposition points to a historical institutionalist explanation. Expert interviews and policy document showed a strong commitment out of the liberal-market tradition to prefer voluntary regulation over mandatory requirements. While as an LME, the UK is open to the concepts of CSR and BHR, the traditions clearly prescribe a voluntarist understanding of the two. This matches the historical institutionalist logic, which stresses an "institutional organization of the polity or political economy as the principal factor structuring collective behaviour and generating distinctive outcomes" (Hall & Taylor, 1996, p. 937).

The policy analysis uncovered that the government, led by the British Conservative Party, was keen on sticking to this tradition, even in cases where a different transposition would have led to a more efficient outcome. When the government was deciding on the scope for the UK reporting requirements, the most value-maximising solution would have been to extend the scope of the EU requirements and match them with the previously existing UK requirements. For businesses, this solution would have reduced complexity the most (Interview 9). However, this solution would have been in conflict both with the voluntarist tradition and with the Conservative Party's priority to keep state intervention in the economy minimal. Therefore, it was dismissed by the responsible Secretary of State for Business Greg Clark (ibid). This example is consistent with a historical institutionalist, rather than a rational choice explanation of the British transposition. The underlying logic of the UK government's transposition behaviour contains both functional and power-political elements. Predominantly, the quick and transparent transposition process favoured structural and procedural factors over agency. At the same time, the political position of the conservative party was consistent with the functional transposition logic. Only cases such as the decision on the scope for the reporting requirements added power-political elements to the British transposition logic.

7.1.1.2 Denmark

The transposition results for Denmark also show large degrees of consistency. In line with expectations for the *nordic sustainability consensus* archetype, Denmark made the most use of non-binding human rights provisions. For the public procurement directives, Denmark received the second-highest human rights score of 158 (3.42 per provision) and made balanced use of the transposition tools and disregarded the least voluntary measures. For the NFR-Directive, Denmark has a score of 37 (4.11 per provision), which is also the second-highest score. Notably, Denmark adopted reporting requirements with the farthest-reaching scope of the four member states considered. On average and across all directives, the Danish government received 3.77 points per directive provision, which is the highest score of the four countries considered in this analysis. Therefore, Denmark showed the highest willingness to impose human rights-related regulations on its businesses.

The interesting aspect about the Danish case is that two completely different transposition processes led to similar transposition outcomes, as the testing of the hypotheses has shown. When comparing the two transposition processes, only two IVs tested for show similar values, namely the policy misfit and the institutional misfit. The most important factor when trying to understand the difference between the two transposition processes was the degree of political salience within the policy subsystem. For the transposition of the procurement directives, the Danish government excluded pro-human rights advocacy groups from the committee that prepared the draft law. While labour unions and employers' associations were included, the process was described as not transparent and closed-off. According to interview evidence from representatives of a Danish NGO and the Danish Institute for Human Rights, the government focussed mainly on reducing public expenditures and on simplifying procurement procedures (Interviews 8 and 11). For the transposition of the NFR-Directive, the government conducted an open consultation process and held a public hearing in the Danish parliament. In the discussions within the policy subsystem, strong corporate sustainability guidelines played a central role and were closely associated with Denmark's model of a sustainable economy. The far-reaching transposition was connected to the expectation that compliance with high international sustainability standards would give Danish companies a competitive advantage in the global economy. Therefore, the Danish transposition of the NFR-Directive is the only case in this study where a policy transfer from international BHR agreements to the national transposition process could be determined.

Despite the differences in procedure, Denmark still received a medium transposition score with both the public procurement directives and the NFR-Directive. Even though the transposition score per provision is higher for the NFR-Directive, the outcome for the public procurement directives is still the second-highest among the four countries considered.[2] This can be attributed to two factors: First, the high degree of corporatism in Denmark and the strong Danish consensus culture within the transposition committee and throughout the transposition process allowed labour unions to include more regulatory rules and promote a more balanced transposition outcome. Second, due to the Danish common practice to transpose EU directives with delegated legislation, the provisions from the Utilities and Concessions Directives directly became Danish law. This had a similar effect as the British transposition of voluntary clauses, as the flexibility provided for in the directives was largely passed on to the Danish contracting authorities. Party politics turned out to be of low relevance for the Danish transposition outcome. Due to the Danish consensus culture and the fact that Danish minority governments are reliant on cooperating with the opposition, the transposition outcomes were not dependent on the political orientation of the political party in power at the time.

From a theoretical perspective, the Danish transposition also points to a historical institutionalist transposition pattern. The hypotheses for the policy misfit and the institutional misfit could be confirmed for both transposition processes. Especially the low institutional misfit, determined by a high degree of corporatism, proved to have high explanatory power for the Danish transposition outcomes. Both the Danish self-conception as a front runner of corporate sustainability and a pronounced consensus culture overrode party-political considerations. The different degrees of political salience within the policy subsystem did not lead to divergent transposition outcomes, as one would have expected from a rational-institutionalist perspective. Instead, corporatist institutions enabled a medium outcome as well. Yet, like any

[2]Nonetheless, NGO representatives were not satisfied with the transposition outcome, stating they would have expected a farther-reaching Danish transposition of the public procurement directives (Interviews 8, 11).

policy process, the Danish transposition process was not one-dimensional and cannot solely be reduced to path dependency. The impact of policy transfer on the NFR-Directive also points to sociological influences, while conservative politicians' intention to promote corporate responsibility as a means to provide Danish businesses with a competitive advantage in the global economy also added rational elements to the transposition process. Nonetheless, in light of the entire processes and outcomes, the structuralism that is inbuilt in Denmark's polity and political economy was dominant in shaping the Danish transpositions. Accordingly, I hold that the Danish transposition processes followed a functional transposition logic.

7.1.1.3 France

Unlike the UK and Denmark, the case of France does not show a consistent transposition outcome but two contrary transposition scores. This result is puzzling, because from France's tradition of state intervention, as portrayed in the description of the archetype *regulated sustainability*, one could have expected a high transposition outcome for both directives. However, a high transposition score was only determined for the NFR-Directive, where France over-transposed the most provisions and has the highest human rights score of the four countries (40).[3] The opposite observation can be made regarding the procurement directives. Here, France ignored 24 out of 45 voluntary directive provisions and showed, with a human rights score of 83, the lowest transposition outcome of the four countries. Still, on average and across all four directives, France transposed the second-most directive provisions (3.14) of the four countries considered.

To understand the divergence between the two transposition outcomes, I contrasted the transposition processes and revealed a number of similarities to the Danish case: The political salience within the policy subsystem was low for the public procurement directives, while it was high for the NFR-Directive. For the public procurement directives, interview evidence showed that human rights were never at the heart of the transposition, which was accompanied by a general overhaul of French public procurement legislation. The political priority of this reform was to reduce costs by simplifying procurement procedures and to decrease the regulatory burden for bidding companies. Due to this focus, as interview evidence suggests, the government was more open to demands from actors that stressed competitiveness rather than to the calls arguing for a comprehensive transposition of the social clause. Hence, the low political salience of the human rights clauses within the policy subsystem overrode other factors that would have been conducive to a far-reaching outcome, namely a low policy misfit and a socialist government that was in principle in favour of state intervention in the economy.

---

[3]Considering the fact that the French socialists were in power during the public procurement legislation and LREM! during the transposition of the NFR-Directive, one could even suggest a higher score for the public procurement transposition.

Regarding the transposition of the NFR-Directive, the situation was completely different. Within the policy subsystem, the human rights-related aspects of the transposition law were highly salient. Pro- and anti-regulatory actors were very active during the transposition process and took part in the public consultation process, which led to several cases of over-transposition. While industry demands were also respected regarding the scope of the new reporting requirements, the government's overriding priority, in unison with other actors within the policy subsystem, was to adopt far-reaching non-financial reporting requirements. The adoption of strong rules for the promotion of corporate responsibility and fair supply chains had been one of the campaign promises by president François Hollande, which is why the transposition law was given high political priority. Like in Denmark, the French government's approach to the NFR-Directive was characterized by the ambition to establish France as a front runner of corporate sustainability. Contrary to the transposition of the public procurement directives, this political goal was consistent with the low policy misfit. However, interview evidence made clear that the low policy misfit was not a decisive precondition for a far-reaching transposition, but the consequence of the high political priority that French governments hat devoted to a strict sustainability reporting framework.

While there are many similarities between the Danish and French transposition processes, there is one important difference. In Denmark, the high degree of corporatism and the prevalent consensus culture prevented a minimalist transposition of the public procurement directives. In the absence of political salience within the policy subsystem, the Danish transposition committee still balanced out the interests of pro-regulatory and anti-regulatory actors. The lack of such a consensus culture in France facilitated the minimalist transposition, even though the French government had set up a special CSR platform (*Plateforme RSE*) to foster dialogue among actors in the policy subsystem. As a French policy expert made clear in an expert interview, the confrontational debates about the transposition of the social clause took place along ideological lines (Interview 16). Due to a low willingness to reach common ground, the discourse did not lead to a consensus but left the decision to the government. Therefore, the institutional misfit variable, operationalized as the degree of corporatism, can explain a crucial difference between the Danish and the French transposition outcomes.

From a theoretical perspective, I argue that the French case is best to be explained through the rational institutionalist lens. To recall:

> [T]he logic of rationalist institutionalism suggests that Europeanization leads to domestic change through a differential empowerment of actors resulting from a redistribution of resources at the domestic level. (Börzel & Risse, 2000, p. 2)

In accordance with this logic, the public procurement directives and the NFR-Directive led to different empowerments within the policy subsystems. For the NFR-Directive, the directive was in line with the political preferences of the government and most other actors within the policy subsystem. The human rights clauses of the NFR-Directive were given high relative importance and led to a far-reaching transposition of voluntary directive provisions. The key actor within the policy subsystem that was originally opposed to a far-reaching transposition, the MEDEF, was *satisficing*. It tried to meet context-specific expectations and to achieve the optimal solution within the confines of the political institutions. Regarding the public procurement directives, domestic interest formation was determined by a low political salience of the human rights provisions within the policy subsystem. This promoted the empowerment of the anti-regulatory actors, such as the MEDEF, and their influence on the French government. Within an institutional setting that did not promote consensus, the negotiations among interest-oriented actors led to a deadlock and thereby enabled a minimalistic transposition outcome.

The difference between the two transposition processes highlights the ambiguity of the French political economy. Even though it is marked by a low degree of corporatism, it also reveals substantial differences to a LME such as the UK. Scholars of comparative capitalism have positioned France in between CMEs and LMEs and labelled the French system as *state capitalism* (Schmidt, 2003). Schmidt (2003) states that on the one hand, French firms are even more autonomous than German or even British firms. On the other hand, the French state still retains an active and often interventionist role and tries to "moralize" (p. 547) labour and business relations (ibid). Such an actor-centred system is in agreement with the rational institutionalist explanation provided above, as it promotes the differential empowerment of actors who are confined by an understanding of a potentially interventionist state. While the degree of corporatism was an insightful indicator to explain the French transposition outcomes for this book's empirical analysis, these considerations show that researchers need to pay particular attention to the French case, when attempting to draw conclusions for transposition behaviour from the setup of the political economy.

7.1.1.4 Germany

Like in the French case, the German transposition outcomes reveal a large divergence between the public procurement directives and the NFR-Directive. However, in the German case, the transposition of the public procurement directives led to a medium transposition score, while the government transposed the NFR-Directive in a minimalistic fashion. For the public procurement directives, Germany received 158 points, which is the highest human rights score of the four counties (3.51 points/provision). Here, the analysis revealed a balanced use of transposition tools. Of the 45 provisions, nine provisions were over-transposed, in twelve cases the discretion was passed on, seven provisions were regularly transposed, and 17 were not transposed. The German transposition of the NFR-Directive was much more one-sided. Like the UK, Germany received a transposition score of 16, which is close to the lowest score possible (13). While in two out of nine cases, the discretion to apply voluntary human rights regulations was passed on, all other provisions were regularly transposed. With a transposition score of 1.78 points per provision, the German transposition of the NFR-Directive stands in stark contrast to the transpositions in Denmark (score of 4.11 per provision) and France (score of 4.44 per provision). On average and across all directives Germany receives a human rights score of 2.64 points per directive provision, which is the second-lowest of the four countries considered.

To understand the large difference between the two outcomes, the political salience of the human rights clauses within the policy subsystem proved, again, to be the decisive factor. The German transposition of the public procurement directives showed striking similarities with the Danish transposition of those directives. Like in Denmark, the aspect of human rights was not at the centre of the policy debates surrounding the transposition. The transposition law was accompanied by a profound reform of German procurement law, which received more attention among actors within the policy subsystem. According to interview evidence, both the consultation process and the policy debates were characterized by a fact-based and constructive atmosphere, in which all actors sought to establish a balanced compromise. Like in Denmark, the corporatist institutional arrangements facilitated the integration of pro-regulatory and anti-regulatory actors. At the same time, several rounds of inter-ministerial coordination led to an outcome that represented the middle ground between the conservative (CDU/CSU) and social-democrat (SPD) coalition partners. While representatives of the Green Party and NGOs criticised that more of the discretionary room could have been used, Germany still received a medium transposition outcome.

The German transposition of the NFR-Directive was less consensual. Here, the political salience was higher for all actors within the policy subsystem, which also led to a more confrontational transposition process. Both pro-regulatory and anti-regulatory interest groups were very active in the consultation process and engaged in lobbying activities. Representatives of the German industry used the low policy misfit as an argument in the negotiations with the government. As interview evidence suggests, representatives of employer associations acted as veto players as they intervened directly at the ministerial level, arguing that the 'regulatory jump' of a far-reaching transposition would be too high. In many respects, the German transposition of the NFR-Directive was similar to the UK's transposition of the same directive, as businesses representatives warned the government about the dangers of excessive regulation to competitiveness. Another similarity to the UK was that the German transposition guideline, according to which all EU directives have to be transposed 'one-to-one', was used as an argument for a minimalist transposition by a ministry official and a deputy of the ruling CDU. Interestingly, the same rule did not appear to have played a role regarding the public procurement directives. A last difference between the transposition processes was that with the NFR-Directive, the CSU/CSU group, the larger political group within the governing coalition, exerted a larger sway over the transposition outcome than in the transposition of the public procurement directives.

As these considerations show how different degrees of political salience within the policy subsystems led to two completely different transposition processes and two divergent transposition outcomes. From a theoretical perspective, each process requires its own interpretation. For the public procurement directives, the explanation for the transposition outcome is concise and points to a historical institutionalist explanation. Like in Denmark, the medium policy misfit and the corporatist institutional arrangements facilitated a consensual policy outcome. The involvement of the classical 'social partners' was consistent with the high degree of corporatism determined for Germany. The transposition of the NFR-Directive, on the other hand, can rather be explained through the rationalist institutionalist lens. Instead of the balancing coordinative process that took place with regard to the public procurement directives, the result of the NFR-transposition was achieved through confrontational negotiations among actors that strictly pursued their preferences. Like in France, the high degree of political salience within the policy subsystem led to a differential empowerment of actors. However, unlike in France, anti-regulatory actors within the government and outside the government were empowered, which resulted in a low transposition score.

7.1.2 Cross-Country Transposition Patterns

These country-specific conclusions have already highlighted how the IVs that I tested in the empirical analysis have differently affected the transposition processes in the four countries analysed. However, to be able to draw wider conclusions that might be instructive for other studies of directive transpositions, be it in the BHR policy area or in related areas, it is worth examining the effects of these factors individually. This sub-section discusses the most pertinent IVs, leaving aside administrative effectiveness, which turned out to be of little relevance for the transposition outcome.

7.1.2.1 Political Salience Within the Policy Subsystem

The factor that proved to be most relevant across the eight transposition cases was the degree of political salience within the policy subsystem. This is a noteworthy finding, as only few directive transposition studies have so far paid specific attention to this factor. Moreover, those authors that focus on salience, such as Spendzharova and Versluis (2013), measured the degree of salience within the wider public, for example, by examining media or newspaper coverage. The influence of political salience *within the policy subsystem* has, to my best knowledge, not yet been investigated as an explanatory variable in a directive transposition study.

As the empirical analysis has shown, the degree of political salience changed the transposition logic in a member state and altered the policy dynamic between actors in the policy subsystem. The direction of this change was not consistent. None of the two competing hypotheses I tested for political salience could be confirmed for all eight transpositions analysed. Therefore, I cannot ascertain for all cases if a low degree of political salience within the policy subsystem was conducive for a high transposition outcome or a low transposition outcome. What can be said with certainty is that in all four countries, political salience affected the transposition dynamic. In the UK, the salience was low for all directives, but due to a 'shadow of politicization' the government was anxious to avoid cases of over-transposition. In Denmark, the degree of political salience affected the transposition processes, but the transposition result was balanced out by the Danish consensus-based decision making. The effect was most notable in the contradictory cases of France and Germany, where the degree of political salience within the policy subsystem was responsible for changing the dynamic and empowerment of the policy actors. In France, the low degree of political salience promoted a minimalist transposition, because in the absence of a consensus culture and strong opposition, anti-regulatory actors were able to influence the government to disregard several voluntary provisions. In Germany, the high degree of political salience empowered anti-regulatory actors inside and outside the government to focus on competitiveness. Moreover, the high salience within the policy subsystem 'activated' the high policy misfit as an important argument in policy debates. Hence, political salience within the policy subsystem can either act as a facilitating factor or a constraining factor in the directive transposition process. While this finding does not allow us to predict transposition outcomes in other directive transposition studies, it shows that political salience within the policy subsystem can serve as an indicator for counter-intuitive transposition outcomes. Moreover, this result should encourage policy-makers and scholars to pay more attention to this factor.

If a factor is salient within the policy subsystem depends on a range of country-specific factors individual for each case as well as on directive-specific features. Regarding the directives analysed in this study, it has become apparent that the NFR-Directive received more relative attention by policy-makers than the human rights-related provisions in the public procurement directives. Objectively, this is surprising because public procurement carries a heavy economic weight. As was shown in Chap. 2, it accounts for 14% (Denmark and UK) and 15% (France and Germany) of GDP in the countries considered, which is why human rights criteria in procurement legislation have widespread economic implications. I identify two other factors that can explain why the NFR-Directive received nonetheless more attention among policy-makers. First, the NFR-Directive is a single-issue directive, while the public procurement package deals with a broad and complex subject area that touches on several kinds of public expenditures. The responses to national public consultations showed that interest in the procurement directives came from a diverse range of business sectors. The public procurement directives are long and complex pieces of legislation in which the human rights-related provisions are only one aspect among many. The NFR-Directive, on the other hand, only addressed sustainable reporting and is relevant for a fixed set of large companies. Since it addresses only corporate responsibility and sustainability, the directive was also much more closely associated with the BHR agenda.

The second factor is the transfer of political salience from the EU level to the domestic policy-making context. Interview insights showed that the issue-specific experts in the national administrations that were leading the transposition process were also closely involved during the directive negotiations in the Council. Actors from interest groups and civil society also work in close coordination with their national counterparts. Moreover, national business associations, especially those from large member states, also tried to influence the negotiations on the directives from their offices in Brussels and are also represented in EU umbrella associations such as *BusinessEurope* or *Eurochambres*. Similarly, national NGOs and national human rights institutions coordinated their activities with their European umbrella organisations. For example, the European Coalition for Corporate Justice (ECCJ) was the voice of NGOs in during the negotiation of the NFR-Directive. At the same time, the ECCJ sent detailed guidance to national NGOs, explaining which issues could be addressed during the national transposition processes. The expert interviews suggested that through such channels, a higher political salience was transferred from the EU level to the domestic level for the NFR-Directive than for the public procurement directives.

7.1.2.2 Policy Misfit

Unlike political salience within the policy subsystem, the policy misfit, which early Europeanization studies have portrayed as a universal explanatory factor for transposition outcomes, did not play a dominant role across cases in explaining the transposition outcomes. In five out of eight transposition cases, the corresponding hypothesis could be confirmed, but interview evidence and policy documents validated the significance only in three cases, namely the Danish, French, and German transpositions of the NFR-Directive. Only in these three cases did the policy misfit have a relevant effect on the transposition outcome. In the French and Danish transpositions of the NFR-Directive, where a low policy misfit (France), and a medium policy misfit (Denmark) coincided with far-reaching transposition outcomes, previous rules on non-financial reporting were cited to have been important for the governments' ambitions to establish strict non-financial reporting regimes. Previous national rules also induced the French and Danish government to try to 'upload' their respective policies to the EU level. In the German transposition of the NFR-Directive, the high policy misfit was used as an argument by anti-regulatory actors against a far-reaching transposition. They stressed that a far-reaching transposition would result in high administrative efforts that would be prejudicial for businesses. In these three cases, the path-dependency of the policy misfit, therefore, influenced the transposition outcome. Still, even in these cases, the policy misfit did not appear to have been the *cause* of the transposition outcome. Instead, it coincided with the governments' political priority. Rather than being the reason for the transposition outcome, the policy misfit was the result of a previously made policy commitment that was later also decisive in determining the transposition outcome. Thus, for the policy misfit, I can confirm Mastenbroek and Kaeding's (2006) critique of the misfit hypothesis explained in Chap. 3, according to which the relationship between the misfit and the transposition is spurious, because "both variables are contingent on domestic preferences or beliefs" (p. 347).

In the other five transpositions analysed in this study, the policy misfit turned out to be even more irrelevant for the transposition outcome. In the French transposition of the public procurement directives, the misfit hypothesis could even be clearly rejected, because despite a low misfit the government opted for a minimalistic transposition outcome. Moreover, one interviewee stated that a low misfit can even complicate the transposition processes (Interview 9), because instead of just copying an EU rule, policy-makers have to go through considerable coordination efforts to align national rules with EU rules.

Therefore, I conclude that for this empirical analysis, the policy misfit is not a relevant factor to explain national transposition outcome. The hypotheses testing and the policy analysis show that the policy misfit was only relevant as an auxiliary factor if it coincides with the political priority of the government. Policy-makers appeared to use the policy misfit as an argument in the process of policy formation, whenever it suited their respective interests. Otherwise, an incongruous misfit could also be ignored and did not play a role in the transposition process.

7.1.2.3 Institutional Misfit

The institutional misfit, on the other hand, turned out to be a more significant factor. In six out of eight transpositions, the institutional misfit hypothesis, which postulated that a high degree of corporatism leads to more transpositions of voluntary directive provisions, was confirmed. In all of these cases, the interpretation of evidence from expert interviews and policy documents revealed that the degree of corporatism was indeed a good indicator for explaining the transposition of the BHR directives. While it was not explicitly cited as a factor in policy documents or expert interviews, it became clear that the institutional misfit shaped the approach governments took with the national transpositions. Unexpectedly, I discovered not one but two mechanisms through which the degree of corporatism affected the transposition. First, as I explained when establishing the institutional misfit hypothesis, the level of corporatism affected how policy-makers interpreted BHR policy. As the account in Chap. 2 has shown, the policy area of BHR policy is characterized by an inherent ambiguity between voluntary incentives and mandatory regulation. This mechanism could be observed in the UK, where policy-makers interpret BHR policy with a focus on voluntary measures. In Denmark, and to a lesser extent in Germany, it is more widely accepted to rely on binding BHR regulation. The policy analysis suggested that the institutional setup of the political economy and the collective understandings attached to them affected how policy-makers set about the transposition process.

The second and less expected mechanism was the effect of corporatism on the transposition policy process. Here, the starting point for countries with a degree of corporatism was to actively include 'social partners', i.e. employers' organizations, labour unions into the policy process. NGOs also benefited from a corporatist approach but to a lesser extent. As the transpositions of the public procurement directives in Germany and Denmark have shown, this consensual approach facilitated far-reaching transposition outcomes, even if the human rights clauses were not highly salient within the policy subsystem. In the absence of such corporatist arrangements, the French transposition of the public procurement directives led to a minimalistic outcome.

The only two cases where the institutional misfit hypothesis could be rejected were the transpositions of the NFR-Directive in France and Germany. As already explained, in these cases the political salience within the policy subsystem altered the policy dynamic between actors and led to a differential empowerment of domestic actors. In both cases, policy-makers within and outside the government made substantial political efforts to achieve transposition outcomes that contradict the institutional misfit hypothesis. Therefore, these cases can be considered as exceptions that confirm the rule rather than undermine it.

7.1.2.4 Composition of the Domestic Government

The IV that tested the relevance of political parties, operationalized using the CHES-indicator, which measures the position of political parties on state intervention in the economy, turned out to have only limited explanatory power for the transposition outcome. The respective hypothesis (H3) could only be confirmed for four out of seven cases[4]: The position of the governing party or parties on state intervention in the economy matched the transposition outcome only in the cases of the UK (both directives), the German public procurement transposition and the Danish NFR-Directive transposition. However, the relevance of this factor was validated by interview and policy document evidence only in three cases. In the two British transpositions, the free-market agenda of the British Conservative party was cited as a relevant reason for the minimalistic transposition. In German transposition of the public procurement directives, the combined position of the CDU/CSU and SPD matched the transposition outcome and was also a relevant factor. Here, the compromise between the two parties was part of a larger consensus process in which ministries, labour unions, business associations, and NGOs coordinated their respective positions. For the Danish transposition of the NFR-Directive, on the other hand, the position of the governing party turned out to be of low relevance. Due to the Danish consensus culture and the fact that Danish minority governments are reliant on cooperating with the opposition, the governing party's position was not decisive for the transposition result.

In the three remaining cases, the hypothesis testing the positioning of the governing political could be rejected. In the Danish transposition of the public procurement directives, the conservative government was opposed to strict state intervention in the economy, but due to strong corporatist institutions and a medium policy misfit, the government still adopted a medium transposition outcome. Similarly, in Germany, the combined measure of the governing political parties' position on state intervention in the economy would have suggested the opposite transposition outcome for the NFR-Directive. In sum, the orientation of the governing political party could not be established as a reliable factor to explain national transposition outcomes.

[4]For the French transposition of the NFR-Directive the hypothesis could not be tested, because.

7.1.2.5 Policy Transfer

The final factor I employed analysing the transposition outcomes was the effect of policy transfer from international BHR agreements on national transposition processes.[5] The Danish transposition of the NFR-Directive is the only case where policy transfer from international BHR agreements to the national transposition process could be determined. As was explained, this policy transfer was contingent on a distinctive combination of factors. The government and other actors within the policy subsystem were already in agreement about a far-reaching transposition. Then, the transposition was connected to the expectation that compliance with high international sustainability standards would give Danish companies a competitive advantage in the global economy. In this respect, policy transfer was also 'activated' by the high level of political salience within the policy subsystem. Moreover, the policy transfer was promoted by the fact that Denmark is a small country and therefore more reliant on complying with international standards than larger economies.

7.2 Theoretical Conclusions

The empirical analysis that was outlined above has shown the complexity of the individual transposition processes. In order to account for the range of possible explanatory factors and the combinations thereof, I adopted a pluri-theoretical approach that builds on the theoretical assumptions put forward by the literature on Europeanization and policy transfer, as well as on the assumed connection between the setup of a political economy and member state behaviour in the policy area of BHR. The underlying assumptions about institutional change were derived from New Institutionalist Theory. I translated the assumptions and main theoretical arguments of the theory into hypotheses that were used to test the validity of the independent variables. The research design followed a deductive reasoning, as it inferred from the general to the particular, to answer this study's research question: How and why do EU member states differ regarding the degree to which they transpose non-binding provisions of Business and Human Rights regulation in EU directives? After having presented and discussed the empirical results of the empirical analysis, we can now move back up the ladder of generality and assess, which theoretical inferences can be drawn from the hypothesis testing.

The empirical results show that a combination of historical institutionalism and rational choice institutionalism is best suited to explain the transposition variation of non-binding provisions in the considered EU directives. Both the British and Danish transpositions, as well as the transposition of the public procurement directives in Germany, are best accounted for through the historical institutionalist lens. While the

[5] Administrative effectiveness was also employed as a control variable. But, as has been explained in Chap. 6, I was able to disregard this factor as there was no evidence to support the respective hypothesis.

policy misfit was only of limited explanatory power, the institutional misfit determined the structure and the actor constellations for the transposition processes in line with previously determined institutional arrangements. As was already indicated, the historical institutionalist imprint on the transposition process is twofold. First, the corporatist structure of the *political economy*, or the lack thereof, served as the starting point for the transposition process and influenced actors' expectations about the degree to which voluntary BHR provisions should be transposed. In the UK, the institutional arrangements of a liberal market economy and the long-established tradition to provide businesses with maximum flexibility shaped actors' expectations and left even pro-regulatory NGO representatives in no doubt about the eventual transposition outcome. In corporatist countries, pro-regulatory actors, advocating for strengthening social rights, and anti-regulatory actors, warning not to curb competitiveness by over regulating businesses, sought to find a consensus, each anticipating the position of the other.

Moreover, as I already suggested in the previous section, the corporatist institutional structure of the *polity* structured the transposition process as well. In the UK, interest groups took part in an open and pluralist system of interest group representation. Due to an institutional promotion of a competitive and transparent consultation process, all interest groups, including pro-regulatory NGOs, took an active part in the transposition process. However, the disproportionate access to decision-making processes by anti-regulatory actors led to a transposition outcome that is in line with the market-liberal tradition of a LME. In the CMEs Denmark and Germany, the institutional structure ensured the integration of the corporatist 'social partners', which then facilitated a consensual transposition outcome. While the approach favours a balanced transposition outcome, such processes can be excluding actors other than the classical social partners, such as NGOs.

However, the historical institutionalist approach is not able to explain all transposition processes analysed in this study. For both transpositions in France and the transposition of the NFR-Directive in Germany, rational choice institutionalism is better suited to provide a conceptual clarification. In these cases, the transpositions were not shaped by previously established institutional arrangements, but by independent actors, conducting themselves according to bounded rationality, i.e. to rational behaviour within the confines of institutions. As was explained in Chap. 3, rational choice institutionalism assumes that "Europeanization leads to domestic change through a differential empowerment of actors resulting from a redistribution of resources at the domestic level" (Börzel & Risse, 2000, p. 2). In the cases of the German transposition of the NFR-Directive and the French transposition of the public procurement directives, the EU directives empowered anti-regulatory actors that stressed the need for competitiveness. While institutional arrangements provided the 'political space' in which interest-oriented actors operated, they did not determine their behaviour or compel them to seek consensus with competing actors. Actors that were not empowered by the European input were side-lined and had little access to the decision-making processes. In the French transposition of the NFR-Directive, the EU input was combined with the political objective of key governmental and societal actors within the policy subsystem to achieve a far-reaching transposition.

Anti-regulatory employer associations such as the MEDEF, which were previously opposed to a far-reaching transposition, were *satisficing* and tried to achieve optimal solutions within the confines of the political space provided for them. They tried to meet context-specific expectations that are embedded in political institutions by changing their position towards the directive and openly supported stricter reporting requirements and hoped that similar transpositions across the EU would level the playing field. Danish anti-regulatory actors within the policy subsystem behaved similarly for the transposition of the NFR-Directive, even though here it was less relevant for the overall transposition.

In sum, a combination of the historical institutionalist and the rational choice institutionalist approaches is best suited to explain both the transposition processes and outcomes. It is noteworthy that in those cases for which rational choice institutionalism applies, the political salience within the policy subsystem was a crucial factor and changed the dynamic of the transposition process. This observation suggests that a high political salience within the policy subsystem is a scope condition for rational choice institutionalism in directive transposition studies. This suggestion is in agreement with a proposition by Mastenbroek and Kaeding (2006), who argue that in their model of EU adaptation, which combines sociological and rational choice institutionalism, saliency is scope condition for rational choice institutionalism (p. 348).

Sociological institutionalism did not turn out to be suitable to explain the divergence between the national transpositions. Policy transfer could only be determined for the Danish transposition of the NFR-Directive, and in this case, it was not a decisive factor. Nonetheless, the transposition processes were not devoid of normative elements. In the field of BHR, collective norms and values play a central role in the coordination and alignment of pro-regulatory actors. NGOs, national human rights institutes, and other civil society organizations acted as 'norm entrepreneurs' and underlined the normative legitimacy of the human rights-related directive provisions. However, for the explanation of the eight transposition processes considered in this study, the sociological institutionalist approach was not relevant.

Beyond the specific conceptual explanations for the empirical findings, this study also contributes to the literature on Europeanization and directive transposition in several other respects. First, like most Europeanization studies, I have contributed to the misfit debate by showing that for the four EU directives in the field of BHR the policy misfit did not play a relevant role in explaining the transposition outcome. In combination with the institutional misfit or with domestic political factors, most notably with the political salience within the policy subsystem, the policy misfit did play a part in affecting the transposition outcome. Based on this result, I agree with Falkner and her colleagues (Falkner, Treib, Hartlapp, & Leiber, 2005), who label the misfit hypothesis a 'sometimes-true-theory'. At the same time, the insight that the institutional misfit, operationalized as the degree of corporatism, turned out to be a highly significant factor in this analysis. This insight can inform future directive transposition studies both in the field of BHR and in other policy areas.

Second, in this study, I paid particular attention to the role of domestic political factors in transposition processes. While I found the political position of the political party to be only of subordinate relevance, the factor political salience within the policy subsystem was decisive in altering the transposition logic in most cases I analysed. Many of the recent studies on directive transposition that analysed the importance of domestic political factors, paid little or no attention to the influence of political salience (Mastenbroek & Kaeding, 2006; Steunenberg & Rhinard, 2010; Zhelyazkova, Kaya, & Schrama, 2016). Those directive transposition studies that did focus on the effect of salience, such as Saurugger (2014a), Spendzharova and Versluis (2013), and Thomann (2015), only investigated the salience of issues for the general public. However, directive transposition laws usually address policy specific and often technical issues that do not receive wider attention by the public and are rarely covered by newspaper articles or TV news.

Nonetheless, for policy-makers and policy-specific stakeholders, the salience of directive transpositions can still vary. Therefore, I addressed this gap in the literature and investigated the relevance of political salience within the policy subsystem in this analysis. One reason for the restriction of previous directive transposition studies to salience for the general public is the prevalence of quantitative methods in directive transposition studies. Political salience is then measured by including data on newspaper coverage of Eurobarometer results in regression analyses. However, for the assessment of political salience within the policy subsystem, qualitative studies are much better suited, as they rely on expert interviews and other qualitative methods of policy analysis, to gauge political salience within the policy subsystem. Therefore, I argue that in order to address this research gap, more qualitative directive transposition studies should investigate the relevance of political salience within the policy subsystem.

Third, this book contributed to the few studies so far that have analysed flexible handling of EU rules. Thomann (2015) demanded that directive transposition studies need to move beyond compliance in order to "gain a fuller understanding of these often neglected, more fine-grained patterns of Europeanization" (p. 1384). With this book, I respond to this demand by proposing a refined framework that allows researchers to measure the degree to which member states make use of the discretionary room in EU directives. Instead of assessing transposition outcomes using binary coding, I propose to rely on four categories (non-transposition, transposition, discretion-passed-on, and over-transposition), which also captures the option that the discretion how to implement a specific transposition is passed on to the implementing authorities. This measure allows for a more precise estimation of transposition outcomes and, in addition, can serve as useful information for studies that analyse the practical implementation of EU directives. In this study, the measure has revealed that the four member states considered in this study have not turned the voluntary frameworks of the directives into mandatory ones. Instead, the four countries have, to varying degrees, contributed to the voluntarism of the directives, as more than half of the voluntary clauses have either been ignored, or the discretion was passed on to the implementing actors. Taking into account the typology of European policy-making by Knill and Lehmkuhl (1999), the findings suggest that the public procurement directives and the NFR-Directive can be positioned in between positive integration and framing integration.

Next to the lessons for research on Europeanization and directive transposition, this study also contributes to the BHR research agenda, as it was the first study of EU directive transposition in the field of BHR policy. A central research concern in this field is the question of how international agreements on BHR, and most importantly the UNGPs, can effectively be implemented by national governments and local communities. In this respect, I tested if international BHR obligations affected the transposition of EU directives in the field of BHR policy. I found policy transfer from the international level to have little to no influence on national transposition processes in the policy area of BHR, where international norms served as the source for EU BHR policy. The only case where a transfer of policy was determined was the Danish transposition of the NFR-Directive. In this case, the transfer coincided with a favourable government, a medium misfit, a high political salience, and the political realization that as a small country it is economically beneficial for Denmark to abide by international standards. Apart from this case, I could not determine instances of policy transfer from international agreements to the national directive transposition.

A more relevant theoretical conclusion for the BHR research area was the finding that the degree of corporatism in a country can serve as a suitable indicator to explain directive transposition outcomes. According to the empirical results, institutional characteristics of a country's political economy proved to be the most suitable starting point to make assumptions about the behaviour of governments in the field of business regulation aimed at the protection of human rights in global supply chains. The results suggest that countries with a high degree of corporatism are more likely to adopt binding measures of BHR regulation than countries with a low degree of corporatism. Further research on the implementation of BHR policy in EU member states and in other countries is needed to examine if this conclusion can be validated for other policy measures as well.

7.3 Political Conclusions

Beyond the theoretical inferences, several political conclusions can also be drawn from this study. First, the results allow us to assess how far member states were willing to adopt more stringent regulation for their national businesses to ensure the protection of human rights in global supply chains. The average human rights score per provision suggests that Denmark, with a score of 3.77, is most committed to adopting regulatory prescriptions that are potentially unwanted by businesses, but that aim at ensuring more socially responsible business conduct. In this respect, France shows the second-highest commitment, with a score of 3.14, followed by Germany (2.64), and the UK (2.06). However, these results should not suggest that globally operating British businesses are more involved in human rights violations than Danish businesses. In fact, due to a long British tradition of CSR, the presence of many corporate sustainability experts, and the personal dedication of some chief executives, many British companies are front-runners in the field of socially responsible business conduct. Therefore, the results of this study are not meant to indicate the impact of a country's businesses on human rights, but rather about the propensity of governments to regulate this impact.

Second, I have argued that domestic political factors, in general, and the political salience within the policy subsystem in particular, are highly relevant for the outcomes of transposition processes. At the same time, the level of salience varies between member states and between directives. In the public conception, the transposition of EU directives is often still understood as a functional and apolitical process. While functional elements will remain to be relevant in directive transpositions, the depiction of country-specific results has underlined the political character of directive transpositions. Especially the transposition processes in France and Germany followed a power-political logic. From a political perspective, more legitimate transposition outcomes could be achieved, if policy-makers, journalists, and actors from civil society paid more attention to the politics of transposition processes. The recognition that the transposition of EU directives is a communicative discourse shaped by public contestation could contribute to a different understanding of the impact of EU law on member states. Comprehending the transposition of directives merely as a functional process will continue to undermine the legitimacy of EU rules in the national perceptions. National policy-makers often support such an understanding, which feeds the misleading narrative that EU rules are decrees from Brussels that are external to legitimate domestic democratic processes. Instead, EU directives, since they are neither purely supranational nor completely national (Ciavarini Azzi, 2000), represent the culture of compromise that has been crucial in the history of European integration.

The third political conclusion addresses the implications of voluntary directive provisions for the coherence of EU BHR policy. The results of this study suggest that the Commission's goal to ensure coherence in EU BHR policy (see European Commission, 2015, p. 16f) was not achieved for the public procurement directives and the NFR-Directive. As indicated, only 13% of the directive provisions are solely mandatory, while the rest are either completely voluntary (57%), or mandatory with discretion (30%). While the four member states were to varying degrees willing to adopt the voluntary rules beyond the required legal minimum, more than half of the transpositions either ignored the voluntary provisions or passed the discretion on to the implementing actors. It is still too early to tell in how far this voluntarism affected the impact of the four directives. The effectiveness of many discretionary rules now depends on the implementation by national authorities, regional authorities, and companies, who have been empowered to interpret voluntary provisions. On the one hand, this transfer of authority allows local authorities and businesses to align the new rules with the practical realities of public procurement and company reporting. Due to the *shadow of hierarchy,* contracting authorities and businesses might assume that discretionary regulations will become mandatory after the next revision and implement voluntary rules as 'pre-law'.

On the other hand, a flexible allocation of authority inevitably leads to large regional and sectoral disparities and decreases regulatory cohesion both between and within member states. The large amount of leeway was already criticized after the adoption of the directives (Kinderman, 2015; Spießhofer, 2014). The results of this study confirm this early scepticism, as they indicate the patchwork of national, regional, and sectoral regulations that followed from the transposition of the public procurement directives and the NFR-Directive. This policy incoherence does not only run the risk of undermining the purpose of the directives, but it also fails to create a level playing field for companies that compete in the internal market.

The purpose of EU directives in general and the goal of EU BHR policy in particular is to progressively harmonize national regulations. In the upcoming legislative revisions of the NFR-Directive and the public procurement directives the Commission should aim at increasing the policy coherence. Based on the observations made in this study, I formulate three policy recommendations to the Commission. First, during the public consultation process, the Commission should ensure that the human rights-related provisions in the public procurement directives are discussed among BHR stakeholders and receive the same amount of attention as single-issue directives in the area of BHR. Both pro- and anti-regulatory interest groups coordinate their activities between the EU level and the national level, which is why a higher political salience within the Brussels policy subsystem can have a harmonizing effect in the member states. Second, the legislative proposal and the Commission's position during trilogue negotiations should actively promote policy cohesion. The Commission should advocate for streamlining the regulatory frameworks and propose that voluntary provisions should either become mandatory or be scrapped if evidence certifies a low level of effectiveness.

Third, during the transposition phase of the new directives, the Commission should foster exchange and coordination between representatives of the national governments. The expert interviews conducted for this book have shown that horizontal exchanges among member states and vertical exchanges with the Commission were rare and practically insignificant for the transposition outcomes. While the Commission organized informal meetings on the development of implementation guidelines, interview partners stressed that such meetings did not go beyond equivocal exchanges of views. Participants reported that while they found those meetings to be interesting, they did not affect the national transposition processes in any way. Two interviewees reported that they would have preferred more formal exchanges and collaboration during the transposition process. These insights show that policy coherence could be increased if national administrations coordinated the level to which they seek to make use of the discretionary room in EU directives.

Concrete measures to promote policy coherence that strengthen the credibility of EU BHR policy would also have implications for the EU's human rights regime in general. Chapter 2 of this book has highlighted the complicated development of the EU human rights regime, which was not only driven by normative considerations but also by concrete political goals. With the EU Charter, arguably the most extensive and modern catalogue of human rights, the EU has endowed itself with a strong normative foundation and presents itself as a global standard-bearer and protector of human rights. At the same time, scholars have observed a 'compliance gap' between the rhetoric and the actual performance of EU human rights policy. According to de Búrca (2011, p. 651), the Commission, in cooperation with civil society and other actors, seeks to address this gap by strengthening the institutions for human rights protection, whereas member states have been described as being resistant to such efforts. However, the member states are at the centre of the EU's human rights regime, both from a legal and political perspective. A voluntarist approach to EU BHR policy that is reliant on the interpretation of national governments, therefore, runs the risk of sustaining the gap between the publicly stated commitment to human rights and the concrete implementation of human rights policy.

7.4 Outlook

In this book, I conducted a comparative analysis of EU directive transpositions in a new and contentious policy area. The analysis has revealed a great degree of variation regarding the extent to which the UK, France, Germany, and Denmark have transposed the three public procurement directives and the NFR-Directive and allowed an assessment of their willingness to impose BHR regulations on national businesses. Future research needs to complement these findings with insights from other member states. Especially evidence from central and eastern European member states, where the concept of corporate responsibility was mostly introduced through Europeanization processes, would be insightful to gain a more complete picture of the domestic impact of the four directives. Moreover, concrete policy implications can only be observed after the directive provisions have been implemented and applied in practice. Coming investigations could, therefore, shed light on how national and regional contracting authorities and large corporations interpreted the discretionary provisions, for example, by analysing public tender documents, or the non-financial statements published by TNCs.

While the analysed directives were chosen as representative examples of EU BHR policy, other studies on the adoption, transposition, and implementation of EU BHR policy are needed to paint a more complete picture of this emerging policy area. Insightful research objects could be the National Action Plans on BHR, which are published by member states and whose submission is organized by the Commission through the OMC. Such studies could compare how the treatment of voluntary measures differs from the usage of the voluntary directive provisions analysed in this book. Moreover, researchers could investigate how the 'conflict minerals regulation', the most recently adopted legislative BHR measure, is applied by TNCs.

The EU's policy on Business and Human Rights is still in a formative phase, which coincides with political controversies about the interpretation and enforcement of fundamental rights in the EU. Due to the recent refugee crisis, the universality of human rights, including the right to asylum (Article 18, EU Charter), has come under threat in the EU. In addition, the Commission has started legal proceedings against Poland and Hungary, claiming that recent laws in these countries violate fundamental rights of the EU. During this time, an effective and credible BHR policy can be a countervailing force, not only because it touches on aspects related to refugees' causes of flight. BHR policy also establishes a tangible connection between the interactions EU citizens have with globally operating companies, as customers, employees, or taxpayers in public tenders and the protection of human rights by these companies. Such a concrete connection is crucial for the public acceptance of the universality of human rights.

In public discourse, human rights are often portrayed as apolitical, neglecting the fact that the protection of universally applicable human rights depends on implementing policies. In the EU, these processes will continue to take place on the national level in the foreseeable future. The continuing reliance on voluntary regulation, as examined in this study, supports the understanding of the EU as a system of 'differentiated integration' (Schimmelfennig, Leuffen, & Rittberger, 2015). On the one hand, this assessment recognises the fact that in the EU, member states will continue to be the most important place for the formation of the public will. On the other hand, the disparities among member states can unbalance the relation of 'community and autonomy', undermine a 'level playing field' for businesses, and challenge the coherence of the EU's commitment to human rights.

References

Börzel, T., & Risse, T. (2000). When Europe hits home: Europeanization and domestic change. *European Integration Online Papers, 4*(15).

Ciavarini Azzi, G. (2000). The slow march of European Legislation: The implementation of directives. In K. Neunreither & A. Wiener (Eds.), *European integration after Amsterdam: Institutional dynamics and prospects for democracy* (p. 384). Oxford: Oxford University Press.

de Búrca, G. (2011). The road not taken: The European Union as a global human rights actor. *The American Journal of International Law, 105*(4), 649–693.

European Commission. (2015). *Commission staff working document on implementing the UN guiding principles on business and human rights—State of play*. Brussels.

Falkner, G., Treib, O., Hartlapp, M., & Leiber, S. (2005). *Complying with Europe. EU harmonisation and soft law in the member states*. New York: Cambridge University Press.

Hall, P. A., & Taylor, R. C. R. (1996). Political science and the three new institutionalisms. *Political Studies, 44*(5), 936–957.

Kinderman, D. (2015). The struggle over the EU non-financial disclosure directive. *WSI-Mitteilungen, 8*(2015), 613–621.

Knill, C., & Lehmkuhl, D. (1999). How Europe matters. Different mechanisms of Europeanization. *European Integration Online Papers, 3*(7), 1–19.

Majone, G. (1996). Regulating Europe. London: Routledge.

Mastenbroek, E., & Kaeding, M. (2006). Europeanization beyond the goodness of fit: Domestic politics in the forefront. *Comparative European Politics, 4*(4), 331–354.

Saurugger, S. (2014a). Europeanisation in times of crisis. *Political Studies Review, 12*(2), 181–192.

Saurugger, S. (2014b). *Theoretical approaches to European integration*. Basingstoke: Palgrave Macmillan.

Schimmelfennig, F., Leuffen, D., & Rittberger, B. (2015). The European Union as a system of differentiated integration: interdependence, politicization and differentiation. *Journal of European Public Policy, 22*(6), 764–782.

Schmidt, V. (2003). French capitalism -transformed, yet still a third variety of capitalism. *Economy and Society, 32*(4), 526–554.

Siaroff, A. (1999). Corporatism in 24 industrial democracies: Meaning and measurement. *European Journal of Political Research, 36*(2), 175–205.

Spendzharova, A., & Versluis, E. (2013). Issue salience in the European policy process: What impact on transposition? *Journal of European Public Policy, 20*(10), 1499–1516.
Spießhofer, B. (2014). Die neue europäische Richtlinie über die Offenlegung nichtfinanzieller Informationen - Paradigmenwechsel oder Papiertiger? *Neue Zeitschrift Für Gesellschaftsrecht, 1281*(33), 1281–1320.
Steunenberg, B., & Rhinard, M. (2010). The transposition of European law in EU member states: Between process and politics. *European Political Science Review, 2*(3), 495–520.
Thomann, E. (2015). Customizing Europe: Transposition as bottom-up implementation. *Journal of European Public Policy, 22*(10), 1368–1387.
Zhelyazkova, A., Kaya, C., & Schrama, R. (2016). Decoupling practical and legal compliance: Analysis of member states' implementation of EU policy. *European Journal of Political Research, 55*(4).

Appendix A
List of Expert Interviews

No.	Date	Name	Position	Country	Institution
1	26.04.2016	Sarah Lincoln	Researcher	Germany	Brot für die Welt (NGO)
2	27.04.2016	Christoph Strässer (SPD)	Deputy	Germany	German Parliament
3	27.04.2016	Cornelia Heydenreich	Team Leader—Corporate Accountability	Germany	Germanwatch (NGO)
4	12.05.2017	Prof. Dr. Heribert Hirte (CDU)	Deputy	Germany	German Parliament
5	06.04.2017	Jerôme Chepalier	Coordinator	EU	European Coalition for Corporate Justice (NGO)
6	29.05.2017	Dr. Thomas Solbach	Head of division	Germany	German Federal Ministry for Economic Affairs and Energy
7	12.04.2017	Marilyn Croser	Policy adviser	UK	CORE (NGO)
8	02.06.2017	Sanne Borges	Policy adviser	Denmark	Amnesty International Denmark (NGO)

(continued)

P. Drahn, *Adoption of EU Business and Human Rights Policy*,
Contributions to Political Science, https://doi.org/10.1007/978-3-030-46935-1

(continued)

No.	Date	Name	Position	Country	Institution
9	12.07.2017	N.N.	Staff member	UK	UK Financial Reporting Council
10	20.09.2017	N.N.	Official	Denmark	Danish government
11	09.10.2017	Cathrine Bloch Veiberg	Policy adviser	Denmark	Danish Institute for Human Rights
12	11.10.2017	N.N.	Official	EU	European Commission
13	1.11.2017	Anja Halbleib	Official	Germany	German Federal Ministry of Justice
14	3.11.2017	Michel Capron	Emeritus Professor	France	Université Paris Est
15	21.12.2017	Rasmus Horskjær Nielsen	Official	Denmark	Danish government
16	22.12.2017	Gérard Brunaud	Policy expert on responsible procurement	France	Former Secretary General of the *observatoire des achats responsible* (OBSAR) and member of the National Platform for CSR
17	25.1.2018	Christopher Schuller	Policy adviser	Germany	German Institute for Human Rights
18	20.03.2018	Katharina Dröge (Alliance 90/The Greens)	Deputy	Germany	German Parliament

Appendix B
Briefing note by the European Coalition for Corporate Justice (ECCJ) on the transposition of the NFR-Directive

ECCJ internal briefing—January 2016

Advocating for an Ambitious Transposition of the Non-financial Reporting Directive

Introduction

> While the battles over the Directive at the EU level are over for the time being, the battles over transposition are just getting started. With few exceptions, national industry associations support a minimalist transposition of the Directive. If these organizations are able to maintain or step up their lobbying activity across the EU in the coming years, there is a good chance that they will be able to ensure that the EU Directive will be implemented restrictively and end up as "a paper tiger."[1]

The new EU rules have been published in the EU Official Journal in November 2014.[2] These rules represent a step towards more transparent, responsible and accountable business. This reform is a major success for European civil society[3] but its effectiveness depends on how States will translate the requirements into national laws and how business will implement them.

A directive is quite a flexible instrument. It obliges Member States to achieve a specific result but leaves them a certain level of flexibility in the way they will transpose and implement these requirements into internal law. Civil society advocacy can result in making improvements, and avoid weakening in areas where the Directive

[1] *Daniel Kinderman, Who Cares about Society and the Environment? The Struggles over the EU's Non-Financial Reporting Directive and The Politics of Corporate Accountability and Upward Regulatory Harmonization. University of Delaware, 2015.*

[2] Official text in all languages: http://eur-lex.europa.eu/legal-content/EN/TXT/uri=uriserv:OJ.L_.2014.330.01.0001.01.ENG. Votes in the Council and the European Parliament: http://www.votewatch.eu/en/term8-directive-of-the-european-parliament-and-of-the-council-amending-council-directives-78-660-eec-and-8.html.

[3] See ECCJ internal assessment of the Directive—available upon request to the ECCJ Secretariat. This briefing includes a comprehensive assessment of the different articles and identifies interpretative problems.

P. Drahn, *Adoption of EU Business and Human Rights Policy*,
Contributions to Political Science, https://doi.org/10.1007/978-3-030-46935-1

makes requirements optional or leaves room for interpretation. It is also where the enforcement mechanism will be defined.

Member States have until December 2016 to transpose it into national law. The first full year of company reporting in accordance with the new requirements will be 2017, with reports expected in first semester 2018. The revision of the Directive will take place in 2019 based on a Commission report on the implementation of the Directive to be published by December 2018.

Priorities for Transposition Into National Law

Main elements of the Directive:
*Large undertakings which are public-interest entities exceeding on their balance sheet dates the criterion of the average number of 500 employees during the financial year**[SECTION 1—scope]**shall include in the management report a non-financial statement containing information to the extent necessary for an understanding of the undertaking's development, performance, position and impact of its activity. **[SECTION 2.1—materiality]**relating to, as a minimum, environmental, social and employee matters, respect for human rights, anti-corruption and bribery matters, including:*

(a) *a brief description of the undertaking's business model**[SECTION 2.2—business model]***
(b) *a description of the policies pursued by the undertaking in relation to those matters, including due diligence processes implemented*
(c) *the outcome of those policies**[SECTION 2.3—policies and due diligence]***
(d) *the principal risks related to those matters linked to the undertaking's operations including, where relevant and proportionate, its business relationships, products or services which are likely to cause adverse impacts in those areas, and how the undertaking manages those risks**[SECTION 2.4—reporting on risks]***
(e) *non-financial key performance indicators relevant to the particular business**[SECTION 2.5—KPIs]**.*

*Where the undertaking does not pursue policies in relation to one or more of those matters, the non-financial statement shall provide a clear and reasoned explanation for not doing so**[SECTION 3—comply or explain]**.*

*Member States may allow information relating to impending developments or matters in the course of negotiation to be omittedn exceptional cases where, in the duly justified opinion of the members of the administrative, management and supervisory bodes, acting within the competences assigned to them by national law and having collective responsibility for that opinion, the disclosure of such information would be seriously prejudicial to the commercial position of the undertaking, provided that such omission does not prevent a fair and balanced understanding of the undertaking's development, performance, position and impact of its activity**[SECTION 4—safe harbor clause]**.*

In requiring the disclosure of the information referred to in the first subparagraph, Member States shall provide that undertakings may rely on national, Union-based or international frameworks, and if they do so, undertakings shall specify which frameworks they have relied upon ***[SECTION 5—use of frameworks]****.*

The Commission shall prepare non-binding guidelines on methodology for reporting non-financial information, including non- financial key performance indicators, general and sectorial, with a view to facilitate relevant, useful and comparable disclosure of non-financial information by EU undertakings. In doing so, the Commission shall consut relevant stakeholders ***[SECTION 6—EU guidelines]****.*

Where an undertaking prepares a separate report corresponding to the same financial year whether or not relying on national, Union-based or international frameworks and covering the information required for the non-financial statement as provided for n paragraph 1, Member States may exempt that undertaking from the obligation to prepare the non-financial statement laid down n paragraph 1, provided that such separate report:

(a) *is published together with the management report in accordance with Article 30; or*
(b) *is made publicly available within a reasonable period of time, not exceeding six months after the balance sheet date, on the undertaking's website, and is referred to in the management report.*

[SECTION 7—integrated or separated report]

The Directive doesn't provide for any specific enforcement mechanism ***[SECTION 8—enforcement mechanisms]****.*

1. The Scope Should Not Be Limited to Public Interest Entities (PIEs) with More than 500 Employees

Public interest entities (PIE) are listed companies, credit institutions, insurance undertakings and any other entity designated by an EU member state as a PIE (for example because they are of significant public relevance due to the nature of their business or size).

National law should have a wider scope, which encompasses both listed and non-listed companies with more than 250 employees. State-owned enterprises should also be covered. Some MS may consider applying the rules to companies benefitting from state support (public procurement, export credit…) and smaller companies operating in high risk sectors.

This wider threshold may be phased during a transition period.

Key arguments

- The current scope only covers 6,000 companies, a small fraction of the 42,000 large European companies.[4]
- 250 employees is the usual threshold for the EU definition of a large company.
- The Directive's threshold is arbitrary and it is a result of political compromise. Originally the Commission's proposal covered a larger number of companies as it encompassed all companies with more than 500 employees, both listed and non-listed.
- Reporting obligations will eventually apply to smaller and non-listed companies as well. Adopting early (or phasing the application of the Directive to different classes of companies) might provide domestic business with advantage in adjusting to the future reporting model.
- Leaving out non-listed companies is problematic in principle because it implies that transparency around companies' social and environmental performance matters only to shareholders. Large non-listed companies may be exposed to or create the same risks as listed companies. The information on these risks is as relevant to their shareholders as to the shareholders of listed companies. Likewise, the impacts of large non-listed companies on society and on the economy, as well as information on their due diligence, is of the same importance to the public and to regulators as is the case for listed companies. Making this distinction would go against the objective of leveling the playing field among large European companies—if in the short-term benefiting from externalites provides a competitive advantage to companies that don't care, then we need better transparency to help responsible companies.
- Why should a non-listed textile company like Mango not be subject to same requirements than listed company Zara, which operate in same sectors with similar supply chains, posing similar risks to society?
- When the proposal was adopted by the Council, Belgium, France, Denmark and Slovenia made a statement calling for an inclusion of non-listed companies in the scope.[5]

Useful examples

- Denmark: 50 companies based on EU threshold but will ultimately apply to **1050** companies. In 2016, state-owned enterprises will be added to the EU-defined scope. In 2018 all companies with more than 250 employees will have to report, as well as the Danish Export Credit Agency.
- There might be good precedents in other national legislations to be used. In the UK, the Modern Slavery Act passed a few months before the adoption of

[4]See table provided in Daniel Kinderman, op. cit.

[5]"Contrary to the initial proposal of the Commission, the text does not include in its scope large unlisted companies although their activities may have a substantial impact in the social and environmental field or in the field of human rights. A scope encompassing large listed and unlisted companies is also essential to ensure a level playing field between companies and to avoid creating wrong incentives with regards to the access to financial markets while helping promote best practices".

the NFR Directive. It sets a useful precedent because it covers both private and publicly-listed companies.

2. Legislation Should Ensure Robust Reporting on Due Diligence and Risks, Including in Supply Chains, Building on the Redefined Approach to Materiality

2.1 Definition of Materiality

Directive departs from usual understanding of materiality which is a guiding principle of the Accounting Directives (information relevant to companies' financial performance). It adds that non-financial information should allow for an understanding of the *impact of company's activity.* This redefined materiality clause specifies what kind of information companies should disclose—risks to human rights, environment posed by its activities and not just risk to its business. Another way how to put it is that the Directive says that severe risks are always material. However, it is very likely that accounting professionals, business lobbyists, and many policy-makers will insist that despite this clear text, non- financial reporting should be subject the traditional test of materiality.

Civil society therefore must ensure that the national law confirms new principle and possibly makes it clearer. Voluntary sustainability and human rights reporting frameworks can provide useful referential points (see also text under letter (d) in Sect. 2.2). Furthermore, Recital 3 and 8 in the Preamble of the Directive clarify the aforementioned definition d impacts on society. Ideally, the transposition law should include the language in these recitals and an explicit statement that disclosure of non-financial information is not subject to the financial materiality test.

2.2 Description of the Business Model

This provision is not explained elsewhere in the Directive. Its transposition provides an opportunity to specify that companies should describe:

(a) their social purpose that goes beyond profit maximisation is and how these two are related;
(b) whether and how their business model considers and adjusts to the concept of the planetary boundaries.

(c) how the aforementioned is organised and demonstrated.

Useful examples

- B-corporation model and similar profit-with-purpose business models may be used as inspiration for clarifying the expected content.

2.3 Description of Policies, Including Due Diligence Processes, and the Outcome of Those Policies

The description of policies should include, ideally,

(a) a description of overall goals of company's engagement with these matters as well as statement of specific objectives of company's policies; and
(b) an explanation why these specific policies and objectives were selected with reference to the severity of impacts associated with company's activity.

The description of outcomes of policies should be concrete. It should be connected with company's choice of KPIs, which is required in letter (e) (see below).
2.4 Reporting on Risks
From the perspective of business and human rights, this is the key provision. The formulation rephrases the definitions of corporate responsibility in the UN Guiding Principles on Business and Human Rights and OECD Guidelines for Multinational Enterprises, and reflected in the EU Communication on Corporate Social Responsibility. Two issues deserve particular attention:

(1) The phrase *where relevant and proportionate* is used but not defined in the Directive. It potentially opens a loophole which would allow companies to ignore impacts that occur in their value chains, i.e. majority of impacts. The transposition law could either avoid using this term or try to clarify it. Such clarification should build on the definition of (human rights) due diligence provided in the UN Guiding Principles on Business and Human Rights (see in particular GPs 17 and 19 and their Commentaries). The key in this respect is reference to the severity of impacts. This connection is suggested in Recital 8 of the directive. This Recital also clarifies that business relationships are meant to cover companies full subcontracting and supply chain. In addition, the application of *'where relevant and proportionate'*can be specified in the transposition law by a reference to sector specific standards as guidance for interpretation.

With respect to the environmental footprint, the interpretation of phrase *'where relevant and proportionate'* can be put into context with the concept of product's life cycle. This connection could be ideally made directly in transposition law.

(2) The definition of what constitutes *principal risks* is not clear. Again, the text of Recital 8 provides a useful language that should not be lost in the transposition. It clarifies that the main test is the severity of impacts, building on the definition in the UN Guiding Principles. Furthermore, it stipulates that companies should provide information about risks of impacts that may materialise along with those that have already materialised which is not entirely clear from the very text of the new Article 19a.

With respect to human rights impacts, the concept of "salient human rights issues", as proposed in the UN GPs Reporting framework[6] provides another useful referential point. This framework is arguably the best tool available for reporting based on UNGPs. According to this Framework, salient human rights issues are *those human rights that are at risk of the most severe negative impacts through a*

[6]http://www.ungpreporting.org/consult-the-reporting-framework/download-the-reporting-framework/.

company's activities or business relationships, measured by impacts scale/gravity, scope, and irremediability. The framework requires companies to report on the occurrence of severe impacts as well as examples illustrating how effectively each salient issue was managed.
Significant financial impact on the organization. Instead they refer to the existence of 'significant impacts' that *refer to those that are a subject of established concern for expert communities, or that have been identified using established tools such as impact assessment methodologies or life cycle assessments.*

Key arguments

- Companies should not judge risks only from the perspective of short-term financial interests that often do not capture the risks to and impacts on society of a large company's operations. A report from the UN Global Compact[7] stresses that "*risk assessment processes should consider risks to society and the environment arising from company activities, rather than solely risks to the company itself'* while also recognising that often these risks to society will in most cases eventually represent *"reputational, legal and financial risks* to the company. These risks might be linked to the company through its own activities or its business relationships.

2.5 Key Performance Indicators
The Directive does not specify in detail what and how key performance indicators (KPIs) should be used. Article 2 and Recital 17 of the Directive refer to European Commission's obligation to prepare non-binding guidelines that should address this matter. However, the Commission is very careful in this respect lacking appropriate expertise. It is likely that its guidance will be minimalistic. Therefore, it would be useful to clarify main principles for use of KPIs in the transposition.
In principle, companies are expected to use KPIs that reflect principle risks, their non-financial policies and outcomes. KPIs can serve two different objectives. First, they should be used to track specific, quantifiable impact that is common to all companies generally or in a specific industry. This is the case for many environmental impacts. Recital 17 refers to 4 key environmental footprint indicators which were adopted by the European Commission in its 2011 Resource Efficiency Roadmap. They are: land use, water use, greenhouse gas emissions and the use of materials. The methodology for their measurement is missing, nevertheless, the transposition laws should explicitly mention these indicators and require those companies with significant environmental impacts to use them.
In human rights area, for some typical, industry-specific human rights issues KPIs can be standardized and mandated, but for many issues such approach is not desirable. The second way of using KPIs is to track effectiveness of company's policy to address salient/significant/severe human rights issues/risks. The law should be specific about this.

[7] *Building a Business Engagement Architecture for the Post-2015 Agenda.* http://www.un.org/News/Press/docs/2013/sgsm15300.doc.htm.

3. Comply or Explain

This "comply or explain" provision is a fundamental principle of the Directive that was supported by all Member States. Although it is a loophole which allows for excessive flexibility and has been criticized by CSOs, our understanding s that the current wording doesn't free a company from the obligation to identify and disclose principal risks. Comply or explain provision remained limited to disclosure of companies policies, which is reasonable in the context of reporting legislation: companies should have policies in areas where they have significant impacts. In transposition it is important to ensure that:

(a) Comply or explain principle is not extended to reporting on principal risks to non-financial matters; and
(b) The requirement to provide a clear and reasoned opinion should specify that such opinion should respect the Directive's requirement to understand company's impact and it should be based on analysis of principal risks of severe impacts outlined in letter (d) and explained in Recital 8.

4. The "Safe Harbor Clause" Could Render NFR Requirements Meaningless and Should Be Left Out

Clause, it is important to ensure that it does not add new, more expansive protection than the existing commercial secrets legislation and case law, and that is indeed limited to *impending developments or matters in the course ol negotiation.*
In addition, any decision of a management body not to disclose information should be explained in a reasoned opinion and it should be verifiable, and any prejudice to the company's commercial position should be weighed against the public interest in disclosure.

Key arguments

- This "safe harbor clause" is vague and provides a broad escape clause that could render non-financial reporting requirements meaningless.
- The SHC sends the wrong signal to companies and directly works against one of the key aims of the reform which is to enable companies to better manage the principal risks of their operations to society and to enable stakeholders to assess these risks. The overarching principle of the Commission's non-financial reporting proposal is to require companies to provide a fair, balanced and comprehensive review of their business.
- Given the "comply or explain" approach and the non-prescriptive approach regarding indicators and use of existing frameworks, the Directive already guarantees a sufficient level of flexibility on what and how companies will report.

Useful examples

- In Denmark the SHC has been left out of the NFR law.

5. Clarify the Use of Standards

Recital 9 refers to a number of standards including EMAS, UN Global Compact, UN Guiding Principles, OECD Guidelines, ISO 26000, ILO Tripartite Declaration, GRI, and others. These standards have different objectives, contenl and intended use. However, the Directive does make such distinction. In the transposition it would be desirable if the differences between these standards are explained and if it is clarified how these standards relate to different obligations outlined in the Directive. For example:

- UN Guiding Principles, OECD Guidelines and ILO Tripartite are government sanctioned standards for corporate responsibility that specify the scope of due diligence and have implications for company's analysis of risks and selection of policies. UN Global Compact is a simpler, voluntary initiative that may help companies understand main issues and principles related to sustainability that they should consider.
- Global Reporting Initiative is a voluntary reporting tool intended to help companies to establish reporting methodology and select appropriate general KPIs for tracking performance.
- EMAS and ISO 26000 are guidance for management systems developed on the basis of certain understanding of scope of corporate responsibility with some implications for disclosure.

It could be made clear that use of any of these standards doesn't relieve company from fulfilling Directive's requirements. They are merely tools intended to help companies.

6. EU and National Guidance

The EU is expected to publish non-binding guidelines on methodology for reporting by December 2016. Such guidance is necessary, as the Directive provides a framework, but a lot of work remains on the content. It could be both general and issue-specific. However, the Guidance may also result in watering down the content of the NFR Directive. Therefore, if there is a good opportunity, it would be helpful if Member States issue their own guidance clarifying key principles of the Directive and further specifying reporting obligations where the Directive is not specific—for instance focusing on specific sectors and risks therein.

The content of such guidance should address main issues outline above in recommendations for Transposition. That is:

- Promote the use of common sets of indicators: companies must identify these themselves—but the guidance must assist them by setting out that a company should identify existing and potential risks and impacts to human rights, and then set out how it intends to address those. The company should then set out what KPIs it will use to track how it is addressing the risk, and the effectiveness of its actions. The guidance should clarify at least key principles for the

use of indicators, in particular the "resource use indicators" mentioned in the preamble.
- Present the best practice for the publication of the report, specifically how it is linked to the annual report and the timing of the publication of the two reports. The directive currently allows companies to publish the non-financial report six months after the Annual Report—so the non-financial report may not be available to shareholders at the AGM.
- Directive prescribes that parent company should report on the whole group (consolidation). This is a good approach, however where serious impacts and risks have been identified by a subsidiary, this should be disclosed in a separate report—otherwise certain impacts will not be disclosed—this could be the responsibility of the parent company to ensure the reporting takes place.

One option to pursue in the development of the guidance would be to take a couple of key principles from SHIFT's UNGPs Reporting Framework, which represents an authoritative interpretation of the UNGPs and has been developed to assist companies with reporting on their implementation of the UNGPs, and use those to press on the content of the guidance. It may be a useful tool to clarify the concept of HRDD in the context of reporting.

7. Non-financial Statement Should Remain Fully Integrated in the Management Report and Not Be Presented in a Separate Report

Member States may allow companies to provide a non-financial statement that is separate from the management reporl and provided within 2 months after the management report. Member States should leave out this option in the national law.

Key arguments

- The reason why ECCJ tried to keep non-financial statements integrated in the management report was that company's management is legally responsible that it is drawn up in accordance with legal requirements in accordance with Article 33 of the Accounting Directive. It is unclear if this responsibility applies to a separate non- financial statement provided outside of the management report at a later stage. It is not explicitly provided in the directive, although such reading may be circumventing the law.
- Allowing separate reports would go against the growing trend to better integrate financial and non-financial information in companies' strategies. Leading companies know that non-financial issues are intrinsically linked to the corporate bottom line.
- Commission's proposal called for having the non-financial report included in the management report.
- Report should be made available to shareholders at the AGM.

8. Monitoring and Enforcement Mechanisms Need to Be Put in Place

The monitoring and enforcement of the obligations is very much left to Member States that are responsible for putting in place effective procedures to enforce compliance and prevent disclosure of misleading information. EU text only requires that the auditor checks whether the information has been provided, and refers to the general requirements applicable to the management report.

This legislation cannot succeed in the absence of legal mechanisms to ensure compliance and disclosure of relevant information. MS shall define adequate and effective laws, regulations and administrative provisions to enforce full, accurate and credible disclosure of non-financial information by companies in compliance with the provisions of this Directive. Such means shall include

- Independent third party verification of reports. The option exists in the EU Directive but needs to be confirmed and operationalized by Member States.
- This Directive and/or bring such failure to disclose before an administrative authority competent either to decide or complaints or to initiate appropriate legal proceedings. Even though our proposal has not been reflected in any Article it has been inserted in the recitals (7a). The call on Member States is rather aspirational. It gives Member States full flexibility to define what constitutes a 'legitimate interest'.
- Another approach could be to establish a mechanism through which domestic authorities would review annually a sample of companies reports.

Advocacy Tips

- **Remind the government that the transposition process should be transparent and provide for an effective consultation of stakeholders**: each state has its established rules and mechanisms for consulting on new legislations, and may provide for additional opportunities for civil society to be involved prior to the drafting of the national law, and to comment on the draft law. The process may include public consultation (UK, Germany?), discussions in relevant national councils which gather different stakeholders (Danish CSR Council), parliamentary hearings (Denmark?), roundtables or workshops (Belgium, Germany), meetings with stakeholders, expert group including representatives from all interested parties.
- **Get figures**: find out the number of companies which will have to report, who these companies are. Often a good argument for a larger scope.
- **Engage with MPs**: they can raise questions, organize hearings, support your proposed amendments,—use politica debate in the parliament.
- **Get public attention**: NFR is a low profile political discussion (quiet politics) often left to experts and organized interes groups—such low salience usually tend to give more influence to business.
- **Build on the political contacts**: that your organization and/or ECCJ established during the EU negotiations.
- **Engage with other NGOs and stakeholders**: suggested collaborations include EU-wide campaigning consortiums such as "Supply CHainge—make

supermarkets fair", Trade Unions, (Socially Responsible) Investors, academics (for instance the "Sustainable Companies" project).

- **Engage with business or refer to business support**: in case NGO voices are disregarded, it is useful to use supportive business voices, such as we did with IKEA and Unilever during the EU negotiations.[8]
- **Find out about key issues raised by your government**—during the negotiations in the Council in 2013-2014, during the transposition workshops organized by the Commission or visits of Commission policy officers to capital cities—and in the impact assessment (we heard some governments are doing it but we don't know which ones).
- **Use parallel processes or policy debates**: some are directly or indirectly related to NFR, and are setting precedents with regards to corporate transparency (for instance, modern slavery act in UK, bill on duty of vigilance in France, debates on trade secrets in several countries…).
- **Seize the opportunity to set the corporate responsibility standard and engage with business**: transposition and implementation of NFR could be used to engage in discussions with companies on their responsibility.
- **Counter the political argument towards increasing flexibility and reducing cost and administrative burden**: very common argument made by governments that NFR law should ensure large level of flexibility to companies, should be aligned with "Better regulation" agenda (avoid "gold-plating"),etc.

  - NGOs must bring arguments to show that it's manageable; that robust NFR is inherent to sound risk management by companies; that leading companies are already doing this; that the cost is only a small portion of the cost of doing the financial report; etc.
  - Argument of trade secrets has been raised in some countries—ECCJ needs to analyze whether this is indeed a dangerous argument against reporting on certain issues.

[8] *Letters sent by IKEA and Unilever to decision makers available upon request to the ECCJ Secretariat.*

The manufacturer's authorised representative in the EU is Springer Nature Customer Service Centre GmbH, Europaplatz 3, 69115 Heidelberg, Germany. If you have any concerns regarding our products, please contact ProductSafety@springernature.com

Printed and bound by CPI Group (UK) Ltd, Croydon, CR0 4YY
30/09/2026
02225510-0007